I0132067

*Disruptive Voices and
the Singularity of Histories*

Histories of Anthropology Annual

EDITORS

Regna Darnell

Frederic W. Gleach

EDITORIAL BOARD

Lee D. Baker, *Duke University*

Sally Cole, *Concordia University*

Alexei Elfimov, *Russian Academy of Sciences*

Geoffrey Gray, *University of Queensland*

Robert L. A. Hancock, *University of Victoria*

Richard Handler, *University of Virginia*

Erik Harms, *Yale University*

Curtis M. Hinsley, *Northern Arizona University*

Christer Lindberg, *Lund University*

Jonathan Marks, *University of North Carolina, Charlotte*

Marie Mauzé, *l'Ecole de Hautes Etudes en Sciences Sociales*

Stephen O. Murray, *El Instituto Obregón*

Robert Oppenheim, *University of Texas*

Vilma Santiago-Irizarry, *Cornell University*

Joshua Smith, *University of Western Ontario*

Susan R. Trencher, *George Mason University*

Disruptive Voices and the Singularity of Histories

Histories of Anthropology Annual, Volume 13

EDITED BY REGNA DARNELL AND
FREDERIC W. GLEACH

University of Nebraska Press | Lincoln

© 2019 by the Board of Regents of
the University of Nebraska

All rights reserved. ∞

Library of Congress Control Number: 2019932102

CONTENTS

ILLUSTRATIONS

This thirteenth volume of *Histories of Anthropology Annual* continues to problematize the plurality of histories and the entailed impossibility of arriving at a monolithic understanding of "what really happened" in the past. The location of this work, bridging anthropology and history, brings to bear a compound set of interests and methods that together offer a richer view of our past. The characteristic anthropological emphasis on ethnographic voice resonates with widespread attention across the humanities and social sciences to the contingencies underlying both specific events and the processes of emergence underlying them. Historicist approaches to texts and process ground the work and infuse dynamism into synchronic events. Most scholars in our disciplinary history deploy both sets of tools and strategies, but individual experience and perspectives produce competing narratives of anthropology's history that can provide a critical point of access to social dynamics.

Over recent decades, the historical disciplines have ventured beyond grand narratives of warfare, commerce, and empire to explore the impact of epic-scale events on particular individuals grounded in equally particular local contexts, often disrupting previous and official histories. Social and cultural historians unravel the complexity of women's history, Indigenous history, national traditions, and oral histories to juxtapose what we understand of the past with its present continuities. This changing focus requires historians to look beyond the intentions recorded in archival documents to what was omitted because it did not seem to be historically significant to participants at the time. Retrospectively, however, historians can synthesize individual and community perspectives that are only accessible from a distance of time and immediate context.

Literary models exemplify the explanatory power of combining micro and macro perspectives in this way: Leo Tolstoy's *War and Peace* documents Napoleon's march on Moscow; Herman Melville's *Moby Dick* grounds multiple positions within the whaling industry at its peak to lend heroic proportions to the confrontation between nature and human will; Albert Camus's *The Plague* dissects the escalating impacts of contagion and quarantine on a community. Similarly, many historians of anthropology approach archival records using ethnographic methods to tease out social and cultural contexts inherent in them and combine insights from multiple archives to disrupt the uniqueness of any single interpretation of "the same" facts. Like archaeologists, archival scholars cannot interrogate their research subjects directly, but traces of past actions and motives remain as grist for the investigator's mill across disciplines and distances.

From its inception, *HoAA* has addressed how history-of-science disrupts comfortable readings of the past: from national traditions; to individuals holding seminal positions in events later judged to be significant; to disciplines and subdisciplines of anthropology, history, and related fields. The "disruptive voices" we emphasize in the title of this volume are not unique here, nor is any individual author necessarily seeking to be disruptive. Taken together, the contributions here continue the project of using specific studies to shake up our understandings of the discipline.

Claudia Salomon Tarquini meticulously documents Indigenous studies in Argentina through the lens of an amalgam of anthropology, history, and ethnohistory, three disciplines that are inextricable in the Argentine context. World anthropologies rarely import categories without such adaptation to local conditions. The hegemony of North American and European traditions recedes as new anthropological traditions emerge and interact across national boundaries.

Sharon Lindenburger examines how Franz Boas navigated his Jewish identity through the intersection of German and American anthropology. Her inferences from Boas's own statements, or lack thereof, problematize the variations within Judaism itself during Boas's early education and family exposure to the revolutionary ideals of 1948, his professional choices at different periods of his life, and his changing relationship to his homeland during two world wars (from pacifism to antiracism). She argues that Reform Judaism, then and now, shared much of Boas's own ambivalence, openness to assimilation, and engagement with the Ethical Culture movement of Felix Adler in New York City.

Frederico Delgado Rosa reexamines the concept of the primitive in anthropology in a sophisticated "comparative history of anthropology" that goes beyond particular case studies to interrogate the "allochronism" around which Johannes Fabian organized his 1983 critique of the anthropological conceit of the ethnographic present. Both text and footnotes abound with exemplars; cases particular to Indigenous North America can be found in the "Voicing the Ancestors" chapters in this volume. Rosa argues that the methodology of the Americanist tradition that grew up around Franz Boas and his students has permeated the discipline beyond the study of Native Americans. His conclusions set the continuity of such traditions within a shared space-time of (post-) modern anthropology and contemporary Indigenous adaptations.

Anthropologists and historians obtain their data through multiple methods that produce surprisingly parallel results across shared questions of historicity. Kathy M'Closkey is a fieldworking anthropologist with long-term relationships to Navajo weavers and weaving as craft, cultural identity, and economic resource. She deploys this lived experience to interrogate archival documents revealing the socioeconomic exploitation of Navajo weavers. The viability and value of Navajo rug designs to their creators and their communities disrupts easy acceptance of cheap knockoffs of Navajo rug designs in a neo-capitalist economic era. Archival and ethnographic evidence combine to resituate Navajo community at the core of the critique.

Deana Weibel uses her family genealogy as the great-granddaughter of impresario Richard Schneidewind with the Bontoc Igorot of the Philippines to explore the contrived contexts of observation and performance, deployed by both researchers and their collaborators—especially experienced interpreter and ethnographic assistant Antero Cabrera—as actors in a living exhibit at a series of World's Fairs and Expositions. Weibel catalogues the publicity gimmicks of exoticism, illusion, metaphor, and misrepresentation as cultures meet in an artificial performance context that intersects with realities back home in the Philippines and belies the early twentieth-century narrative of the vanishing savage.

From the archive of John P. Harrington, a notorious packrat, Nancy Parezo ferrets out fascinating documentation of the personal side of the southwestern U.S. fieldwork of James and Matilda Coxe Stevenson. When long-term fieldworkers and archival historians pore over documents in search of evidence on other matters, familiarity with larger contexts often allows them to recognize and reframe matter out of place, the document that does not belong where it is found.

HoAA policy normally accepts no more than three chapters from any given conference or conference session because of our commitment to span the range of potential histories of anthropology rather than encourage a series of thematic volumes. We make an exception in this volume because each of the chapters on the perspectives of Native North Americans as studied populations reflects themes that recur across multiple earlier volumes of this series. Although each paper stands on its own, their juxtaposition challenges a simple narrative of interpretive voice. Native American intellectuals (as well as ordinary people) have persistently and often stridently disrupted the right of outsiders to speak for them and have disputed the accuracy and validity of what has been spoken and written about them. These chapters argue that the persistent challenge to the legitimacy of the anthropological voice is resolved, to the extent that it is, by collaboration with Indigenous communities and those of their members open to sharing cultural expertise in the hope of enhancing cross-cultural understanding. Ira Bashkow provides an overview of the commonalities of such collaborations, despite their dramatic surface variation over time and across particular scholars and ethnographic sites. Several contributors are Indigenous and reflect their insider standpoint. Because Bashkow presents more extensive framing of the collective intentions of the six chapters that follow, they are treated briefly here.

Ira Jacknis returns to the canonical collaboration between George Hunt and Franz Boas to reveal how the two men, each for his own reasons, worked together to establish Kwakwaka'wakw material culture in a museum context intelligible to a non-Indigenous public audience.

Margaret Bruchac emphasizes how what was once dismissed as ethnographic salvage today functions to reawaken past knowledge for use in contemporary revitalization contexts and assesses the ambivalent legacy of Frank Speck in northeastern ethnology as both activist and gatekeeper.

Saul Schwartz considers the consequences for Indigenous communities of the distance implicit in Boas's vision of anthropology and its changing interpretation as contemporary Indigenous communities return to ethnographic records to support cultural and linguistic revitalization.

Mindy Morgan chooses Ruth Underhill's O'Odham texts from among the many others that might exemplify what can be brought back into the present and documents the cumulative record from three generations of women ethnographers speaking to multiple audiences, both professional and public.

Sebastian Braun and Robert Hancock, in quite different ways, approach the seminal figure of Vine Deloria Jr. as a catalyst for the relationship of Indigenous voices to Indigenous control over Indigenous knowledge and its dissemination. Crucially, Indigenous anthropologists and historians struggle to insert their disruptive voices and to destabilize mainstream knowledge through a more stereoscopic lens. The histories of anthropology are indeed plural. Braun provides background context for the political maelstrom underlying Deloria's often strident voice, whereas Metis anthropologist and historian Robert Hancock, in the cameo method perfected by George Stocking, explores Deloria's satiric voice in a single session at the American Anthropological Association meetings, defining it as a call to collaborative action alongside Indigenous allies and colleagues.

We trust that readers will find in this volume perspectives, interpretations, and specific cases that will articulate in productive ways with their own experiences. Some may reinforce, while others may challenge each individual's understanding of the discipline's histories. As always, we encourage others to read and write on their particular and collective aspects of disciplinary history and to submit their work for future volumes in this series.

REGNA DARNELL

FREDERIC W. GLEACH

Disruptive Voices and
the Singularity of Histories

FREDERICO DELGADO ROSA

1

Totalitarian Critique

Fabian and the History of Primitive Anthropology

The main thesis of the epoch-making book, *Time and the Other: How Anthropology Makes Its Object* (1983), is that the history of our discipline reveals an overall tendency to create in discourse a temporal distance between the *Observer* and the *Observed* that contradicts ethnography's basic epistemological condition of sharing the same time.[1] "Allochronism" and "allochronic" are neologisms created by Johannes Fabian from the ancient Greek words ἄλλος (other) and Χρόνος (time), to mean the anthropological devices that place 'the Other' in time different from that of the anthropologist and his or her society. He forged a complementary neo-Greek concept, combining σχίζω (to split) and γένεσις (origin): anthropology's schizogenic use of time creates a split between the shared time in the field and the distant one in print form. Fabian hopes that his own alert contributes to liberate the discipline from its own legacy, by refocusing it in a radically new direction: "Like other myths, allochronism has the tendency to establish a total grip on our discourse. It must therefore be met by a 'total' response, which is not to say that the critical work can be accomplished in one fell swoop" (Fabian 1983, 152).[2]

Considering the vastness of the anthropological archive, Fabian asks the reader not to take his book, or a specific chapter, as "an historical account" of the intellectual currents under scrutiny and anticipates the possibility of unfairness "to an author or an issue" (Fabian 1983, 38, xi). After all, *Time and the Other* "is too short for its ambition" (Fabian 1991b, 21). And yet, the (so called) strategies of allochronism are "documented from the writings of anthropologists (especially M. Mead, E. T. Hall, and C. Lévi-Strauss) whose claims to speak for established anthropology are widely accepted" (1983, 38). Step by step, however, Fabian reaches the conclusion that allochronism is or was everywhere and that its tendency is or was to establish "a total grip on our [not his] discourse." Aren't his readers liable to forget the precautions against generalization and to take those selected cases for accurate historiography?

In his preface to the 2002 reprint edition, Fabian "confess[es] that [he] never felt secure about this attempt to take on an entire discipline" and that he had written *Time and the Other* "more with [his] guts than with [his] brain" ([2002] 2014, xxxiv). But the book's success had two connected side effects. First, *Time and the Other* kept on haunting its author, in the sense that Fabian often came to be identified with it alone, and there was insufficient attention paid to his subsequent work and afterthoughts. Second, Fabian's acknowledgment of the book's shortcomings—even if he had "no regrets" about it ([2006] 2014, 173)—didn't prevent the cohort of his admirers from taking it as an authoritative overview of the history of anthropology. Even though Fabian's critical reflections were made at the height of anthropology's self-reflexive period, which has since gained a historical status,[3] *Time and the Other* remains a *magnum opus* of enduring impact (Bunzl [2002] 2014; Bensa 2006; Birth 2008; Criado and Estalella 2018). That is why the present essay is focused on the work's "flaws."[4]

The project of dismantling the ideological and colonial foundations of anthropology presents itself as radical or total. The choice by Fabian of the word *total* stimulated, *a contrario*, the present essay, the purpose of which is to identify a recurrent (not universal) strategy in the domain of the critique of anthropology: allochronism that is not focused on the observed or studied peoples, but toward classical anthropologists. "Affirmations of coevalness," Fabian says, "will not 'make good' for the denial of coevalness" (1983, 156). Perhaps a taste of his own medicine would be pertinent here: the rhetorical respect for dead anthropologists does not change the fact that Fabian's critique is allochronic. Occasionally, the verdict of "dated and destined for oblivion" comes to the surface (1983, 46). A contrasting intellectual attitude, indeed a warning to one-dimensional or generalizing views of the history of anthropology, may be found in the opening words of Regna Darnell's *Invisible Genealogies*: "I want to reclaim the history of anthropology so that it can serve anthropologists as a means of constructing contemporary professional identities upon continuity with the past" (2001, 1).[5]

A more empathic reading of the archive is possible if one is attentive to nearing (instead of distancing) devices in spite of apparently allochronic words such as *primitive, savage, archaic, traditional* and so forth. There are other ways of listening to the echoes of the old evolutionist terminology and of connecting the twentieth and the nineteenth century. We can get a first hint of that possibility through a perusal of the fifth edition of the famous *Notes and Queries on Anthropology* (1929). Practicing anthropologists of that period still used profusely the word *savage*, while affirming the need to understand different modes of thought; but propinquity was also accentuated. It is almost disconcerting to notice the use of the prehistorical past as a means of connecting the observer to the observed, not only theoretically speaking, but as a sympathy device on the field. Perhaps more than any other passage in the archive of our discipline, the following one contradicts Fabian's notion of a schizogenic dimension in classical anthropology:

> It may be advisable to tell them something about our forefathers in the stone ages, how rudely and simply they lived. The informants may be pleased to recognize the similarity, and this may spur them on to give voluntary information concerning the similarities and the differences between the two cultures. (BAAS 1929, 20)

This chapter has seven sections. The first suggests the existence of ill-assumed legacies connecting postcolonial to colonial anthropologists, on the very issue of radical transformation of the discipline for ethical reasons related to power asymmetries. The second section challenges the deep-rooted idea that evolutionism *ipso facto* accentuated the distance between *savagery* and *civilization*. The third section puts in perspective Fabian's critique of the way anthropologists used native languages as a means for extracting information and thereby expurgated their texts from the human encounters on the field. The fourth section highlights the centrality of vernacular records and open readings to the detriment of theoretical representation, particularly in the Americanist tradition. The fifth section complements the previous one by suggesting that vernacular records and open readings may be spotted in different traditions and unexpected places of our discipline's archive, whether modern or premodern. The sixth section puts forward indigenous participations in anthropological projects and in the empiricist and representational episteme. The last section addresses Fabian's critique of salvage ethnography as tangential to contemporary communities and explores the ethical paradoxes of postcolonial social theory. An epilogue briefly articulates the whole argument.

A CURSED GENEALOGY?
FABIAN'S COLONIAL FORERUNNERS

When Fabian diagnoses allochronism as an "illness," is he not denying legitimacy to the sick? (Fabian 1983, 30, 150). The disease metaphor is self-explicit: the superiority of the critic manifests itself in the critique. As a distancing device, it exerts its power through the additional use of words or expressions such as "naïve," "epistemological naïveté," "failure," "illusions," "logical inconsistencies," and "mistakes and shortcomings," therefore suggesting a lack of sophistication in the reasoning or in the assumptions of our forerunners.[6] In a word, the critic feels brighter than the criticized and, the truth is, he does not hide it. The identification of the adversaries' flaws leaves no room for admitting them as equal interlocutors in today's anthropological arena. One could argue that the history of anthropology has always been like that, but Fabian insists on suggesting that his procedure transcends the standard and old practice of identifying scholarly weaknesses or limitations in earlier writings. Instead, the denial of coevalness is considered by him to be a case of "bad epistemology," meaning that it "advances cognitive interests without regard for their ideological presuppositions" (Fabian 1983, 32). That is why Fabian considers the anthropologists of the colonial period to be inescapably caught in a web.

And yet, we may find a connection between this generation gap and former ones. A case in point is the posthumous compilation, *The Dynamics of Culture Change: An Inquiry into Race Relations in Africa* (1945). Let us remind ourselves that this work was a call to contemporaneity against the "antiquarian" sensibility. Malinowski, a forerunner in the use of the word *invasion* applied to colonialism, distanced himself from "the old anthropologist" and recognized that the previous focus on pre-European institutions, far from mirroring the ethnographic present, was but a tentative historical reconstruction that obliterated "the real issues" (Malinowski 1945, 2). While acknowledging that change and contact were permanent factors of human societies and cultures, he considered that the intensity scale of twentieth century colonialism demanded the anthropologist, sensitive as he was (or should be) to the fate of colonized peoples, to assume his political responsibilities. Even though this kind of preoccupation had other forerunners in British anthropology, at least since the 1920s, it was Malinowski who contributed the most to surpass the previous focus on the "untouched primitive," that "began to be treated as a weakness to be repudiated or else admitted only in a rather shamefaced way" (Mair [1957] 2002, 229).

Let's leave aside the debatable reasons why Fabian (briefly) mentions *The Dynamics of Culture Change* as an example of implicit allochronic thinking. What is of more interest here is the fact that Malinowski had already been heavily criticized, before the publication of his ill-fated diary but after his death, for having a simplistic notion of the colonial situation in Africa. Max Gluckman inaugurated the critique (1947), which was taken over by others, like Georges Balandier, in *The Sociology of Black Africa: Social Dynamics in Central Africa* (1955).[7] Gluckman's article, "Malinowski's 'Functional' Analysis of Social Change," opened in the following way:

> There can be no single right analysis of social change. The data are so complex and our tools yet so crude that we must expect to work with various hypotheses and many types of abstractions. . . . I immediately distrust such works as this latest polemic of the late Professor Malinowski's which is written in the strident terms of the one and only orthodoxy. (Gluckman 1947, 103)

Through the rest of the article, however, Gluckman committed exactly same fault by judging Malinowski's ideas as unacceptable. While affirming that the subject in question was "humbling," his verdict, making use of epithets like "sterile" and "naive," was quite arrogant: "This is a bad book" (Gluckman 1947, 121). Malinowski's conception of the colonial field "in terms of culture" deviated anthropology from the right path and could not have a place in anthropology as a legitimate perspective among others.[8] Following on the footsteps of Gluckman, it is worth noting that Balandier's theoretical critique of Malinowski was also inseparable from the political dimension:

> As Gluckman has pointed out, the conceptual system elaborated by this famous anthropologist in no way lends itself to the recognition of conflict.... It should be noted how easily a theoretical position of this kind can, in a situation characterized by domination and unequal relations between colonizers and colonized, become a source of error. We then see that the notion of 'maladjustment' is regarded as a strictly cultural phenomenon—resulting from the *cultural* incompatibilities created by contact and the rhythm of change—without sufficient attention being paid to the underlying conflict between groups or races. (Balandier [1955], 42–43)

The case of the Ba-Kongo Kimbangist church, studied by Balandier in *The Sociology of Black Africa*, would be a perfect illustration of Malinowski's alleged "error," in the sense that this prophetic-messianic movement in Belgian Congo, dating back to the 1920s, only followed a collision course with the European missions after and as a consequence of the repressive measures taken by the colonial authorities. Certain groups even detached themselves completely from Christianity; and this could not be a matter of "cultural incompatibility," since the church had started by declaring itself Christian and in debt to the white missionaries' teachings. If we read *The Dynamics of Culture Change* without a *parti pris*, we may nonetheless question the validity of Balandier's critique of Malinowski.[9] In fact, Malinowski wrote that Africans could "begin often by adopting Western ways eagerly and wholeheartedly" (referring explicitly to the case of religion) and "end by reacting" against those ways in movements "directly hostile to the Whites" (Malinowski 1945, 12). This shows that to him the "maladjustment" was not a simple matter of cultural incompatibility; it was instead a political reaction.[10]

It is therefore conceivable to spot the existence of an invisible genealogy between him, Balandier, Gluckman, and Malinowski.[11] In all four, we find a discourse of rupture that intertwines the theoretical and moral problems of earlier schools, authors, or texts. This does not mean that *The Dynamics of Culture Change* is "faultless," but simply that the overbearing attitude of actively searching for its "faults," of not admitting the legitimacy of any of its vistas, generates historiographic distortions that strongly affect the way anthropologists relate themselves, both politically and heuristically, with their discipline's past. Balandier can be a "pioneer" (Fabian 1998, 142), but Malinowski cannot.[12] As Fabian writes, "it was not until the interdisciplinary critique of anthropology's culturalism (and functionalism) had prepared us to 'remember the present' that we began to perceive and appreciate African contemporary culture in its many creative expressions" (Fabian 2007, 71).

In spite of being counter hegemonic, this moral dimension of the postcolonial critique is hegemonic by nature or potentially so; in any case, it became effectively hegemonic. It may be detected, for example, in the association of Sahlins's culturalism to "nationalist movements or even fascist politics" (Kumoll 2013, 72). It can also be illustrated by one of the reactions to Herbert S. Lewis's seminal 1998 article, "The Misrepresentations of Anthropology and Its Consequences." Instead of focusing on the misrepresentations themselves, as identified by Lewis's counter-critique, Sandy Toussaint practically accuses him of silencing the role of women anthropologists and overlooking the importance of past anthropology to contemporary indigenous land claims. In short, Lewis is allegedly guilty of not reading the history of the discipline with a postcolonial ethos: "We must . . . be careful not to romanticize that past" (Toussaint 1999, 606). In his response, Lewis reacted to this particular passage by saying, "where Dr. Toussaint warns us 'not to romanticize that past' (with which I must also agree), the point of my article was to warn against the prevalent attitude that demonizes that past" (Lewis 1999, 609).

There is a synonymy between demonizing and totalizing, since today's anthropologists have to make sure that younger generations do not identify themselves with any classical idea or sentiment. But teachers and professional anthropologists may take part in the process as self-censored, not just censors. In fact, the presumed political righteousness of the hegemonic counter hegemonic argument connotes discordant views with a bygone era of the discipline. And since the past was colonial, the act of developing a positive relationship with past anthropologists is easily targeted as a form of colonial nostalgia or, at best, naïveté. Romanticizing, as we just saw, is still another word for it—"and that feels oppressive."[13] Alternative standings risk ostracism, and what could be worse than not belonging to our time?

PREHISTORICAL COEVALNESS: ANIMISM AS A NEARING DEVICE

Considering the importance of evolutionism in Fabian's thesis as the "founding" paradigm of both anthropology and allochronism, it is surprising that no single evolutionist author or work is properly analyzed in *Time and the Other*, so that contrasting sensibilities within sociocultural evolutionism are overlooked. In a provocative manner at their time, some major figures of this broad intellectual movement, particularly Edward Tylor and his disciples, insisted on the proximity, not the distance, between *savagery* and *civilization*. Besides, any attempt to restrict the concept of animism to non-European cosmologies fully contradicts the spirit of the original theory. According to Tylor, every religion was animist, the two words being synonymous in his anthropology.[14] For each animistic category, he presented illustrations from *savage* to *civilized*, in chapter after chapter of *Primitive Culture*, so there were no sequential stages of religious evolution for him but only permanence, through a very complex, varied and inconsistent transformation of the pre-historical heritage.

Tylor's Huxley, Andrew Lang, resumed this intellectual sensibility with a more literary skill: "Man can never be certain that he has expelled the savage from his temples and from his heart" (Lang 1887, vol. I, 338). Lang also writes, "We cannot escape from him in any field of activity; we repeat his theories without knowing" (Lang 1907, 1). This Victorian principle should be read as revolutionary: one could not escape *from him*, meaning the *savage*, not only because *he* was genealogically connected to our creeds and our most venerable institutions, including kingship in Great Britain, but also because *savagery* was part of us, psychologically speaking. Contrary to what Fabian says, the Tylorian concept of animism was not "a means to indicate that an opponent is no longer in the contemporary arena of debate" (Fabian 1983, 152). In spite of his modern rationality, Tylor knew that he was surrounded by animists in one way or another and that he was not immune to (the creed in) spiritual beings himself.[15] Fabian warns his readers against the illusion of interpreting evolutionism (or, for that matter, colonialism) as "incorporative" in the sense that it created "a universal frame of reference able to accommodate all societies" and insists that it was founded "on distancing and separation" (Fabian 1983, 26). An opposite view is that evolutionism, in one of its most significant branches, "invented" animism (Fabian 1983, 152) as a nearing device, not as a distancing one.[16]

The most daring aspect of the Tylorian theory was the perception that animism, whether by development, survival, or revival, would linger on and forever, anchored as it was in the functioning of the human mind and in the power of custom. As Tylor put it, "The thing that has been will be" (Tylor [1871] 1903, vol. I, 159). If the "central question" for many evolutionist anthropologists "was how civilization triumphed over savagery" (Kuper 2011, 41), this was not the case for many distinguished ones. While Tylor's anthropology could present itself as a "reformer's science," this formula had to do precisely with the resilience of animism in the present time. In any case, he was aware that animism would never be overthrown: at best, it could still evolve.[17] If transformation and continuity were two sides of the same coin, the strong attachment of all peoples to their specific animist legacies was much more than historical. This idea was taken over by several of Tylor's disciples, such as Ernest Crawley:

> As to "survivals" of primitive speculation and customs into civilized periods, the term is misused when it is implied that these are dead forms, surviving like fossil remains or rudimentary organs; the fact is that human nature remains potentially primitive, and it is not easy even for those most favored by descent to rise above these primitive ideas, because these ideas "spring eternally" from permanent functional causes. (Crawley 1902, 4)[18]

Everything could be embellished or developed in time, keeping more or less of its original crudity, but in the end animism—not to mention magic—was "destined to last as long as the human race" (Hartland

1909–10, vol. 2, 285). And if animism had its inevitable place in the here and now, as well as in the future, then there is no necessary contradiction between evolutionist categories and the epistemological condition of ethnography as a shared time. Fabian's idea that evolutionism established itself "as a discourse on distance, on remoteness in space and time" contradicts one of the fundamental principles of Tylorian anthropology (Fabian 1991a, 197).

Different levels of amalgamation occur in *Time and the Other*. After neglecting the diversity within evolutionism, Fabian identifies diffusionism's *Gründerzeit* as identical and then proceeds to a search of allochronic sameness in the modern critiques of both currents. The new schools are presented, "for the sake of brevity" (Fabian 1983, 20), under the labels of British functionalism, American culturalism, and French structuralism.[19] What happened, says Fabian, is that the denial of coevalness turned "from an explicit concern into an implicit theoretical assumption" (Fabian 1983, 38), recognizable in the recycling of an idea of difference that, in spite of a new synchronic focus, kept a barrier between the anthropologist and the alleged Other. "In this respect there is little that divides otherwise opposed schools of anthropology" (Fabian 1983, 160). An academic code emerged through which human communities were pushed to the status of a research object, observed by a new category of professionals who therefore held back the communication experiences actually shared on the field. Real time vanished under such circumstances; the denial of coevalness even became "intensified," in comparison with evolutionism's more explicit allochronism. Whether the word *primitive* was abandoned or kept, anthropology continued to serve as a "time-machine" (Fabian 1983, 38).[20] And the fact is that, more often than not, the word primitive was maintained, betraying in this way the promiscuity between modern spatialization and nineteenth century allochronism. However, an alternative reading of the archive is possible.

THE POETICS OF INTERSUBJECTIVE TIME

Fabian admits that "generations of anthropology students have received, and followed, advice to learn the language," and he acknowledges that "this is sensible advice," considering that conversational skills are the heart of any proper fieldwork experience (Fabian 1983, 106). The identification of linguistically deficient ethnographies at the heart of our discipline's history, particularly Evans-Pritchard's *The Nuer* (1940) and Meyer Fortes's *The Dynamics of Clanship among the Tallensi* (1945), puts into question any idealized picture of the anthropology's communicational abilities.[21] It is doubtful, however, that the ethnography of Africa or, for that matter, of any continent, can be fairly appreciated by "evidence contained in writings considered exemplary" (Fabian 1983, 33; Owusu 1978, 312). The vastness of the ethnographical archive makes this consideration simply irrelevant. If we evoke, for example, the enormous intellectual tradition of folktale collecting, we find for Africa alone a spectrum that had its standard in bilingual publications, at least since Henry Callaway's pioneering Zulu and English works, *Nursery Tales, Traditions, and Histories of the Zulu* (1868) and *The Religious System of the Amazulu* (1870). There is no need to remind ourselves that this tradition "survived" all through the twentieth century in many countries, often if not always in significantly transformed ways, around the polemical concept of oral literature (Baumgdart and Derive 2008; Finnegan 2007), with or without proper attention to the performative dimensions of orality.

Notwithstanding their detractors, folklore studies are part and parcel of anthropology's history, which is a further point against generalization.[22] All the more so that linguistic deficiencies were seldom an issue in Europe, where most folklore collectors spoke the same language as the peasantry or a variant of it. Any critique of anthropology as a colonial project misses the point if it disregards the vastness of European ethnography at home since the nineteenth century—a crucial and enduring chapter of our discipline, with theoretical implications that are far from negligible. The same applies to several non-European settings, from Cuba[23] to Vietnam,[24] where the anthropologists' social background could be different from that of the communities they studied, while sharing the same mother tongue.

Considering that the present chapter is an exercise in comparative history of anthropology and not a case study, there's no need to say that any illustrations are but pointers to the diversity and the complexity of the archive. The discipline's past obviously requires great caution as regards the connections between linguistic, conceptual, and methodological dimensions.[25] Even the skills and goals of the Boasians varied enormously, with modesty prevailing among those who did not choose linguistics as their main subfield.[26] Besides, linguistic competence or incompetence is not a dichotomy: it has all sorts of shades and representatives, including interpreters and nonprofessional ethnographers with many years of field experience and vernacular fluency, before or after the consolidation of anthropology's modern currents. Human proximity, including the share of cultural knowledge and wisdom, does not depend perforce on speaking the same language but implies a wide range of factors. Above all, the comparison of ethnographic results is (and it will always be) a matter of perspective and sensibility, both between different schools and within the same school.[27]

But Fabian does not seem to agree with this; on the contrary, it appears that, according to his worldview, intellectual and political legitimacy may only be gained if the anthropologist, after creating a certain kind of intersubjective experience in the field, keeps it at the center of his or her discourse. Because humans are human, phenomenological intersubjectivity can be pretty much anything, so the problem does not seem to be the classical anthropologists' incapacity of truly shared moments, but their final discourse as a Western structuring of alleged data. Only by generating that kind of praxis, and by further pursuing it in the textual form, can the anthropologist finally negate Otherness as a pathological category. Otherwise, the native languages are but "a *tool*," a regrettable "means to extract information" (Fabian 1983, 106).[28] And if conversation, and therefore coevalness, is an obvious condition of ethnography as fieldwork in one way or another, the final written forms of the monograph are criticized by Fabian for disavowing that experience through an allochronic discourse, let alone for leaving it totally aside.

If the actual situations of dialogue did not permeate a monograph, we should however be attentive to the fact that more often than not there were pivotal passages that reflected the human, coeval relationship between the anthropologist and his or her interlocutors, thereby resolving the presumed paradox.[29] In his 1945 book, *The Dynamics of Clanship Among the Tallensi*, Meyer Fortes thanked the men, women, and children who assisted him and his wife, for their "confidence," for "the devotion with which they instructed us in the way of life of their people." Remembering with gratitude their "patience, tolerance, tact, and friendliness," he added, "They welcomed us to their homes, their domestic occasions, and their esoteric and public religious gatherings. We learnt more from them about humanity than I have the skill to write of" (Fortes 1945, xii).[30] Similar affirmations of coevalness—actually all sorts of explicit references to intersubjective time, whether brief or long, whether in prefaces, in footnotes or in the main body of a book or article—may be found in plenty of classic texts. Fabian suggests that they were contradictory, if not simply rhetorical—a harsh judgement when one considers the existence of poignant testimonies in that lot, such as Nancy Lurie's description of her visits to Mitchell Redcloud Sr. in 1945:

> I visited him frequently and my questions about Winnebago culture helped relieve the tedium of existence in a hospital ward. In time he came to believe that our association had been preordained. . . . He was eventually scheduled for surgery, and fearing that he might not survive the operation, presented me with a cherished and valuable legacy—adoption as his daughter. (Lurie [1961] 2005, xii)

The very aim of a passage like this was to reveal the shared praxis upon which the anthropological discourse was built.[31] This is not a matter of fieldwork anecdotes but of a deep, entangled interaction that was in no case perceived as antagonistic to the published results. After all, Fabian himself insists in saying that dialogue as a literary form does not "automatically preserve the dialogical nature of the knowledge process" (1990a, 764). If this is so, the reverse should also be true: dialogue as an event is not undermined by the absence of dialogue as a genre.

A comparison between Alfred Kroeber's *Handbook of the Indians of California* (1925) and his *Yurok Myths* (1978) would not only be revealing, but also symbolic. This posthumous book—with several references to intersubjectivity in its biographical descriptions of all twenty-nine informants and collaborators—even emphasized differences of personality and creativity between his Yurok informants, thereby rejoining, for once, Paul Radin's insistence on the importance of the individuals. This represents perhaps Kroeber's maximum from this point

of view, considering that the methodological and theoretical foundations of his anthropology consisted in "omit[ting] the human agents"
(Kroeber 1952, 133).[32] But when we remember that his work includes
more than 550 published texts, we should abstain from simplifying the
matter. In her "Foreword" to *Yurok Myths*, Theodora Kroeber reveals
to us that, "once the myths were published," her husband meant to
write "a history at once more personal, psychological, and biographical than any he had yet undertaken" (T. Kroeber 1978, xiv). And the
reason why he never did it encapsulates his deep sense of coevalness
toward the Yurok: "Perhaps I cannot write of the Yurok in this way. I
feel myself too much a Yurok" (T. Kroeber 1978, xiv). Here is a sample
of Kroeber's intersubjective passages about Lame Billy of Weispus:

> I need hardly say that Billy dictated his tales to me without interme-
> diary. He took obvious pleasure in relating them, and the pay was
> welcome to a man deprived of practically all earning power. Several
> times he showed jealousy when I ceased coming to see him, in order
> to work temporarily with someone else. (Kroeber 1978, 16)

FROM HEARING TO WRITING

Fabian believes that one of the main problems of anthropology, which
can be traced "to some of the fundamental convictions of Western culture," is the epistemological overevaluation of sight to the detriment of
hearing (Fabian 1983, 159). The "contemplative view," or "visualism," is
actually perceived by him as "an ideological aberration," for it ideologically accentuates the anthropologist's superior capacities of ordering
the world, instead of exploring the communicative side of the ethnographic experience, forcibly conditioned by language skills (Fabian 1983,
159; Fabian 1991a, 200). His conviction "that we are on the threshold
of some major change in our conceptions of the history and the present role of anthropology" is thus related to the final praise of dialogical
modes of expression that take hearing as man's "noblest sense." Only
in this way, Fabian believes, can we properly perceive and transmit
"the radical contemporaneity of mankind" (Fabian 1983, xiv, 162, xi).[33]
    What about humble modes of hearing at the core of classical anthro-
pology? And what happens when these modes of hearing leave open

the ways of reading in ways that transcend anthropology itself? In her identification of the "Distinctive Features of the Americanist Tradition," considered as a living intellectual heritage in a line of "continuity to contemporary praxis," Darnell reminds us that the Boasian program was, first of all, a search for the Native words and their transformation into text through the collaboration between anthropologists-linguists and Native individuals.[34] Even though the Native collaborators who worked with the Boasians had varying statuses as cultural representatives and experts, that does not invalidate the prevailing perceptions of the "sophistication and complexity" of these interlocutors' narratives (Darnell 2001, 19). It was the anthropologist's interpretation that had to be put aside as potentially falsifying, and so we should not presume any simple hierarchical relation between the observer and the observed or, more precisely, between the listener and the speaker. There are varied sensibilities within this complex and multifarious current, at any time and up to now,[35] but we may say that contemporary representatives of the Americanist tradition are at odds with Fabian's contention that there was and is a prevailing, insurmountable tension between presence and representation, even when writing "engages in and acknowledges co-authorship," namely of texts "transcribed from recordings in the field" (Fabian 2007, 24; Valentine and Darnell 1999).[36]

In the past, the informants and collaborators usually did not appear as actual coauthors of the anthropological publication, but their word was presented as such in any case, so "it is unnecessary," Darnell adds, "to denigrate the textual work done throughout the twentieth century simply because its sensitivities to aboriginal-white relations are not those of our own time" (Darnell 2001, 19). Obviously, when many people were involved, a full sharing of authorship was as unrealistic in the early twentieth century as it is today, but we cannot make generalizations about the way in which the Native informants and collaborators were acknowledged by the Boasians, or how their names were actually mentioned or not, for it varied considerably between anthropologists as between works written by the same anthropologist. There was also here an entire spectrum of possibilities, from brief mentions of anonymous elders to actual appearances on the cover of a book. The autobiographies of American Indians (or, for that matter, of other native individuals around the world)[37] are a case in point, with two paradigmatic cases: Crashing Thunder's, edited by Paul Radin in 1920,[38] and Mountain Wolf Woman's, edited in 1961 by Nancy Lurie.

The anthropologists' commitment to the production of vernacular records as a heuristic priority implied not only "the coevalness" (Darnell 2001, 14) of such collaborations as interaction during fieldwork, but also and above all as a resulting text. This ethnography that wrote down indigenous words, representative as it was of a significant, apparently a theoretical trend in North America (Valentine and Darnell 1999), was in itself a materialization of a praxis between the informants and collaborators, and their anthropologist.[39] Even if the views of the Boasians on the centrality of strictly vernacular records varied as well,[40] any work could have (and usually had) this kind of quotation, so that the fieldwork experience of speaking and listening was always implied in the written form, which cannot be reduced to the Fabian's labels of "information" or "taxonomy."[41]

Each Americanist record also allows and even invites new explorations by future readers. And if the anthropological text remains open, not closed or strictly representational, Fabian's idea that "the emergence of Culture as a guiding concept in anthropology signaled the victory of representationism" might be discarded (Fabian 1991a, 203; Fabian 1990a).[42] In some sense, ethnographical texts as "documents of communicative events, of performances and conversations" have always been at the core of Culturalism—and they may concern other currents as well. This perspective on the history of anthropology may help resolve Fabian's problem: classical outputs do not, in any simple manner, replace the confrontational nature of field research by an observational artifice.[43] As "a practitioner of language-centered anthropology," for whom ethnography is working "with texts" (Fabian 2007, 33, 134), Fabian could acknowledge instead that his own worries are far from being new in the field.

BEYOND TRAVELOGUES AND
SCIENTIFIC MONOGRAPHS

According to Fabian, the "schizogenic" dimension of anthropology—the paradox between the mandatory coevalness of the field experience and the allochronic presentation or manipulation of the results—characterizes a discipline that claimed "a unified existence," meaning the combination by the same professionals of those two activities. "This certainly was not always the case," he clarifies. "After all, travelogues and armchair synthesis coexisted side by side during most of the early history of anthropology without being practically united in the same person or institution" (Fabian 1983, 72). In later works, Fabian finishes by stressing the fact that this understanding of the history of anthropology is artificial: the scientific monograph did not simply replace the travelogue (Fabian 2001, 142). And one of the reasons for this nuance is that professional ethnographers kept fieldnotes just as travelers kept diaries. The problem, Fabian adds, is that the professional ethnographers, unlike the travelers, never or seldom reproduced passages from those records of real-life experience.[44]

Indeed, the history of ethnography is complex. "Pre-modern" ethnographies (and not just travelogues of "en route" experiences) were no mere data collection at the service of armchair thinkers; many of their producers participated in the discipline and made use of anthropological ideas in their monographs (Gosden, Larson, and Petch 2007), including explicitly allochronic, evolutionist formulas in titles such as *With a Prehistoric People: The Akikuyu of British East Africa* (1910), by William and Katherine Routledge. The ethnographies in question ran a gamut of possibilities between the vernacular components and the theoretical implications. In the second place, the exclusion of fieldnotes from modern monographs is counterbalanced by this: anthropologists could organize capital parts of their written work as a *corpus inscriptionum*—to use Malinowski's formula—while attributing to it theoretical implications that it, after all, always had in one way or another.

In their introduction to *Theorizing the Americanist Tradition*, Lisa Valentine and Regna Darnell insist on the need to move beyond "a simple equation of Americanist anthropology with the work of Franz Boas and his students," by taking into account not only its antecedents in the United States, but also the applicability of its principles and ethics in other contexts and within other trends, with increasing illustrations "from other parts of the world" (1999, 6, 16). This idea may be extended by suggesting that the humble dimension of the anthropological praxis, crucial as it was and still is to the Americanist tradition (in spite of its variants), somehow transcends it. The written transcription of what was once heard—and listened to—may appear in the most unexpected places within the archive of our discipline, whether in modern or "premodern" traditions, in different amounts, for sure, sometimes subordinated to theory, but other times excluding it on purpose.

And perhaps the Boasians (at least some of them) were aware that they did not invent the wheel on this particular point. Paul Radin's 1952 compilation, *African Folktales*, is an illustration of that invisible genealogy.[45] It was a selection of eighty-one tales "recorded in the original or by individuals who knew the native language well." They came from thirty-one monographs (most of them with many other chapters apart from the tales) published between 1864 and 1931 by different kinds of colonial agents, some of whom were anthropologists of the first academic generation in Great Britain, like Major A. J. N. Tremearne, or by those personally connected to anthropologists, like Reverends John Roscoe and Edwin W. Smith. Even if "the anthropologists and the laymen who have collected aboriginal folktales tell us, as a rule, very little about their informants except that some have the reputation of knowing more, some of knowing fewer narratives, and that some are good, some poor narrators," the indisputable fact remains that they heard them and wrote their words down (Radin [1952] 1983, 11). Note that Radin used the expression "as a rule," therefore acknowledging different kinds of references to the Native informants or collaborators and to the intersubjective experiences between them and the ethnographers. Indeed, this labyrinth of variations may be imagined as neverending or, at least, as capable of confronting us with unexpected forms of coevalness.

One illustration is the compilation by the Swiss missionary and U.S. commercial agent Héli Chatelain, who lived between 1885 and 1907 near Malanje (then Portuguese Angola) and whose *Folk-tales from Angola* were published in 1894 by the American Folklore Society in Kimbundu with a "literal English translation" (one of the folktales was selected by Radin). Chatelain insisted on the need to give a voice to "the principal, the offended side"—that is, the Africans, not by "unwarranted generalization," but by listening to the "unwritten, oral literature" of particular groups (Chatelain 1894, 16–17). The following passage from the introduction encapsulates, curiously enough, the priority of the sense of hearing to the detriment of vision.[46] We may take it today as a warning against narrowing perspectives about the archive's diversity, particularly about nineteenth century ethnographies apart from travelogues:

> Books of African travelers have been prominent before the public for the last two decades, but, as a rule, only such accessory parts of folk-lore as strike the sense of sight—native dress, arms, and strange customs—have been described, and seldom accurately at that. The essential constituents of folklore, those embodied in words, have been ignored, and the moral and intellectual world of Africa is, today, as much a *terra incognita* as geographical Africa was fifty years ago. (Chatelain 1894, 16)

SALVAGING THE FUTURE

In *Time and the Other*, Fabian takes up the idea that anthropology is the child of colonialism, to the point of equating ethnography with the politics of invasion and exploitation. He believes that the notion of an advanced time, irradiating from the metropolis, underlies the anthropological appropriation of indigenous knowledge, duly subtracted from its underdeveloped context and forward to Western academia and publishing circuits. That is why the informants were not properly informed about the salvaging project they were taking part in; nor were they notified that their knowledge was to be "disseminated for public scrutiny" (Biolsi and Zimmerman 1997, 8). In some cases, for sure, this accusation is pertinent;[47] but in other cases the publishing universe, even the white academy, was part of indigenous people's worldview at least from the late nineteenth and early twentieth centuries. Variety, not homogeneity, has once more to be taken into account.

For example, there is a strong case for the inextricability between Maori and Pakeha projects of salvage ethnography in New Zealand in that period, as Jeffrey Holman sustains in *Best of Both Worlds: The Story of Elsdon Best and Tutakangahau* (2010).[48] In his reconstitution of the passage of these two men between communicable worlds and interests,

Holman highlights the fact that Tutakangahau, who had witnessed cultural transition in his youth, saw Elsdon Best "as an opportunity and not as a threat." The old *tohunga* [sage] of romanticism was, after all, "a modernizer anxious to preserve the old ways in print," someone who felt "the need to commit to paper the knowledge he had" (Holman 2010, 15, 128). According to this reading, the predatory dimension of ethnography (as Fabian and other postcolonial critics puts it) should give way to the collaborative one, all the more so that Tutakangahau invested himself and Best, respectively, with the halo of master and disciple, of ultimate donor and legatee of the vanishing knowledge. Alongside archival material,[49] Holman cites a passage of a 1909 article where Best reproduced the following words of Tutakangahau to himself: "O son! I alone among Tuhoe know of these things, and now for the first time I tell them. I have never divulged them before. You alone know them, and you shall remain as a *tohunga*" (Holman 2010, 160). Holman fully dismisses the hypothesis that Best invented this and, on the contrary, calls attention to the fact that the ethnographer spent the rest of his life, after Tutakangahau's death, as "scribe and recorder of the vanished world he had pursued" (Holman 2010, 217).[50]

What we should keep in mind is that, in several contexts where salvage ethnography took place, native individuals could be aware that books were not only read in the present but constituted a legacy to future generations, both of white and indigenous peoples. Instead of being passively manipulated for a few dollars, powerless before the anthropologists, some informants and collaborators were "passionately interested in the old ways" and participated in salvage ethnography as a project that actually mattered, that concerned their lives and their communities (Lowie [1935] 1985, xxi)—in a word, as a praxis.[51] Whether old sages or young "mixed-blood" interpreters, they might be interested in the ethnographical process for additional reasons of their own and articulate different historical times differently, but these reasons and articulations could be in dialogue with the anthropologist's salvaging sensibility.[52]

The informed, negotiated, sometimes proactive participation of native individuals in anthropological projects has been highlighted in different ways and in different contexts; and it might concern not only the fieldwork praxis, but the printed results as well. In her 2001 book on the ways anthropology "has been captured by Africans," Lyn Schumaker recalls Max Gluckman's anecdote about his own *Judicial Process among the Barotse of Northern Rodhesia* (1955), a monograph that the Lozi experts considered to be their own, hence their surprise upon the arrival of a later researcher interested in the same subject: why was he "wasting their time asking questions about their law when they had written a book about it"? (Schumaker 2001, 234). Having herself revisited several field sites in Zambia in the 1990s, Schumaker concludes that quite a few anthropologists' books had become part of local cultural history.[53] Without any intent of generalizing this illustration, let's just admit that the problematics encapsulated in the title, *When They Read What We Write* (Brettell 1993), is actually a much older story than late colonialism.[54]

In order not to replicate the power asymmetries of the colonial period (see Jezequel 2007), we should be attentive to the risk of downplaying the legitimate involvement of colonized people with ethnography, anthropology or, for that matter, historiography, which have methods and theories that many Indigenous individuals obviously and willingly have adopted. This includes local defenses of an empiricist and representationist episteme, whether these options are identified as Western-like or a mixture of indigenous and non-indigenous visions. The kind of anthropology that Fabian abhors, has had "Indigenous" followers or continuators, without forgetting, obviously, researchers of mixed descent, like Peter Buck/Te Rangi Hiroa or J. N. B. Hewitt. As Ned Blackhawk and Isaiah L. Wilner write, in their introduction to *Indigenous Visions: Rediscovering the World of Franz Boas* (2018), "It is time to peel away the racial and colonial assumptions that have obscured our view of these seminal thinkers" (xiii). This anthology seeks to recenter the vast set of Indigenous[55] actors who did more than participate in the Boasian project and Western science: they contributed to the making of (anthropological) modernity through "a conceptual vernacular for envisioning shared forms of belonging" (xiii). This contribution was therefore in dialogue with the interaction that many classical anthropologists forsake; it is different from, but in a sense deeper than the one Fabian idealizes: the interaction that resulted from seeing actually distant human beings as near, as portrayers of a wisdom that implied a critique of Western society, let alone an answer to understand humanity itself (Lewis 2014).[56] In one of his afterthoughts on the "collateral damages" of *Time and the Other*, Fabian admits that radical critique should not obliterate the fact that some of the words— including *primitive*—that he "took to be evidence for unwarranted allochronism" could be "part of discourses that were critical of blind faith in reason or civilization and of a mindless celebration of modernity" ([2006] 2014, 173–74).

And there are, finally, two additional reasons why field intersubjectivity, along with a (potentially narcissistic) fetishization of the ethnographic moment, should not be the sole criteria to "redeem" anthropology and its past. First, texts create intersubjectivity beyond their authors' own expectations and imaginations, both in their time and after their deaths. And secondly, this open intersubjectivity—that is, the intellectual, emotional, and spiritual human bonds—created by the trajectory of a book (or any other text) in time and space, often concern communities and individuals distant from the original cultural and social contexts.[57] Labeling those bonds colonial for all eternity seems quite a violent option. Fabian himself has some afterthoughts about the problem of giving "little consideration" to the readers: "What happens to their freedom . . . to talk in and out a text (something which the classical monograph permitted and even encouraged)?" In the preface to *Power and Performance*, after stating the "hard-fought victory" against the colonial representational epistemology encapsulated by the classical monograph, he alerts against the risks of "veer[ing] off into hidden conservatism of postmodern playfulness" (1990b, xiii). Is that enough?

Thanks to the way Fabian demonizes Western (colonial) components of anthropological projects, it appears that he does not admit the dialogical dimensions of modern and premodern anthropology (with the exception of travelogues). This seems to imply that the discipline has to correspond to his own picture of coevalness between the human beings implied or be nothing—that is, an illegitimate endeavor. And this is why his critique risks charges of totalitarianism. Now, not all anthropologists feel comfortable with his idea of becoming "itinerant bards, clowns, or preachers" (Fabian 1990a, 767); and that does not make them any less legitimate anthropologists. Believing that one has to expel the empiricist vices in order to get along with "non-Western people" corresponds, after all, to the very allochronism that Fabian seeks to strike down.

PRECOLONIAL VERTIGO: EXCLUDING THE ANCESTORS

Fabian maintains that anthropological literature, resulting from an obsession with precolonial authenticity to the detriment of actual living people, is perceived as "tangential" by their descendants; and this "is yet another symptom of the denial of coevalness" (Fabian 1983, 92).[58] Certainly any anthropologist, Fabian included, is aware of the existence of other, contrasting attitudes to the ethnographical archive. For example, in his contribution to Stocking's *Volksgeist as Method and Ethic*, Thomas Buckley transforms his own critical analysis of "The Epistemological and Moral Contexts of Kroeber's Californian Ethnology" into something else when he explores Native contemporary readings of the original project, such as this statement by a Yurok elder: "Thank God for that good Doctor Kroeber . . . and those other good white doctors from Berkeley who came up here to study us. If they hadn't taken an interest in us and come up here and written it all down we wouldn't know a thing today about who we really are" (Buckley 1996, 294). When juxtaposed with cases of actual extinction (who can deny it?), or irreparable linguistic or cultural loss, words like these cause a problem for anthropologists who systematically belittle the classical projects of salvage ethnography.

Isn't it pitiful that contemporary anthropologists frequently choose to interpret similar statements by Native representatives as an ill-fated heritage or mimicry of the colonial period worldview? And this happens in spite of William Bissel's warning (2005) that the political significance of "colonial nostalgia"—including the romanticization of pre-colonial worlds—should not be presumed as conservative, particularly when ex-colonized peoples express any of its variants. Fabian himself seems to be aware of such a dilemma in his reflection on "World Anthropologies," while at the same time implying that concepts such as culture, tradition, or authenticity only matter to anthropologists in order to "maintain a dialectic tension" (2007, 3). While acknowledging that colonialism is not over (and never was) in the United States, Thomas Biolsi and Larry Zimmerman go to the point of enumerating power concepts and power theories—for example, Eric Wolf's, that are deemed to be not only irrelevant but "threatening" by contemporary communities:

> Even when anthropologists and other intellectuals consciously choose to engage in research critical of colonization and colonial power relations, they do not have the same interests as native peoples; they do not bring the same questions to the research setting. Ironically, some of the most critical and radical thought in anthropology makes Indian people most uncomfortable. (Biolsi and Zimmerman 1997, 15–16; Kumoll 2013; Deloria Jr. 1997)

In a 2008 article, "The Creation of Coevalness and the Danger of Homochronism," Kevin Birth sustains that anthropologists should open their minds to different, even contrasting, temporal conceptions that emphasize "enduring characteristics, everlastingness, eternity, or infinite repetition." These may be "disconcerting" to our postmodern sensibility, marked as it is by "a sense of change as central to being-in-the-world" and by predominant notions of "transience, fragmentation, and instability" (Birth 2008, 11, 15). He thereby attempts to go a step further than Fabian in the avoidance of distancing devices. In retrospect, after twenty-five years of *everybody* trying to create coevalness,[59] he reaches the conclusion that Fabian's critique "did not prevent homochronic writing," meaning by this "a displacement of those people who are ethnographically represented out of their temporality and their assimilation into academic discourses of history." In any case, only the encountering of a common ground between the anthropologist's Time and the informant's Time result in true coevalness, since the phenomenological present of a communicative encounter is not "a sufficient means" for establishing it (Birth 2008, 16, 7; Augé 1994, 74).[60]

"To create coevalness," Birth adds, "it is crucial to adopt the local conceptions that organize the past and relate them to 'general social theory'" (Birth 2008, 17).[61] But what is general social theory exactly? If the result of such an adoption amounts to the identification of "other people's" alleged essentialism or primordialism and, in the end, an implicit demonstration of "our" superior understanding of its true meaning, the result remains allochronic—or, for that matter, homochronic. Anthropology then may have a serious ethical problem in its way of dealing with native forms of "resistance" (Dirks, Eley, and Ortner 1994, 17) against contemporary social theory such as Linda Tuhiwai Smith's rejection of the anthropological (undeniably pejorative) definitions of essentialism and authenticity. The same applies to her defense of alternative, indigenous notions, following a "humanist" perspective according to which the "strategic" dimension of claiming an essence has to be equated in terms of "human rights and indigenous rights," embracing decolonization from within (Smith [1999] 2012, 74).

In the history of anthropology, we are finally confronted with several layers of bringing the past into the present, which is something very different from allochronism as a projection of coeval communities into the past.[62] When all is said and done, the anthropological archive and the history of Indigenous communities are intertwined in ways that should not receive overconfident rejoinders. If there still is, and perhaps will always be, an "inescapable political linkage between anthropologists and disempowered peoples," then we should avoid feeling superior to our forerunners, who had a complex relationship with colonialism (Biolsi and Zimmerman 1997, 13). This discussion concerns the notion that salvaged oral traditions are a "permanent record of human achievement" both from the point of view of language and culture (Darnell 2001, 15). Denying the legitimacy of searching for a community's past by any historical means available is refusing the irruption of another Time into the present and even into the future, for the simple reason that the uses and the interpretations of the archive are not the monopoly of today's academic elites. The archive's potentialities are unpredictable.[63] Bissel's warning should be extended so that it may include the political significance of anthropology's variants as a science of the past.

Alfred Kroeber is again a case in point. His Californian project was, explicitly, a study of the past, not of the present: "it attempts to be a history" (Kroeber 1925, v).[64] If he adopted the present tense in his Yurok descriptions, it was because in the vernacular conception past events and persons "were living, present reality" (T. Kroeber 1978, xvi); and this is quite a rebuttal of the critique of allochronism and homochronism that might fall upon him. In utter contrast, many anthropologists nowadays feel comfortable with shutting their eyes to hundreds or thousands of years of other people's history as if they were irrelevant or, in any case, out of reach. Fabian is far from standing alone in his rejection of precolonial studies implied in the critique of anthropology as "a discipline with a negative object" or "a science of disappearance" (Fabian 1991a, 193, 196). The word itself—*precolonial*—is deemed allochronic by Fabian; however, as Marshall Sahlins alerts, anthropologists who tend to reduce the past of (ex)colonized peoples to colonialism "mimic on an academic plane the same imperialism they would despise." They "do in theory just what imperialism attempts in practice" (Sahlins 2000, 478).

In *Memory against Culture*, Fabian insists in opposing any views of our discipline that may be connected in any manner to the "stones and bones" of popular stereotype: "I am convinced that anthropology's present and future task is to become a human science of presence" (2007, 117). Considering the predominant lack of interest from today's anthropologists in the ancestors of Native peoples, the risk that Fabian's project of a radical contemporaneity of mankind excludes them seems real enough. Nonetheless, Indigenous peoples had a past of their own. Today, one is no longer allowed to hear it—and that feels oppressive.

EPILOGUE: PROGRESS AND REMEMBRANCE

Totalitarian critique has been creating a chasm between the present and the past of anthropology. Through a Manichaean view of "the scandal of domination and exploitation of one part of mankind by another" (Fabian 1983, x), the critics consider themselves to be not just intellectually but also morally right, and they constantly invoke power as a neutralizing strategy. By doing this, the counter-hegemonic critique transforms itself into "an absolutism at work" (Griffin 1989, 623). A good demonstration is Fabian's pathologizing of the alleged denial of coevalness, even though allochronic frames are not incompatible with ethnographical time. We might quite as well affirm that his thesis is an illusion caused by the homophony of the word *time* in two very different senses and by the utterly misleading perception that classical anthropologists thought in terms of radical alterity, as opposed to a suitable "epistemological" equating of otherness (2007, 27–28). Perhaps Foucault should be evoked on the subject of illness; and perhaps that is why Sahlins (2002) says that undergraduate students keep being lobotomized by the defendants of the power paradigm.

We have seen that Fabian's allochronism toward anthropologists of the colonial period has a diametrical opposite in the way they brought past cultures into the present. His critique may be seen as a distancing device in the sense that it denies coevalness both to the discipline's ancestors and to Indigenous ones. Those who were interested in precolonial studies and salvaging projects are deemed by Fabian to be tangible and therefore *passé*—not to mention the actual precolonial ancestors. The critique also affects present day communities and Indigenous individuals who relate with their past in ways that are compatible and entangled with the anthropological archive. It is to Fabian's credit that he admits the unwilling, "negative consequences" of critical anthropology—namely, that it may "endanger people with whom we work" (1991a, 248). This recognition of "impasses, paradoxes and dilemmas" is related to his affirmation that "the critique is not cumulative," so that "the notion of a 'critical tradition' should fill us with suspicion" (1991a, 247–48). In *Memory against Culture* he adds, "*Time and the Other* definitely was not the end of the game, neither for the discipline nor for myself" (2007, 23; [2006] 2014, 174). The problem is that Fabian's desire for a utopia—an anthropology that "needs to be 'reinvented', not once in a while but every time" (1991a, 248) is intrinsically allochronic, not only toward our predecessors but toward those who today accept the intellectual challenge of learning something from them, from their writings. Invisible genealogies or transformative continuities are at stake, instead of definite ruptures.

Radical critique may have made historical sense in the 1970s and 1980s, but it is quite extraordinary that almost a half century later so many anthropologists keep evoking the "mortal sin of essentialism" (Sahlins [1993] 2000, 45) as characteristic of an intellectual, faraway Other (the classical anthropologist) that helps in constructing their identities. The generalization and amalgamation of the history of anthropology in the colonial period is, after all, a form of ethnicity;

the critique is based on the false premise that anthropology had identical flaws that distinguish its representatives *from us*. Considering the part played by so many classical anthropologists in the battle against ethnocentrism, racism, and other forms of discrimination, one might even wonder if it is not dangerous in the Trump era (not to say ridiculous) to keep our forerunners as an intellectual and political target, and to insist on "Otherizing" them.[65]

In spite of the antagonisms that may be detected between Western self-critique and non-Western critique, the rejection of the history of anthropology's legacy seems to be not only a major ingredient of both, but also a significant part of the problem. On the side of the "ex-colonized," it engenders at best an estrangement of important intellectual allies and, at worst, a neglect of crucial historical sources, namely the vernacular. On the side of the "ex-colonizers," it contributes to a lack of understanding of contemporary differences in terms that are meaningful and empathic outside the Western academies. A better relationship with the history of anthropology's archive, from both sides (internal and external) of the contemporary postcolonial critique, would help create a third path—a path of dialogue, reconciliation, and construction. Ultimately, the postcolonial sensibility should surpass itself and admit there is much more to anthropology in any period than being a colonial distancing machine. If it is difficult to follow those who reject Western knowledge for being Western, it's because indigenous knowledge is part of it—is incrusted in its vernacular record whether one likes it or not. Vincent Crapanzano has eloquently associated this historical dimension of the archive to his mistrust of a constant search for anthropology's cutting edge:

> I must confess that whenever I hear the phrase "cutting edge," I think less of a frontier of knowledge than of the aggression that lies behind a singular approach to knowledge, research and innovation. When applied to a discipline like anthropology that relies on intimate relations with informants, it is especially disquieting. (Crapanzano 2011, 119)

Both the ideographic and theoretical richness of the archive are threatened by a hidden belief in progress, but remembrance is an unexpected time: "When we were children my father used to tell us stories in the evening. Whenever we showed signs of restlessness he stopped. Here are some of the stories that I remember" (Crashing Thunder 1926, 41).

NOTES

1. This chapter was originally a paper presented at the panel "Writing the History of Anthropology in a Global Era [History of Anthropology Network]" of the 15th EASA Biennial Conference, Stockholm, Sweden, August 2018. I thank the insights of the panel participants and of the *Histories of Anthropology Annual* peer reviewers. Paper financed by FCT/MEC, following the strategic plan of the Centre for Research in Anthropology UID/ANT/04038/2019.

2. In this particular passage, everyone understands that Fabian does not include himself in the expression "our discourse"—quite the contrary. Besides, the use of "us" instead of "them" is a common literary device in the critique of anthropology. It is a kind of verbal *trompe l'œil* of inclusion, when exclusion or distancing between us (the critics) and them (the so-called classical anthropologists) is actually intended. More than a few instances of such a device could be compiled here, at least since the 1970s and still in full vigor today. One example: "*Our* conception of culture almost irresistibly leads *us* into reification and essentialism" (Keesing 1994, 302; italics added).

3. See Lewis 2014 and Bunzl [2002] 2014 for a historicization of *Time and the Other*.

4. Fabian also admits that "critique is not cumulative, it needs to be thought and formulated again and again" (Fabian 2001, viii). So it is to be hoped that the counter-critique or defense of anthropology may also contribute to "improve" the critique by making it more dialogical and less totalizing.

5. Marshall Sahlins's dissenting views and his use of the epithet "totalizing" in *Waiting for Foucault, Still* ([1993] 2002, 61) have also been inspirational, among other works of sympathetic historiography or deliberate reaction to the postcolonial critique of anthropology (Spiro 1996; Darnell 1995; Sidky 2003; Varisco 2008; Vermeulen 2015). The following passages of the recent compilation of Herbert S. Lewis's writings, *In Defense of Anthropology*, intended to be *An Investigation of the Critique of Anthropology*, particularly ignited my imagination: "The critics have done unto anthropology what they claim anthropology does

unto Others: essentialize, totalize, stereotype, 'otherize.' . . . The follow-ers of Foucault, Edward Said, Johannes Fabian have managed to do to anthropology what Said says Westerners have done to the Orient and to the Other: invent something that never existed in order to dominate it" (Lewis 2014, 5, 23). Mine is but a humble, additional contribution to previous defenses of anthropology, also as an occasion to recall a few dead people. I would like also to express my debt to the thought of Clyde Holler (1995), even if it is not specifically a counter-critique of anthropology.

6. Another of Fabian's allochronic expressions is "the rubbish heap of positivism" (1991, 198).

7. See Mair (1957), 236.

8. "It is irrelevant if the unskilled labor is European, African, Malayan, or Chinese," Gluckman said, because "within all the areas where it oper-ates capitalist enterprise produces similar results" (Gluckman 1947, 112, 113). In so far as Malinowski's analysis was "tied always to a particular and unique reality," it imprisoned anthropology in a purely descrip-tive dimension that obliterated the understanding of conflict and the penetration of power mechanisms through sociological comparison (Gluckman 1947, 116).

9. This is not entirely coincident with Gluckman, who actually resolved the inconsistency of his own critique by stating: "I am aware that examples from his [Malinowski's] writings can be cited against this statement, but these are the fruits of his inconsistency" (Gluckman 1947, 109).

10. He often referred to the importance of developing anthropological studies on conflict and hostility toward the colonizers, without mini-mizing, on the contrary, "forward movements" such as "the African revolt against European innovations," "African nationalism and the development of autonomous African churches," or "the recrudescence of tribalism." These forces "which are growing, which are real now and may become important in the future" were considered by Malinowski to be "a dominant factor in the situation" (Malinowski 1945, 9, 32). For a more detailed analysis of the power dimensions of the "new Malinowski," see Carlo Rossetti (1985). See Schumaker (2001), chap-ter 4, for the critique of Gluckman to Malinowski.

11. Other figures make part of it, for example Malinowski's disciples God-frey and Monica Wilson, whom Gluckman acknowledged as legiti-mate contributors to the study of social change in Africa.

12. Fabian also acknowledges his debt to other figures of the "dissident, rather leftish" Manchester School (Fabian 1998, 7–9). They are the exceptions that confirm the rule.

13. This sentence was repetitively pronounced by Irish drag queen and LGBT activist Panti Bliss (Rory O'Neill) in her/his (already famous) post-show oration at the Abbey Theatre (National Theatre of Ireland) on February 1, 2014.

14. This means a belief in spiritual beings.

15. A few extreme cases, such as some forms of Spiritualism, could be seen as savage revivals, in contrast to the sophisticated, moral refinement of Christianity's animistic developments.

16. The debate over Tylor's understanding of the psychic unity of mankind goes on (See Oesterdiekhoff 2015; Di Brizio 2017). My reading of *Primitive Culture* is basically in accordance with Stringer's (1999). See Rosa 2003.

17. Opler criticizes Stocking's idea that Tylor viewed the English society of his time as the pinnacle of civilization (1964).

18. Or James Frazer: "If there is savagery in our customs, in our ideas, in our religions, it is simply because there are savages amongst us . . . that is people who, while trying to keep a civilized appearance, reproduce in their most inner self the ways of thinking and feeling of the savages" (Frazer 1931, 272, my translation). The huge impact of James Frazer's *The Golden Bough* (1890) had to do with the fact that it subtly revealed the *savage* foundations of the world's most famous "dying god," Jesus Christ, while Sydney Hartland's *The Legend of Perseus* (1894) did the same with His/his supernatural birth (Rosa 2016).

19. Including the French sociological school of Durkheim and Mauss. Later on, Fabian decided to "stick to cultural or social anthropology in its Anglo-American variety" (2007, 17).

20. The allochronic logic is identifiable, says Fabian, in a truly dichotomous terminology that goes through the entire history of anthropology: in place of the nineteenth century savage and barbarian, one finds categories like traditional, scriptless, tribal, archaic, rural, mythical, oral, Stateless, etc., with their Western counterparts: modern, urban, scientific, industrial, democratic, and so on. In these categories, the time dimension is implied, but crucial: they are a form of typological time.

21. Maxwell Owusu (1978) is quoted in *Time and the Other* for having daringly pointed the finger to these two eminent anthropological figures.

Owusu intends to show, on the basis of the analysis of their monographies, that "a great majority" of allegedly "authoritative" ethnographies of the colonial period were put together without a proficient knowledge of local vernaculars (Owusu 1978, 312). Again, a historical generalization is at stake, considering his conclusion that "few ethnographers, if any . . . had any appreciable control of the native languages" (Owusu 1978, 315). Owusu does not demonstrate that linguistic deficiencies actually provoked serious ethnographical inaccuracies. He presumes so on the basis of the "commonsense truth" that different worldviews cannot be understood if the same language is not shared (Owusu 1978: 316, 327, 329). The "representative textual references" that he selects for analysis are those in which Fortes and Evans-Pritchard acknowledged their own linguistic deficiencies. Owusu finds it paradoxical that both of them perceived these to be a serious obstacle and at the same time presented the results as well-informed, if not, scientific.

22. Richard Dorson synthesized the polemics with this provocative formula, intended to be a critique of the anthropologists' arrogant attitude toward folklore studies and the very word *folklore*: "The fact is, anthropologists do not know what folklore is" (1972, 17).

23. Take the case of Lydia Cabrera, a bourgeois white female who was to flee the Castrist revolution but whose works, based upon her prior, intimate ethnographic experiences with Cuban *santeras* "were decisive to acknowledge the importance, the legitimacy and the specificity of the afrodescendants' cultural contribution to Cuban and Caribbean history and identity" (Ortiz 2018, 1).

24. Unpredicted echoes of cultural relativism resonate within Vietnamese anthropology from the French colonial era, namely on the issue of anthropology being perceived as a Western project with "good" political ends or, in this case, consequences. The following words by an insider historian of anthropology may sound shocking to some readers: "Thus, colonization provided the Viets with an unrivaled opportunity for openness to other cultures" (Ngoc 2017, 215).

25. It would be interesting to recover a quite forgotten chapter of nineteenth century anthropology around Friedrich Max Müller's identification of a "new epoch" in the history of the discipline. Its paramount principle was that "no one is in future to be quoted as an authority on the customs, traditions, and, more particularly, on the religious ideas of uncivilized races, who has not acquired an acquaintance with

their language, sufficient to enable him to converse with them freely on these difficult subjects" (Müller, 1892, 151–52). Müller's final recommendation to those who perused ethnographical records was a poisoned gift to anthropology: he suggested that a time would come when no student would venture to write on any religion without having acquired some knowledge of the language of the people in question. In other words, it was not enough that the ethnographer did acquire that knowledge; the anthropologist at home should do the same. This was obviously a transposition of the academic rigors of Sanskritists, Hellenists, Latinists, and so on, to the non-Indo-European realms of Africa, Oceania, or the Americas. Should we resent him for establishing a principle that, when pushed to its limits, would simply erase most anthropological projects, whether of the nineteenth or the twenty-first century?

26. Alfred Kroeber, for example, "made no claim to control a speaking knowledge of Yurok" because his standard was "realistic"—meaning very high. His wife Theodora has nonetheless witnessed his "longish exchanges" in Yurok (T. Kroeber 1978, xv; T. Kroeber 1970, 157–60).

27. For example, Raymond Firth tacitly positioned himself as a brighter, theoretically informed authority on Maori subjects, to the detriment of a previous generation of ethnographers, in particular Elsdon Best, whose fluency in Maori was, however, much superior. Firth's acknowledgement of the fact that he had but a "slight" acquaintance with "the people and their language" only accentuates, on that regard, the gap between the amateur expert and the professional benighted (Firth [1929] 1959, 17–18; Rosa 2018b). Another illustration would be that of Evans-Pritchard in comparison with the colonial administrator and ethnographer Percy Coriat, who spoke Nuer fluently and produced, in the 1930s, an alternative reading of Nuer history, namely as regards the impact of the Arab slave raiding (Johnson and Coriat 1993).

28. The same applies to participant observation, since the only reason for participating, says Fabian, is to observe better.

29. The introduction of Malinowski's *Argonauts of the Western Pacific*—the *putting aside camera, notebook and pencil and joining in what's going on* should be read in this way.

30. Another illustration is Paul Philip Howell's description of his "peculiar and perhaps unique relationship with the Nuer." He was "addressed by his 'bull-name,' greeted as an intimate by men and women of all ages, praised, but often severely criticized, by the chiefs. A Nuer 'bull-name'

is a passport to the most intimate circles in any Nuer cattle camp or village. I often felt that it was I who had to struggle to maintain at least a vestige of the culture from which I had come" (Howell 1954, 3). Howell was Southern Sudan's District Commissioner with a PhD in anthropology. He was totally fluent in Nuer, among whom he lived between 1942 and the independence of Sudan in 1955–56. He corroborated most of Evans-Pritchard's ethnography.

31. Just like Fabian's own equivalents, even though he intends them to mark a rupture with former habits of the discipline. An example: "To acknowledge debts to Tshibumba Kanda Matulu by expressing the usual gratitude to him as 'my informant' would be inappropriate. The briefest glance at our relationship, as evidenced in the texts presented here, shows that we were engaged in a common task" (1996, xiv).

32. As a man who symbolizes both the apogee of the culture concept and its "fall" in North American anthropology, let alone for having died in 1960, Kroeber may be seen as an intellectual ghost or demon whose ideas haunt the field as the exact opposite of all in which so many (if not most) contemporary anthropologists believe. While acknowledging the tensions between real life individuals, he was not interested in that dimension and demanded the right for his anthropology to exist, not as an exclusive, totalitarian project, but as a legitimate one. Different perspectives and different disciplines complemented each other in the treatment of the same subjects. That's why he insisted in saying that he treated culture *as if* it was autonomous. The anthropologist as "culturologist" operated "as if individual personalities did not have a hand in cultural events," while in reality they had: "In the main he is justified in this procedure. He is certainly justified in proportion as his view is long-range. . . . As the range contracts and the segment of culture examined begin to be minute, the role of individuals, under the microscopic dissection being carried on, looms correspondingly larger. *Here is an equally legitimate method of study; but, of course, it yields results of a quite different order.* . . . each has its own kind of fruitfulness" (Kroeber 1952, 133, 135, emphasis added).

33. This does not imply, obviously, a rejection of the sense of vision, only of the "ideology" that overestimates it. "No, I am not to pluck out my eyes," Fabian answered to a critic (1991b, 21; Richardson 1990, 18).

34. "Sapir, Boas, and their contemporaries were convinced that texts provided evidence of the Native point of view that would not be falsified by the standpoint of the observer. The resulting texts could be ana-

lyzed and reanalyzed, or they could simply be valued for their own sake—as distilled records in the words of particular individuals of the knowledge systems of their cultures" (Darnell 2001, 17).

35. In 2004, under the impulse of Darnell's *Invisible Genealogies*, a group of scholars was brave enough to launch the idea of a "Neo-Boasian Anthropology for the 21st century" (Bashkow et al. 2004). It is interesting to note that most of them accentuated the power dimensions of Boasian writings. They are right in identifying this dimension, but not as a *sine qua non* condition to promote a renewed dialogue between the present and the past of the discipline. In spite of their "precaution," some (bad) reactions followed, such as Verdon's (2007) accusation that Boas's cultural history is not for the present, but "obsolete."

36. In his 2005 *Guide to Collaborative Ethnography*, Luke G. Lassiter places the Americanist tradition "on the roots of ethnographic collaboration" (Lassiter 2005, 26–47).

37. One example: *Baba of Karo: A Woman of the Moslem Hausa*, edited by Mary Smith (1954).

38. In the preface, Radin made explicit the deep, human dimension of the collaboration. Here is but a glimpse of the relationship between the two men: "[Crashing Thunder] wove my presence among the Winnebago just then, into the whole fabric of his life. I was the preordained one who had sensed what was the proper time to come to the Winnebago, and this legend he diligently disseminated among all his relatives and subsequently embodied in certain autobiographical snatches I obtained from him" (Radin [1920] 1926, x). Is the anthropologist's integration in the Winnebago man's time no more than a rhetorical device "to neutralize time," to make it "harmless"? (Fabian 1991a, 198). In Fabian's mind, this may well be the case, considering that he includes among allochronic strategies the assumption "that each society is encapsulated in its own representations of time" (1991a, 198). For a critique of Radin's claims to ethnographic authority and authenticity, see Burnham 1998. An alternative view is that Radin's endeavor is a true affirmation (not a denial) of coevalness. And in spite of his status as a maverick among the Boasians (Vidich 1987), there are reasons to believe *Crashing Thunder* is not an exception.

39. Besides, transcriptions by the Boasians were often inseparable from phonograph recordings. "I always tape what I consider truly important," Fabian writes in an article meant to highlight his idea that "context must be constituted in a practice that is individually and therefore

historically situated and determined" (1995, 45, 58) But if note-taking can leave aside the all-important oral inflections, among other performative dimensions, the same applies to other methods. Couldn't we demand videotapes to fill gaps in audio recordings, for example? Pushed to the limits, this kind of question risks becoming ridiculous. After all, the misunderstandings of context are but a spectrum of possibilities that varies with context, precisely, more than with the vehicles of oral texts.

40. The polemic between Mead (1939) and Lowie (1940) resumes the subject.

41. Here is an example, from Kroeber's 1908 *Ethnology of the Gros Ventre*. In the chapter, "War-Experiences of Individuals," we find but a very brief mention of intersubjective time: "It must be remembered that the narrators were not asked to describe the engagements and expeditions in which they were involved, but to narrate their personal share in them." But then, there is a transition to "Black-Wolf's Narrative," followed by Bull Robe's and Watches-All's. The first person transports us to the original, shared, coeval experience of talking, listening, and writing down: "When I was a boy I heard about great deeds in war, and resolved to follow in the tracks of such men" (Black-Wolf in Kroeber 1908, 197).

42. According to Fabian, culturalist anthropologists created a chasm between *our* (their) time—the time of a science that considers itself to be superiorly capable of encompassing each different culture as a whole—and the time of the *others*, who only *live* that difference, who can be granted the status of informants but not the actual authorship of anthropological texts. The holistic dimension of culturalism is at stake.

43. In her contribution to *The End of Anthropology?*, Patricia Spyer suggests that "a new, less colonially inspired, and more nuanced approach to otherness, and therefore as one intimation of how anthropology might productively revamp parts of its classical heritage" would consist of accentuating "the ability to listen" rather than the conventional project of understanding through academic theoretical categories. By contrast with this ambition, listening "would engage otherness without trying to subsume or tame it" (Spyer 2011, 64, 65). But if, as she herself acknowledges, this amounts to revamping parts of the classical heritage, why the need to argue that anthropology as a discipline and as a practice "is coming to an end"? (Spyer 2011, 61).

44. I have decided to leave aside Fabian's argument in his equally celebrated book, *Out of Our Minds: Reason and Madness in the Exploration of Central Africa* (2000), which would demand a chapter by itself.
45. It is quite meaningful that Radin's comparative reading made him recognize in African tales an "emphasis upon the contemporary scene" (Radin [1952] 1983, 4). The storytellers constantly reformulated the traditional subject-matter "in order to bring it up to date, to make it understandable and palatable to a contemporary audience" (Radin [1952] 1983, 16). And if this adaptation was found elsewhere, in Africa it had a specific momentum in relation to the continent's turbulent history, from the slave trade to more recent European encroachments. It is remarkable that Radin, mirroring Boas's political mission, wanted to contradict the Western laymen's enduring perception of African cultures "as primitive in every sense of that much-abused term" (Radin [1952] 1983, 1). The sophistication of the tales spoke for itself.
46. There is possibly a Protestant undertone in his distrust of vision.
47. For example, when one thinks of Baldwin Spencer and Francis Gillen, who published material, including photos, on the Arunta/Arrernte most sacred items that should not be seen by women and uninitiated men. The harshest postcolonial critique of Spencer, equating ethnography and ethnocide, is Patrick Wolfe's (1994). For a counter-critique, see Lewis 2014.
48. His thesis is that "we can never know" what words meant before literacy, when they had power beyond meaning; but when he states that literary versions are "only pointers to this vanished world" he is also acknowledging that they are pointing to something real, to something that existed (Holman 2010, 284). In short, the precolonial time is not a mere colonial chimera. That is why a subtext may be detected all along his monograph: that salvage ethnography is a legitimate link between the past and the future. One has just to realize and accept that the Maori/Pakeha construction of the archive, back in the nineteenth and early twentieth centuries, was a transitional translation, not a direct access to the "unwritten innocence" of tradition (Holman 2010, 285).
49. Like the following excerpt from one of Tutakangahau's last letters: "And you shall make a book—a large book—of these things. And that book shall remain for our descendants to gather information from" (Holman 2010, 218).
50. It is a well-known fact that this is a delicate subject in current New Zealand/Aotearoa, where several Indigenous researchers, along with

some Pakeha, sustain the opposite view of an unbroken chain of Maori spirituality, independent from salvage ethnography (see Rosa 2018b). See the last section.

51. Murray Wax uses the word "alliance" to express the way in which the anthropologists' projects could be representative and advantageous to Indian communities, but he also stresses the risks of estrangement. Vine Deloria's manifesto (1969), in this sense, represented an ultimate crisis (Max 1997).

52. The case of Robert Spott may be taken as paradigmatic of Indian initiative (see Buckley 1996).

53. Schumaker, whose thesis is that African collaborators could "control research to a considerable extent" (16), has Fabian in mind when she calls into question the idea of a gap between fieldwork experiences and publications, namely within the Rhodes-Livingstone Institute tradition (253).

54. In 1868, Henry Callaway wrote in the preface to his book, "The issue of the First part [of *Nursery Tales, Traditions, and Histories of the Zulus*] aroused a spirit of enthusiasm among the natives of the village who were able to read, and several came and offered themselves as capable of telling me something better than I had printed. From this source of information thus voluntarily tendered I have obtained by far the best part of the contents of this volume." Fabian focuses on the colonial dimensions of the "missionary linguistics," including the creation of a literate class that in turn "could become an instrument of power and control" (1986, 75–76).

55. In a broad sense of the word, which includes descendants of slaves, colonized individuals, immigrants, and other informants or translators, ethnographers and anthropologists, and community hosts and leaders. Their visions are termed Indigenous "because they draw their energy from the nonstate communities who served as anthropology's core research subjects" (Blackhawk and Wilner 2018, xiii).

56. Many variants of this leitmotif may be found, including in sociologically minded armchair anthropologists with a foot in the nineteenth century, from Durkheim's Arunta/Arrernte "discovery" of the sense of religion to Mauss's praising of the Maori gift as the best demonstration that people could give to one another through things. The epithets *elementary* and *archaic* should not hide the fact that the remote in space was catapulted to the here and now. In his "Essai sur le don" (*The Gift*), Mauss believed that not everything was lost to capitalism;

the survival of the old spirit of the gift was still detectable among us as a token of our own humanity. In his plea for a return of the gift, he quoted a Maori proverb that was far from being the only piece of the vernacular record that he explored. He was actually extremely sensitive to its significance and to its potentialities. The same applies to the *old* Malinowski, who is obviously a paramount representative of modern anthropology's philosophical affirmation of the *savages'* coevalness. One could always say, with an inevitable dose of cynicism, that true coevalness may only be found in Malinowski's *Diary in the Strict Sense of the Term*; but the closing paragraphs of *The Argonauts of the Western Pacific* encapsulate the proper meaning of Otherness in modern anthropology, a meaning in diametrical contrast with colonialism's civilizing project. Contrarily to a current confusion in contemporary critique, difference and radical difference are not the same thing, and that is why Malinowski believed that the Trobrianders and their neighbors could and should change the Europeans after WWI.

57. As an illustration, let's evoke the case of Frank Edgar's three volume compilation of vernacular fables, originally published without any translation, *Litafi na Tatsuniyoyi na Hausa* (1911–13). It was under the impulse of Lord Lugard's Indirect Rule in Nigeria that a whole host of British officials strove to compile considerable amounts of oral traditions. Edgar's was but "the most extensive collection" and its purpose at the time (apparently with no academic interests and no intention of interpreting the materials beyond the vernacular categories of classification) was "first to provide British Administrative Officers with suitable materials for Hausa language study, and secondly to increase their knowledge of Hausa society and culture" (Smith 1969, vii–viii). Even though the Nigerian emirates had a literate Muslim intelligentsia for centuries, many tales and fables (*tatsuniyoyi*) were indeed handed down orally: "for their preservation among the Hausa, these tales depend on their appeal and their meaningfulness for Hausa narrators and audiences" (Smith 1969, xv). Much of their meaning, purpose, and dynamics was surely lost without the performative context, which could be public or intimate, sometimes with old women and children as protagonists; but Edgar's corpus, like so many others, creates bridges that otherwise wouldn't be there. Besides, it is quite obvious that only a considerable amount of "ethnophilia"—which is a kind of love (Belleau 2015)—can explain the magnitude of Edgar's ethnographic feats. Insisting too much on the (debatable) colonial utility of

his collection would make him a unidimensional character, amounting to a negation of his humanity. In 1969—nine years after the independence of Nigeria—an English translation was eventually published, signed by the ex-colonial officer Neil Skinner, who had been encouraged to do it by the anthropologist William Bascom. In his forward, Michael Garfield Smith (1921–93) encapsulated but one of those unfinished bridges: "For folklorists and others not directly concerned in Hausa culture history, these abundant materials invite and permit other analysis, thematic, stylistic and distributional, independently or in comparative contexts" (Smith 1969, xxi).

58. Some postcolonial critics go to the point of affirming that salvage endeavors are, if not destructive, at least damaging, an idea that echoes Vine Deloria Jr.'s famous statement that "the Indian people begin to feel that they are merely shadows of a mythical super-Indian" (Deloria Jr. 1969, 82).

59. For a "highly incomplete list of important recent ethnographies that are indebted to Fabian's work" see Bunzl [2002] 2014, xxvii.

60. As a matter of fact, one may suspect that Birth's article is an ironic critique of Fabian. We should consider Birth's previous attacks on the postmodern assumption that modern ethnographic authority was unethical (1990).

61. It is curious to note that Birth's progressive view of anthropological thought organizes those two "defaults" as surmountable stages toward a better theory. His addition to *Time and the Other* is enriching in one point in particular: the diagnosis of a specific, predominant fear among those who, influenced by Fabian, have been trying to create coeval and yet homochronic ways of relating to the Other's time: "Coevalness based on a homochronism in which the ethnographer places the Other into a scholarly style history, then, is a distancing construction, much like its predecessor, allochronism. Like its predecessor, homochronism reflects the dominant teleology of the intellectual climate out of which it emerged: *a fear of concepts of time that emphasize endurance, if not eternity, coupled with a desire to document change*" (Birth 2008, 18; emphasis added).

62. For many of its practitioners, anthropology was a historical science not because native peoples were in the past, but because *they were not*. If we pick the Boasians, there is no doubt that most of them understood that the line between the precolonial and the colonial periods was blurred and that it varied enormously, but they knew there was a line.

This was a form of knowledge, in the sense that it was *a* perspective. That is why many would reject in black and white the idea that they were observing (see, for example, Lowie 1915, 5).

63. *Black Elk Speaks* (Neihardt 1932) is a good example of a vernacular record that, in spite of meaningful gaps between the original interviews transcript and John G. Neihardt's final version, had an amazing destiny both in the academy and among the Lakota. Recent endeavors to recover Black Elk's textual words reinforce this perspective (See Holler 2000).

64. If Kroeber usually kept a safe distance to the Boasian subfield of acculturation studies, it was not because the Native Americans' present did not affect him. It was, on the contrary, because the suffering of concrete individuals—with Ishi at their head—and the negative impact of colonialism affected him *too much*, to the point of not being able, avowedly, to control his emotions and produce what would be, in his eyes, a valid anthropology on contemporary or recent transformations corresponding to his famous (not infamous) formula of "the little history of pitiful events" (Buckley 1996).

65. In "Franz Boas as Theorist" (2017), Regna Darnell spots the persistence of several distorting stereotypes about Boas and identifies the subtle transformations of his scientific responses to racism and to antisemitism, both in the U.S. and the Third Reich. Boas, however, "does not make explicit the sharing of popular prejudices by [pseudo] science and statesmen" (20). Darnell herself leaves this connection implicit as regards Trump's era—but the innuendo is there.

REFERENCES

Augé, Marc. 1994. *Pour une anthropologie des mondes contemporains*. Paris: Aubiers.

Baba of Karo. 1954. *Baba of Karo: A Woman of the Moslem Hausa*, edited by Mary F. Smith. London: Faber and Faber.

Balandier, Georges. (1955) 1970. *The Sociology of Black Africa. Social Dynamics in Central Africa*. London: Andre Deutsch.

Bashkow, Ira, Matti Bunzl, Richard Handler, Andrew Orta, and Daniel Rosenblatt. 2004. "A New Boasian Anthropology for the 21st Century," *American Anthropologist* 106, no. 3: 433–34.

Baumgardt, Ursula, and Jean Derive, eds. 2008. *Littératures Orales Africaines*. Paris: Éditions Karthala.

Belleau, Jean-Philippe. 2015. *Ethnophilie: L'amour des Autres Nations*. Rennes: Presses Universitaires de Rennes.

Bensa, Alban. 2006. "Avant-propos." In *Le Temps et les Autres. Comment l'anthropologie construit son objet*, by Johannes Fabian, 7–13. Toulouse: Anacharsis Édtions.

Biolsi, Thomas, and Larry J. Zimmerman, eds. 1997. *Indians and Anthropologists: Vine Deloria Jr. and the Critique of Anthropology*. Tucson: University of Arizona Press.

———. 1997. "Introduction. What's Changed, What Hasn't." In *Indians and Anthropologists. Vine Deloria Jr. and the Critique of Anthropology*, edited by Thomas Biolsi and Larry J. Zimmerman, 3–23. Tucson: University of Arizona Press.

Birth, Kevin K. 2008. "The Creation of Coevalness and the Danger of Homochronism." *The Journal of the Royal Anthropological Institute* 14, no. 1: 3–20.

———. 1990. "Reading and the Righting of Writing Ethnographies." *American Ethnologist* 17, no. 3: 549–57.

Bissell, William Cunningham. 2005. "Engaging Colonial Nostalgia" *Cultural Anthropology* 20, no. 2: 215–48.

British Association for the Advancement of Science. 1929. *Notes and Queries on Anthropology*. London: The Royal Anthropological Institute.

Buckley, Thomas. 1996. "'The Little History of Pitiful Events': The Epistemological and Moral Contexts of Kroeber's Californian Ethnology." In *Volksgeist as Method and Ethic: Essays on Boasian Ethnography and the German Anthropological Tradition*, edited by G. W. Stocking Jr., 257–97. Madison: University of Wisconsin Press.

Bunzl, Matti. (2002) 2014. "Foreword: Syntheses of a Critical Anthropology." In *Time and the Other: How Anthropology Makes Its Object*, by Johannes Fabian, vii–xxxii. New York: Columbia University Press.

Burnham, Michelle. 1998. "'I Lied All the Time': Trickster Discourse and Ethnographic Authority in *Crashing Thunder*." *American Indian Quarterly* 22, no. 4: 469–84.

Callaway, Henry. 1870. *The Religious System of the Amazulu. Izinyanga Zokubula; or Divination as Existing Among the Amazulu, in Their Own Words, with a Translation into English, and Notes*. Natal: J. A. Blair.

———. 1868. *Nursery Tales, Traditions, and Histories of the Zulus, in Their Own Words, with a Translation into English, and Notes*. Natal: J. A. Blair.

Chatelain, Héli. 1894. *Folk-tales of Angola. Fifty Tales, with Ki-mbundu Text, Literal English Translation, Introduction, and Notes, Collected and edited by Heli Chatelain*. Boston: G. E. Stechert.

Crashing Thunder, and Paul Radin. 1926. *Crashing Thunder: the Autobiography of a Winnebago Indian*, edited by Paul Radin. New York: Appleton.

Crawley, Ernest. 1902 *The Mystic Rose: A Study of Primitive Marriage*. London: MacMillan.

Criado, Tomás Sánchez, and Adolfo Estalella, eds. 2018. "Introduction." *Experimental Collaborations: Ethnography through Fieldwork Devices*, 1–30. New York: Berghahn.

Darnell, Regna. 2017. "Franz Boas as Theorist: A Mentalist Paradigm for the Study of Mind, Body, Environment, and Culture." In *Historicizing Theories, Identities, and Nations*, edited by R. Darnell and F. W. Gleach, 1–26. Lincoln: University of Nebraska Press.

———. 2001. *Invisible Genealogies: A History of Americanist Anthropology*. Lincoln: University of Nebraska Press.

———. 1995. "Deux ou trois choses que je sais du postmodernisme: 'Le moment expérimental' dans l'anthropologie nord-américaine." *Gradhiva* 18: 3–15.

Deloria, Vine, Jr. 1997. "Conclusion: Anthros, Indians, and Planetary Reality." In *Indians and Anthropologists: Vine Deloria Jr. and the Critique of Anthropology*, edited by Thomas Biolsi and Larry J. Zimmerman, 3–23. Tucson: University of Arizona Press.

———. (1969) 1970. *Custer Died for Your Sins: An Indian Manifesto*. New York: Avon.

Di Brizio, Maria Beatrice. 2017. "Un anthropologue en chambre? Vie et œuvre d'Edward Burnett Tylor." In *Bérose, Encyclopédie en ligne sur l'histoire de l'anthropologie et des savoirs ethnographiques*. Paris. IIAC-LAHIC, UMR 8177.

Dirks, Nicholas B., Geoff Eley, and Sherry Ortner. 1994. "Introduction." In *Culture/Power/History: A Reader in Contemporary Social Theory*, edited by Nicholas B. Dirks, Geoff Eley, and Sherry B. Ortner, 3–45. Princeton: Princeton University Press.

Dorson, Richard. 1972. "Introduction." In *African Folklore*, edited by Richard Dorson, 3–67. New York: Garden City.

Edgar, Frank. 1911. *Litafi na Tatsuniyoyi na Hausa*. Belfast: W. Erskine Mayne. 3 vols.

Evans-Pritchard, E. E. (1940) 1969. *The Nuer: A Description of the Modes of Livelihood and Political Institutions of a Nilotic People*. Oxford: Oxford University Press.

Fabian, Johannes. 2008. *Memory against Culture: Arguments and Reminders*. Durham NC: Duke University Press.

———. (2006) 2014. "Postscript: The Other Revisited." In *Time and the Other: How Anthropology Makes its Object*, 167–86. New York: Columbia University Press.

———. (2002) 2014. "Preface to the Reprint Edition." In *Time and the Other: How Anthropology Makes Its Object*, xxxiii–xxxv. New York: Columbia University Press.

———. 2001. *Anthropology with an Attitude: Critical Essays*. Stanford: Stanford University Press.

———. 2000. *Out of Our Minds: Reason and Madness in the Exploration of Central Africa*. Berkeley: University of California Press.

———. 1996. *Remembering the Present: Painting and Popular History in Zaire*. Berkeley: University of California Press.

———. 1995. "Ethnographic Misunderstanding and the Perils of Context." *American Anthropologist* 97, no. 1: 41–50.

———. 1991a. *Time and the Work of Anthropology: Critical Essays 1971–1991*. Chur: Harwood Academic.

———. 1991b. "Reply to Michael Richardson." *Anthropology Today* 7, no. 1: 21.

———. 1990a. "Presence and Representation: The Other and Anthropological Writing." *Critical Inquiry* 16, no. 4: 753–72.

———. 1990b. *Power and Performance: Ethnographic Explorations through Proverbial Wisdom and Theater in Shaba, Zaire*. Madison: University of Wisconsin Press.

———. 1986. *Language and Colonial Power: The Appropriation of Swahili in the former Belgian Congo 1880–1938*. Cambridge: Cambridge University Press.

———. 1983. *Time and the Other: How Anthropology Makes Its Object*. New York: Columbia University Press.

Finnegan, Ruth. 2007. *The Oral and Beyond: Doing Things with Words in Africa*. Chicago: University of Chicago Press.

Fortes, Meyer. (1945) 1969. *The Dynamics of Clanship Among the Tallensi: Being the First Part of an Analysis of the Social Structure of a Trans-Volta Tribe*. Oxford: Oxford University Press.

Frazer, James G. (1890) 1900. *The Golden Bough: A Study in Magic and Religion*. London: MacMillan. 3 vols.

———. 1931. *Garnered Sheaves: Essays, Addresses, and Reviews*. London: MacMillan.

Gluckman, Max. 1947. "Malinowski's 'Functional' Analysis of Social Change." *Africa: Journal of the International African Institute* 17: 103–21.

————. 1955. *The Judicial Process among the Barotse of Northern Rhodesia.* Manchester: Manchester University Press.

Gosden, Christopher, Frances Larson, and Alison Petch. 2007. "Origins and Survivals: Tylor, Balfour and the Pitt Rivers Museum and their Role Within Anthropology in Oxford 1883–1905." In *A History of Oxford Anthropology*, edited by Peter Rivière, 21–42. New York: Berghan.

Griffin, Robert J. 1989. "Ideology and Misrepresentation: A Response to Edward Said." *Critical Inquiry* 15: 611–25.

Hartland, Edwin Sydney. 1909–1910. *Primitive Paternity: The Myth of Supernatural Birth in Relation to the History of the Family.* London: David Nutt.

————. 1894. *The Legend of Perseus: A Study of Tradition in Story, Custom and Belief*, vol. 1. London: David Nutt.

————. 1891. *The Science of Fairy Tales: An Enquiry into the Fairy Mythology.* London: Walter Scott.

Holler, Clyde. 2000. *The Black Elk Reader.* Syracuse: Syracuse University Press.

————. 1995. *Black Elk's Religion: The Sun Dance and Lakota Catholicism.* Syracuse: Syracuse University Press.

Holman, Jeffrey Paparoa. 2010. *Best of Both Worlds: The Story of Elsdon Best and Tutakangahau.* North Shore: Penguin.

Howell, Paul P. 1954. *A Manual of Nuer Law, Being an account of Customary Law, its Evolution and Development in the Courts established by the Sudan Government.* London: Oxford University Press.

Jezequel, Jean-Hervé. 2007. "Voices of their own? African participation in the production of colonial knowledge in French West Africa, 1910–1950." In *Ordering Africa: Anthropology, European Imperialism and the Politics of Knowledge*, edited by Helen L. Tilley and Robert J. Gordon, 145–72. Manchester: Manchester University Press.

Johnson, D. H., and Percy Coriat, eds. 1993. *Governing the Nuer: Documents by Percy Coriat on Nuer History and Ethnography 1922–1931.* Oxford: JASO.

Keesing, Roger M. 1994. "Theories of Culture Revisited." In *Assessing Cultural Anthropology*, edited by Robert Borofsky, 301–10. New York: McGraw-Hill.

Kroeber, Alfred L. 1978. *Yurok Myths.* Berkeley: University of California Press.

————. 1952. *The Nature of Culture.* Chicago: University of Chicago Press.

————. (1925) 1976. *Handbook of the Indians of California.* New York: Dover.

————. (1908) 1978. *Ethnology of the Gros Ventre.* New York: AMS Press.

Kroeber, Theodora. 1970. *Alfred Kroeber: A Personal Configuration*. Berkeley: University of California Press.

———. 1978. "Foreword." In *Yurok Myths*, by Alfred L. Kroeber. Berkeley: University of California Press.

Kumoll, Karsten. (2010) 2013. "Indigenous Research and the Politics of Representation: Notes on the Cultural Theory of Marshall Sahlins." In *Beyond Writing Culture: Current Intersections of Epistemologies and Representational Practices*, edited by Olaf Zenker and Karsten Kumoll, 69–88. New York: Berghan.

Kuper, Adam. 2011. "The Original Sin of Anthropology." In *The End of Anthropology?*, edited by Holger Jebens and Karl-Heinz Kohl, 37–59. Wantage: Sean Kingston.

Lang, Andrew. 1907. "Edward Burnett Tylor." In *Anthropological Essays Presented to Edward Burnett Tylor in Honour of his 75th Birthday Oct. 2 1907*, edited by W. H. R. Rivers, R. R. Marett, and N. W. Thomas, 1–15. Oxford: Clarendon Press.

Lassiter, Luke Eric. 2005. *The Chicago Guide to Collaborative Ethnography*. Chicago: University of Chicago Press.

Lewis, Herbert S. 2013. *In Defense of Anthropology: An Investigation of the Critique of Anthropology*. New Brunswick: Transaction.

———. 1999. "A Response to Sandy Toussaint's Commentary: 'Honoring Our Predecessors: A Response to Herbert Lewis's Essay on 'The Misrepresentation of Anthropology and Its Consequences.''" *American Anthropologist* 101, no. 3: 609–10.

Lowie, Robert H. 1940. "Native Languages as Ethnographic Tools" *American Anthropologist* 42: 81–9.

———. (1935) 1983. *The Crow Indians*. Lincoln: University of Nebraska Press.

———. (1915) 1978. *The Sun Dance of the Crow Indians*. New York: AMS Press.

Mair, Lucy. (1957) 2002. "Malinowski and the Study of Social Change." In *Man and Culture: An Evaluation of the Work of Bronislaw Malinowski*, edited by Raymond Firth, 229–44. London: Routledge.

Malinowski, Bronislaw. 1945. *The Dynamics of Culture Change: An Inquiry into Race Relations in Africa*. New Haven: Yale University Press.

Mead, Margaret. 1939. "Native Languages as Fieldwork Tools." *American Anthropologist* 42, no. 2: 189–205.

Müller, Friedric Max. 1892. *Anthropological Religion*. London: Longman, Green.

Neihardt, John G., and Black Elk. 1932. *Black Elk Speaks: Being the Story of a Holy Man of the Ogalala Sioux, as told to J. G. Neihardt.* New York: William Morrow.

Ngoc, Nguyen Phuong. 2017. "Adopting Western Methods to Understand One's Own Culture: Social and Cultural Studies by Vietnamese Scholars of the French Colonial Era." In *Historicizing Theories, Identities, and Nations,* edited by R. Darnell and F. W. Gleach, 199–218. Lincoln: University of Nebraska Press.

Oesterdiekhoff, Georg W. 2015. "The Nature of 'Pre-Modern' Mind: Tylor, Frazer, Lévy-Bruhl, Evans-Pritchard, Piaget and Beyond." *Anthropos* 110: 15–25.

Opler, Morris E. 1964. "Cause, Process, and Dynamics in the Evolutionism of E. B. Tylor." *Southwestern Journal of Anthropology* 20: 123–44.

Ortiz García, Carmen. 2018. "Biographie de Lydia Cabrera, conteuse, folkloriste et anthropologue 'noire et blanche.'" In *Bérose, Encyclopédie en ligne sur l'histoire de l'anthropologie et des savoirs ethnographiques,* Paris, IIAC-LAHIC, UMR 8177.

Owusu, Maxwell. 1978. "Ethnography of Africa: The Usefulness of the Useless." *American Anthropologist* 80, no. 2: 310–34.

Radin, Paul, ed. (1952) 1983. *African Folktales.* New York: Schocken Books.

Richardson, Michael. 1990. "Enough Said: Reflections on Orientalism." *Anthropology Today* 6, no. 4: 16–19.

Rosa, Frederico Delgado. 2018b. *Elsdon Best, l'ethnographe immémorial. Sauvetage et transformation de la mythopoétique maorie.* Les Carnets de Bérose, n° 9. Paris: Lahic / DPRPS-Direction générale des patrimoines.

———. 2016. "Dead and Living Authorities in *The Legend of Perseus*: Animism and Christianity in the Evolutionist Archive." In *Local Knowledge, Global Stage,* edited by Regna Darnell and Frederic Gleach, 31–52. Lincoln: University of Nebraska Press.

———. 2003. *L'Age d'or du totémisme: Histoire d'un débat anthropologique (1887–1929).* Paris: Centre National de la Recherche Scientifique, Maison des Sciences de l'Homme.

Rossetti, Carlo. 1985. "B. Malinowski, the Sociology of 'Modem Problems' in Africa and the 'Colonial Situation.'" *Cahiers d'études africaines* 25, no. 100: 477–503.

Routledge, W. Scoresby, and Katherine Routledge. 1910. *With a Prehistoric People: The Akikuyu of British East Africa. Being Some Account of the Method of Life and Mode of Thought Found Existent Among a Nation on Its First Contact with European Civilization.* London: Edward Arnold.

Sahlins, Marshall. 1999. "What is Anthropological Enlightenment? Some Lessons of the Twentieth Century." *Annual Review of Anthropology* 28: i–xxiii.

———. (1993) 2002. *Waiting for Foucault, Still.* Chicago: Prickly Paradigm Press.

———. (1993) 2000. "Goodbye to *Tristes Tropes*: Ethnography in the Context of Modern World History." In *Culture in Practice: Selected Essays,* 471–500. New York: Zone Books.

Schumaker, Lynn. 2001. *Africanizing Anthropology: Fieldwork, Networks, and the Making of Cultural Knowledge in Central Africa.* Durham NC: Duke University Press.

Sidky, H. 2003. *A Critique of Postmodern Anthropology: In Defense of Disciplinary Origins and Traditions.* Lewiston NY: The Edwin Mellen Press.

Smith, Linda Tuhiwai. (1999) 2012. *Decolonizing Methodologies: Research and Indigenous Peoples.* London: Zed Books.

Smith, M. G. 1969. "Foreword." In *Hausa Tales and Traditions: An English Translation of Tatsuniyoyi na Hausa, Originally Compiled by Frank Edgar,* edited and translated by Neil Skinner, vi–xxi. London: Cass.

Spiro, Melford E. 1996. "Postmodernist Anthropology, Subjectivity, and Science: A Modernist Critique." *Comparative Studies in Society and History* 38, no. 4: 759–80.

Spyer, Patricia. 2011. "What Ends with the End of Anthropology?" In *The End of Anthropology?*, edited by Holger Jebens and Karl-Heinz Kohl, 61–80. Wantage: Sean Kingston.

Stringer, Martin D. 1999. "Rethinking Animism: Thoughts from the Infancy of Our Discipline." *Journal of the Royal Anthropological Institute* 5, no. 4: 541–55.

Toussaint, Sandy. 1999. "Honoring Our Predecessors: A Response to Herbert Lewis's Essay on 'The Misrepresentation of Anthropology and Its Consequences.'" *American Anthropologist* 101, no. 3: 605–9.

Tylor, Edward B. (1871) 1903. *Primitive Culture: Researches into the Development of Mythology, Philosophy, Religion, Language, Art, and Custom.* London: John Murray. 2 vols.

Valentine, L., and R. Darnell, eds. 1999. *Theorizing the Americanist Tradition.* Toronto: University of Toronto Press.

Varisco, Daniel Martin. 2008. *Reading Orientalism: Said and the Unsaid.* Seattle: University of Washington Press.

Verdon, Michael. 2007. "Franz Boas: Cultural History for the Present, or Obsolete Natural History?" *Journal of the Royal Anthropological Institute* 13: 433–51.

Vermeulen, Han. 2015. *Before Boas: The Genesis of Ethnology in the German Enlightenment.* Lincoln: University of Nebraska Press.

Vidich, Arthur J. 1987. "Introduction." In *The Method and Theory of Ethnology: An Essay in Criticism,* edited by Paul Radin, vii–cxx. South Hadley MA: Bergin and Garvey.

Wax, Murray L. 1997. "Educating an Anthro: The Influence of Vine Deloria, Jr." In *Indians and Anthropologists: Vine Deloria, Jr., and the Critique of Anthropology,"* edited by Thomas Biolsi and Larry J. Zimmerman, 50–60. Tucson: University of Arizona Press.

Wolfe, Patrick. 1994. "'White Man's Flour': Doctrines of Virgin Birth in Evolutionist Ethnogenetics and Australian State-formation." *History and Anthropology* 8, nos. 1–4: 165–205.

2

Ich Bin Jüdischer Abstammung (I Am of Jewish Lineage)

The Conflicted Jewish Identity of the Anthropologist Franz Boas

In 1933, as Nazi ideology tightened its grip on Germany, the renowned German Jewish anthropologist Franz Boas, who had been living in the U.S. for several decades, wrote a letter to the German president Paul von Hindenburg. Alarmed by Hitler's rising fascistic menace, Boas began the letter with a forthright statement: "Ich bin jüdischer Abstammung," then quickly added, "aber in Fühlen und Denken bin ich Deutscher" (I am of Jewish lineage, but in my feelings and thoughts I am German) (Hart 2003, 94). In this quote, Boas conveyed that he had always been proud to be German, but that in light of what was happening in Germany vis-à-vis Hitler and growing anti-Semitism, he felt a deep sense of shame regarding being German: "Ich schäme mich, ein Deutscher zu sein" (I am ashamed to be German).

Needless to say, Hindenburg was unimpressed and offended by the letter. In that same year, brownshirt storm troopers burned hundreds of books by Jewish authors such as Albert Einstein, Sigmund Freud, Karl Marx, and numerous others (including some, such as Ernest Hemingway, who were not Jewish). Among the books burned were also, allegedly, writings of Franz Boas (*The History Place* 2001). It seems that this reporting may have had *some* validity. In "Complicity and Conflict: Columbia University's Response to Fascism, 1933–1937," Stephen Norwood indicated that *The Spectator*, the student newspaper of Columbia University, reported that the Nazis had burned some of the works of Franz Boas, who was at that time a Columbia professor.

It seems, as Norwood suggests, that the Nazi regime took offense to Boas's claim in a 1925 article, "Nordic Nonsense," that social context and environment rather than "race" determines human capabilities. Further, writes Norwood, "the University of Kiel, where Boas earned a PhD in 1881, removed his books from its library, prior to staging its own book-burning" (254). One can only speculate about the effect on Boas's psyche of having his intellectual work thoroughly rejected by the nation (whether or not his books were actually burned) with which he had so closely identified. Indeed, Joseph Goebbels reportedly declared, "The era of extreme Jewish intellectualism is at an end" (*The History Place* 2001). Thus, Boas was categorized by his own country as an "extreme" Jewish intellectual, a threat to the Third Reich's Aryan ideology.

In Volume I of *The Franz Boas Papers* (Darnell 2015), Jürgen Langenkämper's chapter, "Franz Boas's Correspondence with German Friends and Colleagues in the Early 1930s," details this tumultuous period, describing Boas's copious correspondence with various influential Jewish intellectuals seeking to exit Germany. Boas was instrumental in helping many of them reach America. Langenkämper also narrates the story of Boas's letter to Hindenburg and its aftermath. Boas had planned to donate his personal library to the Museum für Völkerkunde in Hamburg. However, this was not to be, as Boas's response to the rise of the Nazi regime in Germany was to fight back, first with a widely hailed speech at the University of Kiel, entitled "Rasse und Kultur" (Race and Culture), in which he decried the insidious racial theories that he saw rising in Europe and in America (278). But it was the letter to Hindenburg that was the lit match to the gasoline. Criticism arose from several German scholars who took exception to Boas's leanings toward racial and cultural plasticity and who responded to him with blatant anti-Semitic bias. For example, Langenkämper relates the comments of the Hamburg eugenicist Walter Scheidt, who stated blatantly to Boas, "a wise government eliminates the conflict in that it removes the Jews . . . of those key positions [of influence]" (285). The director of the Hamburg Museum of Ethnology, Georg Thilenius, declared that there was "a Bolshevism in art and literature . . . whose bearers were Jews" (285). In light of the vehement rejection of his letter to Hindenburg, Boas changed his will regarding the donation of his library, and the bulk of his works never arrived in Germany.

At first glance, it would appear that Boas's distress, alarm, and passionate response to what he saw going on in his country of origin would place him fully in solidarity with his Jewish background. However, Boas's wording of his letter to Hindenburg was entangled with a key discourse around Boas: how he saw his Jewish identity and its relationship to what he regarded as his wider identity as a German (and in the U.S. as a German American). The heart of the discourse appeared to revolve around the perception that Boas actively sought to downplay or even seemingly to reject his Jewishness in favor of an entirely secular and assimilationist stance reflected both in his theories of race and culture and in his own life. For example, Leonard B. Glick's influential article, "Types Distinct from Our Own: Franz Boas on Jewish Identity and Assimilation" (1982) appears to have had, as Mitchell Hart (2003) puts it, "a long life, having been taken up and repeated by numerous commentators on the relationship between Boas's Jewishness and the cultural turn in American anthropology" (91). Glick proposes that Boas felt it was crucial to uphold enlightened German ideals and "pride in their national origins and cultural heritage" (546). However, at the same time, Glick insists, Boas "advocated assimilation to the point of literal disappearance for the Jews" (546). No doubt the argument that Boas disregarded his "Jewish identity" has also fueled itself from the thrust of Boas's work itself, particularly his avid stance of challenging, and indeed subverting, any kind of racial or ethnic determinism, and instead focusing on culture as the framework by which to understand human differences.

Thus it is all the more startling to see Boas in the Hindenburg letter lead off with a direct statement of his Jewishness *before* asserting his German identity. Could this assertion of his Jewishness, despite years of downplaying it, have to do with his awareness of the dangers within antisemitism that were reaching a particular boiling point at that juncture of history? Perhaps. However, this was not the first time that Boas had encountered antisemitism. As a young university student in Kiel, Germany, Boas was aware of anti-Semitic movements within the student body (Cole 1999). Despite attempting to distance himself from anti-Semitic attacks, Boas involved himself in circulating a petition against "Jew-haters" and refused to sit at the same table as anti-Semitic leaders (60). Further, Boas bore facial scars as the result of duels involving aggression against Jewish students—specifically, as the *Worcester Daily Telegraph* reported in 1891, "three scars, each over an inch in length, crossing in something the shape of a six-pointed star" (61). One could equally wonder, then, if part of Boas's desire to not be seen as Jewish was a desire to avoid future anti-Semitic sentiment directed at himself. Stanley Freed, in *Anthropology Unmasked* (2012), implies that Boas may not have been entirely successful in avoiding antisemitism in the U.S., either. Pointing to various difficulties Boas had in gaining and keeping employment, Freed tells us that Boas was unceremoniously "chucked out" of the Columbian Field Museum in Chicago, and that it took the combined efforts of his two mentors—Dr. Frederic Putnam and Boas's uncle Dr. Abraham Jacobi (who had married into the decidedly non-Jewish Putnam family)—to secure Boas a key position at the American Museum of Natural History (AMNH). At that time in New York, even with its large Jewish population, anti-semitism (both overt and covert) was not uncommon. Indeed, in New York, antisemitism began intensifying in the 1870s. Following World War I, American xenophobia restricted immigration and closed many venues such as clubs and universities to Jews (Gritz 2007).

Throughout the twentieth century and into the twenty-first, New York Jewish life, overall, has been a complex mix of continuing acculturation, assimilation, and revitalization, although not immune to anti-Semitic discrimination within society. We could speculate that Boas likely encountered anti-Semitic sentiments but did not want to admit this. One example of persistent antisemitism that was underplayed can be found in a comment by the Rev. Chas E. Coughlan in 1938. Jews, wrote Coughlan, "have no nation of their own, no flag [this is prior to the establishment of the state of Israel]. [They are] a closely woven minority in their racial tendencies . . . a minority endowed with an aggressiveness, an initiative which, despite all obstacles, has carried their sons to the pinnacle of success in journalism, in radio, in finances, and in all the sciences and art" (Quinley 1977, 46). Though couched in seemingly rational-sounding language, Coughlan's comments are suspiciously reminiscent of the numerous conspiracy theories of Jewish domination in certain industries, a trend that was growing stronger in the late 1930s with the rise of the Third Reich.

However, Boas's employment difficulties could equally have reflected his overall rather difficult temperament. Known to have a "combative personality," Boas did not like "working under" some of his colleagues. Freed asserts that Boas "saw the world as focused on him" (138). While Boas's colleagues were hired by the University of Chicago, Boas was not, reflecting perhaps a comment attributed by Freed to W. R. Harper, who complained that Boas did not take direction well. Further, it is equally possible (and this is again speculation) that the lethal "new" antisemitism erupting in the Third Reich perhaps did force Boas back into his original identity in a move of unconscious solidarity with other Jews.

What, then, is "Jewishness," and can we make a case that goes counter to Boas's own strategy of disavowal (except under the dire circumstances of the Third Reich)? Any question about the degree of Boas's identification with his Jewishness can, as I indicated, only be speculative at best. There is, however, one possible plausible context by which we might shed light on the ambivalence of Boas's Jewish identity. In this chapter, I argue that Jewishness likely played more of a role in Boas's sense of identity than he was prepared to admit. Moreover, I maintain that his assimilationist and secular stance is actually *paradoxically consistent* with some aspects of Jewish identity itself, particularly the rise of modern developments within Judaism, most prominently the influence of Reform Judaism (more on this later in the chapter).

Boas's efforts to downplay Jewishness need not be seen as a complete denial of Jewishness at all, but rather as his attempted solution aimed at removing the strife-ridden aspects of Jewish life during this period. The orientation of his work was always toward the subversion of ideas of race and ethnicities. He asserted that "race" is a construct, not a biological or genetic reality, and that ethnic differences were a result of culture, not intractable qualities. Moreover, he articulated an ideal that all persons should meld into a common humanity. Thus for him, "racial" inequalities would disappear among, for example, African American and Indigenous communities, by a process of continual, mixed intermarriages among all kinds of populations. He did not contend that cultural ethnicities would completely disappear, but that they had considerable plasticity. His ideals seemed to embody those of a universal humanism. In challenging the reality of "race" and insisting on the plasticity of cultures, Boas was a man well ahead of his time, with many of his ideas regarding race now being supported by biological and genetic research.

It is not surprising that Boas would focus the same lens on "Jewishness." The Jews, he contended, are not a race; and their cultural diasporic differences are highly variable. In his chapter "The Jews" in *Race and Democratic Society* (1969), Boas sought to clarify misconceptions of Jews based on race: "People who concern themselves with the so-called "Jewish question" are accustomed to consider the Jews as a homogeneous race with definite characteristics different from the European groups among whom they live, and possessed of anatomical and mental traits which are hereditary features of the race. This view is based upon a complete misconception of what constitutes a race" (38). Jews, suggested Boas, were distinguished by social factors, not nonexistent racial factors. He did not suggest that Jews could assimilate; he instead argued that they were *already* assimilated. He asserted that Jews manifested a variety of types, not just one; and that they have always demonstrated considerable variability: "The Jews of North Africa are, in their essential traits, North Africans. The Jews of Europe are, in their essential traits, Europeans" (40).

Amos Morris-Reich (2007) shows how holding these views led Boas to an inevitable conclusion: "By claiming that Jews have assimilated thoroughly into their local surroundings, Boas implied that contemporary Jews share no common racial denominator and thus cannot manifest any particular 'racial difference'" (147). Although Morris-Reich shows that Boas's theories were an effective counter-narrative to the Nazi-driven views of Hans F. K. Günther, who argued that Jews were racially distinct, Morris-Reich also contends that Boas had his own ideological agenda, albeit a much more benign one than Günther's. In fact, Morris-Reich suggests that taking a thoroughly assimilationist view was Boas's *deliberate* strategy, buttressing his arguments about race and culture throughout his work. In other words, to make his theories consistent, Boas had to downplay Jewish identity as being anything special. As Morris-Reich explains,

> Boas's article on Jews and his references to Jews in his attempts to refute racialist, racist, and anti-Semitic theories did not have Jews as their object of study. Rather, they made use of Jewish characteristics in order to refute theories he objected to. What made Jews particularly valuable for Boas was the fact that, unlike some other objects of prejudice—Asians, Native Americans, and African Americans—they lacked any phenotypical common denominator. Because his work in this sphere was primarily negative, refuting views he opposed, Jews were the strongest case in his arsenal. . . . His general conception of Jews was guided by a refusal to see a "Jewish difference." . . . Boas employed his method to argue on behalf of an *a priori* conviction. (159)

It follows from this that Boas would have almost inevitably had to de-emphasize his own Jewishness, and in doing so gave rise to a number of different discourses about whether Judaic traditions or Judaic thought played any role in his mind and identity. Despite Boas's forward-thinking challenges to "race"—his accurate claims regarding the variabilities of ethnicity, and the plasticity of cultures—the question of "Jewish identity" is a good deal more complicated than simply asserting a solution of total assimilation. Jewish identity has remained a complex discourse, not solvable by the deconstruction of "race" alone or by arguments of variability. "Being Jewish" has not, and is not likely to, disappear—nor is antisemitism.

THE COMPLEXITY OF BEING JEWISH

Judaism has been identified as many things—a religion, a culture, a moral outlook, and an ethnicity of various types. Most credible scholars of world religions side with Boas in asserting that Judaism is not, and never was, about being a "race." In *A Concise Introduction to World Religions* (2007), Oxtoby and Segal write, "the idea that the Jews constitute a genetic race, which was one of the bases for their persecution in the twentieth century, simply cannot be substantiated. Ever since the ancient Hebrew kingdoms, people of diverse origins have converted or married into the community. Jews today exhibit a vast range of physical characteristics . . . identification on the basis of biology is fraught with error" (63). Jews are often referred to as the "People of the Book," meaning the *Tanakh* (the Hebrew scriptures), the Talmud, and the process of Midrash (commentary on the scriptures). Judaism is also frequently identified as more a way of life in *this* world, as opposed to "salvation" in the next. The prophetic writings within the *Tanakh* and other Jewish sacred documents exercise considerable influence on observant Jews—an "ethical monotheism" that has both secular and religious forms of understanding. Moreover, almost the entire moral value system of the Western world is Judeo-Christian in origin (and remains so, even while immigration from other cultures is changing the dynamic). Northrop Frye once quipped that in the Western world, "We think like Greeks, we strategize like Romans, and we moralize like Jews" (pers. communication, 1971).

Some contemporary Jewish scholars ponder what is meant by the word "Jewish" in current times, and they reference its complexity. One such author is Bernardo Sorj, a Uruguayan-born social scientist at the Federal University of Rio de Janeiro and Director of the Edelstein Center for Social Research. Much of Sorj's scholarly work addresses Jewish-related issues in South American cultures (and is mostly written in Spanish). However, he has, on occasion, written some more general texts aimed at the general public that attempt to account for the complexity of the question, "Who is a Jew?" In his brief 2010 book, *Judaism for Everyone*, Sorj in part echoes Boas in asserting the enormous diversity within groups termed "Jewish." Judaism, Sorj suggests, "is a reality constantly under (re)construction . . . it contains the diversity of each individual's experience . . . and by extension the culture and psychology of an entity that has three thousand years of history behind it" (12). While acknowledging the diversity and indeed the effects of modernity, Sorj, *unlike* Boas, gives considerable weight to "three thousand years of history." Sorj would not find it surprising that Boas would have an assimilationist stance, for "Germany was the principal arena for discussion of the process through which Judaism would absorb modern values" (56). Further, he adds, "the Reform position was that the essence of Judaism was ethics" (56). Jews, suggests Sorj, have always been "living in two worlds" (85), cautioning also that "the social ascent of Jews did not bring an end to stigma and prejudice" (85). Much of the effect of modernity and post-modernity on Jewish identity can be found in the rise of humanistic Judaism, which Sorj sees as "offering non-oppressive ways to identify, rooted in the natural, humanistic, and scientific culture of our time" (85). Sorj's description of humanistic Judaism reflects much of Boas's stance.

In an earlier article, Sorj identifies what he sees as quite possibly the most salient aspect of Jewish experience and Jewish identity: the diasporic consciousness. Again writing for the general public in "Judaism(s), Identity(ies), and Diaspora(s)" (2001), he suggests that while early Judaism—what he calls "pre-modern traditional Judaism"— was oriented to religious precepts and rabbinical leadership within a somewhat self-contained community, modernity transformed being Jewish "into an existential, ideological, and psychological condition and problem. This change was determined by the transformation of the Jews (independently of their wills) into citizens of nation-states, being obliged to define themselves in relation to the new secular values and ideologies of liberalism, socialism, and nationalism" (1). In other words, the daily reality of modern Jews became that of Diaspora. I would suggest, however, that the seeds of diasporic experience were scattered even within the earliest days of traditional Judaism. The vast narrative of the *Tanakh* depicts the history of the Hebrews—the followers of YHVH—as struggling for religious and cultural dominance among many other Semitic and non-Semitic peoples, along with brief sojourns of stability (including the relatively short-lived Davidic reign) combined with long periods of exile (e.g., Egypt, Babylon). Their history is one of almost continuous wandering and displacement. But the word "diaspora" as we know it today in regard to Jewish experience more readily connotes a scattering out of the Middle Eastern lands where their history began, into non-Semitic cultures and areas. As Sorj writes: "The subjective experience of Judaism in modern times, which posed the questions of what it means to be a Jew, why be a Jew, and how to be a Jew, is related to the difficulties of translating the Jewish condition of a diasporic people. . . . Individualistic liberalism, state-based nationalism or internationalist socialism were incapable of including within their categories the existence of diasporas as a meaningful concept and a basis of identity" (2). Sorj suggests that attempts to normalize Jewish experience within Diaspora led to the "repression, denial, and concealing of some aspects of the Jewish tradition and experience" (3), and that secular Judaism sought "to build a 'naturalized/lay' form of Judaism without religious content" (3).

An earlier article by Daniel and Jonathan Boyarin, "Generation and the Ground of Jewish Identity" (1993) frames Jewish history as comprising three stages: first, the tribal perspective in which a people begins to see itself as "special among humanity" (722) and its land as equally special; second, the "tribe" finding its position untenable because of being in contact within that land with other cultural, sociological, and political communities; and, third, "diasporic existence" (722). The Boyarins see diasporic existence as a strength, proposing "a privileging of Diaspora" that is a "disassociation of ethnicities and political hegemonies as the only social structure that even begins to make possible a maintenance of cultural identity in a world grown thoroughly and inexplicably interdependent. Indeed we would suggest that Diaspora, and not monotheism, may be the most important contribution that Judaism has to make to the world" (723). That is to suggest the possibility that Diaspora creates the awareness that "peoples and lands are not naturally and organically connected, [and] could help prevent bloodshed . . . Diaspora can teach us that it is possible for a people to maintain its distinctive culture, its difference, without controlling land, *a fortiori* without controlling other people or developing a need to dispossess them of their lands" (723). Interestingly, whereas the Boyarins connect Diaspora to helping diasporic peoples maintain their distinctive cultures (although current extremist religious strife associated with Islam's encounter with the West belie this somewhat), Boas saw Diaspora as a smoothing-out path of assimilation. He observed that wherever Jews have settled, the majority develop a strong assimilation between themselves and where they are living. Is Boas deliberately de-emphasizing the long history of pogroms and persecution of the Jews at the hands of "Christian" cultures? Did the specter of massive state-driven antisemitism arising in the country of his birth in the lead-up to World War II cause Boas to reevaluate the position of Jews within modern society? We cannot know for sure. Boas, who died in 1942, did not live to see the full impact of the *Shoah* and thus we cannot gauge how that deadly reality might have resonated with his awareness of himself as born Jewish. His statement to Hindenburg (Ich bin jüdischer Abstammung) does suggest a disturbance in Boas's sense of full assimilation.

Certainly Boas, from his birth in 1858, was ensconced in the highly assimilated, yet diasporic community of Jews within Germany, and when he emigrated to North America, it was the similarly assimilated yet diasporic community of Jews in New York City where he circulated, although it must also be said that he formed many friendships and associations outside New York Jewry as well. Boas, like his other Jewish colleagues, was a Jew in Diaspora. New York was, and still is, the location of both the oldest and largest Jewish community in North America, growing sixfold between 1899 and 2017 (from approximately one million to over seven million), yet the entire Jewish population in the U.S. is just 2.1 percent of the entire U.S. population (Jewish Population in the United States by state 2017). New York City alone, however, accounts for over one-third of all Jews in the U.S., comprising 8.9 percent of the population of that state, with the largest New York Jewish component being German Jewish. As history has shown, though, despite the Boyarins proposed scenario that Diaspora can foster a benign cultural identity, the opposite has most often proven true with the long history of worldwide antisemitism wherever there have been significant communities of diasporic Jews. Before considering how Boas's sense of his own Jewishness, with all its contradictions and assimilatory drive, may have been as valid a form of "being Jewish" as other aspects of Jewish tradition, I want to look briefly at some of the hermeneutical narratives of some individuals who helped create the discourse on Boas's Jewishness. Specifically, I will focus on their critique of him and their efforts to understand why he perceived himself in the manner he did.

BOAS'S JEWISH IDENTITY DISCOURSE—SOME EXAMPLES

Due to length restrictions, I have chosen briefly to highlight some of the interpretive efforts that have proposed explanations and motivations regarding the Jewishness of Franz Boas. Douglas Cole, the biographer of Boas's early life, states that Boas arrived in America already committed to an assimilationist stance. He identified as a German, both intellectually and socially (Cole 1999). But his Jewishness was another matter. While sensitive to antisemitism, Boas, according to Cole, went out of his way not to identify himself as a Jew: "Boas did not wish to be set apart; he did not like the feeling that 'the term Jew assigns to the bearer an exceptional position'" (280). He accepted the fact that he was born a Jew, but claimed Jewish traditions had only a small part to play in his upbringing and, similar to many of his German Jewish contemporaries, he showed very little interest in affirming Jewish traditions. Even his marriage emphasized that he seemingly placed little importance on perpetuating a Jewish identity. He wed Marie Krackowizer, who was an Austrian Catholic, the daughter of a prominent Austrian physician (69–70). Indeed, Jewish tradition would dictate that having married a "Gentile," his children would not be Jewish, as Jewish ancestry is construed as being passed down from the mother, not the father.

Cole maintains that although Boas had youthful encounters with antisemitism, he refused to consider whether any of his professional difficulties were related to anti-Semitic attitudes: "while his early career coincided with a rise of anti-Semitism in Germany and America, his difficulties can all be explained by other factors. Significantly, Boas never attributed any of them to prejudice" (281). Boas insisted that there was never anti-Semitic bias among his colleagues. Cole recounts that while it was the case that attitudes toward Boas were likely filtered through common ideas and biases about Jews, Boas's early adult life paints a picture of a man whom others saw through the filter of being Jewish. Boas himself did not ascribe his Jewishness to any kind of difficulties. Moreover, Boas, says Cole, did not consider his Jewishness to be an ethnicity. According to Cole, Boas's attitudes were typical of those of the secular German middle class during a time when there appeared to be a coming together of Jewish values and the enlightened philosophies circulating in Germany. Boas shared these views with others of German Jewish descent, views that Cole describes as "a redefined identity based upon the Enlightenment and *Bildung,* and thus subscribing to individualism, rationalism, humanism, and universalism" (282). This, suggests Cole, was what it was to be a German Jewish intellectual of the time. However, he points out that these German Jewish values were also "shared among a large group of European and American liberals," most of whom were not Jewish (e.g., Gladstone in Britain and Jefferson in America). Cole's depiction of Boas's Jewishness, then, is almost synonymous with secular Enlightenment culture, which implies that Boas was already perceiving himself as beyond his Jewish roots before he ever arrived in America (his family of origin included grandparents who were "pious Jews" who observed dietary customs and kept the Sabbath, but Boas's parents, Sophie and Meier Boas, became progressively more assimilated, resulting in a milder approach to Jewish custom and a greater participation in secular life). However, could we equally argue that, notwithstanding the move toward secularism, the exposure to "piousness" on the part of his grandparents, and the fact that the Boas household continued to adhere to *some* Jewish traditional practices, had to have some effect on Boas's childhood formation? Is Cole too easily asserting the facility of total assimilation in Boas's life?

Leonard Glick, in "Types Distinct from Our Own: Franz Boas on Jewish Identity and Assimilation" (1982), contends that Boas's assimilationist belief that he was fully German in identity belies the many ambivalences present in German society during Boas's youth. Glick speaks of German Jewish communities striving to make themselves "presentable" to the mainstream culture: "they did everything in their power to convince the German people that though remaining Jewish, they could assimilate. There is considerable evidence that at no time did they succeed nearly as well as they hoped and perhaps imagined" (548). Glick observes that during Boas's university life, antisemitism remained pervasive, and he suggests that Boas's eventual migration to America was motivated by a desire to leave antisemitism behind. Glick speculates that Boas's feeling of German society being overly restrictive, particularly to Jews, was part of the context for his feelings about Jewish identity. However, Boas's statements of pride in his German identity seem to contradict Glick's view. Nevertheless, Glick's observation that antisemitism was a continual undercurrent in much of European society is accurate.

Boas's passion for assimilation was, in Glick's view, being taken to an extreme in the sense that Boas "advocated assimilation to the point of literal disappearance for Jews" (546) and that Boas "was determined not to be classified as a Jew" (554). Glick contends that Boas's research regarding Jews ignored key aspects of Jewish history and contexts. Boas, he claims, maintained "bipolar attitudes" toward the two most important aspects of his identity as German and Jewish. Privileging the German identity (and later German American identity) over the Jewish identity led to Boas committing himself not to be bound by any tradition or "to be classified as a member of any group" (560). Thus, interprets Glick, Boas was either unable or unwilling "to confront fully the elements of his own identity," resulting in Boas's "efforts toward defining Jews out of existence" (560), a bias that inserted itself into Boas's research. Glick describes how Boas conducted research on immigrant children, through recourse to anatomical studies, and drew conclusions derived from minor changes in head shape. As Glick argues, "Paradoxically, by concentrating in this manner on physical anthropology, to the virtual exclusion of the historical, economic, and cultural factors that shaped European Jewish identity over nearly two millennia, Boas was employing the very principle to which he was most fundamentally opposed, that "racial" type is the fundamental consideration in national identity, in order to reach conclusions precisely opposite to those of his racist antagonists here and in Germany" (560).

The thrust of Glick's hermeneutic, then, is that Boas harbored a deep ambivalence about being Jewish, was not prepared to face this ambivalence, and used his research methods vis-à-vis Jews to buttress his desire for one-hundred percent assimilation and thus the "disappearance" of the Jews as an ideal outcome. Glick's interpretation, however, raises some questions about its own motivations. First of all, much of Glick's writing in his article on Boas almost approaches psychobiography—an attempt to put together the inner motivations of a person based on events in his or her life. Ironically, it was Boas's contemporary, Sigmund Freud, who created the genre of psychobiography by writing a long essay in 1923 to "psychoanalyze" Leonardo da Vinci, all the while warning his analysis trainees of the dangers of analyzing someone who is not actually an analysand on the couch. Similar to Freud's attempt to explain da Vinci's genius by projecting into what he surmised was going on in da Vinci's unconscious, Glick uses the same strategy with the same pitfalls. Writing long after Boas's death, Glick did not have primary source evidence of Boas's motivations. He had evidence of Boas's written views on race and culture, but no inkling of Boas's inner thought processes. The ambiguities, contradictions, and omissions in some of what Boas wrote about Jews, and in his self-presentation as German (later German American), downplaying the Jewishness, are evident in the external facts of Boas's life and writings. However, Glick seems to want to attribute this to a type of self-delusion in Boas, when it might equally have been a thoroughly conscious strategy motivated by the desire to be seen solely as a brilliant scholar without labels attached to him. In other words, Boas perhaps did not want to boxed in or categorized as a Jewish scholar, but merely as a scholar dedicated to universal humanity, just as in academia today we are seeing African American scholars not wanting to be identified as "black historians" or "black cultural theorists," but instead merely as historians and cultural theorists. As Regna Darnell writes in "Mind, Body, and the Native Point of View" (2015), "Boas ... claims a personal identity as a scholar working within 'our' mainstream American, white, northern European heritage; Judaism was merely a religious category that could be shed along with other 'trammels of culture'" (8).

Gelya Frank in "Jews, Multiculturalism, and Boasian Anthropology" (1997), offers another lens concerning Jewish identity by describing a seeming correlation between Jewish scholars and the history of anthropology as a whole, particularly in the early years of development in this field. Frank suggests that the discipline of anthropology had a decidedly Jewish influence: "the preponderance of Jewish intellectuals in the early years of Boasian anthropology and the Jewish identities of anthropologists in subsequent generations have been downplayed.... The development of American anthropology appears part of Jewish history" (732). Among the first generation of Boas's students, half or more were Jewish, "including Alexander Goldenweiser, Alexander Lesser, Edward Sapir, Paul Radin, Leslie Spier, Robert Lowie, and Melville Herskovits" (732).

Boas's father Meier was an affluent merchant, described by Boas as "liberal." Boas received a nominal religious education; the family, like many in Germany at the time, was far more secular than religious. The Boas family favored assimilation and wanted to be thought of as Germans. Describing Boas as "a cultural hybrid" (732), Frank speculates that Boas's leaning toward a German identity and playing down a Jewish identity had a role in his later challenges to concepts of race and his commitment to "fighting racist stereotypes to the extent of ruling out a cultural approach" (732).

Frank refers to Boas's early encounters with antisemitism as a way to emphasize that, despite assimilationist views, Boas could not escape awareness of his Jewishness. As a young man, as discussed earlier in this chapter, Boas got involved in fights with non-Jewish students and sustained some facial injuries. He was also aware of the prominence of Adolf Stoecker, born near Boas's birth city, who was the court chaplain to the emperor. Stoecker held repugnant anti-Semitic views. Frank proposes that the tension between Jewish identity and cultural assimilation led to the sense of Jews being seen as "racially ambiguous" or, as Frank puts it, "ambiguous whites" (735). Frank seems to suggest that no matter how much Boas insisted that he was German (and later in America, a German American), it was the ambiguousness of Jews not being seen as fully "white" that fueled the development of their vulnerability "to that form of racism known as anti-Semitism" (738). Boas was thus able to draw upon the ambiguities of both his origin and his culture to fuel his convictions about the plasticity of race, moving anthropology toward an "explicitly antiracist science" (741). Frank concludes that Boas's position as an "ambiguously white European Jewish intellectual" (741) allowed Boas to spearhead an anthropological turn that emphasized plasticity, inclusion, and the breaking down of cultural boundaries.

Frank's viewpoint shares much in common with that of George Stocking, who in "Anthropology as *Kulturkampf*: Science and Politics in the Career of Franz Boas" (1992) speculates that Boas's interest in assimilation in his own life was in fact driven by his awareness of the very Jewishness he sought to eliminate. According to Stocker, Boas was able to transmute his personal origins, from his upbringing to his struggles to establish dominance in the field of anthropology, into the concepts of racial and cultural plasticity for which he became famous. Indeed, suggests Stocker, the experience of assimilation in Germany illustrated to

Boas that a group thought to be ostensibly distinct (Jews) were in fact heterogeneous and thus could readily assimilate into German culture.

This same refrain is taken up by Herbert Lewis in "The Passion of Franz Boas" (2001), as Lewis asserts that Boas's pivotal values that would drive his entire career were forged in the crucible between German assimilationism, Enlightenment ideals, "Romantic-Liberal" movements, and the Jewish prophetic tradition that, despite assimilation, remained an undercurrent in Jewish families and communities (451). Lewis points out that "Boas himself would probably have been hesitant to acknowledge the last, however" (451).

Can we connect these numerous interpretations of Boas's Jewish experience (of which we have only touched on a few of many) wherein Boas expressed a distancing ambivalence toward himself? Was his insistence on his own powers of near-total assimilation, first in Germany and later in the U.S., merely an outgrowth of a commitment to secularity and humanism that would take him away from any kind of identification that might have something to do with a religious tradition? Into this realm of interpretive speculation, illustrated by the few (of many) I have referenced here, I insert my own suggestion that, contrary perhaps to his own self-presentation, Boas *did* carry a Jewish identity; further, that his assimilationist stance was rooted not in a departure from Judaism, but in a movement *within* Judaism itself—namely Reform Judaism.

REFORM JUDAISM: TENSIONS BETWEEN SECULARITY AND TRADITION

As Enlightenment values took hold in Europe and political centralization in the eighteenth and nineteenth centuries gained ground, there were profound implications for Jewish communities. Fed by a desire to adapt to both the centralization and the secularization of European society, among many Jews there was a move away from observing Jewish traditions as stringently as in the past. In the words of an article on the origins of Reform Judaism, published by the *Jewish Virtual Library*:

Usually viewed in contrast with Orthodoxy, Reform Judaism was the first of the modern responses to the emancipation of the

Jews, a political process that occurred over an extended period. Because of its stress on autonomy—both of the individual and of the congregation—Reform Judaism has manifested itself differently in various countries. Nevertheless, Reform communities throughout the world share certain characteristics. Reform Jews believe that religious change is legitimate and that Judaism has changed over the centuries as society has changed. While in the past this evolutionary process was subconscious and organic, in the modern world it has become deliberate.

Modern Jewish scholars, such as Michael Meyer (1995) and Gunther Plaut (2015), feature some of the following characteristics emerging from their work on the history of Reform Judaism: the human origins of the Torah in the language of its own time, the rationality of humanity, egalitarianism, and a commitment to ethics, morals, and social action.

Reform Judaism grew very rapidly both in Europe and in America. It is highly likely that Boas was familiar with the Reform Jewish developments in the Germany of his youth. We know that his family moved toward a more assimilationist and secular stance but still kept some Jewish customs. More to the point, however, by the time Boas was born, Reform Judaism was much in evidence in the area where his home city was located. In fact, it was in Germany where Reform Judaism manifested its first expressions.

In the early 1800s, Rabbi Abraham Geiger in Germany sought to modernize Jewish observance. He is considered by many to be the major mover in creating and evolving Reform Judaism. Meyer asserts that "crucial doctrines of Reform Judaism developed within the more turbulent personality and brilliant intellect of Abraham Geiger" (89). Geiger felt that there was a need to update "antiquated Judaism" (91). In Meyer's estimation, Geiger wanted "to instill Jewish self-respect and loyalty by pointing to Judaism's universal values and hopes." Geiger was "willing to be consciously ahistorical," advocated "the free development of the inner moral force," and believed that the values of the Enlightenment and humanism must be brought into Judaism (95–97). Between 1810–30, Jewish groups in Seesen, Hamburg, and Berlin began discarding traditional Jewish practices: removing the Hebrew language from observances and replacing it with German, relaxing the practice of *kashrut,* and viewing one's country of residence as a place of allegiance to become its own Promised Land. In other words, under the influence of the growing Reform movement, many Jewish families, similar to Boas's family, identified the "homeland" with the country into which they felt assimilated.

In the mid-1800s, German Jewish reformers started emigrating to the U.S. They soon became the dominant Jewish cultural expression of American Jews at that time. By 1880, more than 90 percent of U.S. synagogues were Reform. Boas gravitated to New York; he lived and taught there, and he was thoroughly networked into the New York Jewish society of the time. The majority of New York's Jews were Reform—assimilationist, given to humanist world views, and continually modernizing. To this day, especially in the U.S., Reform Judaism manifests a tension between secularity and humanism, and the emphasis on maintaining tradition. Just as Glick, Frank, Stocking, and Lewis noted what they saw as a profound ambivalence within Boas as to his "Jewishness," the article "The Origins of Reform Judaism" in the *Jewish Virtual Library* asserts the marked presence of ambivalence regarding Reform Judaism as a whole, and its interface with both more "traditional" types of Judaism (such as Conservative and Orthodoxy) and secularity.

A key characteristic of Reform Judaism is its commitment to ideas of openness, tolerance, enlightened education, and social justice. It tends to view the world with a wide lens and to think of humankind as a whole rather than giving heavy emphasis to being separate. Instead of thinking of Boas as a person who wanted to reject his Jewishness, we can perhaps see him as manifesting an ambivalent pattern within Judaism itself; that is to say, his attitude was fairly congruent with aspects of Reform Judaism and its ambivalent struggles.

Indeed, Boas became allied to an organization that had strong Reform Jewish roots. In America, Boas developed a close friendship with Felix Adler, who was the founder of the New York Society for Ethical Culture. Felix Adler was the son of Samuel Adler, America's most prominent Reform rabbi. Felix was also on the way to becoming a rabbi himself, but similar to Boas, he eventually gravitated toward a more secular orientation. The website of the Society for Ethical Culture (sec) states that, through Felix Adler, the organization was founded on Reform Jewish values. Boas's friendship with Adler led to Boas participating in fundraising for the SEC and enrolling his children in SEC schools. Adler, like Boas, came to reject traditional Judaism in favor of secularity; he advocated reason, progress, justice, and human rights—all values of the Enlightenment. Adler claimed, in his own words, to be "in favor of a humanistic faith embracing all of humanity . . . Judaism was not given to the Jews alone, but that its destiny is to embrace in one great moral state the whole family of men" (Glick 556). To Adler's writing, Glick adds, "This was, in fact, wholly within the spirit of Reform Judaism."

J. R. Stallones (2009) does not see Felix Adler's departure from the religious aspects of Judaism as any kind of definitive "break" with his father, Rabbi Samuel Adler. Instead it was an evolution that might not have totally pleased the elder Adler. But Samuel Adler's commitment to the idea that "moral principles, not obedience to laws or adherence to doctrinal propositions, was the essence of Judaism" had a profound effect on Felix to the point where "Felix Adler ultimately jettisoned all but morality" (239). Felix Adler's "Jewish roots are clear," and eventually the "moral perfection of all humankind became Adler's lifelong goal, even after he renounced Judaism and created the Ethical Culture Society as the means to this end" (240). It is understandable that Franz Boas would have been attracted to Felix Adler's ideas and to the organization that grew from these ideas. In addition to fundraising for the SEC schools and sending his own children there, Boas also contributed to the organization's publication *The Ethical Record*, specifically a 1904 article, "What the Negro (sic) has done in Africa."

Today, the SEC acknowledges its historical ties to Adler and his family, and the SEC director claims that Boas was actively involved with SEC (pers. communication, 2016). The current SEC also asserts that the founding principles of the organization were based on secular Reform Jewish values. However, telephone enquiries with SEC personnel reveal that SEC does not have an official archivist and that no one has sorted through the boxes of historical material in the SEC's basement. The organization claims that most of Adler's papers were given to Columbia University (where both Adler and Boas taught) and some to Harvard. Further, a staff person at SEC, who did not want to be named (because of a past controversy concerning Adler's descendants), stated that several years ago, the Adler descendants ceased all contact with SEC because of a conflict about which she would not elucidate further. We do know, however, that Adler and Boas had some sort of long-standing relationship. Boas's involvement with SEC and his connection to the Adler family does seem to indicate that, at the very least, Boas was comfortable with Adler's very secular and assimilationist interpretation of Reform Judaism.

Briefly, it is also interesting to look at the contrast between Boas and another major Reform Jewish figure, Kaufmann Kohler. In "Franz Boas and Kaufmann Kohler: Anthropology and Reform Judaism" (1986), Ellen Messer compares the humanism of Boas to the dedicated Reform Jewish outlook of the German Jewish scholar Kohler, who later became a prominent Reform rabbi. Kohler's dedication to Reform Judaism led him to engage in reconciling traditional Jewish values with a wider worldview that would modernize both Judaism and societies in general. Kohler believed that using the "New Knowledge" of science, evolution, history, and social science would help keep the Jewish faith alive. However, unlike Boas, he did not see a conflict between science and modern religion. He believed that Judaism, as well as other faith traditions, could only survive if they were willing to interface with "the realities of the times" (Messer 133). Boas did not share Kohler's commitment to religious faith, but both scholars "also had to deal with the problem of how one could be universal in outlook through participation in a particular cultural (or religious) community. Boas concluded that one could not, and thus was forced into intellectual individualism. Kohler concluded that one could, but had to convince himself that he could be 'universal' and Jewish without the shackles of tradition" (138). The two men, then, can be depicted perhaps as part of a Reform Jewish spectrum: Kohler pursued modern ideals while retaining religious faith, albeit with a much wider lens; while Boas, like Felix Adler, shed tradition, uprooting and discarding almost all vestiges of belief, in favor of scientific enquiry and an overwhelmingly secular commitment. Messer tells us that "the common feature of both Kohler's and Boas's their background" had them posing similar questions about human nature and culture; and that they also shared the "perception that the one 'advance' in human progress that one could hope to see would be the universalization of ethics and values" (136). Further, she writes, "On the issue of race, Boas and the Reform Jewish scholars seem to have entertained parallel ideas" regarding the plasticity of race and culture and holding an ideal of a universal humanity (136). Whereas Kohler wanted to retain aspects of distinctive identities, Boas wanted a melting pot in terms of race and a complete plasticity in terms of cultures. Messer concludes that both individuals were symptomatic of the embedded tension between Reform Judaism and its struggles to remain Jewish, contrasted with its assimilationist and universalist drive. She concludes, "Both anthropologists and American Reform Jews continue to deal with these problems which earlier thinkers clearly identified but could not resolve" (139).

Similarly, I suggest that the tension within Boas himself—in his statements about his secularity and the de-emphasizing of his Jewishness, contrasting with his passionate response toward other Jews who were endangered by the evils of the Third Reich, a passion that led him to *assert* his Jewishness to Hindenburg in that ill-fated letter—is perhaps a small window into issues of his Jewish identity that he himself never really solved.

CONCLUSION

In considering how to evaluate or elucidate Boas's Jewish identity, I have taken several things into account. First, there is what has been written about Boas's ambivalence toward Jewish identity and its influences in his life, and the development of his thoughts on race and cultural plasticity that in some way grew out of his own awareness that he was often perceived as an outsider. Second, there is his choice to settle in the New York German Jewish community, where there was (and still is) a strong Reform Jewish presence. Third, there is his involvement with the SEC and Adler, suggesting that something in Boas resonated with Adler's values, which owed much to principles within Reform Judaism. Fourth, there is the history of Reform Judaism with its struggle between tradition and a relentless drive to modernize, secularize, and assimilate—a dynamic phenomenon that produces a spectrum of positions from religious Reform Jews to extremely secular Jews who keep some of the values but discard the trappings of the tradition so as to appear completely assimilated. Finally, there is Boas's own fierce battles with antisemitism, his attack on Nazism, and his activism in helping Jewish intellectuals get out of Germany to escape persecution. We can perhaps see Boas's conflicted stance toward his Jewishness as being consistent with many of the same challenges faced by Reform Judaism. Perhaps we can gain a deeper understanding of Boas's Jewishness by seeing him as an individual, similar to Adler, who pushed toward the secular aspects of Reform Judaism. However, we cannot simply label Boas as a Reform Jew *manqué*, for to do so would disrespect the indicators of his self-perception. Rather, we could see him as one who went much further away from the tradition than did many of his similarly conflicted contemporaries. This indeed remains the challenge for Reform Judaism today and for Boas in his lifetime—how far can one push away from the tradition and still be viewed as Jewish in identity? For Boas, *despite* his desire to be a German, and later an American, history will continue to identify him as a highly influential Jew, similar to Freud, Einstein, and numerous other major historical figures given to us by Judaism, and who changed the world for the better. Regarding Boas, we can question whether all the speculation about his Jewish self-identity is as important as the groundbreaking research he did in the field of anthropology or the fact that in his passion for tolerance and justice with a world-oriented view of a universal ethical humanity, he was a man attempting to point the way toward a more humane world, toward which to this day we certainly need to aspire.

REFERENCES

Boas, Franz. (1945) 1969. *Race and Democratic Society*. New York: Biblo and Tannen.

———. 1904. "What the Negro has done in Africa." *The Ethical Record* 5, no. 3: 106–9.

Boyarin, Daniel, and Jonathan Boyarin. 1993. "Generation and the Ground of Jewish Identity." *Critical Inquiry* 19, no. 4: 693–725.

Cole, Douglas. 1999. *Franz Boas: The Early Years, 1858–1906*. Vancouver: Douglas and McIntyre.

Darnell, Regna. 2015. "Mind, Body, and the Native Point of View." In *The Franz Boas Papers, Volume I*, edited by Regna Darnell, Michelle Hamilton, Robert L. A. Hancock, and Joshua Smith, 3–18. Lincoln: University of Nebraska Press.

Frank, Gelya. 1997. "Jews, Multiculturalism, and Boasian Anthropology." *American Anthropologist* 99, no. 4: 731–45.

Freed, Stanley. 2012. *Anthropology Unmasked*. Wilmington OH: Orange Frazer Press.

Freud, Sigmund. (1923) 1957. *Five Lectures on Psycho-Analysis, Leonardo da Vinci, and Other Works*, edited by James Strachey. London: Hogarth Press.

Glick, Leonard. 1982. "Types Distinct from Our Own: Franz Boas on Jewish Identity and Assimilation." *American Anthropologist* 84, no. 2: 545–65.

Gritz, Rothenberg Jennie. 2007. "The Jews in America." *The Atlantic*. Accessed April 8, 2019. https://www.theatlantic.com/magazine/archive/2007/09/the-jews-in-america/306273/.

Hart, Mitchell B. 2003. "Franz Boas as German, American, and Jew." In *German-Jewish Identities in America*, edited by Christof Mauch and Joseph Salmons, 88–105. Madison: University of Wisconsin.

History Place. 2001. "The Triumph of Hitler: The Burning of Books." Accessed April 8, 2019. http://www.historyplace.com/worldwar2/triumph/tr-bookburn.htm.

Jewish Virtual Library. n.d. "The Origins of Reform Judaism." Accessed February 22, 2019. http:// www.jewishvirtuallibrary.org/the-origins-of-reform-judaism.

———. n.d. "Vital Statistics: Jewish Population in the United States, by State (1899–Present). Accessed February 22, 2019. http://www.jewishvirtuallibrary.org/jewish-population-in-the-united-states-by-state.

Langenkämper, Jürgen. 2015. "Franz Boas's Correspondence with German Friends and Colleagues in the Early 1930s." In *The Franz Boas Papers, Volume I*, edited by Regna Darnell, Michelle Hamilton, Robert L. A. Hancock, and Joshua Smith, 277–92. Lincoln: University of Nebraska Press.

Lewis, Herbert. 2001. "The Passion of Franz Boas." *American Anthropologist* 103, no. 2: 447–67.

Messer, Ellen. 1986. "Franz Boas and Kaufmann Kohler: Anthropology and Reform Judaism." *Jewish Social Studies* 48, no. 2: 127–40.

Meyer, Michael A. 1995. *Response to Modernity: A History of the Reform Movement in Judaism*. Detroit: Wayne State University Press.

Morris-Reich, Amos. 2007. "Project, Method, and the Racial Characteristics of Jews: A Comparison of Franz Boas and Hans F. K. Günther." *Jewish Social Studies* 13, no. 1: 136–69.

New York Society for Ethical Culture. 2016. "Our History." Accessed April 8, 2019. https://nysec.org.

Norwood, Stephen H. 2007. "Complicity and Conflict: Columbia University's Response to Fascism, 1933–1937." *Modern Judaism* 27, no. 3. 253–83.

Oxtoby, Willard Gurdon, and Alan F. Segal, eds. 2007. *A Concise Introduction to World Religions*. Oxford: Oxford University Press.

Plaut, W. Gunther. (1963) 2015. *The Growth of Reform Judaism: American and European Sources*. Philadelphia: The Jewish Publication Society.

Sorj, Bernardo. 2010. *Judaism for Everyone*. International Federation for Secular and Humanistic Judaism.

———. 2001. "Judaism(s), Identity(ies), and Diaspora(s): a view from the periphery," www.bernardosorj.com/pdf/judaismidentityanddiaspora.pdf.

Stallones, J. R. 2009. "Struggle for the Soul of Felix Adler." *American Educational History Journal* 36, no. 2: 237–54.

Stocking, George W. Jr. 1992. *The Ethnographer's Magic and Other Essays in the History of Anthropology*. Madison: University of Wisconsin Press.

Quinley, Harold E. 1977. *Anti-Semitism in America, 1878–1939*. New York: Arno Press.

3

A Document in an Unexpected Place

John P. Harrington and the Stevenson Scrapbook

As everyone who searches for documents to study the history of anthropology knows, the information we seek is generally scattered in numerous archives, museums, and libraries. We all spend a great deal of time simply locating relevant materials. Although it would be so efficient if everything we needed were in one place, that never happens. And sometimes our own work habits make reconnaissance more difficult. Plodding our way through mounds of materials searching for a missing letter, or obtaining new possibilities from publication footnotes, we write down the names of new repositories on small pieces of scrap paper. These jotted notes then inevitably become lost in the papers on our desks and forgotten. I did this in 1982 while researching James and Matilda Coxe Stevenson's artifactual collecting activities in the American Southwest. I was compiling information on the life of Matilda Coxe Stevenson, the first female anthropologist employed by the U.S. government. My research was for a paper on how systematic museum collections are formed (Parezo 1987, 1993). One day, sitting in a restaurant I no longer remember, I wrote on a napkin, "Look in LAB-Santa Fe. Stevenson Scrapbook there. How did it get there?"

I did not have the money to go to Santa Fe at the time. And life and other projects got in the way of tracking down this potential data source. The napkin slipped into my personal research records, somewhere in eleven four-drawer file cabinets. It probably would never had made it back onto my desk, but in 2014 my colleague, Catherine Nichols, found the note in a green manila file folder that had nothing to do with Stevenson. She decided to search for the scrapbook. On a trip to Santa Fe, she perused a bound volume labeled, "Personal Scrapbook

A, Newspaper Clippings on the Archaeology of the Southwest," in the archives of the Laboratory of Anthropology, Museum of New Mexico (LAB). She was intrigued by the information it held, although it did not contain the data she sought for her dissertation research (Nichols 2014). Catherine told me to look at the scrapbook the next time I was in Santa Fe. When I did, I agreed. It was interesting.

I eventually visited and perused the scrapbook with my friend, LAB archivist Diane Bird. The name Scrapbook A implies there is a Scrapbook B, probably labeled "Newspaper Clippings on the Ethnology of the Southwest." More precisely, I should say, at least two scrapbooks existed at one time. Hopefully it still resides somewhere, maybe in the house of a descendent of Stevenson's nephew or niece, but it was not in the LAB. There was only the one entry in the catalogued collections and Diane did not remember seeing anything like it in the uncatalogued materials. I also checked the library, but there were no additional scrapbooks.

I was initially disappointed because I had always focused on the Stevensons' ethnographic research and there was still so much to learn about Matilda's activities as a foundational anthropologist. Scrapbook A, however, quickly turned out to be a rich source of information on Southwestern archaeology in the 1880s. In fact, it led to my current research project, conducted along with Nichols, on the joint 1882 United States Geological Survey-Bureau of Ethnology field season on the Colorado Plateau. One of our goals is to analyze how observational field sciences, under the direction of John Wesley Powell, helped the government assess the feasibility of integrating northern Arizona and New Mexico territories into the American socio-political economy. News clippings contained information about how anthropologists, geologists, and geographers presented their findings to help the American public understand the region's lands and population, an amalgamation of Indigenous, Hispanic, Mexican, and in-migrating American peoples.

The existence of Scrapbook A in Santa Fe posed a small mystery for me. I have long been interested in how anthropology's knowledge base came into existence, how the information in which we ground our theories and interpretations has (or has not) been saved. This information is critical because it constitutes the foundation on which anthropology partly claims its professional status as the holder of esoteric knowledge based on firsthand observation and interaction with real peoples. It is the same justification for professional status used by experts in botany, geology, and zoology; these disciplines claim credibility based on the existence of contextualized specimens collected in natural settings that can be used repeatedly by multiple practitioners, thereby increasing scientific validity. I have also been interested in how the professional saving of such information, especially fieldnotes and material objects, has been used by contemporary researchers and how Native communities have had (or not had) access to these data. This is partly a practical problem of not knowing where documentary and photographic materials, as well as collections, are housed. It is also due to a lack of knowledge about the life histories that activated the dispersal of documents produced by a single practitioner. Information access is an intellectual problem: how is knowledge organized and how can it be reclaimed and reassessed in light of theoretical and paradigmatic changes?

These interests led me to ask in 2015 what I had queried in 1982: how did Scrapbook A wind up in Santa Fe and when did it become part of their archival collections? Did Stevenson or someone else place it there? How did it get from one of her homes to this archive? Could it have first been in the National Anthropological Archives (NAA), the place where the records of most Bureau of American Ethnology employees now reside? Could it have been part of a transfer from one institution to another and like a long held "temporary" loan of an artifact used in exhibit but never returned? Had someone in Santa Fe borrowed it for some reason and never returned it? There was no paperwork documenting any formal transfer, but people being people, it was possible.

I initially expected any scrapbooks documenting the careers to be in the National Anthropological Archives (NAA), Smithsonian Institution, which is where I naively assumed in 1982 that *all* of Matilda's and James' extant papers resided. Only correspondence or something she had freely given away should be in other archives, probably after interesting journeys. Why was Scrapbook A not in the NAA? Had I missed a Scrapbook B in Washington—and, if I had, why was this the case? I am usually pretty systematic in my searches. I had many newspaper clippings from the NAA, for I considered newspapers an important source, if properly vetted with contents substantiated by other sources. Most of the newspapers I had seen on several trips during the 1980s, however, were found in records groups that consisted of the contents of United States National Museum (USNM) anthropologists' desks, which had been packed away in boxes after their deaths.

Unfortunately, there was no indication of how or when Scrapbook A wound its way from Matilda's home or BAE office to reside in a Santa Fe archive. Bird knew that the scrapbook came under her care after residing in the Museum of New Mexico Library for many years. This meant that at one time it was part of either Edgar Lee Hewett's or Kenneth Chapman's personal libraries. These both became the basis of the institution's core holdings. Its call number designation falls under the old Dewey decimal system: 571.3 s847. On the inside cover is a stamp: "Library, Museum of New Mexico, Division of Anthropology." These two facts indicate that the scrapbook was in the MNM system before 1930 at a time when there was no separate archive. The question now became: how did the scrapbook come to be mingled with either Hewett's or Chapman's books? I thought it was probably included with Hewett's books, given his archaeological interests. Could Stevenson have given or loaned it to Hewett?

This scenario was possible, but not likely, given that Hewett and Stevenson were not friends who would have shared scrapbooks. However, Stevenson could have had the scrapbook at her ranch, Ton'yo, near San Ildefonso Pueblo and Espanola, New Mexico. She had purchased this ranch in 1907 after she sold her old home on P Street in Washington DC (Miller 2007, 179). It was close to Santa Fe. Maybe Stevenson took the scrapbook to Santa Fe herself and left it with an SAA-MNM staff member or with Hewett when she was researching historic Hispanic documents? These possibilities, however, were unlikely since there is no correspondence between Matilda and Hewett about the scrapbook. But she could have still brought the scrapbook to New Mexico to peruse as a remembrance of her life with her husband, for Stevenson intended her New Mexico ranch to be a combined fieldwork base, working ranch, and a holiday retreat.

This led me to think about another possibility. Stevenson intended to move to Denver in late 1914 to be near her sister and her family so she could concentrate on her writing, and then travel occasionally to Washington DC for work. Maybe Scrapbook B made it to Denver on one of her visits and is now in some trunk in an attic. This is possible, but not likely. As a letter to Stevenson's attorney states, she planned to leave New Mexico due to the expenses, and due to the physical and emotional exhaustion concomitant to her libel lawsuit against Clara True and her mother.[1] In March 1915, she shipped all her possessions and papers to Washington DC. So, if scrapbooks had traveled to New Mexico, they had gone back east. That still did help me speculate on the journey of Scrapbook A from its construction in the mid-1880s to 1915. What about after 1915?

I thought about what I knew of Stevenson's materials in the NAA and how much of it was no longer in her records but incorporated into the monumental files of John P. Harrington. I learned about this particular instance of field record reuse the hard way. When I was a postdoctoral fellow at the Smithsonian in 1981–82, I searched and searched for James Stevenson's 1883 field catalogue and subsequent collection inventories for the Zuni and Hopi. I looked in the UNSM and the Smithsonian Institution's archives (SIA), the NAA, the accession papers in the registrar's, and the deaccession records, for any records with the catalogue cards in the anthropology department. Then I rooted around in the uncatalogued boxes in the collection management area, but I didn't find anything.

On my last day before returning home to Arizona, the archivist working on processing the massive John P. Harrington papers came to me. She was a dedicated person who had been systematically working her way through the hundreds of boxes of disorganized data that had languished since Harrington's death. I wanted to look through them, but they were closed to researchers as she catalogued and organized. There were a couple of inventories of Pueblo materials in Harrington's papers, she told me. However, they were in what she called a "strange" handwriting. She asked if I would see if I could recognize the handwriting and identify to which cultures they referred.

Of course, I did. There, mixed into some other typed lists of objects, were pages of Pueblo materials with James and Matilda's notations on the sides of the pages. One set was the missing 1883 inventory. Ecstatic,

I photocopied at lightning speed, but I did not even make a dent in the other material. There were pages with Zuni names for plants in Matilda Stevenson's handwriting, one plant per page on what were essentially scrap notes attached to larger pieces of paper. Others contained Stevenson's northern Rio Grande Pueblo ethnobotanical fieldnotes that should have been in a manuscript folder that only held a few loose pages in the NAA. There were hundreds of slips of papers with ethnographic information, but no attribution or indication of when and where the information was obtained. None were in Harrington's handwriting. These slips were in Matilda Stevenson's handwriting; we looked at one of her files with intact fieldnotes to be sure.[2]

Harrington had taken Stevenson's fieldnotes and reorganized them by topic, then culture.[3] He interspersed her observations and interview notes with his own. As I left the next day I felt I had left so much undone. The archivist said she would keep looking and start to make cross entries with Stevenson's NAA manuscript records. I had suggested she put them back in Stevenson's papers. She would not consider reintegrating the materials with their original files. This would have affected their provenience, which archival protocol privileges by ultimate donor, and the internal organization when the material officially entered the archive, she argued, even if it meant the earlier donated materials placed in the same institution had been altered and gutted. She would not consider that Stevenson's intellectual record had been torn apart by Harrington's behavior. From her standpoint, his reuse— including taking her name off the information—was now part of the record and should not be destroyed. We both had valid perspectives, but the marginalization and appropriation of Stevenson's material still makes me sad. It renders her invisible. It is as if Harrington had stolen her identity, her labor, and her knowledge—and the archival community condoned the activity. It placed and continues to place Stevenson in a subordinate role as a scholar, someone whom Harrington did not even acknowledge. Unfortunately, although not intended, this archival protocol continues a professional practice of marginalization by institutionalizing the appropriation. Digitization and cross-indexing mitigates the invisibility problem to a degree: the finding aides for the Harrington materials now state that Boxes 890 to 899 of Harrington's records are "Matilda Coxe Stevenson Material." But Stevenson's original work will always be part of Harrington's record, no longer her own.[4]

But back to Scrapbook A. If Harrington had access to Stevenson's raw field data generated during the late 1900s and early 1910s, maybe he had gained access to her scrapbooks. Could he have taken Scrapbook A to Santa Fe? Maybe Harrington, who was friendly with Hewett, loaned or gave him the scrapbook? I needed to look at Harrington's and Stevenson's relationship, then reexamine Stevenson's archived materials. Maybe what Harrington took and what he left intact in her papers held a clue?

I had a possible hypothesis for my little mystery: Harrington brought Scrapbook A to Hewett, who never returned it, but placed it in his library where it was discovered by a librarian, accessioned into the MNM library, and eventually transferred to the LAB-MNM archive. I could even place my idea within larger methodological questions: What had I missed about how archival collections are formed, and how did this affect archival research? Was there some process of institutional or personal movement of professional field documents I had overlooked in my previous research, which if I had been attuned to, would have made my research more efficient and more complete? How did previous professional reuse of fieldnotes affect my database?[5] Should I start thinking about a new type of appropriation—younger scholars taking the fieldnotes of older scholars and transforming them into their own?

RETHINKING STEVENSON'S ARCHIVED MATERIALS

Matilda Coxe Stevenson produced thousands of paper field records, object descriptions, manuscript pages, and photographs during her long career. Her NAA finding aide lists 3,352 catalogued photographic items in various formats produced between 1882 and 1915 in NAA Photo Lot 23, and there were more in other NAA photographic collections. These were personal (pictures of her home at 1303 P Street in 1890, family and personal portraits), as well as 900 field snapshots taken at Zuni and other parts of the northern Southwest.[6] There were hundreds of letters in separate correspondence files, in the Bureau and USNM incoming and outgoing correspondence files, as well as in several record units in the Smithsonian Institution Archives (SIA). Her files also included maps, drawings, watercolors, plant specimens, artifacts, monthly work reports, and annual reports. Documents about her and produced by her were in the papers of numerous individuals like William Henry Holmes, in the National Art Gallery archives, and in her employment and pay discrimination grievance case in the SIA. The main record unit is MS 4689, Stevenson papers, 1870–1910, five linear feet of materials from her estate. And then there were her field records, dozens of topical and manuscript units: Taos vocabulary and grammatical constructions from 1906 (MS 2087); game equipment, 1903 (MS 4948); and notes and sketches, 1896 (MS 2038)—to name but a few files.[7] Notebooks and field diaries contained additional information and observations. I had reviewed about 80 percent of the files in the 1980s, but more had been found and catalogued since then. Information about them is now available online. I rechecked on a later visit to the NAA and found that scrapbooks were listed as a named record group, as components of other record groups, or as separate files in the NAA vertical files.

Scrapbook A consists of seventy-six pages containing forty-six newspaper articles, some with and some without authorship or publication attribution, in addition to news notes and announcements from the early- to mid-1880s pasted into the scrapbook. Scrapbook A also contains a dozen loose newspaper clippings recounting Matilda's life in the early 1900s.[8] The pasted entries deal primarily with James' and Matilda's 1880, 1881, and 1882 Southwestern field seasons. Others discussed cliff dwellings explored by James Stevenson's professional acquaintances. There were also articles on miscellaneous topics: John Bourke's 1881 fieldtrip to Hopi and his ensuing collection, Aztec Ruin with a site map, and a description of ancient Santa Fe. A small subset was written by a Miss Grundy documenting Matilda's work with the Zuni elders who came to Washington with Frank Hamilton Cushing in spring 1882.

Matilda was a fair compiler, but not especially systematic or complete in her source documentation. Some 1880s materials were accompanied by a publication's title and the date, written next to the article in Matilda's handwriting.[9] The fact that Matilda saved these articles meant that she valued them; and her handwritten notations, noting errors or questioning details, (writing "yes" or "no" on the pages next to the articles) indicate that she vetted and assessed each. These activities enhance the scrapbook's usefulness as a corpus of articles containing potentially useful information and indications of the newsworthiness of several topics from Matilda's standpoint.

Stevenson clipped some articles herself at first, but the number of newspapers found in the scrapbook would have meant she was spending a good deal of money on newspapers published in far-flung places. She probably used a subscription clipping service to obtain some articles. It would have been a cost-effective option. According to historian Richard K. Propp, in 1899 clipping services charged five cents per clipping, with a one-cent discount for bulk orders.[10]

Newspaper or press clipping services have been used by Americans for over one hundred and fifty years. The commodity service was begun in 1852 by a Polish newsagent in London, after writers, musicians, artists, and actors came to his shop to search for articles about themselves. As an industry used by American intellectuals, politicians, and bourgeois elites, 1884 is the date scholars agree saw press clippings services gain a foothold in America. Samuel Leavitt established an agency in New York City, followed the next year by the National Press Intelligence Company in 1885. Similar agencies were founded in Boston and Chicago in 1888.[11] This timeline means that Stevenson probably cut out her 1882 entries but used a service for 1884 and thereafter. Articles in Scrapbook A were from a cut and clip service; the article was physically cut from the newspaper and mailed to the subscriber.

In the late nineteenth century, hiring a service to read all national and regional newspapers helped professionals keep track of what was being said about them and whether their activities were being mentioned. Many subscribers were enthusiasts researching a topic; others were publicity seekers assessing their celebrity. For business men, using a clipping service was a way to assess their marketing strategies and keep track of economic, social, and cultural trends. The services allowed scholars to keep abreast of special interests, including the activities of their colleagues. Services usually searched for individual names and content based on scientific discipline and geographical region. In the case of Stevenson's scrapbook, this had been archaeological activities in the American Southwest and articles that mentioned either James or

Matilda. Others were doing the same thing to assess their prestige and public acknowledgement of their activities. This was important for all professionals but especially institution builders like Frederic Putnam and government managers, like John Wesley Powell, James Stevenson, William Henry Holmes, and W J McGee, who needed to convince members of Congress to fund anthropological research activities.[12]

Keeping a scrapbook was an intellectual and emotional activity, a means to ensure remembrance for Matilda of her and James's professional careers. And there was a lot to remember. James (1840–88) was a geological-geographical explorer who began working with Ferdinand V. Hayden in 1856 and remained with him until 1879 when the four great U.S. geological surveys were folded into the new United States Geological Survey (USGS). A competent topographer, James served as Hayden's Chief Executive Officer and helped him survey the Yellowstone region. He was memorialized in American magazines as a daring explorer-scientist and seen by other professionals as a good administrator and data collector. In 1879 Powell hired Stevenson as a research scientist for the new Bureau of Ethnology and sent him to the American Southwest to locate and survey archaeological sites, collect artifacts for the USNM at Pueblo communities (particularly Zuni and Hopi), map landscapes, record geological formations, and begin the systematic collection of ethnographic information on Southwestern cultures. Referred to by Powell as "a man of deeds, not words," James continued these activities as well as served as the Chief Executive Officer for the USGS and Bureau until his death in 1888.[13] His wife, Matilda, often accompanied him to the field from the mid-1870s on, collected and analyzed data, catalogued and organized collections, and wrote artifact inventories in the government laboratories in New York City and Washington DC.

Matilda Coxe Evans Stevenson (1849–1915) is most known for her multiyear ethnographic fieldwork at Zuni, Zia, and Acoma. Trained as a botanist, geologist, artist, and chemist, she was also an unrecognized archaeologist, working alongside James (after their marriage in 1872) as an unpaid assistant on numerous Hayden surveys as well as USGS and Bureau field trips in her early career. An official member of Smithsonian, USGS, and Bureau research expeditions by 1879, she began publishing independently in 1881. After her husband's death in 1888 she was given a permanent paid position in the Bureau in order to continue their research. Matilda retained some of James's papers after his death, which were later incorporated as part of her professional papers at the NAA. Other sections of James's papers—including some of Matilda's field watercolors and their joint archaeological data—found their way into the USGS record group in the National Archives or the Smithsonian Institution archives as part of the papers of the USNM.

Throughout her long career, Matilda continued to occasionally compile data on possible sites for Bureau archaeologists to further explore, but she never considered herself an archaeologist. She generally gave her notes to Powell or his staff at the end of each field season. This information was quickly distributed to USNM and Bureau archaeologists like Cosmos and Victor Mindeleff, Jesse Walter Fewkes, Willian Henry Holmes, and Walter Hough. None of her assigned manuscript units contain archaeological information, although there is some information in her diaries. One could have expected that one of these individuals, particularly her friend William Henry Holmes, might have found Scrapbook A interesting.

But was it something she would have shared with Harrington?

JOHN P. HARRINGTON

Harrington (1888–1961) is one of the most famous (and infamous) linguists, folklorists, and cultural anthropologists to work in the American Southwest and California.[14] He is the epitome of the data-collector scholar who assumed that cultural information and languages had to be salvaged before American Indians disappeared. He believed that gathering precious data was more important than summarizing or interpreting information within a body of theory, although he did publish a great deal. Ambitious, territorial, and manically obsessive, Harrington became increasingly reclusive and paranoid. He felt he had a duty to amass everything he could before other scholars, especially Alfred Kroeber, "stole" his data. He raced from field site to field site in a never-ending attempt to obtain one more word in an Indigenous language or one more fact. As a result, his fieldwork was never concluded, for it never could be.

Harrington studied classical languages at Stanford University (1902–5), under classical philologist Henry R. Fairclough (1862–1938), an important member of the Archaeological Institute of America. Harrington graduated at the top of his class and was elected to Phi Beta Kappa. He seemed to have a natural affinity for languages and phonetics. He earned a living translating Russian for the Immigration Service and tutoring other students in French and German. His career path changed, however, when he attended a summer school taught by Alfred Kroeber and Pliny Earle Goddard in 1903. He became deeply interested in California linguistics. To gain advanced training he studied anthropology and linguistics at Humboldt University in Berlin and Leipzig University in 1906 but never finished his doctoral degree. Instead, he returned to California to work with the Mojave while teaching contemporary languages at a Los Angeles high school. By 1907 he was spending all his free time recording Chumash, Quechan, and Mojave languages and stories. "In his field work he lived with the Indians in their own homes, eating their wood and working with them night and day."[15] The constant travel and often ten to eighteen hours a day of fieldwork, in addition to a full-time job, was tiring and led to health problems.

Deciding to work solely as an ethnographer-linguist, Harrington searched for employment, but few universities or museums were hiring. Given his fascination with Native California, the logical place would have been the University of California-Berkeley under Kroeber, but the two men had already developed a lifelong feud over research territoriality. Harrington turned his eyes east, to the next large community of anthropological activity: Santa Fe. It was an area Kroeber did not control.

HARRINGTON, HEWETT, AND STEVENSON, 1908–15

Santa Fe was a new mecca of anthropological research with institutions and money. Scholars were finding support there for their research projects. "Scholar-entrepreneur" Edgar Lee Hewett (1865–1946) had recently gained control over the Museum of New Mexico (MNM) after being hired as the founding director of the School of American Archaeology (SAA). In 1907, the SAA board told Hewett his mandate was to encourage and oversee regional scholarship.[16] Hewett conducted his mandate exceedingly well, as Don D. Fowler recounts in several works. Hewett directed the exhibits at the San Diego Panama-California Exposition (1911–16), served as founding director of the San Diego Museum of Man, and as founding head of anthropology at San Diego State Teacher's College (1917–28). He helped establish the anthropology departments at the University of New Mexico in 1927 and at the University of Southern California in 1934.[17] Just as Kroeber desired to coordinate research in California, Hewett endeavored to manage research in the American Southwest and train young men through his field schools. He simultaneously strove to protect archaeological sites under the regional control of the state museum with himself as the nationally recognized authority figure and administrator. Fowler argues that Hewett was successful because he was a master coalition builder. Between 1907 and 1910 he worked tirelessly, networking with powerful colleagues, like William Henry Holmes, with whom he had written the 1906 Antiquities Act, and their organizations, in this case seeking an alliance between SAA and the Smithsonian Institution to coordinate and co-fund research.[18] Hewitt was a man Harrington wanted to impress. He called on his old professor. H. R. Fairclough, who provided him with a glowing letter of introduction.[19]

Institution builders do not like researchers who are not under their oversight to work in "their" region. They might not share the same vision of how to prioritize research and might, consciously or inadvertently, sour relations with native communities. The Smithsonian Institution and its constituent units had a long history of research in the American Southwest. One of its main practitioners was Matilda Coxe Stevenson, who had been working there continuously since 1879 and showed no sign of stopping. She was now engaged in producing a massive comparison of Pueblo religions focusing on the northern Rio Grande region—Hewett's backyard. She was a threat to his authority and research vision.

Hewett thought Stevenson stood in the way of his plans to produce basic ethnographic and linguistic descriptions of each Pueblo community. Hewett considered her an unpleasant, obstinate but tenacious individual who could be persuasive and diplomatic when she desired. She was also fiercely independent and not to be underestimated or trifled with. She had shown that she would follow her own research agenda, despite counter administrative orders or suggestions. She had important friends in Santa Fe, like ex-governor L. Bradford Prince, who was not enamored with Hewett's SAA leadership, just as she had powerful Washington DC connections (Miller 2007, 198–99). While she was the senior ethnologist in the Puebloan region he felt she had outlived her research usefulness and was not concentrating on the most important research questions. Hewett respected her work but thought she was slow; he thought it was time for her to retire and leave the field to younger men under his direction.[20] Holmes supported her, however, and Hewett had no established ethnographer to suggest in her stead.

Harrington came to Santa Fe to meet Hewett in 1908 after his high school recessed for the summer and asked for a job. His timing was good; Hewett aspired to expand into California and thought Harrington could help him accomplish this goal, even if he had a reputation as a maverick. Harrington assured Hewett that he could work on Puebloan languages. But before giving the twenty-four-year-old who had not finished his PhD a permanent position, Hewett wanted to make sure that he was as good as his boasts. Hewett required Harrington serve as a "voluntary assistant" for the SAA's summer field school in Canyon de los Frijoles. Hewett asked him to begin a systematic study of Tewa language and mythology. He could use as informants the San Ildefonso men excavating at the SAA-MNM sites.[21] Several weeks remained before the start of the field school, however, and Harrington wanted to use them productively. He asked Hewett where he should work. Using his standard assessment and educational technique of sink or swim (i.e., letting people loose to fend for themselves), Hewett sent Harrington to San Ildefonso (without compensation or per diem) to gauge his linguistic skills. Hewett failed to ask the community if they wanted to interact with a linguist. Unfortunately, smallpox had been detected in the village, so Harrington prudently did not attempt to stay. He had sunk before he took his first stroke.

Hewett made no effort to help the young scholar figure out what to do when his research project fell through. Luckily, Stevenson had heard about Harrington through the local grapevine just as Harrington had learned of Stevenson. He showed up at her ranch one day unannounced. Here Harrington saw a flagpole with an American flag and a sign that read "A U.S. Government Camp—No Trespassing," a designation made to protect Stevenson and her native informants from unwanted intrusions.[22] She invited him to stay.

Stevenson had just returned to New Mexico.[23] In early 1908 she had been in Washington DC working on manuscripts and had returned to her ranch only a week before Harrington arrived. She intended to continue her comparative study of religion, seeking information from Santa Clara, San Ildefonso, and Nambe. Like the communities of Taos and San Ildefonso where she had worked in 1907, these pueblos were used to protecting their beliefs and rituals from outsiders. They were more open about other topics but still not readily forthcoming. She had a wealth of information on subsistence, kinship and social structure, a large list of vocabulary, and plant use. Her research method centered on key informants who would work in secret at her ranch, without participatory observation as she had conducted elsewhere. And she had demanding standards to insure she eliminated personal idiosyncrasies when searching for culturally accepted norms. As she told Smithsonian Secretary Charles D. Walcott, "I never record anything until I have had it from at least three Indians neither one knowing they had spoken with me."[24] As a result, her data collection proceeded very slowly. In fact, she had more success with her former Zuni consultants who came to work with her on several projects.[25]

Stevenson liked Harrington immediately and wrote to Bureau director William Henry Holmes that he was a fine young scholar, very cultured and quite remarkable in his linguistic skills. She suggested that Holmes employ him as an ethnographer.[26] Unfortunately Bureau funds for the fiscal year were already obligated, so nothing came of the request; nor would Holmes have hired anyone sight unseen. Stevenson decided the young man was worth mentoring, and she supported Harrington using her personal and Bureau research funds. In addition, she introduced him to one of her major Taos respondents, Manuel Mondragon, who patiently helped Harrington record and understand the language.[27] Concurrently, Stevenson worked on her studies of Zuni and Tewa ethnobotany, and she influenced Harrington's subsequent interests in these topics. No longer as territorial as she had been in her younger days when she and Frank Hamilton Cushing had a fierce rivalry for authoritative status as Zuni scholars, Stevenson freely shared her data with Harrington. Stevenson appears to have acted much like a professor, especially a dissertation advisor, who shares data and insights with a valued student. Harrington began to emulate some of her data collection methods, especially her topical approach. He gained information on ethnogeography (how native peoples viewed and talked about the land), and began to record place names, plant names, and their uses. Harrington remained with Stevenson for six weeks. He went to the field school and returned to his high school in Los Angeles and his California studies.

Stevenson invested in the young man, even though she was leery of neophytes, who were not committed to ethnography, coming to northern New Mexico. Most stayed a brief time and wrote superficial articles without conducting the years of dedicated research she felt ethnography required.[28] In Harrington she saw a young scholar who understood that studying an indigenous culture takes long-term commitment and that learning the language must always be the first task.

Stevenson spent 1909 in New Mexico working at Santa Clara, San Ildefonso, Cochiti, San Juan, and Nambe. After the academic year, Harrington went back to Hewett. This time, Hewett hired the young linguist for the summer and assigned him to work at Cochiti, probably so he could be introduced to Keresan.[29] Again, the young man took advantage of Stevenson's welcome, using her ranch as his starting place for the weeks before the MNM-SAA field school. She gave him the names of more contacts and supplied a letter of a recommendation; he interviewed Marcial Quintana and Mrs. L. S. Gallup with whom Stevenson had been working. Harrington began to write. He chose as his topic the stone idols of Cochiti. These were located at an archaeological site Stevenson had visited with James in the early 1880s. Stevenson shared the stories she had collected about the stone figures and their importance as a place. Harrington incorporated these materials into his own record files. While he never published a separate article on the stone lions or concentrated on Keresan, he did use Stevenson's data on Tanoan languages. In his first publications, Harrington acknowledges her Zuni publications but not the use of her unpublished Taos materials.[30] It is possible that he had begun to make a distinction in what should be acknowledged—only completed work, not raw data.

Harrington returned to Los Angeles to teach during the fall but quit when he obtained a temporary teaching position at the University of Colorado during the spring 1910. In June through August he taught summer school at the University of Washington. He became an adjunct itinerant scholar who returned to northern New Mexico or California at every opportunity. In the late summer and fall he was hired by the Bureau and SAA to join with Stevenson on her study of Tewa ethnogeography, again based on Stevenson's recommendation. He taught at the University of Colorado on Indians of the Southwest during late fall 1910 and winter 1911, then did a lecture tour in the state before returning to Santa Fe. Hewett finally hired him in September as an assistant curator of the MNM, but the position only lasted through June 1912.

This time, Hewett gave Harrington a sweeping mandate: obtain information from elderly Jemez, Isleta, Isleta der Sur, Piro, and Taos speakers, as well as continue his work in California. Again, Harrington called on Stevenson for data and individuals to interview, and she again helped. Their relationship began to be more like colleagues as Harrington matured. During November 1911, when Stevenson was working in Santa Fe, she and Harrington had long talks about how she should write her Zuni ethnobotany manuscript. He convinced her to arrange the plant descriptions according to Zuni terminology, rather than Latin based nomenclature, for ease of reading and to avoid redundancies. It was a tedious task, but Stevenson took his advice, turning in the revised manuscript to Hodge in July 1912.[31]

After a brief time in Washington, Stevenson returned to her New Mexico ranch in April 1912, and she again met with Harrington. He must have asked for her help, for she again recommended that the BAE hire him. It turned out to be timely request. Hewett and Frederick W. Hodge, the Bureau's new director, came to an agreement to combine the two institutions' research efforts in the Upper Rio Grande Valley.[32] Harrington would now be paid partly from Bureau funds. His assignment was more specific: he was to concentrate on Tewa ethnogeography. He would acquire the rest of the information for the study he had begun in October 1910 based on Stevenson's advice; he had spent several weeks touring Tewa country acquiring Native placenames. Again, Stevenson fully shared her fieldnotes, even though she was not a formal partner in the new cooperative BAE-SAA research group.[33] During the same period, Harrington began to publish in SAA publications and professional journals, like the *American Anthropologist*, to establish a national reputation.[34]

After Holmes left the Bureau directorship, Stevenson found herself increasingly marginalized, while Harrington took over more official Bureau duties as its Southwestern and California ethnographer. But he was still on temporary funds and there seemed to be only one way to obtain a permanent salaried position. Hodge repeatedly encouraged an increasingly ill Stevenson to retire but she refused, and she had too many Washington DC political supporters to be fired. She must had been a very challenging employee, for she increasingly refused to return to her Washington DC office. She spent 1912 to mid-March 1915 in New Mexico working on acquiring information and writing. In addition, she was involved in lawsuits that further drained her savings and energy. Her productivity suffered. She also felt she had little intellectual stimulation in Santa Fe. Her ties to Hewett and his staff—who later "seemed to delight in telling disparaging stories about her" and her "extremely forceful" personality—were likewise tenuous.[35] They saw her as a hindrance to their research agenda. They wanted Harrington. Everyone was going to have to wait for her death or until Hodge had had enough to fight the backlash that would occur. The last straw was a highly public scandal.

HARRINGTON BECOMES STEVENSON'S REPLACEMENT

Hodge had had enough by the end of November 1914. He gave Harrington a permanent Bureau position in December. Hodge's ostensible reason was that funds had been freed up; Stevenson was furloughed for medical reasons. The final straw, however, had been the national scandal stemming from Stevenson's Pueblo religion research. It had begun when Stevenson had presented a paper on the possibility of human sacrifices in Tewa communities at the 1914 TT International Congress of Americanists in Santa Fe. Newspapers were on top of it and asked

Commissioner of Indian Affairs Cato Sells why the Indian Service did not know of the activities and stop them. Sells was so angry that he was ready to ban anthropologists from conducting research and insisted that he would allow "no red tape to interfere with his inquiry" into Stevenson's research and her interpretations. He wanted to know if what she claimed was true; and, if so, to stop the practice. He wanted to see her fieldnotes and interview her. Sells called on Hodge to go through Stevenson's notes as part of his investigation and have Stevenson report to his office. Hodge insisted that Sells had to go through proper channels but told Stevenson to get her documentation ready. Stevenson replied that that was not possible; they were packed in boxes at her niece's house in Maryland and not accessible. Sells told reporters that "no red tape" should "interfere with his inquiry."[36] Hodge and Smithsonian Secretary Walcott wanted to keep the investigation low-key and internal. Stevenson, however, counterattacked Sells's threat to stop research and blamed Congress for not supporting more research to discover indigenous secrets. She told a *St. Louis Post-Dispatch* reporter, "What is needed is for more ethnologists to be sent there. For 30 years I have been struggling alone. We are only beginning to penetrate the secrets of Indian mythology, religion, poetry, and social customs."[37] Stevenson, however, refused to name which village. Stevenson's last months in Washington, from March to June 1915, were surrounded by this controversy, which Hodge knew threated Bureau funding and access to research communities.

Stevenson died on June 24, 1915, of a heart attack without providing her fieldnotes to Holmes and leaving a plethora of unfinished projects in her home as well as in the Bureau offices. She also died interstate while living in a boarding house. Two days before her unexpected death, she had contacted her lawyer, Herman E. Gasch, and had written a letter with her wishes. These were being transformed into a will but since they had not been signed and notarized did not constitute a binding contract. It was going to take the court over a year and a half to decide what to do with any research materials that were not at her office at the time of her death. We can conjecture that she had not yet indicated what should be done with data, research notes or incomplete manuscripts. Gasch was named executor and boxed up all her belongings without separating out the anthropological papers. It is likely the boxes included her scrapbooks.

Harrington did not come to Washington immediately in December 1914 because he was working with Hewett and the SAA-MNM staff on the San Diego world's fair exhibits, teaching at the San Diego Normal School, and involved in intensive bouts of fieldwork.[38] He never saw Stevenson in Washington DC. In 1915, Hodge told him that one of his first assignments as a permanent Bureau employee was to complete Stevenson's projects, if he could, based on the materials she had left in her office.[39] Especially important, according to Hodge, was preparing her massive Tewa ethnography for publication; Harrington was to assess it. He soon told Hodge it included over 970 manuscript pages, 243 prints, and 277 photographs.

Completing his mentor's work was not Harrington's priority; there were data that he needed to collect in Southern California. And it is likely that he did not quite know what to do with the manuscript. He had no access to Stevenson's data for checking facts, especially linguistic nomenclature. Harrington worked on Stevenson's materials intermittently between 1915 and 1918, at least enough to keep Hodge content. Instead of completing and editing Stevenson's work as instructed, Harrington deconstructed it. He chose a few topics, cut the paragraphs from the manuscript, and interspersed the pieces amongst his own data. These pieces eventually were included in his 600-page compilation on Tewa ethnogeography and indigenous knowledge classification systems that he had begun in 1910 with Stevenson's assistance, and any relevant data collected over the years by Stevenson, all unacknowledged. Other books on ethnozoology and ethnobotany and several papers were all published by 1920; all of these on the northern Rio Grande contained Stevenson's data.[40] Harrington began to work on her Taos material more intently, but never dealt with the entire Tewa manuscript nor finished the ethnohistorical sketch.

Harrington treated other portions of Stevenson's materials, as well as those of James (which Matilda had retained upon his death, along with materials that were already archived in the permanent Bureau files in their library), as his own, appropriating the information verbatim without acknowledgment and thereby decreasing its usefulness; he generally did not retain the dates on which observations were made. At other times, he would cut up the pages of her initial notes and reorganize them by topics. He also deconstructed her partial analyses; Harrington transformed some fieldnotes into slipnotes (pieces of paper with one vocabulary word or piece of information). Harrington also appropriated institutional records, including original object catalogues and field inventories, that should have been placed in USNM accession files.

I conclude that after being assigned to use the material in 1915, Harrington apparently decided that Hodge's passing of Stevenson's corpus of information to him meant that he owned it. His logic must have included the fact that Stevenson had freely provided him with her data under their mentor-student relationship, as well as the fact that he always assumed his work was more important than that of others. He does not appear to have felt that the information belonged to the Bureau or that others could have use for the materials. He limited the access of other scholars until his death.[41]

SCRAPBOOK A COMES TO THE BUREAU

It seems logical to assume that Hodge told Harrington to assess the other unfinished manuscripts, organize Stevenson's unanalyzed data, and determine if any of it could be used by Harrington or other Bureau employees as they pursued Bureau approved projects. How Harrington treated Stevenson's materials provides clues about how the scrapbook may have become separated from the other Stevenson papers now in the NAA.

It is unlikely that Stevenson kept any scrapbooks in her Smithsonian office. Stevenson had numerous personnel artifacts and fieldnotes at her Washington DC residence, including the materials related to the human sacrifice scandal. Being interstate led to delays for Stevenson's lawyer, and her executor refused to alienate any materials. Hodge moved quickly to claim all her professional documents at the time of her death before her executors and the courts labeled them as part of her estate, which was to be sold at auction in late 1916 or early 1917. Hodge considered anything that contained ethnographic information Bureau property, since Stevenson had been a salaried employee. This created a legal problem, for it is often hard to separate anthropologists' professional from personal papers; for example, correspondence to relatives often contains large quantities of field observations, written as incidents. Hodge wrote to Gasch but received no immediate satisfaction. The lawyer refused to turn anything over to Hodge, and the issue moved up the administrative ladder. He even refused to let him look at the materials without a court order.[42]

There must have been some question about what was professional and what personal, for the Secretary of the Smithsonian, Charles Walcott, appealed to the U.S. Attorney General to help recover Stevenson's "large body of valuable manuscripts and notes, drawings and photographs" before it was dispersed.[43] The Attorney General took Gasch court to withhold relevant materials from auction. On January 17–19, 1917, Stevenson's private belongings (including her extensive personal collection of Native American art) were auctioned in Washington DC by the C. G. Sloan Company. These did not include professional papers, which the court ordered set aside in a trunk in the office of the executor, Herman E. Gasch, and the American Security and Trust Company, to be returned to the Bureau.[44] It is unknown who decided what was professional and what was not. Even the catalogue for the auction and newspaper accounts of the event listed simply papers and albums without any specificity.

But the Bureau still did not have the materials. Either Gasch and the auction house never got around to having them moved to the Smithsonian or purposefully "forgot" to send the materials over. It took another year of legal negotiation before the auction house released one steamer trunk to Hodge on January 16, 1918.

Hodge told Harrington to see what was in the trunk, and it is my best guess that he found Scrapbook A. Unfortunately, Harrington never made an inventory of what the trunk contained. It is possible that Scrapbook B was there as well. Conversely, it could have been sold under the listing albums in the estate sale. It might have gone with some personal letters the lawyer sent to Stevenson's sister in Denver, along with the proceeds from the auction, the title to the New Mexico ranch, and some shares of what turned out to be worthless stock. There is currently no way to know.

There is one other possibility. It turns out that Herman E. Gasch, Stevenson's executor, did not turn over all of Stevenson's records to the Smithsonian. NAA record group 4689, "Matilda Coxe Stevenson papers, 1870 to 1910," was accessioned into the NAA in October 21, 1961, when Gasch's son, Manning, gifted a second trunk, which had been in their attic for forty-four years. The trunk contained some of James's papers, his rifle, two Zuni fetishes, an 1857 travel narrative of Stevenson's father, attorney Alexander H. Evans, a diary of Matilda's activities at the 1893 and 1904 world's fairs, loose newspaper clippings, all of Stevenson's correspondence with Clara True, the lawsuits, and the papers about her ranch. There were also Pueblo fieldnotes and numerous photographs, including photo albums of famous people like Charles Darwin and Kit Carson and her contemporary actors and actresses.

THE SCRAPBOOK COMES TO SANTA FE

This still leaves the problem of how and when Scrapbook A arrived in Santa Fe. I propose that Harrington, considering it his personal property—as he did all of Stevenson's other documents that he wanted—brought it with him on one of his field trips between 1918 and 1924. Why these years? Following the acquisition of the materials in the trunk, Harrington began intensely using Stevenson's unpublished Taos materials, which I assume were partly in the trunk since Harrington did not work on them from 1915 to 1917. Beginning that summer, he traveled repeatedly to Santa Fe and Taos to fill in lacunae in Stevenson's data and conduct his own ethnographic and library research.

I imagine that Harrington told Hewett about the contents of the trunk in 1918, and that Hewett wanted to see Scrapbook A. In his 1919 trip west, Harrington brought it to Santa Fe and showed it to Hewett as a professional courtesy. He was still trying to impress Hewett and be cordial. Since Harrington did not cut up Scrapbook A, and it dealt with archaeology, he probably lent it to Hewett (one of those long-term "temporary" loans so famous in the museum world). He never retrieved it as he raced off to procure more information from some Native community. It probably had no evidentiary value for Harrington's studies. Scrapbook A had more value to an archaeologist like Hewett. Since

Hewett was also interested in the history of anthropology, he most likely would have found it useful.

Could Harrington have brought the material on a later trip and simply left it in one of the Santa Fe libraries himself? It is possible, but not probable, because this would have happened after 1930. I chose 1924 as the end date for the scrapbook's journey because at that time Harrington seems to have developed obsessive behavior and paranoia. By this time, he had refused to share Stevenson's materials with other scholars, starting with Elsie Clews Parsons. During repeated requests from 1918 to 1924, Harrington made excuses, claiming that Parsons would inadequately edit Stevenson's terms. Parsons argued with Hodge and his successor, Jesse Walter Fewkes, as well, that anthropology needed her to have access; she stated that Harrington was obviously not going to use the data and it was needed. Parsons asked John Swanton, another Bureau ethnographer, to look for the materials in 1922, and he located some 423 pages of Stevenson's fieldnotes on all topics except for the Taos or Tewa manuscripts.[45] Harrington was too engrossed in his linguistic work to take the time to do this himself, for whatever reason, possibly the territoriality between New York and Washington. Stevenson's entire 400-page manuscript is still missing, and it still is; it is most likely deconstructed. Harrington spent the latter half of his career "fearing that colleagues might steal his data."[46] The scrapbook, however, is intact and safe in Santa Fe.

EPILOGUE

I have one other piece of circumstantial evidence to support my scenario of how the Stevenson document wound up in an unexpected archive. There is another Matilda Coxe Stevenson manuscript in Santa Fe. In 2015, at the School of Advanced Research, the librarian and archivist Laura Holt found an unnamed manuscript in a box entitled "School of American Research Miscellaneous Papers." This document (a typed manuscript intended for a book with the name missing) was marked "NAA No. 2093." It turned out to be a missing file for which I had searched in Washington in 1982: the original manuscript of one of Stevenson's last projects on Puebloan clothing. It was a final draft, almost ready to publish, and when I looked at the handwriting along the side of the page with editing suggestions, I noticed it was that of Hodge. Luckily, there had been an earlier copy of this manuscript in another NAA file along with Hodge's typed notes on how the editing should proceed. I thought in 1982 it was a significant contribution that should have been published. In 1986, I edited the manuscript, along with my husband, archaeologist Richard Ahlstrom, generally following Hodge's sage recommendations, then made it available for scholars to use.[47] We had always wondered why the Bureau never published it, and I now think that it was given to Harrington to finish and he never did, preferring to collect and then hide data away than analyze and publish what he found.[48] It must have been in the trunk. Maybe he asked Hewett for advice on what to do with it and, like the scrapbook, he forgot about it?

Until some other corroborating document comes to light, we will never know for sure, just like we will never know for sure about Scrapbook A's travels. Like any story without a definitive ending, it leaves me wondering whether Harrington's actions were common. What about mentors and students? How many other students have used materials loaned or shared by their teachers to help them establish reputations and gain expertise? And does gender enter the equation in instances of male mentors and female students, female mentors and female students, or male mentors and female students? And how many recipients have treated the materials as their own, rather than providing proper attribution? Is unacknowledged appropriation more common if the mentor or teacher is female? Does the passing on of information follow the same patterns and dynamics as between Stevenson and Harrington?

These are questions for a broader study than my small mystery because Harrington is not typical in any sense of the word, and I would never use him as the baseline for disciplinary comparisons. I suspect that Harrington is an outlier for a range of activities. We still have much to learn about the nature of collaboration, authorship, entitlement, and individuals finishing up the projects of others—and how these factors affect how practitioners reuse original data. In the meantime, Scrapbook A's journey—from Stevenson's home or field camp; to her trunk, which was rescued from an estate sale; to the Bureau offices; to Harrington's hands; from Washington to Santa Fe, then into Hewett's hands; and, finally, into the Laboratory of Anthropology and School or Advanced Research archives—makes a good story.

NOTES

1. Matilda Coxe Stevenson to Herman E. Gashin, May 31, 1915. Testimony Paper of Matilda Coxe Stevenson, Superior Court of the District of Columbia. MCS vs Clara True libel case, filed August 24, 1912. Civil Case No. 6398, Santa Fe County, New Mexico State Records Center and Archives. See also Miller (2007, 180, 191–95, 223).

2. I realized later that I should have known to look in the Harrington papers. In 1965, John P. Bodine went to the Smithsonian to locate Stevenson's information on the Taos Blue Lake ceremony which was supposed to be part of her larger unpublished manuscript, "The Taos Indians." He could not find it. Luckily, he looked through Harrington's unorganized papers for other relevant information. Unexpectedly, he found Stevenson's missing text and noted that Harrington had crossed out her name and put his own on it—without altering a word (Bodine 1988, 91, 1967). See also Miller (2007, 188–89); Stevenson, "The Taos Indians," NAA, BAE manuscript 3073. This was a case of my not paying attention to published footnotes.

3. I still have no idea why Harrington took James Stevenson's 1883 artifact inventory, which should have remained with the USNM files. John Peabody Harrington Papers: Taos 1909-circa 1944 NAA accessions 1976–95. See Mills and Brickfield (1986). All the Harrington record groups now list Matilda Coxe and James Stevenson, Carobeth Laird, and Blanche Grant as co-creators.

4. I do not say this to belittle the hard work of numerous NAA archivists who have made this massive and disorganized irreplaceable material available to scholars in 2018 in ways that could not have been envisioned in the 1980s and 1990s.

5. Other scholars have of course been concerned with these processes. See Sanjek (1990).

6. See Isaac (2005).

7. Smithsonian Institution archives. Accessed February 27, 2019. http://collections.si.edu/search/results.htm?q=Matilda+Coxe+Stevenson&fq=online_media_type: Finding+aids. See National Museum of Natural History collections search: http://collections.si.edu/search/results.htm?q=Matilda+Coxe+Stevenson&fq=object_type%3a%22archival

+materials%22&start=20, accessed June 26, 2018. In addition, see Clouse-Radigan (2011) *Cross Index Guide: Matilda Coxe Stevenson*. Collections and Archives Program, NAA, Smithsonian Institution. There are also many pages about Stevenson and her activities in the files of other individuals.

8. My thanks to archivist Diane Bird for allowing me to photograph and copy this scrapbook. I do not know where Stevenson's other scrapbooks are located or if they still exist.

9. While I have tried to track down the unidentified news clippings, I have been only partially successful. Clipping services often did not always provide complete attribution information, nor did people when they made their own notations. Matilda Stevenson certainly did not.

10. Popp (2014, 428). Propp's excellent article discusses how press clipping bureaus built a commercial infrastructure for extracting information for its resale. This was the beginning of data mining and an instance of the consolidation of corporate capitalism with national markets.

11. Pott (2014, 431).

12. My thanks to the anonymous reviewer of this paper who kindly reminded me about the clipping services (press cutting agencies), which scholars used in the 1880s and 1890s to see what was being said about them and their careers. Understanding how these clipping services work helps us assess the data source's validity and comprehensiveness. Today clipping (or monitoring) services cover multiple forms of media: radio, television, the web, and printed forms. In the mid-1880s, as my insightful reviewer stated, a news clipping from a service was usually marked in a colored pencil, usually blue, on the clipping itself.

13. Powell (1889).

14. Information on Harrington's life was obtained from Laird (1975), Victor Golla (1997), and Walsh (1976).

15. Stirling and Glemser (1963, 371).

16. Fowler (2000).

17. Fowler (2003, 1999); Hinsley (1986).

18. Chauvenet (1983, 42); Thompson (2000).

19. Stirling and Glesmer (1963, 371).

20. There is no evidence that Stevenson spoke critically of Hewett. Others had tried to force Stevenson off the Bureau staff in order to open up funding for a young male scholar. See Parezo and Fowler (2007) for an account of how W J McGee tried to remove Stevenson so he could hire Frank Russell but wound up losing his own job.

21. Hewett also felt a reexamination of all Puebloan languages was needed, clearly ignoring and marginalizing Stevenson's research, and since the information could not be obtained in any of the pueblos using Native excavators as anthropological informants, as Jesse Walter Fewkes had done in Hopi communities, (not collaborative consultants) facilitated the study (Hewett 1909, 667–70). Hewett was pleased with Harrington because his data supported his own ideas about the importance of tradition and cultural continuity.

22. Letter: Matilda Coxe Stevenson to Charles Walcott, no date, 1909, MCS papers, MS4689, NAA; See also Fowler (2000, 261–74, 366–71); Miller (2007, 160–95); Parezo (1993).

23. Stevenson had worked at Zuni from January through early March 1907, returned to Washington DC for several months to work on a manuscript, then travelled to New Mexico in August to concentrate on Santa Clara rabbit hunts and Taos history.

24. Stevenson to Charles D. Walcott, November 17, 1908. Smithsonian Institution Archives, incoming correspondence, office of the secretary.

25. Stevenson was also engaged in a lawsuit with BIA schoolteacher Clara True dealing with the distribution of water in the San Ildefonso ditch between their two adjacent ranches. Stevenson countersued and the case gained a good deal of notoriety. Going to court in 1914 took up most of Stevenson's time (*Albuquerque Journal* 1914). This ruined her emotionally and financially as well as stymied her research. Since Hewett sided with True, Stevenson considered him a potential enemy on one level but was always personable when they met.

26. Matilda Coxe Stevenson to William Henry Holmes, July 31, 1908, BAE Letters Received, NAA.

27. Harrington (1910, 17).

28. Matilda Coxe Stevenson to Secretary Charles Walcott, December 1, 1908, MCS Papers, MS 4689, NAA; Stevenson to William Henry Holmes, November 23, 1909, and January 24, 1910, BAE incoming correspondence, NAA.

29. Hewett wanted to undermine Stevenson's claims to ethnographic autonomy but had to work surreptitiously. Harrington, the young linguist, would have seemed a useful tool to obtain this goal. One method was to have Harrington continue to work with Stevenson as a pseudo-apprentice or mentee and report back to Hewett about what she was doing.

30. Harrington does acknowledge the use of the language records housed in the Bureau of American Ethnology. In later articles Harrington

notes the assistance of Barbara W. Freire-Marreco's data but not Stevenson's. He also lists his major Native informants in his texts (Harrington 1910, 1912).

31. Stevenson (1915), Miller (2007, 206).

32. Hewett, Edgar Lee. "Organic Act and Annual Reports of the School of American Archaeology, 1906–1917," 80–81. Special Collections, School of Advanced Research. Hodge also instructed Harrington to continue his research with the Mojave and make an ethnographic artifactual collection for the USNM.

33. At the same time, Hewett urged Harrington to finish his degree, finding the young man brilliant but infuriating. Harrington, however, decided to concentrate on fieldwork; he went to collect information from the Chemehuevi in 1910–11. NAA. BAE manuscripts 2290, 2292, 2295, 2296, and 2318 contain ethnographic fieldnotes and word slips from the 1915, 1916, and 1918 research trips. These files also contain the materials collected by Carobeth Harrington Laird, Harrington's wife at the time and an excellent data collector in her own right. Laird also wrote a 500-page manuscript in 1918. Harrington never gave her credit for any of her work in his publications, even for the materials that she collected, analyzed, and wrote up (see Mills and Brickfield 1986).

34. Stirling and Glesmer (1963).

35. Miller (2007, 222).

36. *The Boston Globe* (1915).

37. *St. Louis Post Dispatch* (1915).

38. Matilda Coxe Stevenson to William Henry Holmes, July 31, 1908, Bureau-Incoming Correspondence 1888–1910, NAA. My thanks to Laura Holt, School of Advanced Research librarian, for helping me research Harrington's association with SAA/MNM.

39. Harrington was also told to be prepared to deal with the Tewa ritual controversy if needed. However, after Stevenson's death, Commissioner Sells did not continue with the investigation, and Hodge never brought the subject up again.

40. Harrington (1916); Henderson and Harrington (1914); Robins, Harrington, and Freire-Marreco (1916).

41. Later in life Harrington became pathologically secretive and felt others were going to "steal" his data. He also developed an antipathy to publishing, feeling his work was never perfect—that is, never finished, something any anthropologist or linguist will acknowledge is inevitable. I contend that Harrington showed the material to Hewett as part of his youth-

ful behavior when he was trying to convince anthropological institution builders like Hewett, Holmes, and Hodge to give him a permanent job (Laird 1975); Stevenson and the BAE are also discussed in Parezo (1993).

42. Hodge to Gasch and American Security and Trust Company, December 24, 1915; Hodge to Bolitha Laws, January 3 and November 6, 1917; Hodge to Sloane and Co., January 16, 1918; Gasch to Hodge, December 26, 1916, and November 5, 1917, BAE incoming correspondence, NAA.

43. Charles Walcott to Attorney General, May 29, 1916, BAE Letters received, MCS, NAA. See also Miller (2007, 228–29).

44. Stevenson's estate probate was No. 22170 in Washington DC filed on March 28, 1917. The attorney was Alfred B. Lett and the other trustee was James F. Hood. The auction included "household furnishings, watercolors by Thomas Moran, W. H. Holmes, Walter Paris and others, bric-á-bric, Canton china, Persian rugs, jewelry, silverware, and a valuable collection of Indian relics and curios" (Santa Fe New Mexican 1917, 2). I assume that the USNM would have liked to have had the collection of relics and curios.

45. John R. Swanton to Elsie Clews Parsons, March 16, 1922, Parsons Family Papers, Rye Historical Society; Elsie Clews Parsons to Jesse Walter Fewkes, October 21, 1918, April 24, 1922, December 3, 1922, January 24, 1921, BAE, letters received; Fewkes to Parsons April 27, 1922, December 23, 1922, BAE outgoing correspondence, NAA. (Miller 2007, 273).

46. Miller (2007, 189).

47. Ahlstrom and Parezo (1987).

48. The other possibility is that Harrington dismantled it and parts are scattered in his papers.

REFERENCES

Ahlstrom, Richard V. N., and Nancy J. Parezo. 1987. "Dress and Adornment of the Pueblo Indians" by Matilda Coxe Stevenson. *The Kiva* 52, no. 4: 275–312.

Albuquerque Journal. 1914. "Raynolds Hears Celebrated Case." April 28, 1914, 3.

Bodine, John. 1988. "The Taos Blue Lake Ceremony." *American Indian Quarterly* 12, no. 1: 91–105.

———. 1967. "Attitudes and Institutions of Taos, New Mexico: Variables for Value System Expression." PhD diss., Tulane University.

Boston Globe. 1915. "Investigation Ordered. 'Human Sacrifice' Charges Stirs Indian Bureau—Mrs. Stevenson Blames Congress." April 18, 1915, 16.

Chauvenet, Beatrice. 1983 *Hewett and Friends: A Biography of Santa Fe's Vibrant Era*. Santa Fe: Museum of New Mexico Press.

Fowler, Don D. 2003. "E. L. Hewett, J. F. Zimmerman, and the Beginnings of Anthropology at the University of New Mexico, 1927–1946." *Journal of Anthropological Research* 59, no. 3: 305–27.

————. 2000. *A Laboratory of Anthropology: Science and Romanticism in the American Southwest, 1846–1930*. Albuquerque: University of New Mexico Press.

————.1999. "Harvard vs. Hewett: The Contest for Control of Southwestern Archaeology, 1904–1930." In *Assembling the Past: Studies in the Professionalization of Archaeology*, edited by Alice B. Kehoe and M. B. Emmerichs, 165–211. Albuquerque: University of New Mexico Press.

Golla, Victor. 1997. "A Harrington Chronology." J. P. Harrington Database Project. University of California, Davis. Internet Archive Wayback Machine. Accessed May 15, 2017. https://web.archive.org/web/20080513230305/, http://www.library.csi.cuny.edu/dept/history/lavender/389/golla.html.

Harrington, John P. 1986. "The Papers of John Peabody Harrington in the Smithsonian Institution, 1907–1957, Volume 4: A Guide to the Fieldnotes: Native American History, Language, and Culture of the Southwest," edited by Elaine L. Mills and Ann J. Brickfield.

————. 1916. *The Ethnogeography of the Tewa Indians*. Twenty-Ninth Annual Report of them Bureau of American Ethnology, 1907–1908, 29–618.

————. 1912. "Tewa Relationship Terms." *American Anthropologist* 14, no. 3: 472–98.

————. 1910. "An Introductory Paper on the Tiwa Language, Dialect of Taos, New Mexico." *American Anthropologist* 12, no. 1: 11–48.

Henderson, Junius, and John P. Harrington. 1914. *Ethnozoology of the Tewa Indians*. Bureau of American Ethnology Bulletin No. 56.

Hewett, Edgar L. 1909. "The Excavations at Rio De Los Frijoles in 1909." *American Anthropologist* 11, no. 4: 651–73.

Hinsley, Curtis, M., Jr. 1986. "Edgar Lee Hewett and the School of American Research in Santa Fe, 1906–1912." In *American Archaeology Past and Future*, edited by David J. Meltzer, Don D. Fowler, and Jeremy A. Sabloff, 217–31. Washington DC: Smithsonian Institution Press.

Isaac, Gwyneira. 2005. "Re-Observation and the Recognition of Change: The Photographs of Matilda Coxe Stevenson." *Journal of the Southwest* 47, no. 3: 411–55.

Laird, Carobeth. 1975. *Encounters with an Angry God*. Albuquerque: University of New Mexico Press.

Miller, Darlis A. 2007. *Matilda Coxe Stevenson: Pioneering Anthropologist*. Norman: University of Oklahoma Press.

Nichols, Catherine. 2014. "Museum Networks: The Exchange of the Smithsonian Institution's Duplicate Anthropology Collections." PhD diss., Arizona State University.

Parezo, Nancy J. 1993. "Matilda Coxe Stevenson: Pioneer Ethnologist." In *Hidden Scholars: Women Anthropologists and the Native American Southwest*, edited by Nancy J. Parezo, 38–62. Albuquerque: University of New Mexico Press.

——— . 1987. "The Formation of Ethnographic Collections: The Smithsonian Institution in the American Southwest." In *Advances in Archaeological Method and Theory vol. 10*, edited by Michael B. Schiffer, 1–47. San Diego: Academic Press.

Parezo, Nancy J., and Don D. Fowler. Forthcoming. *An Archaeological Wedding Journey: Theresa and Frank Russell's Research trip, 1900 and Beyond*. Tucson: University of Arizona Press.

——— . 2007. *Anthropology Goes to the Fair: The 1904 Louisiana Purchase Exposition*. Lincoln: University of Nebraska Press.

Popp, Richard K. 2014. "Information, Industrialization, and the Business of Press Clippings, 1880–1925." *Journal of American History* 101, no. 2: 427–53.

Powell, John Wesley, and James Stevenson. 1889. *Ninth Annual Report of the US Geological Survey, 1887–1888*, 42–44. Washington DC: Government Printing Office

Robins, Wilfred W., John P. Harrington, and Barbara Freire-Marreco. 1916. *Ethnobotany of the Tewa Indians*. Bureau of American Ethnology Bulletin No. 55.

Sanjek, Roger. 1990. *Fieldnotes: The Making of Anthropology*. Cornell University Press, Ithaca

Santa Fe New Mexican. 1917. "Auction Sale of Stevenson Effects." January 24, 1917, 2.

Stevenson, Matilda Coxe. 1915. "Ethnobotany of the Zuni Indians." *Thirtieth Annual Report of the Bureau of American Ethnology, 1908–1909*, 31–102.

Stirling, M. W., and Karlena Glemser. 1963. "John Peabody Harrington (1884–1961) and Bibliography of the Writings of John Peabody Harrington." *American Anthropologist* 65, no. 2: 370–82.

St. Louis Post Dispatch. 1915. "Human Sacrifices Offered near Santa Fe, Says Woman. Government Bureau Begins Inquiry into Report of Practices by Tewa Indians." April 18, 1915, 32.

Thompson, Raymond H. 2000. "An Old and Reliable Authority: An Act for the Preservation of American Antiquities." *Journal of the Southwest* 42, no. 2: 191–381.

Walsh, Jane M. 1976. *John Peabody Harrington: The Man and His California Indian Fieldnotes.* Ramona CA: Ballena Press.

4

Diasporas Of and By Design

Exploring the Unholy Alliance between Museums and the Diffusion of Navajo (Diné) Textile Designs

Without all the rugs she made for years and years, we wouldn't have survived. . . . It's mainly on her account all us kids didn't starve to death.

Tall Woman's family's concluding reflections (Frisbie 2001, 322)

This chapter unsettles narratives of Navajo (Diné) weaving history, critiquing scholars' lack of engagement with long-standing issues of appropriation. As a principal source of outside knowledge, scholars consistently portray Diné as the great borrowers—sheep from the Spanish, the loom from the Pueblos, and designs from traders licensed by the federal government (Bsumek 2004; Denetdale 2007, 20–23). Regrettably, this trope continues to sanction theft of Diné patterns by entrepreneurs who claim "pan-Indian" origins for their designs (Chelsea Goin Papers 1996; Wood 2008). Such appropriations are not examples of cultural intermingling but a forced marriage brokered by entrepreneurs (Stephen 1991a, 1991b, 1991c, 1993, 2005; Henson 2001; Wood 2008, 2017). The assumptions held by authors who scripted "the history of Navajo weaving" reflect the asymmetry of gender relations as constituted historically in the Euro-American West. Weaving is typically described as women's domestic activity, only engaged in for functional purposes, non-sacred because materials were borrowed from external sources, and dominated by traders who ostensibly influenced designs in response to consumer preferences (Amsden [1934] 1975; Kaufman and Selser 1985; Kent 1985; Maxwell [1963] 1984; Rodee 1981). This destructive script neglects the politico-economic domain *and* omits weavers' nar-

Fig. 1. Knock-offs of Teec Nos Pos and Two Grey Hills Navajo rug designs, 2006 Taos NM. Photo by Kathy M'Closkey.

ratives. Indeed, it was comments made during a series of interviews I had with weavers during 1992 that drove me to reassess much of the literature because what I was hearing from them was absent from the published record until recently (Bonar 1996; M'Closkey 2002, 2004; Willink and Zolbrod 1996).

HISTORICAL CONTEXT

As pastoralists for more than four centuries, weaving, wool production, livestock and horticulture provided a major portion of Diné subsistence until the Great Depression (Bailey and Bailey 1986; Iverson 2002; Underhill 1983). By 1800, the Navajo blanket had become the most valuable trade item among southwest tribes (Van Valkenburgh and McPhee 1974). During 1863, in an attempt to "civilize" Diné and open up their homeland for settlement, the federal government forced over ten thousand of them to relocate to Hwééldi (Bosque Redondo) in eastern New Mexico territory (Denetdale 2018, 24). After attempts to farm the alkaline soil failed, a treaty was signed, allowing Diné to return to their homeland reduced by 70 percent (Denetdale 2008). After the formation of the reservation in 1868, straddling Arizona and New Mexico Territories, Diné self-sufficiency was undermined in part because government licensed traders fostered a dependence on expendable commodities (Aberle 1983; White 1983). Wool production more than doubled between 1890 and 1910, yet textile production escalated more than 800 percent (M'Closkey 2002). Government reports confirm that textile production by Navajos was "the most profitable of the native industries . . . and is done by women in their spare time" (Sells 1913). Nevertheless, weavers lost control of the market as commercial trade blanket manufacturers appropriated the form, materials, and designs (Kapoun 1992), selling thousands of manufactured blankets through traders to many Native Americans formerly provisioned by Navajo weavers.

Today royalties from nonrenewable resource extraction provide most of the Navajo Nation's revenue. Over twenty thousand weavers face increasing difficulties finding buyers for their rugs. Their market has been decimated by the volatile investment in historic (pre-1950) textiles combined with the dramatic rise in "knockoffs" imported from twenty countries including India, Pakistan, Romania, Moldova, Thailand, Turkey, and Mexico, and sold via the Internet and retail stores. For decades Navajos' per capita income has stalled at 20 percent of the national average. Over 50 percent of the population of 332,000 Diné reside within the Navajo Nation (U.S. Census 2010). Unlike artisanal production in Australia, Mexico, and Nunavut, Canada, cooperatives are rare, and private enterprise continues to dominate marketing and sales (Graburn 1976; M'Closkey 2002; M'Closkey and Manuel 2006; Mitchell 1996, Stephen 1991c, 1993; Wood 2008).

A HISTORY OF CONNOISSEURSHIP

The early development of a collaboration between ethnologists and commercial entrepreneurs in the American Southwest stimulated substantial commercial markets for both authentic Indian "antiquities" and tourist curios that catered to the demands produced by what C. B. MacPherson calls the "possessive individualism" of nationalism (Handler 1997). Ethnological salvage became a highly commodified, enduring endeavor. Connections initiated during the 1880s among ethnographers, anthropologists, archaeologists, tourists, and the commercial sector continue to have repercussions today (Busmek 2008; M'Closkey and Manuel 2006; McLerran 2009; Mullin 2001). For more than a century, scholars in this field have placed emphasis on entrepreneurs and collectors (Amsden 1934; Blomberg 1988; Hedlund 1997; McNitt 1962; Rodee 1981; Webster 2005; Weigle and Babcock 1996).

The following example reveals how museums continue to elide the relationship between historic works and the realities of contemporary life for thousands of weavers. In 1996, the Heard Museum in Phoenix, Arizona, sponsored a symposium in conjunction with a major exhibit, "Inventing the Southwest: The Fred Harvey Company and Native American Art." The company, founded in 1876, managed dozens of restaurants and dining cars for the Santa Fe Railroad. A publication with essays from twenty contributors accompanied the show (Weigle and Babcock 1996). Although over 60 percent of the papers dealt with important stakeholders involved in the marketing of Native American creations, none of the authors accessed information from the company's Indian Department ledger books that contained thousands of entries related to the purchase and sales of Native American creations acquired between 1900 and 1940. Yet this significant body of primary documents is housed *directly above* the symposium's location, in the museum's library.

I use this anecdote as a catalyst to critique the profound disconnect between the high value accorded Native American antiquities and the low value attached to the politico-economic context of production. For more than a century, a purist mythology dominated the seldom discussed topic of artisanal labor. For example, while he was the editor of *American Anthropologist*, Alfred Kroeber deleted a section of an article on Indian arts that mentioned the impoverishment of the native population (Trump 2001, 174–75). Although Gladys Reichard (1934, 1936, 1939) paints an endearing portrait of several weavers who patiently tutored her in the craft, she neglects to acknowledge the significance of weavers' contributions overall by downplaying the importance of their textile production to the regional economy. When she spoke of weavers' feelings about their work, Reichard couched them in terms of Western aesthetics associated with decorative design—that is, a certain percentage of weavers were "real artists . . . who would experiment with colors for hours" (Reichard 1936, 27). Other than my publications, the most recent substantive study on Navajo artisanal labor was authored by Nancy Parezo in 1983. Yet, Shelton reminds us that "the separation of production from the consumption of material culture short-circuits any full history of an artefact's successive objectifications. The object 'biography' must begin with the process of production" (1992, 28).

DOUBLE JEOPARDY

The tsunami of knockoffs shipped from abroad is perfectly legal according to the federal Indian Arts and Crafts Board Act, as long as they are not labelled "Indian made." Lacking communal property rights protection by the U.S. government, historic Navajo designs reside in the "public domain" and thus are amenable to appropriation resulting in soaring knockoff sales (Henson and Henson 2001; M'Closkey 2010, 2012). Because many Diné endure impoverished living conditions, my critique challenges scholars' overt support for the unauthorized copying of Diné designs by Zapotecs for over three decades (Nash 2000; Stephen 1993, 2005; Wood 2008, 2017). The production of knockoffs is also well publicized in journals and books (Cohen 2000; M'Closkey 2000, 2002, [2008], 2010b, 2012; M'Closkey and Halberstadt 2005; Stephen 1991a, 1991b, 1991c, 2005; Tiffany 2004; Wood 2008, 2017). Yet, no response acknowledging the deleterious consequences of appropriation is forthcoming from the academy. Anthropologists' support for such activity exerts an even greater threat to Diné weavers because it neutralizes copying through the prism of scholarly involvement (Berlo 2006, 38).

The Museum of New Mexico Foundation recently licensed several manufacturers whose designers draw on classic Navajo patterns contained in their collections (Kelly and Thompson 2013). The Museum of Indian Arts and Culture (MIAC) in Santa Fe promotes rugs with Diné motifs sold by West Elm and Williams-Sonoma. Part of an "Aid

Fig. 2. Stacks of Navajo knock-offs, 2007. Photo by Kathy M'Closkey.

to Artisans" program, weavers in India now have their products certi-
fied by a "Craftmark" label (West Elm 2013). This project is part of a
$35 million handcraft purchasing plan funded by the Clinton Global
Initiative (2013). MIAC's collaboration will augment funding for pro-
gramming at the expense of Diné weavers who have seen their market evaporate. How does this square with the museum's mission: "to
serve as a center of stewardship, knowledge, and understanding of
the artistic, cultural and intellectual achievements of the diverse peoples of the Native Southwest" (Museum of Indian Arts and Culture
2017)? The other half of "double jeopardy" for weavers concerns the
vigorous collectors' market for pre-1950s rugs. Old textiles receive far
more exposure, for example, by way of avenues such as the PBS series
"Antiques Roadshow." Antiquities' dealers report robust sales relative
to the collapsing market for contemporary rugs (Antique Tribal Dealers' Association; Baer 2001; Miller 2001). The *Indian Trader* featured
an article on medical doctor-cum-Indian antiquities dealer Mark Sublette of Tucson, Arizona, describing his new gallery in Santa Fe, New
Mexico and his recent success advertising on the Internet: "The arts

and crafts business has never been better . . . we are selling a lot on our website and at our two locations. We sell the higher end stuff and the demand is huge. Our problem is not selling what we have but getting the stuff people want to buy" (Miller 2001, 5). Sublette markets Native American pottery, baskets, and Navajo textiles created between 1850 and 1950. He and his contemporaries cater to a dedicated coterie of collectors who increasingly invest in Indian antiquities as a more reliable and lucrative option than the stock market.

Joshua Baer, of Sante Fe, one of the most active dealers in old Navajo blankets, advertised continually in *American Indian Art*. The quarterly magazine, which ceased publication in autumn 2015, featured the "Auction Block" column, highlighting sales at Sotheby's and other international auction houses. That market, "though vast, is but a fraction of the business" (Johnson 2000, 25). As Baer explains, "NASDAQ stocks lost more than $3 trillion in value during 2000. The biggest losses were sustained by investors with the most to lose. Given the extent of their losses, certain wealthy collectors of Navajo blankets may decide to sell . . . [if you purchase] a great blanket . . . what it says to you while you own it is as much a part of the return on your investment as the profit you realize when you sell it" (Baer 2001). The most arcane details accompany research on individual textiles. For example, Sublette's full-page ad in *American Indian Art* illustrates magnified images of three different types of wool (1994, 27). Accurate identification via electron microscopy may translate into a tenfold difference in the value of an historic blanket, thereby "serving the needs of the discerning collector with the Science of Art" (Sublette 1994, 27).

UNRAVELLING ACADEMIC SCHOLARSHIP AND COMMERCIALISM

Dealers' financial success is abetted by museum curators. In 1981, Marian Rodee, curator at the Maxwell Museum, University of New Mexico, Albuquerque, authored *Old Navajo Rugs: Their Development from 1900 to 1940*. Funded with National Endowment for the Arts support, there are multiple editions of the book. In the preface she writes, "Old Navajo rugs exert an appeal that is frequently lacking in contemporary weaving. In contrast with many modern rugs that are sold as wall hangings, beautiful but remote from their original function, old Navajo rugs remain engaging, well woven, strong. This book is designed to fill a lacuna in their history—the period from 1890 to World War II. I hope . . . to assist both private and public collectors who are turning to this period as 19th century weaving becomes increasingly expensive" (1981, xiii).

Until very recently, anthropologists and popular writers have convinced the reading public that Navajo weavers' patterns are derivative. Such an assumption is reflected in the following quotes taken from textile scholar Kate Peck Kent: "Navajo weaving has no deep historical roots in cultural tradition. Essentially, it has always been a commercial link with other Indians, Spanish and Anglo-Americans. As such, it has thrived on innovation, change and outside contacts [therefore] . . . rugs woven in this century will not tell us anything about Navajo personality or values because Anglo traders and markets have influenced Navajo weavers so much that any meanings or aesthetic styles which may have existed in early weavings were extinguished" (1976, 101). Kent also writes, "Weaving among the Navajo is a secular art. . . . The search for a distinctive Navajo aesthetic ends with the onset of the Rug period [1890]. When weavers ceased to manufacture blankets for their own use and turned to the production of rugs for sale to whites, they accepted Anglo American standards of taste" (1985, 111).

Unfortunately, such published statements by noted scholars have reproduced the power relations that marginalized weavers in the first place. Anthropologist Suzanne Baizerman has written about the escalating interest and shift in type of publication on historic weaving: "Some museum curators and anthropologists became dealers, and some dealers received training in anthropology. . . . It is evident that the museum is the center of publishing on historic Navajo textiles and the trend is getting stronger" (1989, 16). Baizerman also remarks on the recent surge in value of old weaving, stating that dealers and collectors serve on museum boards: "Publications are important, to establish authority and expertise and to provide the publicity necessary to help sustain the value of the product. . . . The rise in the number of publications on Navajo textiles correlates with the rise in their monetary value" (1989, 17).

Howard Bahr's massive Navajo bibliography (1999) contains thousands of references and indexes more than fifty entries about weaving under "Catalogs," "Collections," and "Exhibitions," with only four under "Economics." A review of information referenced in most texts and catalogues reveals just how overdetermined the topic is: typically the same twenty to twenty-five publications are cited, all of which are authored by collectors, dealers, anthropologists, museologists, and textile scholars. Prominent museologists served on the editorial board and published in the *American Indian Art* magazine until 2015. Currently, much of the history of weaving available on the Internet is scripted by collectors and dealers; the mystique of the "Old West" is filtered through gallery authorities including Joshua Baer, Steve Getzwiller, Mark Sublette, Mark Winter, and Len Wood.

As elite stakeholders, collectors, dealers, and curators continue to benefit to the detriment of the descendants of the original creators. In fact, the beautifully illustrated coffee-table books authored by scholars and featuring old textiles are shipped abroad and used as templates for future production of knockoffs (M'Closkey fieldnotes 2011).[1] Juxtaposing the information cited above vis-à-vis current poverty levels evokes Malaysian anthropologist Wazir Karim's (1996) queries voiced at the Oxford Decennial: "what do we do with this social knowledge which we have created through the worlds we represent? Is anthropological knowledge generated to enrich the western intellectual tradition or destitute populations from which this knowledge was appropriated? ... Why is it that as the field of theoretical anthropology is enriched by every new discourse it adopts, the people of the world from which anthropology makes its name become culturally impoverished by the day?" (1996, 120, 129)

Karim's comments are germane to the issues I raise concerning the predicaments faced by thousands of Navajo weavers. Only a handful make an adequate living (Conner 1991; Duus 1987; Frisbie 2001, 322; M'Closkey 2010a; M'Closkey and Manuel 2006; M'Closkey and Halberstadt 2005; Roessel 1983; Woodman 1980). Significant portions of Diné Bikeyah are remote and isolated, and over 80 percent of the roads are unpaved. Over half the population lives below the poverty level, and many residents still lack basic utilities (Satchell and Bowermaster 1994). Until 2002, 80 percent lacked telephone service. With per capita income at 20 percent of the national average, weavers are deeply affected by the decreasing demand for their rugs. The number of dealers who retail contemporary weaving exclusively has declined dramatically over the past thirty years, concomitant with the escalation in the number of galleries and shops selling historic textiles or "knockoffs" (M'Closkey 2012).

THE POLITICS OF APPROPRIATION

In 2001, a lawyer campaigned as a Democratic candidate for Attorney General of New Mexico. He proposed a ban on the sales of knockoffs appropriating Native American artisanal designs. Prior to the runoff, he learned that regional banks and retailers—major stakeholders in the knockoff trade—had withdrawn their support because knockoff sales are far too lucrative. He not only lost the election; he also lost part of his law practice (fieldnotes October 2005).[2]

The object-based aesthetics grounded in Euro-western epistemology fuels connoisseurship, while ignoring the politico-economic relations of long term cross-cultural asymmetrical trade (M'Closkey [2002] 2008, 2010a, 2010b, 2012). Articles published in *American Indian Art* typically depict weavers as "cultural performers" who labor in a virtual economic vacuum (McLerran 2011; Valette 2012). Museologists took the high road and journeyed to the land of connoisseurs. As a feminist political ecologist and weaver focused on a broader context, I travelled to the archives and discovered the proverbial Pandora's box the size of an enormous warehouse stacked ceiling high with thousands of handwoven "pound" blankets and rugs (Hubbell Trading Post Papers; Maxwell [1963] 1984; Frank McNitt Papers; United States Government Annual Narrative and Statistical Reports; Williams 1989). An enormous amount of evidence languishes in a dozen government and business archives, as well as in numerous books and journal articles, which manifest how the harmful effects of free trade over a century ago triggered Navajo impoverishment.[3] After 1890, thousands of women wove one-third of the annual coarse wool clip sheared from *churra* sheep. Weaving served as a means of diversification for dozens of reservation traders coping with fluctuations in the global market due to duty-free imports of over one hundred million pounds of carpet-grade wool annually, much of it shipped from China. This "alternative means to market wool" sustained the trading post system during the 1890s, a decade when one-third of domestic growers went bankrupt because President Grover Cleveland had placed all classes of wool on the duty-free list. In 1898, a high tariff was reinstated on clothing wools (Classes I and II), protecting Anglo growers, but coarse wools (Class III) remained on the free list (Bensel 2000; Taussig 1897). Thus, it is no coincidence that the blanket was transformed into a rug during the free trade era, since Diné were the sole carpet wool growers in the country by that date (M'Closkey forthcoming).

Due to the high volume of production until the 1950s, Diné textiles were placed under the "jobbers" classification, a category cheaper than wholesale. The statistical portions of Indian agents' annual reports to the Commissioner of Indian Affairs include the quantity and value of weaving: the information is embedded in the livestock and wool production figures, demonstrating how bureaucrats perceived weaving as an extension of the livestock industry (United States Government Superintendents' Annual Narrative and Statistical Reports). Propagation of the housewife ideology concealed how many weavers were the principal breadwinners for their families, since they owned over 60 percent of the sheep and all of the goats. Nearly all reservation traders used weaving as an alternative means to market the annual wool clip (M'Closkey forthcoming). Anthropologist Gary Witherspoon (1987) has conservatively estimated that one-hundred thousand women had woven more than one million blankets and rugs over the past two centuries.

Weavers are typically depicted as "cultural performers" in the extant literature, thus conceptually separated from the politico-economic sphere (Dockstader 1978; Hedlund 1993; Rodee 1981; Tanner 1968; Webster 2017; Wilkins 2008; Wheat 1984, Wheat and Hedlund 2003; Whitaker 2002). Such historic silencing perpetuates the false idealism that distorts the conditions under which they labored and their connections to global capitalism (Moore 2015). By 1930, weavers' production totaled over $1 million annually, providing one-third of reservation income (Amsden 1932, 139). The Lorenzo Hubbell family of Ganado, Arizona controlled a significant portion of trade for decades, and their extensive archives housed at the University of Arizona provide a barometer of the regional economy. By the time this catalogue was published in 1902, (Hubbell Trading Post papers Box 545(13)) textile sales comprised 90 percent of Hubbell's business correspondence. And 80 percent of the ledger accounts were in women's names, identified in relation to their closest male kin. Accessible since 1977, these rich archives have been woefully underutilized in gauging the magnitude of production and importance of textile sales to traders' financial success. The Hubbells shipped over two hundred tons of hand-spun woven textiles between 1893 and 1913 (M'Closkey [2002] 2008, 76). Nearly all textiles were acquired from weavers by weight until 1970. Weavers received credit, not cash, and their saddle blankets and rugs were jobbed by traders to pay down their monthly accounts with regional wholesalers (Hubbell Trading Post Papers 1885–1965; M'Closkey [2002] 2008).

Thus thousands of Diné "housewives" subsidized the traders for decades, since Diné wools were in competition with duty-free carpet wool imports from twenty countries. Weavers' participation in the seemingly "informal" economy translated into invisibility. Compelling archival evidence challenges extant narratives continually recycled in the literature—namely, that weavers' productivity rose because of consumer demand ostensibly driven by the Arts and Crafts movement and increasing tourism, facilitated by the railroad (Bsumek 2008; Cottam 2015; Weigle and Babcock 1996; Wilkins 2008). These assertions collapse upon analysis of pertinent archival documents. Both factors partially drove consumption, but free trade in carpet wool drove production.[4] Thus, analysis of traders' business records and correspondence ruptures the master narrative—that traders saved weaving by developing off-reservation markets. Huge shipments reveal the magnitude of gendered injustice, as weavers and their families became increasingly impoverished (M'Closkey forthcoming). This story, embedded in the archives, serves as a classic example of the functioning of a commodity chain, "a network of labor and production processes whose end result is a finished commodity" (Dunaway 2001, 9). Cherokee sociologist Wilma Dunaway (2001) notes that every node in the chain represents a specific production process. In order to engender a commodity chain,

Catalogue and Price List

Navajo Blankets
& Indian Curios

J. L. HUBBELL
INDIAN TRADER

Ganado, Apache County, *Arizona*
Branch Store: Keam's Cañon, Arizona

Fig. 3. Hubbell trading post catalog, 1902.

one must begin with the household, where women are found working longer hours than men to contribute surpluses that do not appear in account books of capitalists or government measurements of GNP. A commodity chain structures the maximal exploitation of underpaid and unpaid labor, thereby permitting the endless accumulation of capital as textiles are sold and resold. Historical geographer Jason Moore's model depicting a tripartite division of labor, reveals how every act of *exploitation* of commodified labor power depends upon an even greater act of *appropriation* of unpaid work and energy from humans and non-humans (Moore 2015, 54). Thus, capitalism serves as a way of

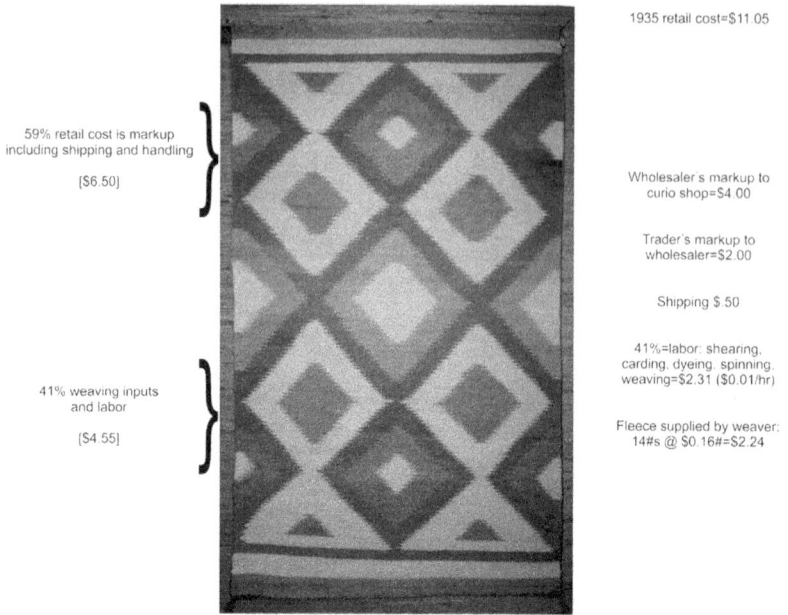

1935 retail cost=$11.05

59% retail cost is markup
including shipping and handling

[$6.50]

Wholesaler's markup to
curio shop=$4.00

Trader's markup to
wholesaler=$2.00

Shipping $.50

41%=labor: shearing,
carding, dyeing, spinning,
weaving=$2.31 ($0.01/hr)

41% weaving inputs
and labor

[$4.55]

Fleece supplied by weaver:
14#s @ $0.16#=$2.24

Fig. 4. Double-saddle blanket cost breakdown, 1930s.

organizing relations between humans and the rest of nature as capitalists relentlessly seek out commodity frontiers. Work is always materialized in and through the web of life—a "world-ecology."

Pauperization continues as thousands of "pound blankets" are recycled in the antiquities markets, depressing the demand for contemporary rugs. The values incorporated here were averaged from dozens of Hubbell ledger entries spanning the 1930s. Many compelling examples illustrate the concealed potential for enormous profits when archival evidence is ignored because authors emphasize weaving as art divorced from its politico-economic context (Hedlund 1997, 1993, 1990, 1989b; McLerran 2009, 2011; Rodee 1981; Webster 2017, Wheat and Hedlund 2003; Whitaker 2002).

HOW PAST PRODUCTIVITY HARMS CONTEMPORARY WEAVERS

Many of the "pound" blankets and rugs jobbed by weight currently fetch very high prices in the volatile art market. Sales increased exponentially after the first exhibit of historic weaving was borrowed from the collections of twenty prominent artists including Kenneth Noland, Frank Stella, and Andy Warhol, and toured internationally from 1972 to 1976 (Berlant and Kahlenberg 1977; Wheat 1974). Extrapolating from Meyer's data, from $70 to $100 million worth of historic weaving has changed hands since that time (Meyer 1973, 81). Emphasis on historic weaving focuses upon individual textiles, their provenance and pedigree, while ignoring the systemic economic problems, both past and present, which are severe. Crucial information located in government and business archives provides evidence of the conditions endured by weavers in order to provision their households historically (Hubbell Trading Post Papers; Donald Parman Papers; United States Government Annual Narrative and Statistical Reports). This evidence receives scant attention, while museologists continue to "order, dissect and classify" by determining the kinds of dyes, yarns, number of warps and wefts, and types of fleece incorporated in historic textiles (Hedlund 1989b; Rodee 1981; Webster 2017; Whitaker 2002). This "boilerplate" discourse occupies center stage and neglects the politico-economic domain entirely. The stories of the makers of these historic textiles that now bring so much money have literally been "swept under the rug."

Swept Under the Rug: A Hidden History of Navajo Weaving ([2002] 2008) incorporates a dozen tables and seven figures detailing the cost of goods at trading posts, and the annual wholesale averages of Navajo livestock products, including textiles, acquired between 1881 and 1943. Hundreds of invoices located in the two tons of Lorenzo Hubbell Trading Post Papers affirm the importance of women's textile production in subsidizing the family's business empire (M'Closkey 2002, 2010a). O'Neill describes how the income generated by weavers often bridged the gap between starvation and family survival (2005, 55–80). Traders and Navajo households were bound together through a system of debt. A century ago, regional warehouses were stuffed with authentic Navajo rugs. Today, they are crammed with knockoffs imported from twenty countries (M'Closkey 2010b, 2012). Meanwhile, antiquities dealers and trading posts located in reservation border towns hold large inventories of historic textiles and unredeemed pawn (fieldnotes 2006).

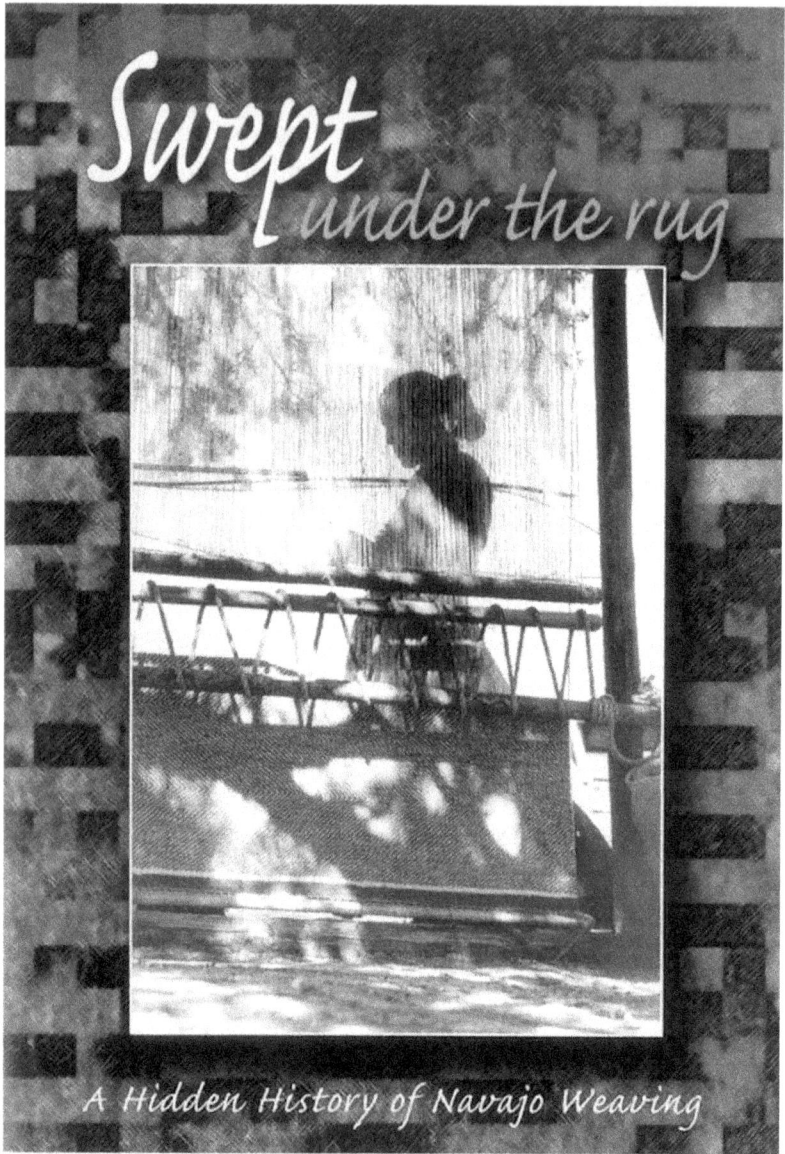

Fig. 5. *Swept under the Rug* book cover 2002.

The following information highlights two vignettes from recent collector activity. An issue of *Architectural Digest* features Ralph Lauren's huge Colorado ranch (Goldfarb 2013). The buildings are adorned with dozens of Navajo "pound" blankets and rugs. *Forbes* estimates his net worth at $6.5 billion. Lauren's brand defines a lifestyle and, for decades, he's mined Diné designs to create his "Beacon Print" line. Singer Andy Williams passed away in 2012. His collection (Hedlund 1997), valued at over $1 million, was auctioned by Sotheby's in 2013 (The Andy Williams Collection of Navajo Blankets 2013). A single "chief's" blanket sold for $221,000. Sotheby's evaluated a double saddle blanket at $2,000. It sold for $13,000. Hubbell had jobbed similar textiles for $4.00 each (Hubbell Trading Post Papers). These examples illustrate how old textiles sell avidly in galleries and at auctions, and internet sales have escalated exponentially (M'Closkey [2002] 2008). Currently, over twenty thousand weavers within the vast Navajo Nation lack an infrastructure to market their rugs because of the trading post system's collapse. Further, there are no reservation-wide co-ops, microfinance programs, or fair-trade organizations to assist weavers with marketing. Elderly weavers with decades of experience auction their textiles monthly at a local school gymnasium in Crownpoint, New Mexico, nearly sixty miles from the closest motel (Klain 2008). Over the past decade, sales averaged $225 per rug. With few exceptions, off-reservation private enterprise continues to control the marketing of rugs, a consequence of the legacy of control exerted by the United Indian Traders' Association, formed in 1931, to thwart the development of cooperatives on the reservation as promoted by John Collier (United States Government, Indian Arts and Crafts Board Records). The number of dealers who retail contemporary rugs exclusively has plummeted. Thus, thousands of weavers are pushed to the periphery as their ancestors' creations are endlessly replicated or sold at auction. Scholars who ignore the context of production unwittingly engage in historical amnesia through their refusal to acknowledge the elephant in the room: the escalation in poverty that occurred in tandem with increased production.

With the implementation of the UNESCO convention on illicit trade in antiquities in 1970 and passage of NAGPRA, the Native American Graves Protection and Repatriation Act, in 1990, archaeologists have become increasingly aware of how their research has serious ramifications in the world of the living. During 2006, the *New York Times* featured a series of articles on the entangled relationships between major museums and the international antiquities trade. Illicit trade in cultural property is widely recognized as one of the most prevalent types of organized crime. On March 6, 2006, the New School in New York City sponsored a panel discussion called "Who Owns Art." Participants included two directors of major museums, a philosopher, an archaeologist, and a *New York Times* art critic. Discussion highlighted the controversy surrounding antiquities and their provenance. SUNY Stoney Brook archaeologist Elizabeth Stone spoke out in criticism of scholarly involvement in authentication: "when you publish, as a scholar, you're authenticating the object. And when you authenticate it, its value goes up. You're participating in the trade." The following portion of my paper critiques how southwestern museologists do just that.

In 1989, Sotheby's auctioned a rare First Phase chief's blanket owned by real estate mogul Edwin Janss for over $500,000. Harmer Johnson, a Sotheby's appraiser, had estimated its value between $100,000 and $150,000. The auction house contacted retired archaeologist Dr. Joe Ben Wheat, acknowledged as the dean of Navajo textile studies. He wrote a one-page description noting that Herman Schweizer of the Fred Harvey Company had sold it to John Collier, Commissioner of Indian Affairs (1933–45). Very few blankets of this type remain in private hands. One surfaced at an *Antiques Roadshow* filmed in Tucson, Arizona in 2002, and the 2012 sale of the Chantland blanket by John Moran Auctioneers set a record at $1.8 million (Montano and Yohe 2017, 25).

The Maxwell Museum at the University of New Mexico, Albuquerque, featured an exhibition titled, "I Can See by Your Outfit, Wearing Apparel and Native Heritage," from July 2005 through February 2006. It was curated by local and regional *dealers* in Indian antiquities. The museum also hosted an arts and crafts appraisal day during which several dealers gave seminars on material culture in their respective areas of collecting. Every exhibition has the potential to increase the value of the art in it. And every book published on Native American antique art that is authored by an academic serves an elite cadre of investors and connoisseurs (Hedlund 1989b).[5] For example, anthropologist Kathleen Whitaker authored *Southwest Textiles: Weavings of the Pueblo and Navajo* (2002). Initially priced at $65, a new copy can fetch $350 on the web.

The Arizona State Museum in Tucson features annual fundraisers that bring prominent dealers and collectors together. Modeled after *Antiques Roadshow*, such events draw hundreds of participants who are anxious to discover the value of their treasures. Museum curators mingle with dealers, and close scrutiny leads to some surprising discoveries (Nichols 2005). The Heard Museum in Phoenix, Arizona also hosts semi-annual appraisal days during which prominent dealers provide a statement of estimated value for a fee (Heard 2017). However, due to the potential conflict of interest such occasions might entail, the University of British Columbia in Vancouver cancelled a similar program. As Ann Stevenson told me, "Before the *Antiques Roadshow* was on TV, we had a regular identification clinic where the public brought in their objects and curators tried to identify them, conservators gave advice on taking care of them, etc. We also gave out names of local appraisers but never gave values or 'authenticated' pieces, per se. After the *Roadshow* began it was clear that expectations for definitive authentications and value were expected so we have not continued" (pers. comm., December 19, 2005).

An important issue is whether dealers' involvement in curating or providing financial support for exhibitions compromises an ethnological museum's integrity. During 2005, the Arizona State Museum mounted an exhibit of historic and contemporary Navajo blankets. Mark Sublette and the Antique Tribal Art Dealers' Association (2005) provided some financial backing for the event, yet in their newsletter the organization posted a warning about knockoffs on eBay advertised as historic rugs. Members were informed that the images were taken from books on historic textiles and told that "Navajo-style weavings done by other cultural groups are not a new phenomenon . . . [and] are perfectly acceptable as derivative contemporary rugs." However, "if these forgeries enter the mainstream market under the guise of genuine antique Navajo textiles, a great deal of harm will be done to a robust and vibrant market and to the textile dealers who market the real antique pieces." The demand for Navajo knockoffs also continues unabated (M'Closkey 2012).

AN ETHICAL CONUNDRUM

In this chapter, I reveal the profound disconnect between the high value attached to old textiles and the low value attached to their context of production. Although we are accustomed to thinking of art as a critical component of civilization, scholars concerned with cultural preservation do not generally think of art collections as potential vehicles of cultural fragmentation. Clearly, museum professionals have a responsibility to consider the potential impact of exhibitions on the markets from which objects are drawn and on the producers of those objects. Websites such as Antiques and the Arts Weekly review exhibitions of historic material culture curated by ethnologists. Gallery owner Philip Garaway encourages collectors to read scholarly books and collect antiquities, since they evoke "a primal link to America's native heritage" and they are much easier to sell (1991, 10). Dating and sourcing of individual textiles are key ingredients, while thousands of historic economic transactions between makers and traders lay buried in traders' and retailers' ledger books. It is difficult to fathom how scholars can contribute to cultural preservation when consorting with the commercial world jeopardizes contemporary producers. Such selective amnesia evokes Kenneth Hudson's critique: "Ethnographical museums may collect widely, but they do not dig deeply. The political consequences of doing so would be too serious, or so it is felt" (1991, 458). His quip brings to mind a comment made by Faith Hagenhofer, librarian for the Nisqually Nation in Washington State. While attending the 2012 Textile Society of America meeting, Faith noted, "It's just amazing that conscientious consumers visiting tourist destinations like Santa Fe know where to buy fair trade coffee, but they haven't a clue about the adverse consequences of knockoffs, or sales of old textiles for Navajo weavers."[6] It should be incumbent upon museologists to become fully aware of the commodification process and avoid market consequences of their activities. By over-valorizing the material part of material culture, scholars separate the Navajo past from the Navajo present.

International art dealers, auction houses, and intermediate dealers rely heavily on museological expertise that may establish and enhance market values to create or augment demand and raise prices (Garaway 1991; Lynott and Wylie 1995). In archaeology, this may lead to looting; when ethnological museums embrace such practices, they facilitate an increase in collectors buying antiquities, precipitating a decline in the purchase of creations by contemporary Native American artists. Yet strangely, museologists neglect to acknowledge how their consorting with the commercial world may jeopardize contemporary producers in ways that they have not envisioned. For example, the Arizona State Museum's mission and values statement "aspires to create authentic, life-enriching experiences that broaden perspectives about and encourage respect for the region's diverse cultural heritage ... [while] upholding ethical standards and anthropological principles" (Arizona State Museum).

THE INVIDIOUS EFFECTS OF DUALISTIC THINKING

The patterns of relations that brought rugs into existence are fractured through adherence to dualisms. Cultural theft has been sanctioned in multiple ways. Currently a way of life is sold to the highest bidder as the old textiles fetch record prices. Through dating and sourcing textiles for auction houses, and authoring books on historic collections, scholars inadvertently sustain this robust market. Such activities are midwifed by the binary between the sacred world of religion and the secular or profane world of commodity production as conceived by scholars such as Gladys Reichard (1934, 1936, 1939), who provided much of the foundation for the construction of "Navajo weaving history" (Hedlund 1989a, 1989b, 1990; Kent 1976, 1985; Wheat 1984, 1996; Hedlund 2003). Adherence to such a research regime, informed by an epistemology that separates cultural patterns from commodities, has reaped devastating consequences. The contexts of interpretation deployed to describe weavers' creations privileges settler history (Amsden 1934; Berlant and Kahlenberg 1977; Blomberg 1988; James 1988; Kaufman and Selser 1985; Kent 1976, 1985; McNitt 1962; Underhill

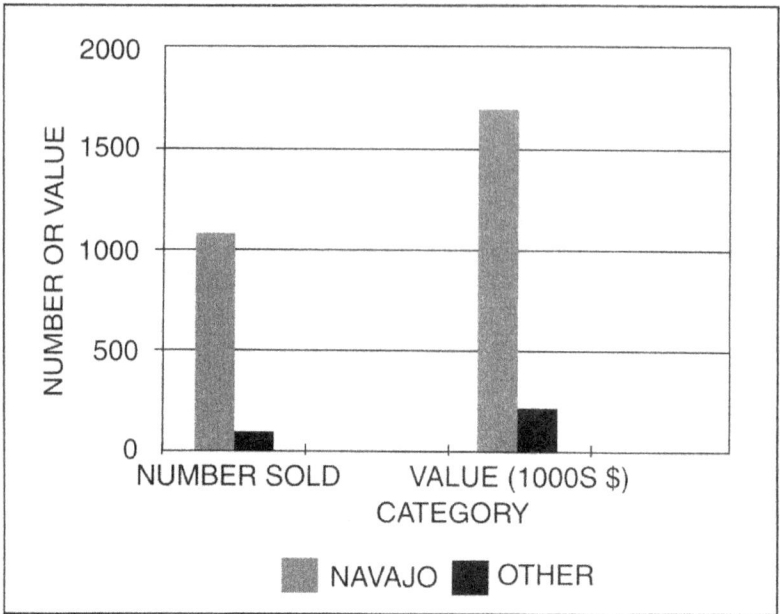

Fig. 6. International antiquities sales, Navajo textiles. From M'Closkey, *Swept*, 177.

1983; Webster 2017; Wilkins 2008). Much of the literature has emphasized the evolution of various styles and traders' ostensible influences
on their development. My analysis of the hidden history, as revealed
in underutilized archives in tandem with weavers' interviews, begs
the question: is the history of style really history? Extant interpretations block a deeper understanding of the value of weaving for Diné.
Research for the sake of research perpetuates narratives of nostalgia,
demonstrating how provenance and pedigree continue to take prece-
dence over concern for poverty.

Complex patterns of relations were occluded through the epistemological lens of the colonizers, including the traders and ethnographers.
The binary of sacred and profane, as constructed by anthropologists
historically, has thrust weaving into an alien field. Although scholars
acknowledged the importance of kin relations (k'e'), they failed to
recognize that the process and products of weaving serve as recursive
enactments of the Diné Creation Story thereby linking cosmology,
kinship solidarity, harmony, *and* provisioning (Denetdale 2007, 93,
130; M'Closkey 2004; Willink and Zolbrod 1996). Weavings are cul-

tural mappings of ecological patterning. In a chapter devoted to Sympoiesis in her recent book, *Staying with the Troubles: Making Kin in the Chthulucene*, Donna Haraway explicates how Navajo weaving serves as an example of multi-species world-making because it "performs worlds with mathematical vitality that remain invisible in the doxa of scholarship on women's fiber practices in settler and colonized indigenous production" (2016, 89). Weaving sustains ecological continuities and that recursive process links ecological aesthetics to epistemology. Thus aesthetic patterns expressed through weaving are epistemological and recursive, rather than objectively distinguished, isomorphic, and autonomous, as typically reflected in museologists' models. In creating their rugs, weavers perpetuate *hózhó*, the order and harmony of the system. This perspective evokes Victor Masayesva's comment, "There is such a thing as an Indian aesthetic and it begins in the sacred" (Leuthold 1998, 1).

In 1996, Navajo linguist Roseann Willink and English professor Paul Zolbrod published *Weaving a World: Textiles and the Navajo Way of Seeing*, the culmination of an eighteen-month project in which sixty Navajo weavers examined two hundred textiles housed at the School of American Research, Museum of New Mexico (Laboratory of Anthropology). Of the dozens of textiles highlighted in the book, weavers acknowledged that a significant number were woven for ceremonial use. For example, a rug depicting snakes was incorporated in the Male Shooting Way and Windway ceremonies (1996, 60). When a prominent New Mexico textile dealer learned of this project, he phoned the governor and warned that if the book were published, state museums risked losing their Navajo textile collections under NAGPRA (Zolbrod, pers. comm.). His concerns were unfounded due to the changes to the act owing to pressure applied during the hearings from the Antique Tribal Art Dealers' Association (ATADA). Vice President James Reid and Sotheby's lawyer Diana Lopez had testified and successfully argued for revisions that narrowed the definition of "sacred" objects to cultural patrimony necessary for the perpetuation of religious ceremonies as practiced by believers *as a group* (McKeown 2012, 196). In one of their 1998 newsletters, ATADA noted that as collectors, both museums and dealers "share mutual concerns and interests" and boasted that "in

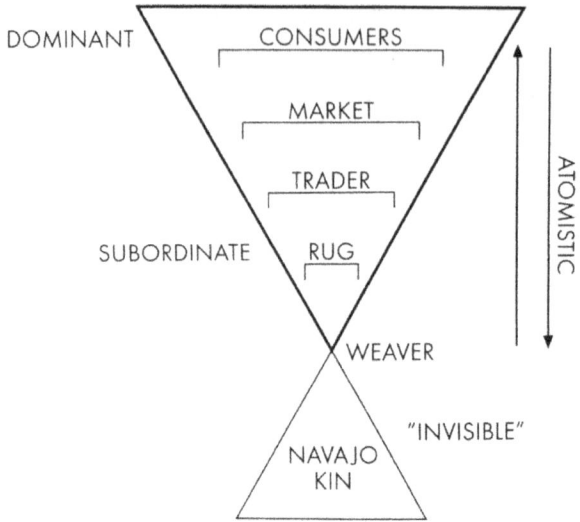

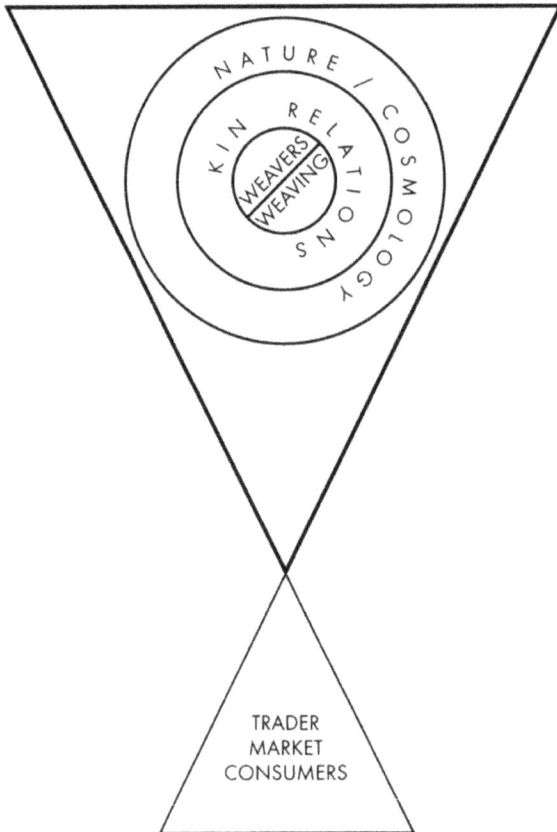

Fig. 7. (*opposite top*) Visible Commodity Relations.

Fig. 8. (*opposite bottom*) Navajo Relations, *k'e*.

Fig. 9. (*above*) Mary & Darcy John, Red Valley, Navajo Nation, 1992. Photo by Kathy M'Closkey.

1990 ATADA *played a major role in re-writing key definitions for* NAGPRA" (Antique Tribal Dealers' Association 1998, 30).

CONCLUSION

The story I relate here serves as a textbook case of how the legacy of settler colonialism, and the indentured poverty it engendered, is sustained. As Dunaway writes, "As we descend down the nodes of the commodity chain, with every link we should call *Her* name, not the brand name of a product" (2001, 23). Diné designs have indeed become "brand" names, linked to designers like Ralph Lauren, retailers such as Urban Outfitters, antiquities' dealers, movie stars, artists, and other wealthy collectors, trade blanket manufacturers,[7] museums "shock and awe" collections, and hundreds of retailers including NOVICA, the fair trade organization associated with National Geographic, which, until recently marketed Navajo knockoffs woven by Zapotec weavers (M'Closkey 2010b). Given the unacknowledged consequences of extensive appropriation that is well over a century old, one wonders how thousands of Diné can possibly survive as weavers in the future in an increasingly globalized, hyper-competitive world, because both commercial markets threaten Diné lifeways and livelihood. Scholars' sustained disengagement with these pressing issues ultimately delegitimizes Diné claims to an essential component of their cultural heritage.

On July 7, 2017, the Senate Indian Affairs Committee held a Hearing in Santa Fe, New Mexico, on Modernizing the Indian Arts and Crafts Act. In her testimony, Navajo weaver and Museum of Indian Arts and Culture curator Joyce Begay-Foss stated that "we can't make a living," due to influx of rug knockoffs legally imported from nearly two dozen countries. She mentioned how appropriation of designs is in violation of the Native American Religious Freedom Act. It also violates Articles 11, 20, and 31 of UNDRIP, the UN Declaration on the Rights of Indigenous Peoples, to "maintain, control, protect and develop their heritage, traditional knowledge and expressions . . . [including] designs, and the intellectual property over traditional cultural expressions."[8] Weavers also face severe competition from the healthy and growing market for historic textiles. Nancy Parezo cautions, "many forms cannot be understood if they are not recognized as commodities that are sold in an international art market specializing in ethnic art; historic and contemporary Native American art must be contextualized in a framework that includes the political economy of collecting" (2002, 221). Expunging the context of the initial acquisition situates the textile exchanges within a milieu of equals: other collectors, dealers, traders, and connoisseurs (Blomberg 1988; Webster 2017).

Thus, it is challenging to shift one's eyes from the "shock and awe" collections housed in museum collections and contemplate how competition from both historic textiles and knockoffs threatens the livelihood of thousands of contemporary weavers. As Isleta artist Andy Abeita (2006) commented, "the world renowned recognition of southwest arts and crafts does not reflect what goes on within impoverished makers' homes." Given that numerous publications authored by generations of scholars working in the southwest were primary contributors to discourses on Native American material culture, this is an astonishing statement. Because poverty among artisans is so under-researched, consumers lack awareness of current circumstances. According to

Abeita, because of such massive appropriation, craft production by Native American artisans, a crucial aspect of cultural preservation, *is being driven to oblivion* (Abeita 2006). The unfortunate circumstances I have outlined above contrast sharply with the current relations between scholars and Aboriginal Peoples from Australia, New Zealand, and Canada. For example, a number of scholars concerned with the protection and repatriation of First Nations cultural heritage in Canada are members of Intellectual Property Issues in Cultural Heritage (IPinCH), an ambitious, long-term project that includes First Nations, anthropologists, archaeologists, and lawyers (Bell and Paterson 2009). Fortunately, Canadian anthropologists have maintained a history of engagement that leaves connoisseurs and antiquities dealers out of the loop.

My paper provides a counterpoint to the movement of indigenous artifacts as described in Maureen Matthew's provocative session at the 2017 joint International Union of Anthropological and Ethnological Sciences (IUAES) and Canadian Anthropological Society (CASCA) conference, "What do Indigenous Artifacts Want?" Navajo textiles remain firmly ensconced in museum collections due to NAGPRA regulations. In contrast, the textile patterns have migrated globally because the federal government placed Indian designs in the public domain over a century ago. The UN Declaration of the Rights of Indigenous People (UNDRIP 2007) may hold the potential to rectify this injustice. Former President Obama signed it in December 2010, noting that actions are needed to match the words affirming Native American aspirations. To date, neither actions nor research are forthcoming from either the U.S. government or southwestern museum scholars to halt the unrelenting appropriation of Diné designs. Thus, the extraordinary production of thousands of Navajo weavers historically, *to cope with the dire consequences of free trade*, threatens the market for textiles created by thousands of their descendants.

NOTES

I am grateful to Regna Darnell for her invitation to submit this paper which was presented at the CASCA/IUAES conference May 2017, hosted by the University of Ottawa. Thank you to Maureen Matthews and Joshua Smith for accepting my abstract and co-chairing three sessions

with the provocative theme "What do Indigenous Artifacts Want?"
This research was funded by the Social Sciences and Humanities
Research Council of Canada (grant no 410–2004–0170, and no. 410–
2008–0964). The Social Justice and Globalization Data Archive at the
University of Windsor offered invaluable assistance, providing office
space and technical support. Although the SJG Data Archive is now
closed, I wish to thank former Director Dr. Suzan Ilcan and data archivist Stephen Richter for their help and support. Many librarians and
archivists at various institutions have assisted me over the years, including the National Archives, Washington DC; the Newberry Library, Chicago; Special Collections, University of Arizona, Tucson; Center for
Southwest Research, University of New Mexico, Albuquerque; Special Collections Cline Library, Northern Arizona University, Flagstaff;
and Ken Wade, American Indian Studies Library, UCLA. I am also very
grateful for the friendship and warmth extended by many Diné who
have shared stories, especially Bonnie Benally Yazzie, Jennifer Denetdale, Roseann Willink, and the Horseherder family of Hard Rock,
Navajo Nation, Arizona. Two anonymous reviewers provided insightful
comments on an earlier draft. And a final thank you to Regna Darnell
and Fred Gleach for shepherding *HoAA 13* into production.

1. An anthropologist working with weavers in the Middle East informed
   me that the large color photographs from two recently published "coffee table" books about Navajo weaving were being used as templates
   for the production of knockoffs. The rug factory owners asked the visitor to forward the names of North American retailers as potential dealers.
2. I interviewed the candidate months before the run-off, and I later
   learned that he had moved to another city after losing the election.
3. The following references contain a portion of the information vital to
   historicizing Navajos as woolgrowers and weavers within an international context of commercial competitiveness: Arizona Woolgrowers'
   Association, Babbitt Brothers Trading Company; Frank Bond & Son
   Records; Bulletins of the National Association of Wool Manufacturers
   1870–1943; Carman et al. 1892; Cole 1941; Connor 1921; Dobson 1976;
   Great Britain Empire Marketing Board 1932; Gross-Kelly and Company Business Records; Holmes 1917; Hultz 1931; The National Woolgrower; Donald Parman Papers; U.S. Tariff Board 1912; U.S. Treasury
   Department 1894; Wolman 1992.

4. Bigelow-Sanford Carpet Company Records; Cole 1926, 1941; Edmund Pike Graves Papers; Gross-Kelly and Company Wool Code Books 1888—; Hubbell Trading Post Papers; Taussig 1893, 1897, 1913; Treasury Department 1894.

5. In a publication devoted to historic Navajo textiles, anthropologist Ann Hedlund noted, "An intriguing by-product of (Joe Ben) Wheat's scholarly work has been the interest shown in the research results by private collectors, gallery owners and others who buy and sell historic textiles. The complex mechanisms of proving authenticity through dating, sourcing and other wise identifying have attracted a wide and supportive audience" (1989b, 134).

6. Hagenhofer made the comment during a discussion following a screening of "Weaving Worlds: Navajo Tales of How the West Was Spun." I served as research director for the award-winning documentary directed by Diné Bennie Klain, funded by Native American Telecommunications and aired on PBS.

7. Pendleton Blankets are the largest trade blanket manufacturers in North America. They now market Zapotec textiles bearing Navajo designs, from saddle blankets to room-sized rugs, on their website, under the "HOME" flat rugs category. https://www.pendleton-usa.com.

8. Wood (2008, 89–95) notes that Michael Wineland, owner of Santa Fe Interiors, appropriated several Navajo designs from Blomberg's 1988 publication featuring William Randolph Hearst's collection. Wineland earned over $1 million in 2000 on the "Hearst Series" sales.

REFERENCES

Abeita, Andy. 2006. "Pressing Concerns for the Future of Native American Arts and Crafts." Navajo Studies Conference, University of New Mexico, Albuquerque, November 2, 2006.

Aberle, David F. 1983. "Navajo Economic Development." In *Handbook of North American Indians*, vol. 10, edited by Alfonso Ortiz, 641–58. Washington DC: Smithsonian Institution.

Amsden, Charles Avery. 1932. "Reviving the Navajo Blanket." *Masterkey* 6: 136–49.

———. (1934) 1975. *Navajo Weaving, Its Technique and History*. Salt Lake City: Peregrine Smith.

Antique Tribal Art Dealers' Association. 2005. "Fake Navajo Rug Alert." Accessed September 23, 2005. http://www.atada.org/news.html.

Arizona State Museum. n.d. "Mission, Vision, and Values." Accessed July 2, 2017. https://statemuseum.arizona.edu/about/mission-vision-and-values.

Arizona Woolgrowers Association 1880–1980. NAU.MS.233, Cline Library Special Collections and Archives Department. Northern Arizona University, Flagstaff AZ.

Babbitt Brothers Trading Company 1880–1999. NAU.MS.83. Cline Library, Special Collections and Archives Department. Northern Arizona University, Flagstaff AZ.

Baer, Joshua. 2001. Advertisement. *American Indian Art Magazine* 26, no. 2. Accessed August 28, 2009. http://www.navajoblanketappraisals.com.

Bahr, Howard. 1999. *Diné Bibliography to the 1990s*. Lanham MD: Scarecrow Press, 1999.

Bailey, Garrick, and Roberta Glenn Bailey. 1986. *A History of the Navajos— the Reservation Years*. Santa Fe NM: School of American Research Press, 1986.

Baizerman, Suzanne. 1989. "The Study of Material Culture: The Case of Southwest Textiles." *Museum Anthropology* 13, no. 2 (1989): 14–18.

Bell, Catherine, and Robert Paterson, eds. 2009. *Protection of First Nations Cultural Heritage: Laws, Policy and Reform*. Vancouver: University of British Columbia Press.

Bensel, Richard Franklin. 2000. *The Political Economy of American Industrialization, 1877–1900*. New York: Cambridge University Press.

Berlant, Tony, and Mary Hunt Kahlenberg. 1977. *Walk in Beauty*. New York: Little, Brown.

Berlo, Janet C. 2006. "'It's up to you—': Individuality, Community and Cosmopolitanism in Navajo Weaving." In *Weaving Is Life. Navajo Weaving from the Edwin L. & Ruth E. Kennedy Southwest Native American Collection*, edited by Jennifer McLerran, 34–47. Athens OH: Kennedy Museum of Art.

Bigelow-Sanford Carpet Company Records. Baker Library Historical Collections, Harvard Business School.

Blomberg, Nancy. 1988. *Art from the Navajo Loom: The William Randolph Hearst Collection*. Tucson: University of Arizona Press.

Bonar, Eulalie, ed. 1996. *Woven by the Grandmothers*. Washington DC: Smithsonian Institution Press.

Bsumek, Erika. 2008. *Indian Made. Navajo Culture in the Marketplace 1868–1940*. Lawrence: University Press of Kansas.

———. 2004. "The Navajos as Borrowers." *New Mexico Historical Review* 79, no. 3: 319–47.

Bulletins of the National Association of Wool Manufacturers 1866–1925. Newberry Library, Chicago.

Bulletins of the National Association of Wool Manufacturers 1926–1943. Baker Business Library, Harvard University.

Carman, Ezra, H. A. Heath, and John Minto. 1892. *Special Report on the History and Present Condition of the Sheep Industry of the United States.* U.S. Department of Agriculture, Bureau of Animal Industry. Washington DC: GPO.

Chelsea Goin Papers. 1996. Harold S. Colton Memorial Library, Museum of Northern Arizona, Flagstaff.

Clinton Global Initiative. "Commitments to Action." Accessed October 14, 2013. http://www.clintonfoundation.org/clinton-global-initiative/commitments.

Cole, Arthur H. 1941. *The American Carpet Manufacturer: A History and an Analysis.* Cambridge MA: Harvard University Press.

———. 1926. *The American Wool Manufacturer,* vol. I and II. Cambridge MA: Harvard University Press.

Cohen, Jeffrey H. 2000. "Textile Production in Rural Oaxaca, Mexico: The Complexities of the Global Market for Handmade Crafts." In *Artisans and Cooperatives: Developing Alternative Trade for the Global Economy,* edited by Kimberly Grimes and B. Lynne Milgram, 129–141. Tucson: University of Arizona Press.

Conner, Debbie. 1991. "An Ethnography of the Crownpoint Navajo Rug Auction." MA thesis, New Mexico State University, Las Cruces.

Connor, L. G. 1921. "A Brief History of the Sheep Industry." In *Annual Report of American Historical Association,* 93–197. Washington DC: Government Printing Office.

Cottam, Erica. 2015. *Hubbell Trading Post: Trade, Tourism, and the Navajo Southwest.* Norman: University of Oklahoma Press, 2015.

Denetdale, Jennifer. 2018. "Naal Tsoos Sani (The Old Paper): The Navajo Treaty of 1868, Nation Building and Self-Determination." *National Museum of the American Indian* 19, no. 2, 24–31.

———. 2008. *The Long Walk: The Forced Navajo Exile.* New York: Chelsea House, 2008.

———. 2007. *Reclaiming Diné History: The Legacies of Navajo Chief Manuelito and Juanita.* Tucson: University of Arizona Press.

Dobson, John. 1976. *Two Centuries of Tariffs: The Background and Emergence of the U.S. International Trade Commission.* Washington DC: GPO.

Dockstader, Frederick J. 1978. *Weaving Arts of the North American Indian.* New York: Thomas Y. Crowell.

Dunaway, Wilma A. 2001. "The Double Register of History: Situating the Forgotten Woman and Her Household in Capitalist Commodity Chains." *Journal of World Systems Research* 7, no. 1: 2–29.

Duus, Gloria. 1987. "Navajo Weavers and Woolgrowers' Study." Window Rock AZ: Office of Navajo Women and Families.

Frank Bond and Son Records. 1870-1958 MSS 133BC 1&2. Center for Southwest Research, University of New Mexico.

Frank McNitt Papers. Coll. 1973–024. New Mexico Commission of Public Records. State Records Center and Archives. Santa Fe NM.

Fred Harvey Company Rug Ledgers 1900–1946. Billie Jane Baguley Library, Heard Museum, Phoenix AZ and the Museum of International Folk Art, Santa Fe NM.

Frisbie, Charlotte J., ed. 2001. *Tall Woman: The Life Story of Rose Mitchell, A Navajo Woman c. 1874–1977.* Albuquerque: University of New Mexico Press, 2001.

Garaway, Philip. 1991. "Collecting Native Southwestern Antiques." *Indian Trader* 22, no. 10: 10.

Goldfarb, B. 2013. "In His Element." *Architectural Digest*, 148–61.

Graburn, Nelson, ed. 1976. *Ethnic and Tourist Arts.* Berkeley: University of California Press.

Edmund Pike Graves Papers, 1865–1919. MSS 761 G 776 Baker Library Historical Collections, Harvard Business School. Cambridge MA.

Great Britain Empire Marketing Board. 1932. *Wool Survey: a Summary of Production and Trade in the Empire and Foreign Countries.* London: His Majesty's Stationery Office.

Gross-Kelly and Company Business Records 1902–1954. MSS 96 BC. Center for Southwest Research, University of New Mexico, Albuquerque.

Haraway, Donna. 2016. *Staying with the Troubles: Making Kin in the Chthulucene.* Durham NC: Duke University Press.

Handler, Richard. 1997. "Cultural Property, Culture Theory and Museum Anthropology." *Museum Anthropology* 21, no. 3: 3–4.

Heard Museum. 2017. "American Indian Art & Artifacts Appraisal Day." Accessed July 3, 2017. http://heard.org/event/appraisal-day/.

Hedlund, Ann Lane. 1997. *Navajo Weavings from the Andy Williams Collection.* St. Louis: St. Louis Art Museum.

———. 1993. *Reflections of the Weaver's World: The Gloria F. Ross Collection.* Denver: Denver Art Museum.

———. 1990. *Beyond the Loom: Keys to Understanding Early Southwestern Weaving.* Boulder: Johnson Books.

———. 1989a. "In Pursuit of Style: Kate Peck Kent and Navajo Aesthetics." *Museum Anthropology* 13 no. 2: 23–28.

———. 1989b. "The Study of Nineteenth-Century Southwestern Textiles." In *Perspectives on Anthropological Collections from the American Southwest: Proceedings of a Symposium*, edited by Ann Lane Hedlund, 121–38. Phoenix: Arizona State University.

Henson, Dusty, and Bonnie Henson. 2001. *Rugs to Riches: The Amazing Story of the El Paso Saddle Blanket Company*. El Paso TX: Trego-Hill Publications.

Holmes, George K. 1917. *Wool: Production, Foreign Trade, Supply and Consumption*. No. 751. GPO: Department of Agriculture.

Hubbell Trading Post Papers 1882–1968 (AZ 375). Special Collections Library, University of Arizona, Tucson.

Hudson, Kenneth. 1991. "How Misleading Does an Ethnographical Museum Have to Be?" In *Exhibiting Cultures: The Poetics and Politics of Museum Display*, edited by Ivan Karp and S. Lavine, 457–64. Washington DC: Smithsonian Institution Press.

Hultz, Fred S., and John A. Hill. 1931. *Range Sheep and Wool in the Seventeen Western States*. New York: John Wiley and Sons.

Iverson, Peter. 2002. *Diné: A History of the Navajos*. Albuquerque: University of New Mexico Press.

James, H. L. (1976) 1988. *Rugs and Posts: The Story of Navajo Rugs and Their Homes*. Tucson: Southwest Parks and Monuments.

Johnson, Harmer. 2000. "Auction Block." *American Indian Art Magazine* 26, no. 1: 20–25.

Kapoun, Robert. 1992. *The Language of the Robe*. Salt Lake City: Peregrine Smith.

Karim, Wazir. 1996. "Anthropology Without Tears: How a 'Local' Sees the 'Local' and the 'Global.'" In *The Future of Anthropological Knowledge*, edited by H. L. Moore, 115–38. London: Routledge.

Kaufman, Alice, and Christopher Selser. 1985. *The Navajo Weaving Tradition 1650 to the Present*. New York: E. P. Dutton.

Kelly, Pamela, and Shelley Thompson. 2013. "Translating Museum Treasures into Products." *El Palacio* 118, no. 1: 24, 32.

Kent, Kate Peck. 1985. *Navajo Weaving: Three Centuries of Change*. Santa Fe: School of American Research Press.

———. 1976. "Pueblo and Navajo Weaving Traditions and the Western World." In *Ethnic and Tourist Arts*, edited by Nelson H. Graburn, 85–101. Berkeley: University of California Press.

Klain, Bennie, director. 2008. *Weaving Worlds: Navajo Tales of How the West Was Spun*. Directed by Bennie Klain, 2008. 56 minutes, color, subtitled. Distributed by VisionMaker Video. http://www.visionmaker.org.

Leuthold, Steven. 1998. *Indigenous Aesthetics: Native Art, Media and Identity*. Austin: University of Texas Press.

Lynott, Mark, and A. Wylie. 1995. *Ethics in American Archaeology: Challenges for the 1990s*. Society for American Anthropology. Lawrence KS: Allen Press.

Maxwell, Gilbert. (1963) 1984. *Navajo Rugs: Past, Present and Future*. Palm Desert CA: Desert Southwest.

McKeown, C. Timothy. 2012. *In the Smaller Scope of Conscience: The Struggle for National Repatriation Legislation 1986–1990*. Tucson: University of Arizona Press.

M'Closkey, Kathy. Forthcoming. *Why the Navajo Blanket Became a Rug: Excavating the Lost Heritage of Globalization*. Albuquerque: University of New Mexico Press.

———. 2012. "Up for Grabs: Assessing the Consequences of Sustained Appropriations of Navajo Weavers' Patterns." In *No Deal! Indigenous Arts and the Politics of Possession*, edited by Tressa Berman, 128–54. Santa Fe NM: SAR Press.

———. 2010a. "Unravelling the Narratives of Nostalgia: Navajo Weavers and Globalization." In *Indigenous Women and Work. From Labor to Activism*, edited by Carol Williams, 120–135. Urbana: University of Illinois Press.

———. 2010b. "Novica, Navajo Knockoffs and the 'Net. A Critique of Fair Trade Marketing Practices." In *Fair Trade and Social Justice: Global Ethnographies*, edited by Sarah Lyon and Mark Moberg, 258–82. New York: New York University Press.

———. 2004. "Towards an Understanding of Navajo Aesthetics." SEE: *Semiotics, Evolution, Energy* 4, no. 1: 91–117.

———. (2002) 2008. *Swept Under the Rug: A Hidden History of Navajo Weaving*. Albuquerque: University of New Mexico Press.

———. 2000. "'Part-time for Pin Money.' The Legacy of Navajo Women's Craft Production." In *Artisans and Cooperatives: Developing Alternative Trade for the Global Economy*, edited by Kimberly Grimes and B. Lynne Milgram, 143–158. Tucson: University of Arizona Press.

M'Closkey, Kathy, and Kevin Manuel. 2006. "Commodifying North American Aboriginal Culture: A Canada-U.S. Comparison." In *Historicizing Canadian Anthropology*, edited by Julia Harrison and Regna Darnell, 226–41. Vancouver: University of British Columbia Press.

M'Closkey, Kathy, and Carol Halberstadt. 2005. "Free Trade + Fair Trade = the Fleecing of Navajo Weavers." *Cultural Survival Quarterly* 29, no. 3: 43–46.

McLerran, Jennifer. 2011. "Clubwomen, Curators and Traders: Early- to Mid-Twentieth-Century Navajo Weaving Improvement Projects." *American Indian Art Magazine* 36 no. 4: 54–92.

———. 2009. *A New Deal for Native Art. Indian Arts and Federal Policy, 1933–1943.* Tucson: University of Arizona Press.

McNitt, Frank. 1962. *Indian Traders.* Norman: University of Oklahoma Press, 1962.

Meyer, Karl. 1973. *The Plundered Past.* New York: Atheneum.

Miller, Layne. 2001. "Visiting the Medicine Man Gallery Website." *Indian Trader* 32, no. 3: 5–7.

Mitchell, Marybelle. 1996. *From Talking Chiefs to a Native Corporate Elite: The Birth of Class and Nationalism among Canadian Inuit.* Montreal: McGill-Queens's Press.

Montano, Roshii, and Jill Ahlberg Yohe. 2017. "Blanketing the Plains: Hanoolchaadi in Indian Country." *First American Art Magazine* 14: 20–25.

Moore, Jason W. 2015. *Capitalism in the Web of Life.* London: Verso.

Mullin, Molly H. 2001. *Culture in the Marketplace: Gender, Art, and Value in the American Southwest.* Durham NC: Duke University Press.

Museum of Indian Arts and Culture. n.d. "Mission and Vision." Accessed July 3, 2017. http://www.miaclab.org/mission.

Nash, June. 2000. "Postscript: To Market to Market." In *Artisans and Cooperatives: Developing Alternative Trade for the Global Economy*, edited by Kimberly Grimes and B. Lynne Milgram, 175–79. Tucson: University of Arizona Press.

The National Woolgrower. Monthly publication of the NWG Association. Salt Lake City, Utah.

New York Times. 2006. "Is It All Loot? Tackling the Antiquities Problem," March 29, 2006, https://www.nytimes.com/2006/03/29/arts/artsspecial/29panel.html.

Nichols, Judy. 2005. "March 18: Native American Art & Artifacts Appraisal Day." *Arizona Republic*, November 17, 2005, http://www.azcentral.com/ent/calendar/articles/1117appraisal17.html.

Nizhoni Ranch Gallery. n.d. "History of Navajo Weaving." Accessed May 10, 2018. http://www.navajorug.com/pages/history-of-navajo-weaving.

O'Neill, Colleen. 2005. *Working the Navajo Way: Labor and Culture in the Twentieth Century.* Lawrence: University Press of Kansas.

Parezo, Nancy. 2002. "Indigenous Art: Creating Value and Sharing Beauty." In *Companion to American Indian History,* edited by Philip J. Deloria and Neal Salisbury, 209–233. Hoboken NJ: Wiley-Blackwell.

————. 1983. *Navajo Sandpainting: From Religious Act to Commercial Art.* Tuscon: University of Arizona Press.

Parman, Donald Lee Papers, 1909–1990. Special Collections. Newberry Library, Chicago.

Reichard, Gladys. 1939. *Dezba: Woman of the Desert.* Glorieta NM: Rio Grande Press.

————. 1936. *Navajo Shepherd and Weaver.* New York: J. J. Augustin.

————. 1934. *Spider Woman.* New York: MacMillan.

Rodee, Marian. 1981. *Old Navajo Rugs: Their Development from 1900 to 1940.* Albuquerque: University of New Mexico Press.

Roessel, Ruth. 1983. "Navajo Arts and Crafts." In *Handbook of North American Indians,* vol. 10, edited by Alfonso Ortiz, 592–604. Washington DC: Smithsonian Institution Press.

Satchell, Michael, and David Bowermaster. 1994. "The Worst Federal Agency." *U.S. News and World Report,* November 28, 1994: 61–4.

Sells, Cato. 1913. Annual Report of the Commissioner of Indian Affairs. Washington DC: GPO.

Shelton, Anthony. 1992. "Constructing the Global Village." *Museums Journal:* 25–28.

Stephen, Lynn. 2005. *Zapotec Women. Gender: Class and Ethnicity in Globalized Oaxaca.* Durham NC: Duke University Press.

————. 1993. "Weaving in the Fast Lane: Class, Ethnicity and Gender in Zapotec Craft Commercialization." In *Crafts in the World Market,* edited by June Nash, 25–57. New York: State University of New York Press.

————. 1991a. "Export Markets and Their Effects on Indigenous Craft Production: The Case of the Weavers of Teotitlan del Valle, Mexico." In *Textile Traditions in Mesoamerica and the Andes,* edited by Margot Blum Schevill, Janet Berlo, and Edward Dwyer, 381–99. New York: Garland.

————. 1991b. *Zapotec Women.* Austin: University of Texas Press.

————. 1991c. "Culture as a Resource: Four Cases of Self-Managed Indigenous Craft Producers in Latin America." *Economic Development and Culture Change* 40, no.1:101–30.

Sublette, Mark. 1991. Advertisement. 1994. *American Indian Art* 19, no. 3: 27.

————. n.d. "Collective Navajo Rugs: An Introduction to the Diverse and Intricate Styles of Navajo Textiles." Accessed May 10, 2018. http://www.medicinemangallery.com/collecting-Navajo-rugs-April-2017.

Tanner, Clara Lee. 1968. *Southwest Indian Craft Arts*. Tucson: University of Arizona Press.

Taussig, Frank. 1893. "The Duties on Wool and Woollens." *The Quarterly Journal of Economics* 8, no. 1: 1–39.

———. 1897. "Tariff Act of 1897." *The Quarterly Journal of Economics* 12, no. 1:42–69.

———. 1913. "Tariff Act of 1913." *The Quarterly Journal of Economics* 28, no. 1: 1–30.

"The Andy Williams Collection of Navajo Blankets." May 21, 2013, http:// www.sothebys.com/en/auctions/2013/so-williams-n08984.html.

Tiffany, Sharon. 2004. "Frame That Rug: Narratives of Zapotec Textiles as Art and Ethnic Commodity in the Global Marketplace." *Visual Anthropology* 17: 293–318.

Treasury Department. 1894. *Wool and Manufactures of Wool*. U.S. Bureau of Statistics. Washington DC: GPO.

Trump, Erik. "'The Idea of Help': White Women Reformers and the Commercialization of Native American Women's Art." In *Selling the Indian: Commercializing and Appropriating American Indian Cultures*, edited by Carter Meyer Jones and Diana Royer, 159–89. Tucson: University of Arizona Press.

Underhill, Ruth. 1983. *The Navajo*. Norman: University of Oklahoma Press.

United Nations Declaration on the Rights of Indigenous Peoples (UNDRIP). 2007. Division for Social Policy and Development, Indigenous Peoples. Accessed July 3, 2017. http://www.un.org/development/desa /indigenous peoples/declaration-on-the-rights of indigenous-peoples. html.

U.S. Census. 2010. Navajo Population Profile. Window Rock AZ, Navajo Nation. Accessed December 2013. http://www.nec.Navajo-nsn.gov /Portals/0/Reports/nn2010populationProfile.pdf.

U.S. Records of the Indian Arts and Crafts Board, 1929-1988. Record Group 435. National Archives, Washington DC.

U.S. Superintendents' Annual Narrative and Statistical Reports, and unpublished correspondence from the Navajo Agencies 1910–1935. Records of the Bureau of Indian Affairs, Record Group 75. National Archives, Washington DC.

U.S. Tariff Board. 1912. Wool and Manufacturers of Wool. Report of the Tariff Board on Schedule K of the Tariff Law. Vol. I. Washington DC: GPO.

Valette, Rebecca M. 2012. "Early Navajo Sandpainting Blankets: A Reassessment." *American Indian Art Magazine* 37, no. 2: 54–82.

Van Valkenburgh, Richard F., and John McPhee. 1974. *A Short History of the Navajo People*. New York: Garland.

Webster, Laurie, et al. 2017. *Navajo Textiles: The Crane Collection at the Denver Museum of Nature and Science*. Boulder: University Press of Colorado.

———. 2007. *Collecting the Weaver's Art: The William Claflin Collection of Southwestern Textiles*. Cambridge MA: Harvard University Press.

Weigle, Marta, and Barbara Babcock, eds. 1996. *The Great Southwest of the Fred Harvey Company and the Santa Fe Railway*. Tucson: University of Arizona Press.

West Elm. "Craftmark Indian Artisans." Accessed March 2, 2019. http://www.westelm.com/shop/collaborations/craftmark-indian-artisans.

Wheat, Joe Ben. 2003. *Blanket Weaving in the Southwest*, edited by Ann Lane Hedlund. Tucson: University of Arizona Press.

———. 1996. "Navajo Blankets." In *Woven by the Grandmothers*, edited by Eulalie Bonar, 69–85. Washington DC: Smithsonian Institution Press.

———. 1984. *The Gift of Spiderwoman: Southwestern Textiles, the Navajo Tradition*. Philadelphia: The University Museum, University of Pennsylvania.

———. 1974. "Navajo Blankets" from the Collection of Anthony Berlant. Tucson: University of Arizona Museum of Art.

Whitaker, Kathleen. 2002. *Southwest Textiles: Weavings of the Pueblo and Navajo*. Seattle: University of Washington Press.

White, Richard. 1983. *The Roots of Dependency: Subsistence, Environment, and Social Change among the Choctaws, Pawnees, and Navajos*. Lincoln: University of Nebraska Press.

Wilkins, Teresa. 2008. *Patterns of Exchange: Navajo Weavers and Traders*. Norman: University of Oklahoma Press.

Williams, Lester. 1989. *C. N. Cotton and His Navajo Blankets*. Albuquerque: Avanyu.

Willink, Roseanne, and Paul Zolbrod. 1996. *Weaving a World: Textiles and the Navajo Way of Seeing*. Santa Fe: Museum of New Mexico Press.

Winter, Mark. "Toadlena Trading Post." Accessed May 10, 2018. http://www.toadlenatradingpost.com.

Witherspoon, Gary. 1987. "Navajo Weaving: Art in its Cultural Context." MNA Research Paper no. 36. Flagstaff: Museum of Northern Arizona.

Wolman, Paul. 1992. *Most Favored Nation: The Republican Revisionists and U.S. Tariff Policy 1897–1912*. Chapel Hill NC: University of North Carolina Press.

Wood, Len. "Gallery of Antique American Indian Art." Accessed May 10, 2018. http://www.indianterritory.com.

Wood, W. Warner. 2017. "Art by Dispossession at El Paso Saddleblanket Company: Commodification and Graduated Sovereignty in Global Capitalism." In *Art and Sovereignty in Global Politics*, edited by Douglas Howland, Elizabeth Lillehoj, and Maximilian Mayer, 169–95. London: Palgrave.

———. 2008. *Made in Mexico: Zapotec Weavers and the Global Ethnic Art Market*. Bloomington: Indiana University Press.

Woodman, Nancy. 1980. "The Story of an Orphan." In *The South Corner of Time*, edited by Larry Evers, 77–88. Tucson: University of Arizona Press.

DEANA L. WEIBEL

5

Mock Rituals, Sham Battles, and Real Research

Anthropologists and the Ethnographic Study of
the Bontoc Igorot in 1900s "Igorrote Villages"

Human curiosity about other humans, particularly those whose culture is dramatically different, can have both positive and negative consequences. For instance, most anthropologists, driven by curiosity,
attempt to explore and understand peoples and cultures, then share
their findings with colleagues and students. On the other hand, human
curiosity about other humans, particularly those who are regarded as
somehow inferior, can lead to sensationalistic portrayals that feed the
need for entertainment, a confirmation of superiority, and many other
dubious desires, rather than fulfilling intellectual inquiries. This type of
curiosity can be disastrous and often deadly. Sometimes the two types
of curiosity I have described come together in strange permutations.
This chapter, which combines the personal with the professional, will
look at anthropological and linguistic research done in the "Igorrote
Villages" run by Richard Schneidewind, my own great-grandfather.

Although I am an anthropologist, I do not claim to be an expert on
the Igorot people, anthropology of the 1900s, or the phenomenon of
"human zoos." I study religion, specifically pilgrimage and people's
relationships with sacred places and objects. Most of my fieldwork
has taken place in France at the Catholic shrine town of Rocamadour.
When I decided to study anthropology (after obtaining a bachelor's
degree in linguistics), it was with almost no knowledge of my family's
involvement with the display of Igorot people. During my childhood
my mother would occasionally mention that her grandfather had been a

Fig. 10. Richard
Schneidewind, photo
courtesy of Richard
Schneidewind Papers,
Bentley Historical Library,
University of Michigan.

showman who had traveled with a band of "pygmy headhunters," but she knew very little about the particulars, and her inaccurate characterization (a guess based on photos she'd seen in her grandparents' sun room in their Detroit home) made it difficult for me to uncover the details once my curiosity drove me to explore this piece of my family history.

My intent in this chapter, therefore, is not to cover the full history of the Western display of "exotic" cultures, but to write from my own rather unusual perspective as an anthropologist who happens to be a descendent of one particular impresario, Richard Schneidewind, who operated "Igorrote Villages" during this period. My academic findings are coupled with information I have gleaned as I have learned more about my genealogical connections to Schneidewind. My two most helpful interlocutors in this case have been Smithsonian anthropologist Dr. Patricia Afable and my mother's first cousin Douglas Fernlock, the family curator of documents, photos, and objects from the days of the fairs. I began collaborating with them in 2007, resulting in my understanding of Richard Schneidewind as a specific case study in the intersecting history of anthropology and the display of non-Western peoples for "education" or entertainment.

I have previously written about my work with Patricia Afable (see Weibel 2014), specifically focusing on the research partnership between an impresario's offspring and an Igorot anthropologist (Afable is a linguistic anthropologist who studied under Harold Conklin at Yale) and what our backgrounds allowed each of us to bring to shared research and presentations during the centennial celebrations of several world's fairs. This paper, however, picks up a thread that caught my interest during our work but was until now largely unexplored: how Schneidewind's "Igorrote Villages" (he used the Spanish *Igorrote* rather than the English Igorot to distinguish his business from that of competitors like Truman Hunt) were sites of anthropological and linguistic research. My access to family histories and documents has given me useful information on the academic repute of these so-called ethnological expositions.

THE ORIGINS OF "ETHNOLOGICAL EXPOSITIONS"

European colonialism contributed to both the creation of zoos and the development of anthropology, stimulating popular interest in the strange and exotic living things that inhabited the far reaches of the globe. Chokri Ben Chikha and Karel Arnaut note that both American and European populations enjoyed the kinds of cultural entertainments that put unfamiliar humans on display, a practice that became widespread in the nineteenth century and continued into the early twentieth century. They argue that the "human zoo enjoyed considerable scientific legitimation, not least because it was often the direct focus of scientific research such as language sampling or anthropometric research" (Ben Chikha and Arnaut 2013, 662).

In his paper on influential archaeologist Frederic Ward Putnam, a mentor of Franz Boas among other notable achievements, Curtis M. Hinsley gives a detailed account of Putnam's role in the presentation of anthropology at 1893's World's Columbian Exposition, also known as the Chicago World's Fair. Putnam is described as a careful, scientifically minded scholar who sought to promote anthropology and saw the Chicago Fair as an opportunity to do so on a grand scale. One of Putnam's projects was an "ethnographic village," a place where he could showcase "contemporary Native peoples, from Tierra del Fuego to the Arctic, living in completely or largely 'traditional' ways" (Hinsley 2016,

20). This idea followed from one of Putnam's primary missions: to educate the public. As Hinsley writes, "Putnam contended that in order to understand and appreciate the astounding material and moral progress of American civilization (and by extension European civilization as well) in the four hundred years since Columbus first made landfall in 1492, the Chicago Fair required a comparative demonstration of the cultural state of the western hemisphere in Columbus's time" (Hinsley 2016, 11). The popularity of the Chicago fair helped ensure that these types of exhibitions would continue into the twentieth century.

POWERLESSNESS AND AGENCY AMONG "PERFORMERS"

Whether or not they led to advances in scientific understandings of humanity or an increase in the ethnological knowledge of the common man, these displays were frequently the stuff of ethical nightmares. One of the best known examples was Ota Benga, a Pygmy man who was essentially sold as a slave to anthropologist Samuel Phillips Verner, displayed as a curiosity at the 1904 St. Louis World's Fair, and put in the Bronx Zoo's monkey house in 1906. Benga left the zoo to receive an education at the "Colored Orphan Asylum" in Brooklyn but ended up committing suicide in 1916 (Buckner 2010, 171). The display of human beings as a form of "exotic" entertainment is clearly problematic. Robert Rydell's *All the World's a Fair* (1984) argues as well that these ethnological exhibitions legitimated colonialism and encouraged a culture of imperialism, harming far more people than those who were actually put on display.

Some researchers, on the other hand, have suggested that under certain conditions, the people displayed were active participants and even involved in the planning behind these shows. Anthropologist Patricia Afable, who is a member of the Ibaloi Igorot tribe of the Philippines, conducted research interviewing the descendants of Igorots who participated in such shows with two impresarios, Dr. Truman K. Hunt and Richard Schneidewind. Her analyses complicate the black-and-white narrative that is often told. For instance, Afable emphasizes that the Igorots who made the journey to the United States did so consensually and with contracts guaranteeing them payment. In addition, she notes, many of the Igorots made multiple journeys, returning home for a while and then heading back to the U.S. Afable claims that the Igorots who were displayed around the country "explored new forms of presenting their traditions, histories, and selves to others," and that their descendants "speak of their ancestors as mostly young adventurers who 'ran away' to Malika, teaming up with their neighbors, families, and other relatives, in the hope of bringing back money and White people's goods" (Afable 2004, 462). Family memories portray the Americans encountered through these "adventures" as mostly kind and gullible, and memories of the Igorots themselves as taking advantage of them by constructing essentially false identities. For example, Afable mentions "young men who became 'chiefs' during the Fairs" and inauthentic practices as a way to attract attention and income.

THE VALIDATING INFLUENCE OF ANTHROPOLOGY

Issues of equality and agency aside, Afable's findings lead to thought-provoking questions about the role of these exhibitions, including the ones led by Schneidewind, in relation to the discipline of anthropology in the early twentieth century. Rydell and others have demonstrated that the practice of displaying the "Other" in fairs and amusement parks, as well as much of early anthropology, stemmed from long-standing European colonialism and nascent American colonialism. Nations seeking to control the resources of other lands believed they would improve their chances of success if they could understand the *people* of those lands. Many early anthropologists not only worked to explain foreign cultures to scholars back home but also worked to create systems that accounted for human difference, including hierarchical distinctions between groups. Lewis Henry Morgan's 1877 categorization of humans into savage, barbaric, and civilized societies is one example. In a neat bit of symbiosis, anthropology gave academic authority to the practice of colonialism, while colonialism, in many ways, promoted and sustained anthropology.

Nancy Parezo and Don D. Fowler recount the long history linking anthropology and the frequently imperialism-promoting fairs and exhibitions, starting with the 1867 Paris Exposition; they also discuss the influence of such scholars as George Brown Goode and Franz Boas on the way material culture could best be displayed and made interesting to the larger public. Efforts to make these displays increasingly appealing led William H. Holmes and his partners first into the creation of lifelike mannequins for museums. Later, working with W J McGee in preparation for the 1904 Louisiana Purchase Exposition in Saint Louis, Holmes (certainly influenced by Frederic Ward Putnam) promoted the display of actual, living human beings. As Parezo and Fowler write, "In Holmes's eyes the mannequin life groups were ideal for museum displays, but for expositions the real thing was better" (2007, 25).

The St. Louis Exposition, of course, eventually included an astounding collection of these "real things," with the Philippine Reservation itself housing "about twelve hundred and fifty individuals" (Parezo and Fowler 2007, 165). Anthropologists weren't just involved in working out the display of the various Philippine tribal groups, but also in arranging for participants. Albert Jenks, for instance, known for his ethnography *The Bontoc Igorot* (1905) had been placed in charge of the Philippine ethnological section of the fair and had, in fact, personally recruited many of the Igorots displayed by Dr. Truman K. Hunt in his "Igorot Village." This village—a mock-up of an actual Igorot village, where "primitive" Philippine people could be seen in a naturalistic, lifelike setting undertaking traditional activities and rituals—was enormously popular with the public.

SCHNEIDEWIND'S INTRODUCTION TO THE FAIRS

Among those admirers of the village, its inhabitants, and the potential of such displays to make money was my great-grandfather, Richard Schneidewind. He had been an Army nurse during the Spanish-American War and had contracted typhoid during his journey to the Philippine Islands, nearly dying before his arrival. He was actually still on the "sick list" when he was discharged in 1899. Rather than returning to his home state of Michigan, however, Schneidewind stayed on in the Philippines, marrying a local woman (who died shortly after giving birth to their son in December 1900), and taking a job as a clerk in a Manila post office. In 1901, Schneidewind was accused of having participated in the smuggling of expensive embroidered fabrics from Manila to San Francisco and was dismissed from his position (McKay 1907).

At this point, it appears that Schneidewind returned to his home in Detroit, leaving his son in the care of his maternal relatives in Manila

Table 1. Schneidewind and Felder's Filipino Exhibition Company Time Line

There were often two groups on different schedules

Lewis and Clark Exposition, Portland, Oregon	1905
Chutes Park, Los Angeles, California	1905–06
Riverview Park, Chicago, Illinois	1906–07
Schneidewind's wedding to second wife, Selma and return to Philippines	Fall 1906
Schneidewind takes 18 "Igorrotes" to Detroit and left a second group with John Kreider at Riverview Park in Chicago	May 1907
Cedar Point, Sandusky, Ohio	July 1907
Canadian National Exposition, Toronto	August–September 1907
Nashville, Tennessee	September 1907
York Fair, York County Pennsylvania	September 1907
Georgia-Carolina Agricultural Fair, Georgia	November 1907
Also in 1907:	
Oletangy Park, Columbus, Ohio	
St. Louis, Missouri	
Jacksonville, Florida (probably Florida Midwinter Exposition)	
Alaska-Yukon-Pacific Exposition	June–October 1909

until he retrieved the child in 1904. A ship's manifest from that year shows that Schneidewind and his son Richard Jr., called "Ding" by his Philippine family (a nickname that continued with his German family in Michigan), arrived in San Francisco together on October 23, 1904, bound for St. Louis (the fair continued until December 1). Schneidewind was, in fact, employed in St. Louis during the fair, selling "High Grade Manila Cigars" at the Philippine Tobacco Concession at the Philippine Reservation. Soon after the close of the fair, Schneidewind returned to the Philippines to work for the colonial government.

Fig. 11. This postcard from Richard Sr. to Richard Jr. from 1908 uses Tagalog nicknames, with "Dick" becoming "Ding" and Papa becoming "Papang." Author's personal collection.

The end of the Spanish-American war, the potential for American imperialism, the rise of anthropology as a discipline, and the popularity of displays showcasing "exotic" peoples at fairs and expositions in the early twentieth century all came together to create a sort of mechanism in which colonialism could provide entertainment; anthropology could make this entertainment seem educational and worthwhile; and public interest in these shows could be used to increase awareness and appreciation of the new anthropological sciences. Not all anthropologists were in favor of these displays. However, as Parezo and Fowler point out, this relationship helped anthropologists "legitimize their field of study, broker their specialized knowledge, and prove their status as 'scientists'" (2007, 8). My great-grandfather's career can be looked at more closely here, providing a case study.

SCHNEIDEWIND AND ANTHROPOLOGY

Without anthropology, Richard Schneidewind would never have been a showman. In many important ways, Schneidewind's career resulted directly from the actions of anthropologist Albert Jenks. Sometime in 1905 Schneidewind started the Filipino Exhibition Company with partner Edmond Felder, and the company's first engagement was that year at the Lewis and Clark Exhibition in Portland, Oregon. In an interview published by the *Los Angeles Times* on January 28, 1906, Schneidewind describes the reason for his first trip to Bontoc to recruit Igorot tribespeople. He explains, "Late in May . . . I heard that Dr. Jenks, chief of the Ethnological Survey for the Philippine Islands, had agreed to the sending of a band of Bontoc Igorrotes to the Lewis and Clark Exposition at Portland, provided he could get someone to bring them over. I was then in the service of the Philippine government, and tendered my services." Once he arrived in Bontoc, while visiting a club frequented by Americans, Schneidewind "encountered Antero, the bright English-speaking native boy, serving as a waiter. When Antero learned my mission he told me he would like to go again to America" (*Los Angeles Times* 1906).

It makes sense that Jenks, who recruited Philippine tribal peoples to go to St. Louis, would continue this role in Portland. He literally wrote the book on the Bontoc tribe, and his need to get Igorots to the Lewis and Clark Exposition opened the door for Schneidewind to enter into the business. Antero Cabrera, who introduced himself to Schneidewind and asked to be included, would become Schneidewind's chief translator and very influential with the press. He already had a history of working with Westerners as not only a servant, but as an ethnographic interlocutor. According to Afable, he had worked with Reverend Walter Clapp on a Bontoc dictionary and had been a houseboy in the Bontoc home of Jenks and his wife, learning excellent English in the process. He had also been part of Hunt's group in St. Louis. Antero's relationship with anthropologist Jenks was largely responsible for his desire to work with Schneidewind (Afable 2004, 459).

Schneidewind appears to have acknowledged his debt to anthropology—or, conversely, taken advantage of the legitimacy the discipline conferred, in many of the materials used to promote his Igorrote Villages. These brochures (which may have been written by Schneidewind, either on his own or working with Felder) discussed such ethnographic details as terraced gardening, headhunting practices, and the ritual of eating dogs. The brochures appear to have used Jenks's ethnography

Fig. 12. Antero Cabrera, photo courtesy of Richard Schneidewind Papers, Bentley Historical Library, University of Michigan.

as source material, although the brochures include information that either goes beyond or contradicts what is found in Jenks's book.

Jenks, for instance, discusses the dog eating ritual of the Bontoc Igorot (the tribe displayed by Schneidewind) as purely ceremonial, taking place at weddings and funerals (1905, 142). A more contemporary account written by Bel S. Castro discusses the ritual consumption of dogs, both in the past and in the present, where it has come to be associated with cleansing rituals after conflict (2007, 74). Neither description of the ritual aligns with the pamphlet distributed by Schneidewind at the 1909 Alaska-Yukon-Pacific Exposition, which argues, for instance, that women are forbidden from eating dog "because it is considered to have a quality which nerves up the fighter for the headhunting expeditions, and the Igorrotes do not care to have their women fight." The pamphlet continues, somewhat sensationally, stating that the Bontoc Igorot would not agree to come to the U.S. until they "exacted a promise that their customs would not be interfered with, and they are allowed to have their favorite dish at the village" (*Igorrote Village* 1909). According to Jenks, the Bontoc preferred chicken, pork, fish, and carabao (a type of water buffalo) to dog, which was certainly not a "favorite dish" (1905, 140). It is possible that Schneidewind and Felder contributed their own ethnographic information gleaned through close contact with the Igorot people they had recruited and managed, but it seems much more likely that the truth was sometimes stretched or even ignored to create better copy.

Despite the tone of the section of the pamphlet on dog eating, other topics presented in the pamphlet do reflect Igorot life of the time more accurately, with passages about trial marriage, governance, and irrigation. Self-consciously anthropological terminology is also used, with a section noting the Bontoc Igorot have no "head man," and another indicating the group's "Malay" race. The perspective taken by Putnam in 1893 Chicago is evident as well. The pamphlet describes the "Igorrotes" as "a people thousands of years backward in the scale of civilization" whose "presence affords visitors . . . an opportunity to study at close range these interesting and likable children of nature, who are still in the childhood of a race" (*Igorrote Village* 1909).

The cover of the pamphlet seeks to attract attention via a portrait of "The Head Hunter's Return," showing a triumphant headhunter grasping his victim's head by its hair (a notation under the image reports that it was copyrighted in 1906 by the Filipino Exhibition Company). A fine line had to be walked between providing educational content and keeping the public titillated enough to purchase tickets.

AN EXPOSITION OF THE LIFE OF A
REMARKABLE PRIMITIVE WILD PEOPLE

IGORROTE VILLAGE

HEAD HUNTING, DOG EATING WILD
PEOPLE FROM THE PHILIPPINES

The Head Hunter's Return
COPYRIGHTED, 1908, THE FILIPINO EXHIBITION CO.

THE STAR FEATURE OF THE PAY STREAK
ALASKA-YUKON-PACIFIC EXPOSITION Seattle

Fig. 13. Pamphlet from Alaska-Yukon-Pacific Exposition, photo courtesy of Richard Schneidewind Papers, Bentley Historical Library, University of Michigan.

Fig. 14. Pamphlet from Alaska-Yukon-Pacific Exposition, photo courtesy of Richard Schneidewind Papers, Bentley Historical Library, University of Michigan.

"Living as They Live at Home"

IGORROTE WAR DANCE

the village teems with the life of a people thousands of years backward in the scale of civilization, struggling to solve the play of the mysterious forces of nature.

THE PEOPLE

AMONG the more than one hundred tribes of the Philippine Islands, the Igorrote is one of the most conspicuous, and easily the most interesting, because of his strange method of life and still stranger customs. So little known is he that today he would be as great a curiosity in the City of Manila as here. He is of Malay origin, the "brown man," without negroid kinship, of a superb bronze color, long straight hair, and remarkable physique, although as a rule not tall. He is the only native man in the Philippine Islands with a keen sense of humor. In all his movements he is singularly graceful. The men wear a breech-clout, called "gee-string," and a picturesque little hat, which is not worn as a head covering, but as a pocket. The women wear a short skirt and queer jacket, made of native woven cloth.

POCKET HAT MAKERS

The Igorrote is a pagan, the basis of his religion being animism, the wide-spread belief of every man in the spirit world. In some strange way he has grasped the idea of one god, Lu-ma-wig, who had a part in the beginning of all things, who lived with them twice as a man in Bontoc and taught them all they know that is worth while, and who still lives in the sky above to care for them. There is no priesthood. Any Igorrote may appeal to Lu-ma-wig direct.

He is a barbarian in culture, having escaped from savagery through the necessity of earning his living. Unable to cultivate the lowlands because of floods, he terraces the mountain sides with stones, forming "sementeras," where he grows rice in the dry season, while others grow theirs in the wet season. This is accomplished by diverting streams so that they will irrigate the sementeras. This is properly shown in the Village on an impressive scale.

Fig. 15. Pamphlet from Alaska-Yukon-Pacific Exposition, photo courtesy of Richard Schneidewind Papers, Bentley Historical Library, University of Michigan.

HUNTS HEADS

FOR generations untold he has been a fierce hunter of human heads. There is constant warfare between neighboring towns, and head hunting is not only a means of self-defense, but, in a measure, a pastime, for after a member has taken and brought home the head of an enemy, a month is given over to happy celebration. There are rites and ceremonies peculiar to the event, and there are constant dances and feasts, which bring to the otherwise hard-worked people relaxation and social intercourse.

EATS DOGS

ALL IGORROTES eat dog. It is a tribal dish. No female, however, is permitted to partake of dog flesh, because it is considered to have a quality which nerves up the fighter for the head-hunting expeditions, and the Igorrotes do not care to have their women fight. Before agreeing to come to this country, the Igorrotes exacted a promise that their customs would not be interfered with, and they are allowed to have their favorite dish at the Village. The dogs are carried to the "a-to," or public building, the throat cut, the dog bled, singed, dressed, cut up, boiled and served in true Bontoc style.

WEAVING NATIVE CLOTHS ON HER SIMPLE LOOM

Fig. 16. Photo of weaver from Alaska-Yukon-Pacific Exposition, photo courtesy of Richard Schneidewind Papers, Bentley Historical Library, University of Michigan.

Perhaps unexpectedly, given Schneidewind's tendency to play fast and loose with ethnographic data on the Bontoc, there are several occurrences in which the villages were used to inform anthropology, reinforcing the notion that these shows were a valuable ethnographic resource. Through my research I have become aware of three instances where academic research was undertaken within the villages themselves, with some efforts being more successful than others. These efforts fit loosely into three categories: cultural anthropology, biological anthropology, and linguistics.

Haddon's Cultural Research

One of the most successful locations for the Igorrote Village in terms of number of visitors and revenue was the Alaska-Yukon-Pacific Exposition held in Seattle, Washington in 1909. Newspaper reports from Seattle published that summer recount a series of events involving Cambridge anthropologist Alfred Cort Haddon, who was teaching a summer class, "Stages of Cultural Evolution around the Pacific," at the University of Washington. Haddon appears to have used the exposition as a source of field trips for his class. Throughout the summer, he took students to see various cultural groups on display. According to the reports, Haddon brought a dog with him on a reconnaissance visit to the village in order to obtain permission for the dog to be used for the infamous "dog feast" of the Igorots while his class of twelve students observed. Before permission could be obtained, however, Haddon's dog was slaughtered, requiring him to find a second dog to be eaten during his class field trip. The *Seattle Times* takes a humorous tone, making fun of the absentminded professor and his "students of a strong ethnic bent," but notes that Haddon claimed the observations were being done for science. The article concludes, "While this barbaric spectacle was being enacted, Prof. Hadden [*sic*] and his scientific protégés gravely took copious notes, from which the professor will later draw his material for a chapter to be incorporated in a prospective book on strange fancies about strange tribes" (*Seattle Times* 1909).

CAMBRIDGE DON
DINES ON DOG

English University Instructo
Partakes of Igorrote
Delicacy

'TWAS HIS OWN FID(

Igorrotes Made Him Furnish th
Canine, and It Cost

P.I. — July 18

Prof. A. C. Haddon, reader in ethnology in the Cambridge University, England, dined upon dog yesterday morning, with a dozen Igorrotes as mess-
mates. The canine banquet took place
in the Igorrote village on the Pay
Streak, and, saving the presence of
Prof. Haddon and a half dozen students
of the University of Washington, who
have been in attendance

Figs. 17 & 18. Haddon
news clippings (loose),
photo courtesy of Richard
Schneidewind Papers,
Bentley Historical Library,
University of Michigan.

The article notes that this visit was the last made by Haddon to the exposition. Immediately afterward, he boarded a steamship to take him to study the salmon fishing habits of Washington's North Coast Indi-ans. I have searched for any mention of the Bontoc Igorot tribes and the "dog feast" in Haddon's writings, but have yet to find any references (I don't believe he ever used the phrase "strange fancies about strange tribes" in his work). Whatever Haddon learned from the Igorrote Village in Seattle, he seems to have been kept to himself.

Kroeber's Biological Research

Biological anthropology conducted in one of Schneidewind's Igorrote Villages did result in a publication, albeit a small one. After the Lewis and Clark Exposition in Portland closed, Schneidewind moved the group to Central Park in San Francisco starting on November 4, 1905. In the "Anthropologic Miscellanea" section of the January 1906 issue of *American Anthropologist*, there is a paragraph by Alfred Kroeber, "Measurements of Igorotes," along with an accompanying chart (Kroeber 1906, 194–95). Kroeber includes such information as shoulder height, color, forearm length, and the cephalic and nasal indices of eighteen men and seven women, explaining that the data came "courtesy of Mr. R. Schneidewind, manager of the Filipino Exhibition Company's Igorot village recently displayed in San Francisco." Kroeber's conclusions focused on how close in average height the women were to the men (suggesting that this surprisingly close measure came from the men's group having a "preponderance of very young men") and that the "women gave the impression of being darker than the men."

No ethnographic information was included in this particular document, but it seems likely that this encounter with a group of Bontoc Igorot people had some influence on Kroeber's interest in the peoples of the Philippines. For example, in 1918 Kroeber authored a work titled, "A History of Philippine Civilization as Reflected in Religious Nomenclature." Kroeber's approach in this work seems to have been a linguistic analysis of different Igorot languages with a special focus on religious terminology in order to determine "the cultural relationships of the several Philippine peoples" (39).

Although the Bontoc dictionary compiled by Carl Wilhelm Seidenadel (which will be discussed below) had been published in 1909, and Alfred Jenks published a significant ethnography of the Bontoc Igorot in 1906, Kroeber cites neither Seidenadel nor Jenks in this work (which, to be fair, looked beyond just the Bontoc tribe). Neither does Kroeber appear to be working from any kind of ethnographic data, including his own 1905 visit to the Igorrote Village in San Francisco. Instead, he concentrates primarily on a dictionary of Philippine mythology published by Ferdinand Blumentritt in 1895, describing it as "an assemblage of practically all religious names reported from the Philippines up to 1895" (9). From this source, Kroeber creates a comparative list of terms used by distinct Philippine populations, looking for similarities and differences and discussing what these findings reveal.

Kroeber concludes from this analysis of religious terms in the Philippines that the Igorot tribes have unique characteristics, compared to the rest of the Philippine population, even as individual Igorot vary from each other: "The Igorot group is sharply marked off from all other peoples on the islands. Practically all the terms shared by any Igorot tribe with any other tribe are shared with other Igorot tribes, and with them only" (41), Kroeber goes on to state that the Igorot people are also unusual in the Philippines in terms of "physical type and speech" and remarks that the Igorot people, "in spite of their apparent unity as against the remainder of the Filipinos, and in spite also of the comparative crowding of their several divisions into a small geographical compass, have diversified considerably *inter se*" (42). Some attention is given to the Bontoc people (whose tribe members he encountered at the Igorrote Village in San Francisco), although Kroeber spells their name as Bontok, and only speaks of them to draw comparisons between their group and other Igorot peoples like the Ifugao and Kalinga.

The sole section where his research with Schneidewind's group may have provided any direct influence comes in his section on race. Here, Kroeber follows an argument made by L. R. Sullivan, author of "Racial types in the Philippine Islands," that "the Philippines contain native groups belonging to at least three racial types: the Negrito and two brown skinned, straight haired stocks. Of these two brown stocks, the one prevailing among the interior and less advanced peoples is shorter, longer headed, and broader nosed then the type dominant on the coasts and lowlands among the more advanced peoples" (56). Kroeber considers whether the "less advanced" group resulted from a mixture of the other two groups, but finally argues that the texture of the hair and shape of the head do not support this conclusion. Instead, he theorizes that perhaps the physical bodies of these Philippine peoples became modified due to different physical environments (57).

It is in these passages that we can see some echo of Kroeber's attempts to measure the Igorots traveling with Richard Schneidewind's exhibit, those men and women from whom Kroeber took detailed measurements of height, arm and finger lengths, skin color, head and nostril shape, etc. It would appear that Kroeber was a novice at such physiological studies, however, because in his 1906 article he makes no mention of hair texture, a feature that later seems to be important to both Kroeber and Sullivan in distinguishing between the Negrito and other Philippine types. Putting aside the questionable validity of this type of research, particularly when seen from the perspective of contemporary anthropology, it is clear that although Kroeber visited the Igorrote Village with scholarly intent, and may have even been somewhat intellectually inspired by the visit, it did not lead directly to any major academic findings or publications.

Seidenadel's Linguistic Research

The third example of research done in the Igorrote Village is a linguistic study carried out by Carl Wilhelm Seidenadel. Although Seidenadel was not an anthropologist *per se*, he produced a work, published in 1909, titled *The First Grammar of the Language Spoken by the Bontoc Igórot, with a Vocabulary and Texts, Mythology, Folk-Lore, Historical Episodes, Songs* (sic) that included a large quantity of cultural information and was reviewed by Franz Boas's student Alexander F. Chamberlain for an issue of *American Anthropologist* in 1910.

Seidenadel's large tome includes information on grammar, vocabulary, and texts, totaling 590 pages. In his preface, Seidenadel describes conducting the research at Riverview Park in Chicago (which is, incidentally, where my great-grandparents met) in the summer and fall of 1906 and the spring and summer of 1907.

Interestingly, perhaps to ward off associations with recent sensational news stories, Seidenadel spends a good portion of his preface describing just how ideal the park was for all involved, including the Igorots, a place of "well built houses and humane treatment" (Seide-

HONEYMOON TO BE SPENT WITH BAND OF FILIPINO SAVAGES

MR. AND MRS. RICHARD SCHNEIDEWIND.

Honeymoon journeys in company with a band of Filipino head hunters are not common in America. Yet that is the experience which Mr. and Mrs. Richard Schneidewind are to enjoy.

The groom is a Detroit man and the bride was Miss Selma Eichholz,

Schneidewind has exhibited the people at Los Angeles, Cal., Chicago and other places throughout the country. It was during the stay in Chicago that he became acquainted with Miss Eichholz.

Mr. Schneidewind has become much attached to the head-hunters. He attributes to them a mental ability superior to that of many of the

Fig. 19. Wedding Announcement in *Detroit Free Press*, October 4, 1906. Available through Newspapers.com

nadel 1909, vii) and explaining how Schneidewind's group was joined by another group of Igorots who had been working for Dr. Truman K. Hunt and who, due to abuses suffered under Hunt's management, had been placed with Schneidewind's group by an order of a Federal Court (for an engaging account of the Igorot performers' successful lawsuit against Hunt, see Prentice, 2014).

Seidenadel discusses the initial difficulties he encountered in his research due to the unfamiliarity of the Igorots with English; he explains that his subsequent approach of conducting his research entirely in Bontoc was a "blessing." He was helped further when the aforementioned Antero, who had been traveling with another group, returned to Chicago and assisted Seidenadel with revisions and clarifications of the material he had gathered without the aid of a translator. The work that resulted from Seidenadel's research was considered very successful and a clear improvement on previous attempts to record the language.

MIXED RESULTS

It should be clear from these examples that academic work by anthropologists (and of interest to anthropologists) was indeed attempted within the "Igorrote Villages" managed by Schneidewind. It is interesting to consider, however, whether the research produced work of any lasting value. The influence of Franz Boas and Bronislaw Malinowski was growing, and with it a commitment to studying cultures through fieldwork, specifically participant-observation, ideally in the language of the people being studied. Rather than conducting their research on the Bontoc Igorot peoples in Bontoc, the way Jenks (and later S. C. Simms) did, Haddon, Kroeber, and Seidenadel went to expositions and amusement parks and attempted research in a mock-up of the kind of village that could be found in Bontoc among people who, rather than living their normal, daily lives, recreated the most crowd-drawing elements of their culture, including war dances, spear throwing, tree climbing, fire making, dog feasts, and "sham battles," often completely out of context.

If the goal had been to produce an ethnography of Igorot *performers*, this would have been ideal. However, we find with Haddon, for example, that "research" was being conducted in a single afternoon, in a hurry, and with the focus on an isolated instance of a particular ritual. So-called dog feasts were rare in Bontoc, but public interest resulted in them occurring with great frequency during the shows, often to the irritation of the performers. Although Haddon told the press that he was conducting research for a book, it is clear that his real successes as an anthropologist came from prolonged study among peoples with whom he was much more familiar, such as his work in Borneo. The dog feast in Seattle was probably a diverting field trip, but not much more.

As for Kroeber, although he was an accomplished ethnographer, his work in the Igorrote Village in San Francisco was apparently not an attempt to study Igorot cultural activities. Instead, he gathered information on various physical characteristics of the performers, following Aleš Hrdlicka's *Directions for Collecting Information and Specimens for Physical Anthropology*. Although Kroeber's later studies of Philippine peoples were more ethnographic in nature, context here was probably much less important, and the presence of the village allowed for quick data collection that would not even have taken place had it not been so convenient. This research was successful, but certainly not very ambitious.

In contrast, Seidenadel's work appears to have been conducted over the long term, mostly in the Bontoc language, and with the cooperation of several key informants. Seidenadel was studying language, and the Bontoc performers were active and current speakers of Bontoc. They may have been enacting rituals and other cultural activities as a form of performance, but their use of language and recounting of folk tales were authentic. I feel compelled to add, however, that indispensable interlocutor Antero Cabrera, following the convincing logic of Roger Sanjek's "Anthropology's Hidden Colonialism: Assistants and their Ethnographers," should have been made a co-author of several publications, including Seidenadel's work (Sanjek 1993). Without Cabrera's input, Seidenadel's work would likely have been considerably weaker—Afable (2004) shows this was true for the work of Clapp and Jenks as well.

In the end, it seems that my great-grandfather's career and the discipline of anthropology were intimately entwined, with real research in the "Igorrote Villages" being possible, at least for particular topics, as long as these artificial sets were studied long term and with an appreciation for what was actually taking place.[1] Patricia Afable was able to conduct ethnographic research relating to the fairs after the fact, interviewing the descendants of those persons who traveled with Schneidewind and Hunt, and working to reconstruct the emic perspective. She and I have wistfully discussed the lost opportunity of doing ethnography during the shows themselves to unearth how this strange chapter

The Ev
GRAND RAPIDS, M

EVEN IGORROTES READ THE PRESS

—Staff Photographer.

tero, the Igorrote interpreter, who speaks and reads English, gets his
news from The Evening Press.

Fig. 20. Antero Cabrera, *Grand Rapids Evening Press*, photo courtesy of Richard
Schneidewind Papers, Bentley Historical Library, University of Michigan.

in the history of the Bontoc Igorot people was truly understood from the inside. Despite this missed chance, it is plain that the "Igorrote Villages" and the field of anthropology were mutually beneficial, if only in the very short term.

NOTES

Images from the Bentley Historical Library were donated by Deana L. Weibel

1. Richard Schneidewind ended his career as a showman after 1915, as interest in human zoos began to gradually dwindle. A European tour with the Igorots turned out disastrously, with several Bontoc performers claiming abandonment in Ghent, Belgium, and one performer, Timicheg, dying during the tour (see Weibel 2014). Schneidewind's last stand as an impresario was at the San Francisco Panama-Pacific Exposition of 1915, displaying a group from Samoa (Rydell 1984, 282). His work after the fairs was varied and transitory, including employment with a streetcar company, a clerical job at an office supply business, and—as my mother remembers well—manufacturing industrial disks during the Great Depression using a machine set up in his backyard. He died on January 4, 1949, a few weeks after his seventy-second birthday.

REFERENCES

Afable, Patricia O. 2004. "Journeys from Bontoc to the Western Fairs, 1904–1915: The 'Nikimalika' and their Interpreters." *Philippine Studies* 52, no. 4: 445–73.
Ben Chikha, Chokri, and Karel Arnaut. 2013. "Staging/caging otherness in the postcolony: spectres of the human zoo." *Critical Arts* 27, no. 6: 661–83.
Blumentritt, Ferdinand. 1895. *Diccionario Mitológico de Filipinas*. Madrid: Viuda de M. Minuesa de los Rios.
Buckner, Jocelyn L. 2010. "Ota the Other: An African on Display in America." *Theatre History Studies* 30, no. 1: 154–75.
Castro, Bel S. 2007. "Food, Morality, and Politics: The Spectacle of Dog-Eating Igorots at the 1904 St. Louis World Fair." In *Food and Morality: Proceedings of the Oxford Symposium on Food and Cookery*, edited by Susan R. Friedland, 70–81. London: Prospect Books.
Chamberlain, Alexander F. 1910. "The First Grammar of the Language Spoken by the Bontoc Igórot, with a Vocabulary and Texts, Mythology, Folk-Lore, Historical Episodes, Songs. By Dr Carl Wilhelm Seidenadel." *American Anthropologist* 12, no. 2: 321–23.

Clapp, Rev. Walter Clayton. 1908. *A Vocabulary of the Igorot Language as Spoken by the Bontok Igorots*. Manila: Bureau of Printing.

Hinsley, Curtis M. 2016. "Anthropology as Education and Entertainment: Frederic Ward Putnam at the World's Fair." In *Coming of Age in Chicago: The 1893 World's Fair and the Coalescence of American Anthropology*. Lincoln: University of Nebraska Press.

Hrdlička, Aleš. 1904. *Directions for collecting information and specimens for physical anthropology*, vol. 39. U.S. Government Printing Office.

Igorrote Village, An Exposition of the Life of a Remarkable Primitive Wild People, Head Hunting, Dog Eating, Wild People from the Philippines. Seattle: University Publishing, 1909.

Jenks, Albert Ernest. 1905. *The Bontoc Igorot*, vol. 1. Manila: Bureau of Public Printing.

Kroeber, Alfred Louis. 1918. *The History of Philippine Civilization as Reflected in Religious Nomenclature*. New York: AMS Press.

———. 1906. "Measurements of Igorotes." *American Anthropologist* 8: 194–95.

Los Angeles Times. 1906. "Hard to Get Igorrotes," January 28, 1906.

McKay, J. K. 1907. Untitled Memo, Bureau of Insular Affairs (War Department), June 3, 1907.

Morgan, Lewis Henry. 1877. *Ancient Society; or, Researches in the Lines of Human Progress from Savagery, through Barbarism to Civilization*. New York: Henry Holt.

Parezo, Nancy J., and Don D. Fowler. 2007. *Anthropology Goes to the Fair: The 1904 Louisiana Purchase Exposition*. Lincoln: University of Nebraska Press.

Prentice, Claire. 2014. *The Lost Tribe of Coney Island: Headhunters, Luna Park, and the Man who Pulled Off the Spectacle of the Century*. Amazon Publishing: New Harvest.

Rydell, Robert W. 1984. *All the World's a Fair: Visions of Empire at American International Expositions, 1876–1916*. Chicago: University of Chicago Press.

Sanjek, Roger. 1993. "Anthropology's Hidden colonialism: Assistants and their Ethnographers." *Anthropology Today* 9, no. 2: 13–18.

Seattle Times. 1909. "Headhunters Eat Dog at Fair," July 18, 1909.

Seidenadel, Carl Wilhelm. 1909. *The First Grammar of the Language Spoken by the Bontoc Igorot, with a Vocabulary and Texts, Mythology, Folklore, Historical episodes, Songs*. Chicago: Open Court.

Simms, Stephen Chapman. 1908. "Bontoc Igorot Games." *American Anthropologist* 10, no. 4: 563–67.

Weibel, Deana L. 2014. "A Savage at the Wedding and the Skeletons in My Closet." In *Mutuality: Anthropology's Changing Terms of Engagement*, edited by Roger Sanjek, 99–117. Philadelphia: University of Pennsylvania Press.

6

Indigenous Studies in Argentina

Anthropology, History, and Ethnohistory from the 1980s

In memoriam Raúl Mandrini, Ana María Lorandi, Maria Bechis, and Daniel Villar

This chapter analyzes the development of studies concerning indigenous peoples in Argentina during the last thirty years, since the mid-1980s, when the return of democracy allowed for substantial changes in academic spaces and indigenous peoples' movements started to gain visibility in this country.[1] The first section is devoted to a brief history of native peoples in the country and state policies to provide adequate context, followed by a second section that addresses studies from anthropology, ethnohistory, and history (or historiography), paying special attention to social conditions and academic spaces built to foster new perspectives. A third section focuses on case studies concerning indigenous peoples in the Pampas and Patagonia. My main sources for this section are academic papers, and conference abstracts, combined with semi-structured interviews with historians, anthropologists, and archaeologists, supplemented by their curricula vitae. The methodological approach is mostly qualitative and uses techniques of network analysis and documentary observation.

Any research about indigenous studies in Argentina must start with a few important clarifications. First, there is a wide field of studies concerning indigenous peoples in this country, encompassing different disciplines and approaches, but the term is very recent. One would expect any specialist to describe their own practice as anthropology, history, or ethnohistory, rather than indigenous studies. Second, while the term "indigenous studies" in English has a double meaning—including both studies about indigenous peoples and studies about indigenous peoples made *by* indigenous peoples—that is not the case for Argentina, where most scholars do not have, or acknowledge, native heritage.

Along with a constant growth of studies involving indigenous peoples, Argentinian anthropologists have also started doing research about the history of anthropology and what was called, in an Argentinian context, ethnohistory and historical anthropology. As a result, there are a vast array of papers about many topics: museums and preservation policies,[2] institutional features and group and personal trajectories throughout the twentieth century,[3] theoretical perspectives (Name 2012) and analyses that combine both social and theoretical histories for specific contexts,[4] and studies of the evolution of ethnohistory in Argentina.[5] Historians still have not produced a thorough reflection of the importance of indigenous peoples' history, except for some contributions by Raúl Mandrini (2007, 2015). This paper is situated within this wider background and provides an account of social and academic conditions for the emergence and evolution of indigenous studies in the Pampas and Patagonia, bearing in mind the overall context of social sciences in Argentina and previous experience of key research scholars in the field.

INDIGENOUS PEOPLES IN ARGENTINA

The territory that now constitutes Argentina had—and still has—many indigenous peoples with diverse socioeconomic systems, languages, and cultural practices. The Spanish conquerors adapted their domination strategies to these groups and were more or less successful in imposing their domination, taking into account settling patterns, demographic features, possibilities for Spaniards to obtain valuable resources (mainly gold and silver in mountains), and rivalries among indigenous peoples that could endanger colonial settlements. This pattern of domination characterized the colonial and republican periods until the late nineteenth century, when genocidal practices took place through military attacks, territorial dispossession, and removal of indigenous peoples in Chaco and Pampas and Patagonia.[6] Hence, a brief account of this history is necessary to understand the way in which indigenous studies evolved in Argentina.

In the northwest region of what is now Argentina, by the late fifteenth century, Inca armies had started incorporating some of the indigenous peoples in their powerful empire, but it was not equally successful everywhere. While a certain cultural uniformity was imposed (the use of Quechua language, metal use, agricultural techniques, and the expansion of roads and urban areas), its brief domination could not erase regional differences or old ethnic rivalries (Mandrini 2008, 165). People situated in the south of this area (what is now the eastern part of the provinces Salta, Tucumán, and Catamarca, in addition to the northwest of Santiago del Estero province) witnessed several conflicts between those peoples and some of Amazonian origin. To the south (on the central mountains of the current provinces Cordoba and San Luis) agriculturally based groups shared cultural features with the southern Andes, mainly in the production of textiles. In the north and east, hunting, gathering, and fishing were the main economic activities of people in the Chaco region and in the area besides the biggest rivers in the east (Parana, Paraguay, and Uruguay). In the South, and from what is now the grasslands of Buenos Aires province, La Pampa province, and Patagonia (current provinces of Rio Negro, Neuquén, Chubut, Santa Cruz, and Tierra del Fuego), several hunter-gatherer groups populated the vast plains and the mountains that provided abundant resources (Mandrini 2008; Melia 2000).

The arrival of Spanish conquerors had a tremendous impact on some of these populations.[7] By the mid-sixteenth century, the penetration into indigenous people's territories started on the northwest (following the routes of the Inca empire). But natives peoples' resistance was strong (such as the rebellions of Calchaquí Valleys)[8] and Spanish domination was imposed by the mid-seventeenth century, mainly through *encomiendas*.[9] In the eastern area (Paraguay and part of what is now Misiones province), by the early seventeenth century, Jesuit priests established missions that lasted until the late eighteenth century.[10] In the mid-eighteenth century, this religious order tried to establish a similar system of indigenous labor force exploitation in the south (on Buenos Aires plains), but they were unsuccessful because of native peoples' resistance.

While most of the indigenous population in what now constitutes the provinces of Jujuy, Salta, Santiago del Estero, Catamarca, La Rioja, San Juan, Cordoba, Mendoza, and southern Santa Fe was incorporated into this colonial system, those groups located outside the Potosi-Buenos Aires corridor (see map) resisted and exerted control over their territories until the late nineteenth century. After declaring independence from the Spanish Crown, republican governments were busier in trying to secure their territories instead of conquering new ones, since war among different provinces was common between the 1820s and 1870.[11]

But after national unification (a process that started in the 1860 and was consolidated in 1880), a unified federal policy broke indigenous peoples' resistance. Military attacks took place from 1878–79 and 1881–85 in the Pampas and Patagonia regions, and between 1884 and 1917 in the Chaco region. They were followed by relocations, family and group separations, reclusion in concentration camps, statistical invisibility in the national census, and very small land allotments to individual families in agricultural colonies. Thus, indigenous people were forced to live in marginal areas. In what is now Chaco and Formosa provinces, they survived by fishing, hunting, and gathering. In Pampas and Patagonia, they worked as herders and hunters; and in both areas they labored as seasonal migrant workers with the lowest wages and the worst conditions. The assimilationist policies imposed by the national government were consistent with the political project of eliminating "barbarism" (in Sarmiento's term) from the building of a nation. It would soon become clear that diversity could be included only as long as new inhabitants came from Europe.

This type of foundational narrative located indigenous peoples only in the past—not as a living part of the nation—a project that permeated academic spaces until the late twentieth century. In this context, indigenous peoples' claims over territory and rights were sporadic and rarely collective. But the twentieth century witnessed some attempts for organization, with different levels of success.[12] In the mid-1980s, with the return of democracy in Argentina after the genocidal dictatorship of 1976–83, indigenous peoples had the chance to start taking their claims for their rights to every provincial government and at a national level. During this decade, almost all provincial constitutions included indigenous rights, and in 1989 a first federal law was passed (N° 23.302), creating the National Institute of Indian Affairs (INAI). In 1992, ILO-Convention 169 was ratified by the federal government, and in 1994, when the National Constitution was amended, it incorporated article 75, clause 17, which recognized the preexistence of aboriginal peoples. Although these legal provisions did not solve native peoples' problems, and the last two decades have witnessed both progress and setbacks in the effective application and implementation of their rights, it is true that the indigenous movement has been constantly growing. This, in turn, has influenced research agendas by anthropologists and historians, as I will discuss in the next section.

INDIGENOUS STUDIES IN ARGENTINA

As mentioned in the introduction, studies related to indigenous peoples have taken place within disciplines such as anthropology and, more recently, history, as well as a new field in Argentina since the 1980s: ethnohistory. This section is devoted to such developments in these three areas. It is important to note that in this country, the university system is concentrated in bigger cities such as Buenos Aires, La Plata, Córdoba, and Rosario, where the largest number of researchers and resources are concentrated.

Anthropology

Anthropologists were the first scholars interested in studying indigenous peoples in Argentina. Since the late nineteenth and early twentieth centuries, explorers and naturalists (both Argentinian and European) sought to study indigenous peoples as remnants of a past that supposedly would soon disappear. As such, the creation of the Museum of Natural Sciences at La Plata in 1888 and the Ethnographic Museum in Buenos Aires in 1904 was part of a nation building project that exhibited indigenous peoples' body parts and their cultural artifacts at the same time they were considered a racial obstacle from the past and the present that could hamper the growth of a modern country (Podgorny 1999).

A general periodization of the development of anthropology in Argentina according to Ratier (2010) is the one that locates positivist beginnings between 1880–1930, followed by a predominance of culture-historical diffusionism (1930–59), professionalization (1959–66), censorship (1966–73), politicization (1973–74), repression and theoretical standstill (1974–83), and a renewal since the return of democracy, after 1983.

In general, in can be said that anthropologists in this country paid little attention to the three metropolitan anthropological traditions that would be hegemonic elsewhere during the twentieth century (i.e., British, French, and U.S. anthropologies) and even less to Mexican indigenism. Instead, there was a clear dominance of the German School of diffusion until the mid-1960s and even later. This was due to the arrival of scholars such as Jose Imbelloni (an Italian fascist ethnologist who arrived in Argentina in 1921), Marcelo Bórmida (an Italian fascist who arrived in 1946), and Oswaldo Menghin (an Austrian civil servant during the Nazi regime who fled to Argentina in 1948). These scholars achieved dominant positions in museums and universities due to their connections with the Peronist government (Vezub and De Oto 2011; Lazzari 2004). After World War II, Imbelloni facilitated, from his prominent position at the Ethnographic Museum, the settlement in Argentina of scientists and philosophers associated with fascist regimes in Central Europe (Vezub and De Oto 2011), such as Bórmida.[13]

The professionalization of anthropology was established after the overthrow of the Peronist government in 1955. The discipline started being taught at the universities of Buenos Aires (1958) and La Plata (1957). Jose Luis Romero, the new rector of Buenos Aires University, appointed Alberto Salas as Dean of the Facultad de Filosofía y Letras, whose mission was to reorganize the political, academic, scientific, and institutional situation of this academic unit (Perazzi 2003, 93). Other figures (such as Fernando Márquez Miranda and Enrique Palavecino), who had political and academic differences with the diffusionist group, were promoted to higher positions, but Bórmida retained his position as a tenured professor. Although historic-cultural diffusionism did not lose its significance, the creation of anthropology academic programs and renewal of authorities in national universities gave way to some other perspectives such as those coming from France and the U.S.

The emergence of social anthropology was a crucial change to anthropology in Argentina.[14] According to Guber (2007), this orientation did not come from social demands but rather from a series of factors such as political proscription, radicalization of young university students during the sixties, and the intervention of the executive power in Buenos Aires in 1966. Bórmida and Imbelloni were highly reluctant to incorporate social anthropology at the Institute of Anthropology. Instead, "Social Anthropology" was the name of a course in the Department and Institute of Sociology led by Gino Germani. The course included perspectives by Radcliffe-Brown, Malinowski, Boas, and Steward among others. Ralph Beals was invited to teach this course for a semester in 1962 and was later replaced by Abraham Monk; both of their syllabi featured authors such as Ralph Linton, Alfred Kroeber, Oscar Lewis, Ruth Benedict, and Robert Lowie (Guber 2007, 269). Also, some differences had arisen since Alberto Rex Gonzalez finished his PhD at Columbia University (as a disciple of Julian Steward) and started teaching at universities in Cordoba, Rosario, and La Plata from the 1950s to 1960s.[15] In those contexts, he was a strong influence for young scholars like Ana María Lorandi, to whom we will refer later as one of the main actors in the building of ethnohistory as a field of studies in Argentina. The unrest by anthropology students led to a meeting in Rosario in 1961 where theoretical perspectives expanded beyond diffusionism. Later, selection processes for teaching assistants allowed these young scholars to start introducing students to other readings and professional practices.[16] Moreover, the politicized students who asked for Menghin's removal due to his Nazi background, as well as the arrival of Esther Hermitte in 1965 as a new professor at the Department of Anthropological Sciences, paved the way for a rupture with the long-established tradition of historic-cultural diffusionism (Guber 2007, 281). However, the repression of teachers on the night of July 29, 1966—now known as "La noche de los bastones largos" (long sticks' night)—weakened this renewal, and the dictatorship of 1976–83 would only make things more difficult for scholars in the field of social anthropology. Several professors and students were missing, tortured, excluded from academic environments, and subjected to external and internal exiles. A strong surveillance over those academic programs that were kept (mainly the one in Misiones province, led by Leopoldo Bartolome) was combined with the closing of several programs related to social anthropology (as in Mar del Plata).

It was only by the mid-1980s, with the return of democracy, when some of these scholars came back, that anthropological perspectives were truly reinstated. But the context was now very different. Policies against social anthropology had an impact on social and academic relationships from the 1980s. Those who had taught or received their degrees between 1975 and 1983 were suspected of having collaborated with "anthropology of the dictatorship" and could sometimes be excluded from the new hierarchies that were being established as tenure processes advanced (Bartolome 2007, 21). A differentiation grew between training ages (before and after dictatorship); professorship (teaching or not during the dictatorship); and subdisciplines (ethnology, folklore studies, archaeologists, and physical anthropologists against social or cultural anthropologists). Hence, and especially at University of Buenos Aires, labels such as "ethnologist," "folklore expert," and even "archaeologist" were almost synonyms of dictatorship anthropology, while social anthropology came to be identified with democracy (Bartolome 2007, 22).

The renovation of theoretical approaches introduced the issue of ethnicity, with a strong influence of Brazilian scholars (such as Roberto Cardoso de Oliveira). Some universities, starting in the 1990s, started academic programs for graduate students and offered both MA and PhD degrees. While there was a strong interest among faculty in offering these graduate studies, the limited amount of teaching positions and the absence of institutional mechanisms to change graduate faculty hampered this tendency. Here, Brazil became a space for the formation of Argentinian social anthropologists and as a labor market for young graduates, and joint research programs were developed (Lins Ribeiro 2004; Bartolome 2007).

As a result, new topics were addressed, such as gender, interethnic relations, popular culture, ecology, urban issues, politics, and violence, among others. In that context, studies concerning indigenous peoples were also renovated, and an increasing political visibility during the 1990s made it possible for researchers to pay attention to previously disregarded areas.

Ethnohistory

The area of studies known as "ethnohistory," which some authors have considered to be a discipline, began in Latin America with the Congreso Internacional de Etnohistoria (International Congress of Eth-nohistory) (CEI).[17] Some of the main organizers of these institutions have been Franklin Pease in Peru, Ana María Lorandi in Argentina, José Luis Martínez in Chile, and a group of researchers from the Universidad Mayor de San Andrés (UMSA) in Bolivia.

Franklin Pease's team was based at the Pontifical Catholic University of Peru, and they organized the congresses in Lima in 1996 and 2008.[18] Pease and his colleagues at PUCP have had frequent contact with researchers from the French Institute for Andean Studies (IFEA), including Nathan Wachtel, Pierre Duviols, and Jacques-Poloni Simard. In fact, the first director of IFEA since its foundation in 1940, Jehan Vellard (doctor and ethnographer), taught at PUCP and at the University of San Marcos (Salazar-Soler 2007, 94). In the PUCP, ethnohistorical studies were carried out for the most part by historians.

In contrast, ethnohistorical studies in Argentina were fostered by anthropologists. This process started in the mid-1980s with the creation of the Ethnohistory Section in 1985 at the Institute of Anthropological Sciences of the UBA, under the direction of Ana María Lorandi.[19] This researcher, initially trained in archeology with A. Rex González, had contacted Murra at a conference on rock art in Huanuco in the 1960s and was closely linked to the French line of Andean ethnohistory studies led by Nathan Wachtel. The team—initially constituted by Lorandi, Ana María Presta, and Mercedes Del Río, along with other researchers and fellows—was responsible for the organization of the first Congreso Internacional de Etnohistoria (International Congress of Ethnohistory) (CEI) in 1989, followed by another that took place in Buenos Aires in 2005. Although some historians did participate, Lorandi herself points out that historians' relationship with ethnohistory specialists, and particularly with those at the University of Buenos Aires, had been quite a distant one; and that in Argentina, the area in which it was possible to promote ethnohistory was through institutes of anthropology.[20] Here, most ethnohistorical studies were concerned with Andean indigenous peoples, combining archaeological techniques with the ethnographic reading of historical documents. The University of Buenos Aires was not the only team; some other areas received attention in academic centers located in provinces such as Buenos Aires, Salta, Córdoba, Santa Fe, Mendoza, San Juan, and Neuquén, among others.[21]

The CEI, however, has shown that a growing number of scholars started being interested in other areas besides the Andes. But the CEI itself has had a tough time keeping regular meetings, mainly due to financial difficulties in Latin America. The gap between 1998 and 2005 is an example of this, but so are the complications in materializing the meeting in Arica planned for 2013, which finally took place in 2014. However, the number of presentations, which had been stable at an average of one hundred, increased during the last meeting, as shown in figure 21.[22]

History

Historians in Argentina have not been interested in indigenous peoples as important actors in historical processes. Until the mid-1990s there seemed to be a labor division between historians (who studied colonial settlers in different periods) and anthropologists, who were in charge of examining aspects of native peoples' lives either in the past or the present (Mandrini 2007). However, it is worth noting that some historians, such as Juan Carlos Garavaglia, Raúl Mandrini, Enrique Tandeter, Daniel Santamaria, and Silvia Palomeque were making important contributions since the mid-1980s (Palermo 1992), and they trained younger historians who increased the amount of history specialists working on these issues.

But this tradition of labor division between anthropologists and historians also had an impact on the development of historic archaeology. The early links between scientific archaeology and prehistory, and the period in which archaeology achieved academic status, resulted in archaeology becoming almost synonymous with the study of pre-Hispanic societies (Igareta y Schavelzon 2011, 20). This was, of course, related with the context of a nation-building project that located native peoples in the past. As Irina Podgorny explains, the book *Historia de la Nación Argentina* continued one of the teaching traditions of history established since the beginning of the twentieth century, where 'Argentine aborigines' and the results of archaeological studies car-

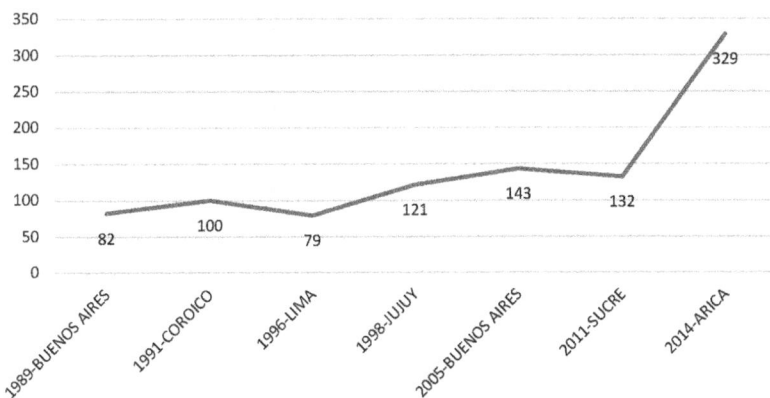

Fig. 21. Number of papers presented at the CEI, 1989–2014. Sources: Programa del Primer Congreso Internacional de Etnohistoria, Buenos Aires, Argentina, 1989; Arze, Silvia, Rossana Barragán, Laura Escobari, and Ximena Medinacelli (Eds.) *Etnicidad, economía y simbolismo en los Andes: II Congreso Internacional de Etnohistoria. Coroico.* La Paz: Instituto de historia social boliviana. HISBOL- Institut français d'études andines. IFEA-Sociedad Boliviana de Historia. SBH- Antropólogos del Sur Andino. ASUR, 1992; AA.VV. *Actas del IV Congreso Internacional de Etnohistoria,* Lima: Pontificia Universidad Católica del Perú, 1998; *Libro de resúmenes del V Congreso Internacional de Etnohistoria,* Jujuy, Argentina, 1998; *Programa del IV Congreso Internacional de Etnohistoria,* Buenos Aires, Argentina, 2005; *Segunda circular del VII Congreso Internacional de Etnohistoria,* Lima, Perú, 2008, accessed June 13, 2013, http://congreso .pucp.edu.pe/etnohistoria/2008/pdf/segunda_circular.pdf; Convocatoria al *VIII Congreso Internacional de Etnohistoria,* Sucre, 2011, accessed June 13, 2013, http://laboratoriodehistoriacolonial.wordpress.com/noticias/viii-congreso-de -etnohistoria-sucre-2011/; *Programa del IX Congreso Internacional de Etnohistoria, Colonización, Descolonización e Imaginarios,* Arica, Chile, 2014. I am deeply grateful to Ana María Lorandi, Roxana Boixados, and Daniel Villar, as well as the IFEA (Instituto Frances de Estudios Andinos, Peru) and the Library of the University of La Pampa for the copies of some of the printed versions of these programs.

ried out within the national territory had been equated with the initial chapter of the history of the nation" (2004, 148, my translation). This kind of tradition prevailed until the late 1980 and early 1990s, when some historians, like Raúl Mandrini, started building links with scholars from historic archaeology and anthropologists, as we will see in the next section.

This section focuses on the conditions of historiographical, anthropological, and archaeological academic production concerning native peoples in the Pampas and Patagonia regions, making a preliminary approximation to the gradual constitution of relations built by researchers and among research institutions. I am particularly interested in providing an account of the conformation of spaces of sociability that fostered exchanges, as well as their limitations.

The Beginnings and Subsequent Years

The history of the indigenous peoples of Pampa and Patagonia was not only of interest to anthropologists in Argentina since the nineteenth century, but also began to gain Argentine historians' attention little by little, though with a theoretical approach that still considered native peoples as a remnant of a barbarianism that would soon disappear. One of the milestones in which the national historiography reviewed the characteristics of the frontier policies was the "National Congress of History on the Conquest of the Desert," that took place in General Roca (Río Negro) from November 6–10, 1979 (Academia Nacional de la Historia, 1980). In the context of the dictatorship, it was a date in which it was hoped by the military rulers that the whole of this production and the congress itself would represent an area of vindication of the military campaigns of 1878–84.[23] For this reason, the proceedings were published in four volumes that included papers about frontier policies; the main creole protagonists of the area such as military officers, politicians, scientists, and technicians (Sarmiento, Álvaro Barros, Santiago Avendaño, Manuel Fernández Oro, Silvano Daza, Lino Oris de Roa, Eduardo Ramayón, among others); the economic aspects and the financing of the military campaign through the analysis of the contributions of provinces such as Buenos Aires, Córdoba, San Juan, Mendoza, Salta; press coverage; literary creations; and the situation immediately after the military campaign in terms of the delimitation of territorial spaces, economic policies; and actions by Salesian missions.

But a few years earlier, in the mid-1970s, initial inquiries had begun by those who would later become key scholars in the area, in some cases in the framework of archaeological research. For example, Daniel Villar, María Teresa Boschín, Lidia Nacuzzi, and Raúl Mandrini argued in their interviews that they were interested in indigenous peoples' history, and the first three had archaeological training. To a considerable extent, the turn toward reading documents as a technique was more related to the adverse conditions in the months before the dictatorship and the later years. Such conditions were related to lack of funding for archaeological research, having been excluded from teaching positions, and, in some cases, suffering internal exiles.

Nacuzzi, for instance, recounts:

> In the second quarter of 1974, I tried to take courses at the Facultad de Filosofía y Letras at the University of Buenos Aires. They were archaeologists and were digging sites in an archaeological rescue plan where the Chocón Dam would be built. They were interested that we, the students, could read about the area, the Limay river basin, to do a work of "ethnohistorical reconstruction." They presented it more or less in those terms. We only got two classes, then the University was intervened and classes were interrupted, among other disasters that happened.[24] In those classes, all the other students were interested in doing lytic typology. María Teresa Boschín and I started thinking about reading travelers' accounts, we were attracted by that proposal. But what definitely convinced us was that, after the Facultad was closed down, we could continue with that work at the National Library.[25]

In a similar vein, Daniel Villar comments:

> By the middle of 1974, I had been assigned for excavation archaeological sites in the Coronel Dorrego district (Buenos Aires province), with the purpose of undertaking the development of the work plan of my future doctoral thesis, a project that became frustrated by the intervention at the National University of the South (February 1975), and then it was abandoned due to the beginning of the dictatorship, when the equipment to which it was incorporated was dismembered. That intervention produced massive unemployment in the area of Social Sciences (which included the current Depart-

ment of Humanities) to which we belonged. Consequently, my teaching activity was necessarily interrupted until fifteen years later. [...] Archaeological activity requires equipment, infrastructure and institutional support that could not be available individually. That reality prevailed and determined my departure from this discipline. I then raised the need to look for issues that, referring also to the native populations of Pampas and northern Patagonia, addressed the problems from a perspective that allowed me to access other data, avoiding the limitations that in that context implied archaeological research.[26]

Several of these researchers suffered layoffs, and the youngest were new graduates who had not begun to work as teachers in the universities. Thus, a good part of them had to resort to work outside the academic scope or face exile, as we have described in the previous section.

It was only by the middle of the 1980s and the beginning of the next decade when they could rejoin national universities and begin to assemble their own teams. The classic works of this early period are those by Martha Bechis, Miguel Angel Palermo, and Raúl Mandrini. Palermo published several key studies between 1986 and 1989 (Palermo 1986, 1988, 1991, 1994, 1999), although he did not continue his activity in academic circles later. Mandrini, a historian specializing in the ancient and classical world, became interested in these issues through Alberto Rex González.[27] While rereading available sources in the light of processes that he knew for other contexts, and remaining in close contact with archaeologists of the Pampas and Patagonia region (such as Diana Mazzanti, Ana Biset, Gladys Varela, and Alicia Tapia among others)[28] he warned that the characterizations of indigenous peoples of the region as equestrian nomads, with an economy based on predation, were incompatible with the construction of dams and social and political indicators of hierarchical divisions, such as the practice of suttée (Mandrini 1994).

Also, by the early 1990s, anthropologist Claudia Briones finished her PhD studies at the University of Texas at Austin, and soon after her return, she assembled a team that would soon renovate perspectives about contemporary indigenous movements and ethnicity.[29] She introduced in Argentina theoretical approaches by Jeremy Beckett, Ana María Alonso, James Brow, and Lawrence Grossberg, among other authors, whose research allowed for a better understanding of social relationships, indigeneity, ethnicity, hegemony, and state building in local contexts.

The contacts between some of these scholars would soon take place, and in that sense the spaces of academic sociability described in the next section were fundamental. Throughout the decade of 2000, and within the framework of professionalization tendencies of the academic world in Argentina, numerous disciples of those first researchers finished their doctoral studies, and some of them formed their own teams in several universities of the country, consolidating this line.[30]

This was the way in which research lines were deepened and other related work began at the University of Buenos Aires (with scholars at the Ethnohistory Section such as Ingrid de Jong and Lidia Nacuzzi, and those at the Ethnology and Ethnography Section, such as Diana Lenton and Mariela Rodríguez); the National University of Río Cuarto (with joint work of historians and archaeologists such as Antonio Austral, Ana María Rocchietti, and Marcela Tamagnini); the National University of the Center of the Province of Buenos Aires (Tandil, with greater presence of historians such as Raúl Mandrini and Olavarría, with a greater number of archaeologists such as Gustavo Politis and Rafael Curtoni); the National University of the South in Bahía Blanca (with historians like Juan Francisco Jiménez and Daniel Villar, who was also a regular professor at National University of La Pampa Santa Rosa, La Pampa); the National Patagonian Center of CONICET in Puerto Madryn (with historians such as Julio Vezub and archaeologists such as María Teresa Boschín); the National University of Río Negro (with anthropologists like Claudia Briones, Ana Ramos, and Walter Delrio, among others); the National University of Comahue (with historian Enrique Mases, for instance); the National University of Quilmes (with historian Silvia Ratto among others); the and National University of San Martín (with anthropologist Axel Lazzari).

Spaces of Sociability: Congresses and Seminars

Raúl Mandrini played a key role in building social networks and academic spaces for exchanges during the 1980s. He recalled that one of the first meetings on these subjects was in Tandil: "I'm almost sure it was in 1987. They were Ana María [Biset] and Gladys [Varela], I think Daniel [Villar] and several archaeologists, like Diana Mazzanti, Gladys Ceresole, Monica Berón and, I think, Patricia Madrid. [...] the discussions focused on the Buenos Aires plains, on which I had presented a paper that was published a year earlier in the *Anuario del IEHS* Vol. 2, and the archaeological analysis was crucial."[31]

The second meeting, held in Neuquén from May 26 to 28, 1988, was called "Ethnohistorical and Archaeological Investigations Seminary of the Patagonia and the Pampas (sixteenth through nineteenth centuries)." The meeting was organized by the National University of Comahue, UNICEN, and the Sub-Secretariat of Education and Culture of Neuquén province. According to Raúl Mandrini, these meetings were rather informal but:

> the most formal one, due to its very international character, was the First International Congress of Etnohistoria, which was held in Buenos Aires between July the 17th and 21th, 1989. It was organized by Ana María Lorandi's group and, at the beginning, it was dedicated exclusively to the Andean area. It was I who proposed Lorandi to organize the symposium 'Indigenous society and frontier relations in the southern territories of Argentina and Chile (sixteenth through nineteenth centuries)' which she accepted. He was the only one on these issues in the Congress. . . . What was important was that a group of Chilean researchers who had worked with [Sergio] Villalobos in the volume *Relaciones fronterizas en Araucanía,* and a classic on the subject, attended the Congress. It was important because it was the first direct contact with researchers from that country, and with some of them I continued to maintain contacts for many years, such as Holdenis Casanova, Luz María Méndez and Horacio Zapater. Through them, I was then connected with Jorge Pinto Rodríguez.[32]

Many other scholars were present at this congress, including Martha Bechis, Ana Biset, Gladys Varela, Holdenis Casanova, Eduardo Crivelli Montero, Juan Carlos Garavaglia, José Mateo, Carlos Mayo, Amalia Latrubesse, Luz Méndez Beltrán, Lidia Nacuzzi, Jimena Obregón

Iturra, Luis Parentini, María del Rosario Prieto, Helmut Schindler, and Horacio Zapater.

Another academic space that deserves to be highlighted took place a few years later, when Martha Bechis taught a seminar in 1999 for doctoral students at the University of Buenos Aires, which is mentioned by several researchers as the space in which they met and came together from different geographical and disciplinary backgrounds.[33] Several students in this seminar, who would later become specialists in these subjects, started coordinating symposia and panels at academic meetings in which historians and anthropologists came together without distinction.[34]

Publishing Spaces

Another example of the dynamism acquired by these studies was not only the publication in different foreign magazines but also the construction of publishing spaces at the local level. Studies of the indigenous populations of the Pampas and Patagonia regions gained more weight in history journals such as the *Anuario del IEHS* (which begun in 1986 and in whose editorial team Raúl Mandrini participated) and *Quinto Sol* (the first issue was published in 1997 under the direction of Daniel Villar).[35] Also, anthropology and archaeology journals started to include articles and dossiers regarding these topics. It is worth mentioning some like *Runa: Archivo para las Ciencias del Hombre* (initiated in 1948 by José Imbelloni at the University of Buenos Aires);[36] *Etnia* (started in 1965 by Enrique Palavecino at the National University of the Center of Buenos Aires Province); *Memoria Americana* (launched in 1991, initially directed by Ana María Lorandi and later by Lidia Nacuzzi between 2007 and 2009);[37] and some interdisciplinary ones such as *Identidades* (started in 2011 at the National University of La Patagonia San Juan Bosco);[38] and *Corpus: Archivos virtuales de la alteridad americana* (the first issue was published in 2011, directed by Diego Escolar).[39] The latter, in turn, led to the creation of the Network of Indigenous and Peasant Studies,[40] formed in 2013, which organizes periodic debates on these themes, which were then published in different journals.[41]

Besides these history and anthropology journals, specific publications concerning mostly indigenous peoples in the Pampas and Patagonia regions were created in more recent years. Some of these were TEFROS journal (Ethnohistory Workshop of the Southern Frontier, inaugurated in 2003, under the direction of Marcela Tamagnini, from National University of Río Cuarto)[42] and *AtekNa* (started in 2013 and initially directed by María Teresa Boschín).[43]

Topics and Debates in Recent Research

Anthropologists, historians, and archaeologists have contributed to shape a field of studies with diffuse limits, in addition to multiple articulations and meeting points.[44] Some of the most prominent implications and perspectives of this production were noted by Raúl Mandrini (2007), especially about those texts referring to Pampa and Patagonia in the eighteenth and nineteenth centuries. Although the initial positions were of a descriptive and typological type and were maintained until the 1980s in some cases (for instance Casamiquela 1985), scholars would soon revise these categorizations and concepts.

Among the aspects highlighted by Mandrini for the studies in Pampa and Nordpatagonia, there is the progressive change in the way of understanding the concept of "frontier," which went from a simplistic and superficial vision as a border or line that separated two worlds, to be conceived as a space for social interaction. But scholars also noted that frontier relations could not explain the dynamics and strategies of indigenous peoples. Moreover, the concepts of interethnic and intraethnic relations were insufficient to account for the complexity and evolution of the linkages among indigenous peoples and between indigenous peoples and colonial settlers that were addressed in numerous general and case studies from 1980 to 2000. The bulk of the historiographic and anthropological production of Pampas and Northern Patagonia is focused on these issues.[45] More recently, and since the 2000s, different studies began to deal with the situation of indigenous people after military campaigns and the diverse ways in which these actors positioned themselves in this situation. To do this, scholars began to use previously unexplored sources and oral testimonies.[46]

As for Southern Patagonia, it is worth noting that, until the 1980s, the history of Tierra del Fuego mostly considered issues such as white settlement, the role of the prison, the role of the missionaries, among others; and the narratives were still written largely by lawyers, military, political scientists, amateurs, or from other authors belonging to, or close to, the Catholic Church. Professionalization of scientific research in Argentina was established at the end of the 1980s, and it deepened, in the next two decades, with a renewal of attention to several topics: visions of the "frontier," interethnic relations, and native people's agency and dynamics.

In archeology, scholars began to use long-term perspectives in their research on indigenous peoples in Southern Patagonia. This work articulated different registers and, on a theoretical level, more frequently used the approaches of processual archeology and evolutionary archeology, with the ecological-environmental and biological aspects as explanatory axes. Some common topics included mobility, territoriality, use of space, subsistence, provisioning of resources, technology, distribution, availability and exploitation of raw materials, settlement, social organization and group structuring, and population density and demographic trajectory. Scholars addressed the relationship and synergy between these aspects, as well as the alterations generated by interethnic contacts, always paying attention to displacements and disintegrations. A bioanthropological orientation was fundamental to this research, depending on the possibility of measuring the pathological and sanitary consequences of colonization in indigenous communities.

The most recent works emphasize the social aspects as part of the causalities in historical processes and propose alternative periodizations. These scholars see the twentieth century in perspective and contribute to complex debates about the irreversibility of colonization, attending to the fluctuation and creative evolution of societies in pursuit of their survival. Because of this, the paradigm of "extinction" (Casali 2017) and the biologistic conceptions that dominated a large part of the academic work on Tierra del Fuego are definitely ended.

One of the main contributions of the production of the last four decades is to rescue the indigenous agency in its different modalities, and to overcome inherited typologies and classifications. These approaches show the complexity of the processes carried out by the natives, thus making it possible to put into question those oppositions between native population groups as homogeneous blocks without links among themselves (like the Mapuches and the Tehuelches) for the different periods.

The growth of the field of studies concerning indigenous peoples of the Pampas and Patagonia regions has been constant, and it can be noted in the amount of papers and books published, the multiplication of research nuclei in various parts of the country, and the fluidity of contacts between scholars and the new generations of researchers. The resources provided by the National Scientific and Technical Research Council (CONICET) and national universities during the last decade, especially 2003–15, certainly contributed to this growth, but the ties between researchers, the deepening of discussion, and the opening of new lines of research had started in the 1980s. The return of democracy meant also that several exiled scholars came back to universities, renewing history and anthropology disciplines and incorporating new theoretical approaches. Although much research is still necessary, it seems that this field of study has won a legitimate place in the academy.

NOTES

1. This paper is written within the context of two projects: "Producir cultura, producir regiones: agentes, redes e imaginarios en campos culturales emergentes (La Pampa y Norpatagonia, fines s. XIX-principios s. XXI)" (Producing culture, producing regions: agents, networks and imaginaries in emerging cultural fields (La Pampa and Northern Patagonia, late nineteenth century through early twenty first century) (PIO UNLPAM-CONICET), and "Historia de las investigaciones sobre indígenas en etnohistoria, historia y antropología: un abordaje comparativo," (History of research about indigenous peoples in ethnohistory, history and anthropology: a comparative approach), which is my line of research at CONICET (National Scientific and Technical Research Council).

2. See an account on the literature about the history of Argentinian natural museums in Podgorny and Lopes 2013.

3. For instance, Guber and Visacovsky 1999, 2006; Perazzi 2003, 2011; Fígoli 2004; Garbulsky 2004; Briones 2004; Mazzanti 2005; Guber 2007, 2010; Soprano 2006; Bartolomé 2007; Gil 2010, 2014; Ratier 2010; Bonnin and Soprano 2011; Igareta and Schávelzon 2011; Politis and Curtoni 2011; Martínez et al. 2011; Silla 2012.

4. Lazzari et al. 2015; Milana et al. 2015; Rodríguez et al. 2015; Ceriani Cernadas 2015; Salomón Tarquini and Casali 2015.
5. The reader can follow the evolution of the discussion about ethnohistory in Argentina in these texts: Santamaría 1985; Lorandi and Rodríguez Molas 1985; Palermo 1992; Lorandi and Del Río 1992; Lorandi and Nacuzzi 2007; Lorandi 2010; Zanolli et al. 2010; Lorandi 2012; Zanolli et al. 2013.
6. A brief summary of this period can be found in Tarragó 2000.
7. See, for instance, Garavaglia 1999; Lorandi 2000; Saignes 2000; Wachtel 2000.
8. See Lorandi 2000.
9. This system was a grant by the Spanish Crown to a colonist conferring the right to demand tribute and forced labor from native peoples.
10. See Santamaría 1994 and Vitar 1997.
11. See an excellent analysis of the relationship between native peoples' political processes and the wars held by white settlers against colonial empires during the early nineteenth century in Villar and Jiménez 2002.
12. See Lenton 2015 and Rosas 2016.
13. One of the first works to assess the negative impact of this school on anthropology in Argentina was the one by Boschín and Llamazares (1984).
14. It is worth noting that social anthropology in Argentina did not mean the same as in England and the U.S. (see Guber 2007, 264–65).
15. For further details about Alberto Rex González's trajectory, see Bonnin and Soprano (2011).
16. In Argentina, regular positions in teaching (similar to tenure) are allocated through *concursos* (both for professors and teaching assistants), a competitive examination process after which the teacher retains a more or less permanent position. The duration of this position depends on every university.
17. It should be noted that the orientation of what is called "ethnohistory" in Latin America is rather different than the one developed in the U.S. since the mid-1960s. U.S.-authored texts by scholars working in ethnohistory started circulating in Argentina by the late 1980s, a time by which the Ethnohistory Section had been formed at the University of Buenos Aires, with more focus on Andean studies and archaeological techniques.
18. This included Liliana Regalado de Hurtado, Amalia Castelli, and Teodoro Hempe, among other scholars.

19. Lorandi earned her PhD degree in 1967, and a little earlier she had been appointed as a researcher at CONICET. She had resigned from her position as a professor in 1966, after the repression known as *La noche de los bastones largos* (long sticks' night). During the 1980s, she was asked by A. Rex Gonzalez to start teaching at the University of La Plata and later joined the University of Buenos Aires.

20. This does not mean that during the 1980s there were not historians working on these topics. Raúl Mandrini was one of them, and he coordinated one of the six symposia at the CEI. However, such historians did not work at the University of Buenos Aires.

21. Within the long list of researchers that were actively working on ethnohistory by the late 1980s, we can mention Gustavo Paz, Florencia Roulet, Pedro Krapovickas, Guillermo Madrazo, Myriam Tarragó, José Antonio Pérez Gollán, Sara Mata, Eduardo Crivelli Montero, Gladys Ceresole, Leonor Slavsky, Josefina Piana, Griselda Tarragó, Diana Mazzanti, María del Rosario Prieto, Gladys Varela, Alicia Biset, and Miguel Angel Palermo (Palermo 1992, 148).

22. This table was made with information from the following sources: *Programa del Primer Congreso Internacional de Etnohistoria*, Buenos Aires, Argentina, 1989; Arze, Silvia, Rossana Barragán, and Laura Escobari y Ximena Medinacelli, editors. *Etnicidad, economía y simbolismo en los Andes: II Congreso Internacional de Etnohistoria. Coroico.* La Paz: Instituto de Historia Social Boliviana. HISBOL-Institut français d'études andines. IFEA-Sociedad Boliviana de Historia. SBH-Antropólogos del Sur Andino. ASUR, 1992; AA.VV. *Actas del IV Congreso Internacional de Etnohistoria*, Lima: Pontificia Universidad Católica del Perú, 1998; *Libro de resúmenes del V Congreso Internacional de Etnohistoria*, Jujuy, Argentina, 1998; *Programa del IV Congreso Internacional de Etnohistoria*, Buenos Aires, Argentina, 2005; *Segunda circular del VII Congreso Internacional de Etnohistoria*, Lima, Perú, 2008 (disponible en http://congreso.pucp.edu.pe /etnohistoria/2008/pdf/segunda_circular.pdf); Convocatoria al VIII *Congreso Internacional de Etnohistoria*, Sucre, 2011 (disponible en http:// laboratoriodehistoriacolonial.wordpress.com/noticias/viii-congreso-de -etnohistoria-sucre-2011/); *Programa del IX Congreso Internacional de Etnohistoria, Colonización, Descolonización e Imaginarios*, Arica, Chile, 2014. I am deeply grateful to Ana María Lorandi, Roxana Boixadós, and Daniel Villar, as well as the IFEA (Instituto Frances de Estudios Andinos, Peru) and the Library of the University of La Pampa for the copies of some of the printed versions of these programs.

23. Of course, such vindication was decidedly linked to a need of the military government to legitimize itself after the strong criticism that the dictatorship started in 1976 had received in 1978, when the World Cup championship held in Argentina had called the attention of human rights advocates all over the world.

24. Although the strongest repressive measures were taken by the dictatorship started in 1976, public universities suffered interventions by the executive branch from 1973 to 1975.

25. Lidia Nacuzzi, interview conducted by the author on March 9, 2015. All the interviews quoted in this chapter were in Spanish; translation into English was made by the author of this chapter.

26. Daniel Villar, interview conducted by the author on March 10, 2015.

27. See this reference in his interview published in Salomón Tarquini 2016.

28. The development of archaeology in the province of Buenos Aires was quite important by the mid-1980s. See, for instance, the case of Olavarría (Mazzanti 2005). A list of the main texts that helped foster a renewal of approaches concerning indigenous peoples in the area can be consulted at Mandrini 2007, 35–36.

29. Interview with Claudia Briones, conducted by the author on March 2, 2015. Her notable trajectory and impact in indigenous studies cannot be properly summarized here. In a few years, she built various research groups and trained scholars like Walter Delrio, Axel Lazzari, Diana Lenton, Mariela Eva Rodríguez, Ana Ramos, and Diego Escolar, among others.

30. Some of these, in alphabetical order, are: Sebastián Alioto (2009), María Elba Argeri (2004), Rafael Curtoni (2007), Ingrid De Jong (2003), Walter Delrio (2003), Diego Escolar (2003), Juan Francisco Jiménez (2006), Axel Lazzari (2010), Diana Lenton (2006), Eugenia Néspolo (2006), Ana Ramos (2005), Silvia Ratto (2004), Mariela Eva Rodríguez (2010), Claudia Salomón Tarquini (2009), Marcela Tamagnini (2006), and Julio Vezub (2005).

31. Raúl Mandrini, interview with the author, April 20, 2015.

32. Interview with Raúl Mandrini, published in Salomón Tarquini 2016, my translation.

33. The seminar was taken by about twenty graduate students. It was called "La Etnohistoria como dinámica histórica de situaciones hegemónicas entre alteridades colectivas" (Ethnohistory as historical dynamics of hegemonic situations between collective alterities). Among these students, there were Julio Vezub, Diego Escolar, Walter

Delrio, María Eugenia Néspolo, Diana Lenton, and Ingrid de Jong. I thank Julio Vezub for the program of seminar and his reference about the students who attended it.

34. I do not intend to provide an exhaustive account of these instances, but the following list can be illustrative: X Jornadas Interescuelas / Departamentos de Historia (Rosario, 2005, "Poder, conflicto y redes sociales en espacios fronterizos latinoamericanos, siglos XVIII y XIX," coordinated by Sara Ortelli and Silvia Ratto); 2das Jornadas de Historia de la Patagonia (General Roca, 2006, "Historia de los pueblos originarios," coordinated by Diana Lenton, Walter Delrio and María Andrea Nicoletti); XI Jornadas Interescuelas/Departamentos de Historia (Tucumán, 2007, "Etnogénesis, incorporación estatal y formaciones nacionales siglos XIX–XXI," coordinated by Walter Delrio and Diego Escolar); 3ras Jornadas de Historia de la Patagonia (Bariloche, 2008, "Políticas indígenas en Patagonia: una historia de dos siglos," coordinated by Diana Lenton, Walter Delrio and Claudia Salomón Tarquini); III Encuentro de Investigadores: Fuentes y Problemas de la investigación Histórica Regional (Santa Rosa, 2008, "Sociedades indígenas de Pampa y Nordpatagonia: aportes para un debate interdisciplinario," coordinated by Claudia Salomón Tarquini); XII Jornadas Interescuelas Departamentos de Historia (Bariloche, 2009, "Procesos de etnogénesis, sometimiento e incorporación estatal/nacional de pueblos originarios s.XIX/XX," coordinated by Walter Delrio and Diego Escolar); VIII RAM (Reunión de Antropología del Mercosur, Buenos Aires 2009, "Estrategias Indígenas y Estatales en los Procesos de Expansión Nacional: Enfoques Regionales y Fronteras Conceptuales," coordinated by Izabel Missagia and Ingrid de Jong; "Indigenismos e Políticas Indigenistas nas Américas. Para uma Análise Comparativa das Relações entre Povos Indígenas e Estados nos séculos XX e XXI," coordinated by Guillaume Boccara, Claudia Briones and Antonio Carlos de Souza Lima); 4tas Jornadas de Historia de la Patagonia (Santa Rosa, 2010, "Subalternización y resistencia de los pueblos originarios en Argentina y Chile," coordinated by Walter Delrio and Claudia Salomón Tarquini); and Jornadas 25 años de etnohistoria en la Argentina (Buenos Aires, 2010, "Participación y resistencia en los procesos de conformación de los estados," coordinated by Ingrid de Jong and Lorena Barbuto), among several others.

35. See http://cerac.unlpam.edu.ar/index.php/quintosol. Accessed May 6, 2018.

36. See more about *Runa* in Guber and Rodríguez 2011. Part of the collection is available at http://revistascientificas.filo.uba.ar/index.php/runa/issue/archive. Accessed May 6, 2018.

37. See http://antropologia.institutos.filo.uba.ar/revista/memoria-americana-cuadernos-de-etnohistoria. Accessed May 6, 2018.

38. See https://iidentidadess.wordpress.com/numeros-anteriores. Accessed May 6, 2018.

39. See https://corpusarchivos.revues.org. Accessed May 6, 2018.

40. See https://redreic.wordpress.com. Accessed May 6, 2018.

41. It is worth mentioning *Nuevo Mundo-Mundos Nuevos* (France) (https://nuevomundo.revues.org), accessed May 6, 2018, and *Revista de Indias* (Spain) (http://revistadeindias.revistas.csic.es/index.php/revistadeindias), accessed May 6, 2018, as important publishing spaces abroad where papers about indigenous peoples in Pampa and Patagonia were and are being published.

42. See http://www.hum.unrc.edu.ar/ojs/index.php/tefros/issue/archive. Accessed May 6, 2018.

43. See http://www.atekna.com.ar/2012/12/atek-na-en-la-tierra.html. Accessed May 6, 2018.

44. This section is a brief description of topics and debates in the area, but a larger and deeper exploration can be found at Salomón Tarquini and Casali (2015).

45. Although this is by no means an exhaustive account, some of the most important works in this line are Bechis (1984) 2011; Crivelli Montero 1991; Davies 2013; De Jong 2007; Nacuzzi 1998; Néspolo 2012; Tamagnini 1999; Tamagnini and Pérez Zavala 2012; Varela and Manara 2000; Vezub 2009; Villar 2003; Villar and Jiménez 2002, 2011; Villar, Jiménez, and Ratto 1998.

46. See, for instance, Mases 2002; Delrio 2005; Argeri 2005; Ramos 2010; Salomón Tarquini 2010; Lazzari 2011; Casali 2013; Lenton 2014; Nagy 2014.

REFERENCES

Academia Nacional de la Historia. 1980. *Congreso Nacional de Historia sobre la Conquista del Desierto, celebrado en la ciudad de Gral. Roca del 6 al 10 de noviembre de 1979*. Buenos Aires: Academia Nacional de La Historia.

Argeri, María E. 2005. *De Guerreros a Delincuentes: La desarticulación de las jefaturas indígenas y el poder judicial. Norpatagonia, 1880–1930*. Madrid: Consejo Superior de Investigaciones Científicas.

Bartolomé, Leopoldo. 2007. "Argentina: la enseñanza de la antropología social en el contexto de las ciencias antropológicas." Report for the research: A Distributed and Collective Ethnography of Academic Training in Latin American Anthropologies, Latin American Working Group of the WAN Collective. Accessed March 31, 2017. http://www.ram-wan .net/old/documents/06_documents/informe-argentina.pdf.

Bechis, Martha. 1983. "Interethnic Relations During the Period of Nation-State Formation in Chile and Argentina: From Sovereign to Ethnic. Ann Arbor MI, University Microfilms International." PhD diss., 1983. *Corpus: Archivos virtuales de la alteridad americana* 1, no. 2. Accessed March 6, 2019. https://corpusarchivos.revues.org/1193.

Bonnin, Mirta, and Germán Soprano. 2011. "Antropólogos y antropología entre las universidades de La Plata, Litoral y Córdoba. Circulación de personas, saberes y prácticas antropológicas en torno del liderazgo académico de Alberto Rex González (1949–1976)." *Relaciones de la Sociedad Argentina de Antropología* XXXVI: 37–59.

Boschín, M., and A. Llamazares. 1984. "La escuela Histórico-Cultural como factor retardatario del desarrollo científico de la arqueología argentina." *Etnia* 32: 101–56.

Briones, Claudia. 2004. "Pueblos indígenas y Antropología en Argentina (1994–2004)" *Anuario de Estudios de Antropología Social*: 83–100.

Casali, Romina. 2017. *Conquistando el fin del mundo: La misión La Candelaria y la salud de la población selk'nam, Tierra del Fuego 1895–1931.* Rosario: Prohistoria.

———. 2013. "De la extinción al genocidio selk'nam: sobre Historia e historias para una expiación intelectual. Tierra del Fuego, Argentina" *A Contracorriente: Una revista de estudios latinoamericanos* 15, no. 1: 60–78. Accessed March 6, 2019. https://acontracorriente.chass.ncsu.edu/index .php/acontracorriente/article/view/1605.

Casamiquela, Rodolfo. 1985. "Características de la Araucanización al Oriente de los Andes." *Revista Cultura, Hombre, Sociedad* 1, no. 1, http:// portalrevistas.uct.cl/index.php/cuhso/article/view/141/136.

Ceriani Cernadas, Cesar. 2015. "Flujos teóricos y transformaciones empíricas en el estudio de los pueblos indígenas del Chaco argentino." *Papeles de Trabajo* 9, no. 16: 110–51.

Crivelli Montero, Eduardo. 1991. "Malones: ¿saqueo o estrategia? El objetivo de las invasiones de 1780 y 1783 a la frontera de Buenos Aires." *Todo es Historia* 283: 6–32.

Davies, Geraldine. 2013. Haciéndonos parientes: diplomacia y vida cotidiana entre los linajes indígenas de NordPatagonia y los criollos de Carmen de Patagones (1852–1879). Tesis de Maestría en Ciencias Sociales y Humanidades, Mención en Historia. Universidad Nacional de Quilmes.

De Jong, Ingrid. 2007. "Acuerdos y desacuerdos: política estatal e indígena en la frontera bonaerense (1856–1866)." In *Pueblos indígenas en América Latina*, siglo XIX: sociedades en movimiento, Anuario del IEHS, Suplemento 1, edited by Raúl Mandrini, Antonio Escobar Ohmstede, and Sara Ortelli, 47–62. Tandil: Instituto de Estudios Histórico-Sociales, UNCPBA.

Delrio, Walter. 2005. *Memorias de Expropiación: Sometimiento e incorporación indígena en la Patagonia, 1872–1943*. Bernal: Universidad Nacional de Quilmes.

Fígoli, Leonardo H. 2004. "Origen y desarrollo de la antropología en la Argentina: de la Organización Nacional hasta mediados del siglo XX" *Anuario de Estudios de Antropología Social* 1: 71–80.

Garavaglia, Juan Carlos. 1999. "The crises and transformations of invaded societies: La Plata Basin (1535–1650)." In *The Cambridge History of Native Peoples in the Americas*, vol. II, edited by F. Salomon and S. Schwartz, 1–58. Cambridge: Cambridge University Press.

Garbulsky, Edgardo. 2004. "La Producción del Conocimiento Antropológico-Social en la Facultad de Filosofía y Letras de la Universidad Nacional del Litoral, entre 1956–1966: Vínculos y relaciones nacionales." *Cuadernos de Antropología Social*, 20: 41–60.

Gil, Gastón Julián. 2014. "Relatos antropológicos periféricos. Los antropólogos argentinos y el Handbook of South American Indians," ponencia en el XI Congreso Argentino de Antropología Social, Rosario.

———. 2010. "Neoevolucionismo y ecología cultural: La obra de Julian Steward y la renovación de la enseñanza de la antropología en la Argentina." *Revista del Museo de Antropología* 3: 225–38.

Guber, Rosana. 2010. "Otras antropologías y otras historias de la antropología argentina," *Revista del Museo de Antropología* 3: 169–70.

———. 2007. "Crisis de presencia, universidad y política en el nacimiento de la antropología social de Buenos Aires, Argentina." *Revista Colombiana de Antropología* 43: 263–98.

Guber, Rosana, and Martha Rodríguez. 2011. "Vitrinas del mundo académico: Las revistas de la Facultad de Filosofía y Letras de la Universidad de Buenos Aires entre 1946–1966." *Historiografías* 2: 66–84.

Guber, Rosana, and Sergio Visacovsky. 2006. "The Birth of Ciencias Antropologicas at the University of Buenos Aires, 1955–1965." *History of Anthropology Annual*, vol. 2: 1–32.

————. 1999. "Imágenes etnográficas de la nación. La antropología social argentina de los tempranos años setenta" *Série Antropologia* N°251, Brasilia.

Igareta, Ana, and Daniel Schávelzon. 2011. "Empezando por el principio: pioneros de la arqueología histórica argentina." *Anuario de Arqueología* 3: 9–24.

Lazzari, Axel. 2004. "Antropología en el Estado: el Instituto Etnico Nacional (1946–1955)." In *Intelectuales y Expertos. La constitución del conocimiento social en la Argentina*, edited by Federico Neiburg and Mariano Plotkin, 203–29. Buenos Aires: Paidós.

————. 2011. "Autonomy in Apparitions: Phantom Indian, Selves, and Freedom (on the Rankülche in Argentina)." PhD diss., Columbia University.

Lazzari, Axel, Mariela Eva Rodríguez, and Alexis Papazian. 2015. "Juegos de visibilización. Antropología sociocultural de los pueblos indígenas en Pampa y Patagonia." *Papeles de Trabajo* 9, no. 16: 56–109.

Lenton, Diana. 2015. "Notas para una recuperación de la memoria de las organizaciones de militancia indígena." *Identidades* 8, no. 5: 117–54.

————. (2005) 2014. "De centauros a protegidos. La construcción del sujeto de la política indigenista argentina desde los debates parlamentarios (1880–1970)." PhD diss., Universidad de Buenos Aires, *Corpus: Archivos virtuales de la alteridad americana* 4, no. 2. Accessed March 6, 2019. http://corpusarchivos.revues.org/1290.

Lins Ribeiro, Gustavo. 2004. "Presentación. La antropologa brasileña en América Latina." In *La antropología brasileña contemporánea: Contribuciones para un diálogo latinoamericano*, edited by Alejandro Grimson, Gustavo Lins Ribeiro, and Pablo Semán, 9–13. Buenos Aires: Prometeo Libros-Asociacao Brasileira de Antropologia.

Lorandi, Ana María. 2012. "¿Etnohistoria, Antropología Histórica o simplemente Historia?" *Memoria Americana* 20, no. 1: 17–34.

————. 2010. "Los estudios andinos y la etnohistoria en la Universidad de Buenos Aires." *Chúngara: Revista de Antropología Chilena* 42, no. 1: 271–81.

————. 2000. "Las rebeliones indígenas." In *Nueva Historia Argentina: Tomo II*, edited by E. Tandeter, 285–329. Buenos Aires: Sudamericana.

Lorandi, Ana María, and Lidia Nacuzzi. 2007. "Trayectorias de la etnohistoria en la Argentina (1936–2006)." *Relaciones de la Sociedad Argentina de Antropología* XXXII: 281–97.

Lorandi, Ana María, and Mercedes del Rio. 1992. *La etnohistoria: Etnogénesis y transformaciones sociales andinas*. Buenos Aires: Centro Editor de América Latina.

Lorandi, Ana María, and Ricardo Rodríguez Molas. 1985. "Historia y antropología: hacia una nueva dimensión de la ciencia." *Etnia*: 53–80.

Mandrini, Raúl. 2008. *La Argentina aborigen: De los primeros pobladores a 1910*. Buenos Aires: Siglo XXI Editores.

———. 2007. "La historiografía argentina, los pueblos originarios y la incomodidad de los historiadores." *Quinto Sol* 11: 19–38.

———. 1994. "Sobre el suttee entre los indígenas de las llanuras argentinas, Nuevos datos e interpretaciones sobre el origen y práctica." *Anales de Antropología* 31: 261–78.

Martínez, Ana Teresa, Constanza Taboada, and Alejandro Auat. 2011. *Los hermanos Wagner: Arqueología, campo arqueológico nacional y construcción de identidad en Santiago del Estero, 1920–1940*. Bernal: Universidad Nacional de Quilmes.

Mases, Enrique. 2002. *Estado y cuestión indígena: El destino final de los indios sometidos en el sur del territorio (1878–1910)*. Buenos Aires: Prometeo Libros/Entrepasados.

Mazzanti, Diana. 2005. "La institucionalización de la arqueología desde Olavarría." *Andes* 16: 1–14. Accessed May 10, 2017. http://www.scielo.org.ar/pdf/andes/n16/n16a08.pdf.

Melià, Bartomeu. 2000. "Sociedades fluviales y selvícolas del este: Paraguay y Paraná." In *Historia General de América Latina II: El primer contacto y la formación de nuevas sociedades*, edited by F. Pease and F. Moya Pons, 535–51. Paris: Unesco-Ed.Trotta.

Milana, Paula, María Macarena Ossola, and María Victoria Sabio Collado. 2015. "Antropología social y alteridades indígenas: Salta (1984–2014)." *Papeles de Trabajo* 9, no. 16: 192–226.

Nacuzzi, Lidia R. 1998. *Identidades impuestas: Tehuelches, aucas y pampas en el norte de la Patagonia*. Buenos Aires: Sociedad Argentina de Antropología.

Nagy, Mariano. 2014. *Estamos vivos: Historia de la Comunidad Indígena Cacique Pincén, provincia de Buenos Aires* (Siglos XIX–XXI). Buenos Aires: Antropofagia.

Name, María Julia. 2012. "La historia que construimos. Reflexiones a propósito de una investigación sobre la historia de la antropología en la Argentina." *Runa: Archivo para las Ciencias del Hombre* XXXIII, no. 1: 53–69.

Néspolo, Eugenia. 2012. *Resistencia y complementariedad*. Gobernar en Buenos Aires. Luján en el siglo XVIII: un espacio políticamente concertado. Buenos Aires: Escaramujo.

Palermo, Miguel Ángel. 2011. "La antropología en escena: redes de influencia, sociabilidad y prestigio en los orígenes del Museo Etnográfico de la Universidad de Buenos Aires." *Anthropologica* 29: 215–32.

———. 1999. "*Mapuches, Pampas y mercados coloniales.*" In *Etnohistoria, Número especial de la Revista Noticias de Arqueología y Antropología (Naya), edited by María De Hoyos.* CD-ROM.

———. 1994. "El revés de la trama. Apuntes sobre el papel económico de la mujer en las sociedades indígenas tradicionales del sur argentino." *Memoria Americana.* 3: 63–90.

———. 1992. "La etnohistoria en la Argentina: antecedentes y estado actual." *Runa: Archivo para las Ciencias del Hombre XX:* 145–50.

———. 1991. "La compleja integración hispano-indígena del sur argentino y chileno durante el período colonial." *América Indígena,* LI, no. 1: 153–92.

———. 1988. "Innovación agropecuaria entre los indígenas pampeano-patagónicos. Génesis y procesos." *Anuario del iehs III:* 43–90.

———. 1986. "Reflexiones sobre el llamado 'Complejo Ecuestre' en la Argentina." *Runa: Archivo para las Ciencias del Hombre XVI:* 157–78.

Perazzi, Pablo. 2003. "Antropología y nación: materiales para una historia profesional de la antropología en Buenos Aires." *Runa: Archivo para las Ciencias del Hombre XXIV:* 83–102.

Podgorny, Irina. 2004. "'Tocar para creer': La arqueología en la Argentina, 1910–1940." *Anales del Museo de América* 12: 147–82.

———. 1999. "De la antigüedad del hombre en el Plata a la distribución de las antigüedades en el mapa: los criterios de organización de las colecciones antropológicas del Museo de La Plata entre 1897 y 1930." *História, Ciências, Saúde-Manguinhos* 6, no. 1: 81–101.

Podgorny, Irina, and Maria Margaret Lopes. 2013. "Trayectorias y desafíos de la historiografía de los museos de historia natural en América Del Sur." *Anais do Museu Paulista: História e Cultura Material* 21, no. 1: 15–25.

Politis, Gustavo, and Rafael Pedro Curtoni. 2011. "Archaeology and Politics in Argentina during the last 50 years." In *Comparative Archaeologies: A Sociological View of the Science of the Past,* edited by L. R. Lozny, 495–525. New York: Springer.

Ramos, Ana M. 2010. *Los pliegues del linaje: Memorias y políticas mapuches-tehuelches en contextos de desplazamiento.* Buenos Aires: Eudeba.

Ratier, Hugo E. 2010. "La antropología social argentina: su desarrollo." *Publicar en Antropología y Ciencias Sociales* VIII, no. ix: 17–46.

Rodríguez, Lorena, Roxana Boixadós, and Camila Cerra. 2015. "La etnohistoria y la cuestión indígena en el Noroeste argentino. Aportes y proyecciones para un campo en construcción." *Papeles de Trabajo* 9, no. 16): 152–91.

Rosas, Sabrina. 2016. "Violencia e invisibilidad indígena. La cuestiín de los pueblos originarios durante el primer peronismo." *Anuario del Instituto de Historia Argentina* 16, no. 1: 1–12.

Saignes, Thierry. 2000. "Las zonas conflictivas: fronteras iniciales de guerra." In *Historia General de América Latina II: El primer contacto y la formación de nuevas sociedades*, edited by F. Pease and F. Moya Pons, 269–99. Paris: Unesco-Ed.Trotta.

Salazar-Soler, Carmen. 2007. "La presencia de la antropología francesa en los Andes peruanos." *Bulletin de l'Institut Francais d'Etudes Andines* 36, no. 1: 93–107.

Salomón Tarquini, Claudia. 2016. ". . . Nos falta empezar a hacer una historia de los pueblos indígenas . . ." Reflexiones en torno a la construcción de un campo de estudio y de una carrera académica, entrevista a Raúl Mandrini." *Pasado Abierto* 2, no. 3: 164–79.

———. 2010. *Largas noches en La Pampa. Itinerarios y resistencias de la población indígena (1878–1976)*. Buenos Aires: Prometeo.

Salomón Tarquini, and Claudia y Romina Casali. 2015. "Los pueblos indígenas de Pampa y Patagonia, siglos XVIII–XX. Un breve estado de las investigaciones." *Papeles de Trabajo* 9, no. 16: 22–55.

Santamaría, Daniel. 1994. *Del tabaco al incienso. Reducción y conversión en las Misiones Jesuitas de las selvas sudamericanas siglos XVIII y XVIII*. San Salvador de Jujuy: CEIC-Universidad Nacional de Jujuy.

———. 1985. "La historia, la etnohistoria y una sugerencia de los antropólogos." *Desarrollo Económico* 25, no. 99: 465–72.

Silla, Rolando. 2012. "Raza, raciología y racismo en la obra de Marcelo Bórmida." *Revista del Museo de Antropología* 5: 65–76.

Soprano, German. 2006. "Continuidad y cambio en los estudios en etnología de poblaciones indígenas contemporáneas y comunidades folk en la Facultad de Ciencias Naturales y Museo de la Universidad Nacional de La Plata (1930–1976)." *Anuario de Estudios en Antropología Social*: 23–51.

Tamagnini, Marcela. 1999. "Fragmentación, equilibrio político y relaciones interétnicas (1851–1862). La frontera de Río Cuarto." In *Actas de las Segundas Jornadas de Investigadores en Arqueología y Etnohistoria del Centro-Oeste del País*, edited by Marcela Tamagnini, 199–209. Río Cuarto: Universidad Nacional de Río Cuarto.

Tamagnini, Marcela, and G. Pérez Zavala. 2012. "Dinámica territorial y poblacional en el Virreinato del Río de la Plata: indígenas y cristianos en la Frontera Sur de la Gobernación Intendencia de Córdoba del Tucumán, 1779–1804." *Revista Fronteras de la Historia* 17, no. 1: 195–225.

Tarragó, Myriam. 2000. *Los pueblos oirignarios y la conquista*. Buenos Aires: Sudamericana.

Varela, Gladys, and Carla Manara. 2000. "En un mundo de frontera. La guerrilla realista-chilena en territorio pehuenche (1822–1832)." *Revista de Estudios Trasandinos* 4: 341–63.

Vezub, Julio. 2009. *Valentín Saygüeque y la "Gobernación Indígena de las Manzanas. Poder y etnicidad en la patagonia noroccidental (1860–1881)*. Buenos Aires: Prometeo.

Vezub, Julio, and Alejandro De Oto. 2011. "Patagonia, archivo etnológico y nación en el primero peronismo. Una lectura descolonial." *Otros logos. Revista de Estudios Críticos* 2: 135–62.

Villar, Daniel, ed. 2003. *Conflicto, poder y justicia en la frontera bonaerense, 1818–1832.* Santa Rosa: Departamento de Humanidades (UNSur) y Fac. Cs. Humanas (UNLPam).

Villar, Daniel, and Juan Francisco Jiménez. 2002. "La tempestad de la guerra: Conflictos indígenas y circuitos de intercambio. Elementos para una periodización (Araucanía y Pampas, 1780–1840)." In *Las fronteras hispanocriollas del mundo indígena latinoamericano, los siglos XVIII y XIX. Un análisis comparativo*, edited by Raúl J. Mandrini and Carlos D. Paz. Tandil: UNCPBA (Instituto de Estudios Histórico-Sociales), UNComahue (Centro de Estudios de Historia Regional y Relaciones Fronterizas)-UNSur (Departamento de Humanidades), compact disc.

Villar, Daniel, and Juan Francisco Jiménez, eds. 2011. *Amigos, hermanos y parientes. Líderes y liderados en las sociedades indígenas de la Pampa Oriental (S.XIX).* Bahía Blanca: Centro de Documentación Patagónica, Departamento de Humanidades, Universidad Nacional del Sur.

Villar, Daniel, Juan F. Jiménez, and Silvia Ratto. 1998. *Relaciones inter-étnicas en el Sur bonaerense. 1810–1830.* Bahía Blanca: Depto. de Humanidades Universidad Nacional del Sur/Instituto de Estudios Histórico-Sociales UNICEN.

Vitar, Beatriz. 1997. *Guerra y misiones en la frontera chaqueña del Tucumán (1700–1767).* Madrid: Consejo Superior de Investigaciones Científicas.

Wachtel, Nathan. 1990. "Los indios y la conquista Española." In *Historia de América Latina. 1. América Latina colonial: La América precolombina y la conquista*, edited by L. Bethell, 170–202. Barcelona: Crítica.

Zanolli, Carlos. E, Julia Costilla, Dolores Estruch, and Alejandra Ramos. 2013. *Los estudios andinos hoy: Práctica intelectual y estrategias de investigación.* Rosario: Prohistoria ediciones.

Zanolli, Carlos. E, Alejandra Ramos, Dolores Estruch, and Julia Costilla. 2010. *Historia, representaciones y prácticas de la Etnohistoria en la Universidad de Buenos Aires: Una aproximación antropológica a un campo de confluencia disciplinar.* Buenos Aires: Antropofagia.

Voicing the Ancestors

7

Fieldwork Predecessors and Indigenous Communities in Native North America

Some years ago, while doing research in the Margaret Mead Papers at the Library of Congress, Lise Dobrin and I came across a trove of old photographs from Mead's and Reo Fortune's joint anthropological fieldwork in the Mountain Arapesh region of New Guinea from 1931–32. When we next visited Papua New Guinea, we brought copies of these photographs to the Alitoa community where Mead and Fortune had stayed. Alitoa was in a new location, still atop a steep mountain but much closer to the sea coast and rough vehicular road.[1] We had sent word in advance so a large group was waiting for us, and we were ushered into an open-sided, thatched roof meeting space where a crowd of people sat close together like passengers riding in the open bed of a truck. We sat on the ground in the middle. The first question people asked us was: were we Mead and Fortune's descendants? When we replied we were not, a murmur of confusion went through the crowd. We explained (in all truth) that we had come to know about Alitoa through Mead and Fortune's writings, that Lise was documenting a neighboring variety of their language, and that we were studying and writing about Arapesh ethnohistory and Mead and Fortune's biographies. We then had a long visit and showed people the photographs, recording commentary about them and leaving copies. When we were about to depart, we were asked again about our relationship to the prior anthropologists: "Are you *sure* you are not Margaret Mead's descendants?" one Alitoa man asked us, incredulous in the face of our denials. Initially I was taken aback by this suggestion that we might be confused about our own ancestry, but I soon appreciated that from the man's perspective, we *had* to be related, somehow, to Mead or Fortune. Why else would we have come from as far away as America to renew their long-dormant relationship with Alitoa? We were even bringing their photographs! His question called on us to acknowledge that a descent *of some kind* was implied by our taking the prior anthropologists' place.

When doing fieldwork, an anthropologist enters into relationship with prior fieldworkers. What this means is impossible to pin down in general: the fields that anthropologists constitute through their research are very diverse, and who counts as a predecessor depends on the perspective of the people who are the anthropologist's subjects, reflecting *their* categories of self and other, and their ways of making sense of the arriving researcher in terms of remembered precedents.[2] To the practitioner, what is most salient and interesting in present practice is often the departure from the past—elements of innovation and novelty. But in the eyes of our subjects, these may appear as mere nuances in contrast to the substantial continuity which defines present and past fieldworkers as of a kind. To the anthropologist it can be unsettling to have their identity interpreted with respect to an absent third party from whom they may think themselves distant and with whom they may even strongly disagree. But it is in the nature of anthropological research that the subjects observe and interpret the researcher even as the researcher is observing them, and as George Devereux (1967) observes, the researcher is bound to feel anxiety at being attributed characteristics that differ from the researcher's self-image. Like race, class, and gender, the condition of being an anthropological fieldworker involves negotiating assumptions that are projected onto the self by others. One day you are a graduate student, reading past scholars' writings about your area and criticizing their shortcomings, but next thing you know, you are in the field and being identified as of a kind with those past scholars yourself.

Fieldwork predecessors have scientific importance when a case is restudied or when earlier research is used as a baseline for comparison or assessing change over time. They may also have practical significance in attracting future researchers' attention to a community in the first instance, in forging institutional ties that pave later researchers' way to the field,[3] and in training local field assistants who may come to work for subsequent researchers, too.[4] Fieldwork predecessors are often of heightened concern to later researchers in regard to issues of ethics. A predecessor's ethical reputation may influence how a new researcher is perceived and received by a community. There may be remembered disappointments to be corrected, a legacy of mistrust to overcome, or patterns of interaction and reciprocity that were established and are now expected of newcomers. The predecessor's reputation in the community may or may not accurately reflect their actual conduct; we know that memory is complex. It may be evaluated differently by different individuals, reflecting community-internal divisions and the closer and more distant relationships the researcher had with different families. Finally, there is no guarantee of consonance with the predecessor's scholarly reputation. A past fieldworker may be remembered in the community more for personal characteristics, relationships, and activities in and for the community itself, than for the scholarly products of their research as it is viewed by their colleagues.

The six essays that follow grew out of a conference session titled "Voicing the Ancestors" at the American Anthropological Association meeting in 2016. As in two similar "Voicing the Ancestors" sessions held in prior years, presenters were practicing anthropologists and historians of anthropology who were invited to select a few paragraphs by an intellectual ancestor to read out loud (i.e., to "voice") and to comment on the text's historical context and present significance.[5] For the 2016 session, which was organized by Mindy Morgan and Ira Bashkow, Morgan suggested highlighting the concept of collaboration and the relationship between the discipline of anthropology and Indigenous communities of North America. Thus, the ancestors chosen by the presenters to be "voiced" included Native American scholars as well as anthropologists who had worked with tribal communities and their field consultants, research assistants, or allies.

An important theme that emerged in the session was how anthropologists and their work have been evaluated in different periods by people associated with the communities they studied. Like other scholars, anthropologists are well understood to have *intellectual ancestors*: mentors, teachers, and other formative influences on their ideas and approaches.[6] But they also have forebears of another sort: *fieldwork predecessors*, previous field workers in the communities where they, too, have chosen to do field research. The concept of fieldwork predecessor may be a resource for further opening the historiography of anthropology to the perspectives of those people who have historically been anthropology's subjects. While the concept of an intellectual ancestor emphasizes discipline-internal aspects of mentorship and intellectual influence, that of fieldwork predecessor takes us outside the discipline into the realm of relationships with the studied community, however defined. Indeed, it is triangulated with people who are of that community, at a given time in some meaningful way. It implicates *their* points of view, and to that extent, is not fully in the control of the researcher. Of course, intellectual ancestors, too, are not all strictly elective; many grow out of biographical pathways (like where a person does graduate study) and are associated with long-term relationships of mentorship that are more than solely a matter of their own personal choice. Nevertheless, scholars do enjoy flexibility in constructing their intellectual genealogies as an aspect of fashioning their scholarly influences and identity; their chosen intellectual ancestors contrast with the fieldwork predecessors that may be foisted upon the researcher by others: those they have opted to study. And because this concept of fieldwork predecessor involves sensitivity to these others' viewpoints, it has less to do with the predecessor's disciplinary reputation, or with his or her formal results of research as published in books and journals, and more to do with personal conduct, relationships, reciprocities, and collaborations. It is formed of perceptions, recollections, and oral traditions of what the fieldworker did, as subject to a continuing process of interpretation, evocation, and transmission.

FIELDWORK PREDECESSORS: COLLABORATION, ACTIVISM, AND SALVAGE

The essays in this theme collection take up charged issues surrounding fieldwork predecessors in Native North America. They describe how past anthropologists interacted with research collaborators, consultants, and others in Native American and First Nations communities, exploring how the anthropologists' involvement has been viewed and discussed by community members, leaders, activists, and intellectuals. Four of the essays focus on Franz Boas and his students Frank Speck, Gordon Marsh, and Ruth Underhill in the first half of the twentieth century, while two reconsider the challenge to anthropology in the 1960s by Native American intellectual Vine Deloria Jr. Some of the essays describe fieldwork relationships as they unfolded over a time span of decades, providing perspective on anthropologists' activities in light of their long-term implications.

The essays look afresh at the Boasian fieldwork legacy. As is well known, Boas's vision for fieldwork emphasized the collection of ethnographic "material"—especially texts and artifacts but also photos, recipes, music, and other data—to reveal generalizable cultural processes and illuminate history. This historical orientation reflected Boas's critique of social evolutionism and his intellectual models in German historical science, ethnology, and philology. It also reflected the emergent anthropological discipline's institutional roots in the museum field of natural history. But in the American context, the Boasian aim to preserve traces of past culture of aboriginal peoples resonated with the popular assumption that "the Indian" was "a vanishing race," destined for oblivion and requiring white outsiders' help to "save" and curate the remaining mementos of a romantic "proud past." This idea found endorsement when anthropological fieldworkers were out collecting old artifacts and eliciting and writing down texts encapsulating elderly informants' recollections of the aboriginal past. Such "memory ethnography" had itself become antiquated within anthropology in the 1930s, when acculturation studies and the science of societal "functioning" came into vogue; and by the 1960s, it was criticized as "salvage ethnography" and as an accessory to the imperialistic and genocidal subjugation of Indians in American history.[7] The implied standpoint of such criticism was solidarity with Native Americans, and so a particularly important voice was the Indian theologian, legal scholar, and activist Vine Deloria Jr., who blasted anthropology and anthropologists in the pages of *Playboy* magazine and in a chapter of his bestselling 1969 book *Custer Died for Your Sins*.

One of the overarching lessons of this collection of essays is that the late twentieth century rejection of salvage ethnography takes an overly simplified view of past anthropology. Anthropological fieldwork of all kinds—not only "salvage"—is haunted by a fundamental asymmetry in that its products advance the individual researcher's career and contribute to the collective life of the field of anthropology—as it is renewed continually through publishing, conferences, museum work, college and university teaching, and so on—but these products do not, as a matter of course, play a similar role in supporting the vitality of the communities studied. This troubling asymmetry was taken for granted by the numerous nineteenth and twentieth century scholars who called for efforts to create a record, in bones and artifacts as well as texts, of Native peoples threatened by the depredations of Euro-Americans and Europeans.[8] The justification for creating the record was strictly to preserve data for science—this was the scientific project of salvage anthropology that Deloria (and others) criticized.[9]

But a second, humanistic idea of "salvage" developed alongside it in the mid-twentieth century, justified in different terms: that the record might someday have value for a descendant community of the people studied. In effect, this second idea acknowledged the asymmetry but suggested that, in a situation of cultural disruption, anthropological salvage might enable the documented aspects of culture to be revitalized *later on*. While an improvement, this, too, was not perfect. The value of salvage work continued to be premised on an unattractive pessimism regarding the ability of Indigenous people to preserve and reproduce their own cultures at the time of the research. This evokes skepticism. Who is to determine whether a culture is *dying* or merely *changing*? Anthropologists have often warned in error that the cultures they study are on the brink of demise.[10] Worse, the claim that cultures are dying has been used to deny the robustness and continuity of Native claims to valued resources like land and artifacts. But whether or not it is helpful or accurate to think of whole "peoples" or "cultures" (in the abstract) as "dying," we should not lightly dismiss the fact that specific cultural and linguistic knowledge and genres of activity and creativity do perish, and the essays in this collection by Saul Schwartz and Mindy Morgan attest that anthropological research products sometimes *do* have the claimed value of contributing to cultural and linguistic revitalization. But, crucially, this is not when the culture is "dead": it is when the community itself has cultural activists who of their own accord take up the products of long-ago research and make something of it themselves. The source community, in other words, retakes control of the old products of cultural and linguistic documentation, reactivating, repackaging, and recontextualizing them in revitalization activities. The materials truly do have great potential value, but in order to realize it their use must have a life of its own in the source community—that is, *outside* anthropology.

Another way of ameliorating the asymmetry of anthropological field research is by collaborating with people in the community studied to partially reshape the research process and its products in accord with their own desiderata, needs, and ideals. Such collaborative research involving negotiation and partnership between the fieldworker (or fieldworkers) and individuals in the host community has become popular within anthropology today.[11] The essays in this collection show that certain forms of collaboration have precedents in the research of Boasian anthropologists in North America. Boas himself did not envision collaborative fieldwork in the current sense of the term, and he clearly did not regard service to the community, per se, as a priority for the fieldworker. Nevertheless, as Ira Jacknis shows, there were important collaborative aspects to his own work with George Hunt, who assisted Boas for decades with collecting, documenting, and photographing Kwakwa̱ka̱'wakw (Kwakiutl) material culture. Hunt, whose mother was Tlingit and who married into Kwakwa̱ka̱'wakw, on his own initiative extended and improved upon Boas's instructions and methodological requirements. He also started collecting projects himself, including the use of photography, in which he realized a distinctively percipient Native vision. In Schwartz's essay, where we see Boas in the role of mentor to a fieldworking student, Gordon Marsh, it is again clear that Boas's priority was to obtain a scientifically valued end product—here an extensive corpus of Native language (Chiwere) texts with translation and annotation—but he recognized this could only be done with active, willing help from Native linguistic consultants, who would naturally have their own motivations. Boas's practical advice was oriented to harnessing these motivations by giving them due expression. A particularly striking form of this was to get the consultants to dictate "texts"—a laborious process—by allowing them to say what they wanted for posterity, since, as Boas observed, consultants "are eager to be put on record in regard to questions that are of supreme interest to them."[12] This eliciting practice was not justified by the value of collaboration, as such. Even so, as Schwartz observes, it resulted in the recording of consultants' own discourse on topics like colonization. Here again, we have products of field research that were co-constructed by the field researcher and the people researched: it was not a simply one-sided exploitation as one might imagine a colonial relationship.

We might think of those examples as collaboration in the service of scholarship. But there are also precedents in these essays for collaboration as activism, in service of the community. In Margaret Bruchac's essay, we learn that Frank Speck's famous account of Algonquin and other "family hunting territories" in the early twentieth century originated in an attempt to regain Indigenous hunting rights on lands outside the reservation, which had been severely curtailed by Canada's Indian Act. During fieldwork in 1912, and in correspondence with Edward Sapir, Speck saw that Indians suffered grave hunger because they were barred from their former hunting and fishing places that the government had leased to outsiders. To build a case to restore Indian access to these places, he worked with Algonquin leaders to map the boundaries of hunting "domains" by family, documenting the names, totems, and myths of each group of land "proprietors."[13] In effect, they co-constructed a basis for Native claim to land rights in terms that would make sense to a non-Indian Canadian public: it was, Speck said, "traditional," obtaining since time immemorial. One gets a feel for their translational savvy from the statement Speck quotes by his collaborator Chief Aleck Paul, likening Indian hunters to family "farmers" who solely owned and husbanded the production of their family farm: "The beaver was the Indians' pork; the moose, his beef; the partridge, his chicken," etc. As scholarship, this approach had limitations. Subsequent researchers have criticized Speck's account of the family hunting territories as historically shallow and ethnographically weak (ironically, these arguments undermined Indigenous attempts to retain territorial sovereignty, through whatever means possible). In the final analysis, Speck's research was activism *disguised* as salvage: he dressed his account in the (later-criticized) robes of an inquiry into the custom of yesteryear in order to gain for it the legitimacy of continuity with precolonial times. So in an interesting twist, salvage itself here served as an activist strategy.[14]

If the community's needs are prioritized absolutely, is it still anthropology?[15] In the 1960s the anthropologist Robert Rietz took activist collaboration to the point of dispensing altogether with scholarly knowledge production and an academic career.[16] A student of Sol Tax, Rietz tried to operationalize the principles of "Action Anthropology," putting anthropological field research methods—like active listening, genuine caring, and non-direction within situations where Indigenous people exert control—in the service of helping the Indigenous community of Chicago solve practical problems and improve people's well-being.[17] While directing the American Indian Center of Chicago, he kept his role inconspicuous while working in the wings to facilitate plans set by Indigenous leaders. He assiduously cultivated rapport, not for the sake of research but to build the organization. At times, when individuals spoke to him about personal problems they were experiencing, he searched out common elements and quietly proposed community-level solutions, drawing on his close relationship with the politically well-connected Tax to find sources of funds.[18] Rietz was a prime example of an anthropologist who employed his training and the resources of the field fully in the service of the community. Unfortunately, for this very reason he is little known by anthropologists today.

Salvage anthropology was neither all bad nor all good. To return to Bruchac's essay about Speck, even as Frank Speck was working in close alignment with Algonquin leaders to protect Indigenous patrimonial lands, he was finagling to alienate patrimonial objects elsewhere, by purchasing four Haudenosaunee wampum belts that had been improperly obtained by a French trader from the Mohawk village of Kanesatake. Over the years, when Haudenosaunee chiefs protested, Speck and his successors stonewalled. In this business Speck evidently convinced himself that these tribal leaders were too economically distressed to preserve their cultural patrimony. In the darker spirit of salvage anthropology, he worried they would just "sell the belts again" if they regained them and reasoned that these objects would be safer in museums.[19]

This justification points to a crucial problem with the collecting of unique artifacts that does not apply to the collecting of texts. When a valuable, unique artifact is removed to the possession of an anthropologist or museum, it is no longer available to the source community for use in cultural transmission, a dispossession that is hard to justify except on the presumption that the source community will lose possession of it in any case. But texts are copyable and malleable in ways that facilitate nonexclusive possession (sharing) and use in different ways simultaneously. This contrast between artifact collection and text collection in respect of their potential to support Indigenous cultural revitalization is raised explicitly by Schwartz, and implicitly by Bruchac and Morgan, in this collection. In fact, it was the discovery of text copies that led Bruchac on the journeys by which she pieced together the story of those "lost" Haudenosaunee wampum belts. She travelled to each tribal nation, archive, museum, and auction house that had played a part in their story, along with delving into the faculty files of her own university department. By a mix of persistence and lucky coincidences in the course of this remarkable research, she succeeded in locating the surviving originals of the documents she had seen copies of, along with accompanying documents that helped her establish the wampum belts' provenance and the identities of the multiple collectors whose hands they had passed through on their way to their present location. Turning to activism again, Bruchac parlayed the relationships she had forged on these research journeys—with museums, Indigenous communities, private collectors, and Speck's own department—to lay a path that could facilitate the return of these wampum belts to Kanesatake.[20]

The depreciation of Native peoples, their capacities, and their choices is the most corrosive and galling fault of anthropologists that Vine Deloria Jr. excoriated in his biting critique of the field, which the essays by Robert Hancock and Sebastian Braun clarify. Deloria cast his attack on anthropology in the form of satire. In *Custer Died for Your Sins*, he presents a parody of the white male anthropologist who "heads into Indian country" with his camera and tape recorder to make observations and write scientific books and reports.[21] Overweening yet scruffy, this stereotype anthropologist is overzealous in his regard for the past that he identifies with authenticity. He is so very focused on Indians of the past—and recovering evidence about them that might have value for science—that he all but overlooks the present, evincing little interest in the actualities of life for the people before him. Indeed, he infects the thinking of some Indian youth with his excessive concern for the past, which he associates with "the 'real' Indian," "a mythical super-Indian," so that instead of contributing to the vitality of the community he studies, he harms it: he fosters a tragic "sense of inadequacy" in the present, "burying" the significance of present-day Indians' successes and struggles.[22]

As a remedy, Deloria urges anthropologists, not to stay away—this is a frequent misunderstanding of his critique that Braun and Hancock point out—but to become more "intimately tied in with the community" in its present life.[23] His insistent message is that anthropological fieldworkers must do more to reciprocate Indigenous communities for what these contribute to individual anthropologists' lives and the continuity of anthropology as a collective endeavor. Anthropologists, in other words, must address the asymmetry or imbalance discussed above. But they must do so, first and foremost, through their own conduct. For Deloria, it is almost beside the point what anthropologists publish in their theses, journals, and books that sit on library shelves. Their formal "scholarly productions," he says repeatedly, are "useless and irrelevant" to the contemporary "real life" needs of Indigenous people.[24] What really matters is how fieldworkers comport themselves: how they talk (respectfully?); how they reciprocate the hospitality they receive from people in the community (generously?); and how they react (helpfully?) when called upon to help, especially when important communal goals are at stake, as in land claims cases or the imperative of resisting tribal termination, that exceedingly noxious U.S. policy in the mid-twentieth century.[25] Addressing a meeting of American anthropologists, Deloria instructed: "You have some responsibility to the Indian community . . . to help us when we need help and not simply when *you* want to study us. . . . And we must see it on the basis of friendship."[26] In so saying, Deloria was instructing his audience of anthropologists in their own relationship to the past and the future. He was reminding them that they shared in the ethical estate of anthropological fieldwork predecessors in Indigenous communities. From these predecessors they had inherited a legacy of disappointment and apprehension to overcome. And looking forward, what would be their own legacy as fieldwork predecessors themselves to anthropologists in the future?

I was once asked by the director of a center for ethics in journalism to explain why anthropological researchers give expensive gifts to those they are researching, sometimes buying food for their families, paying school fees for children, even sponsoring health and economic development projects in their communities. Such gifts struck her as compromising the integrity of the information obtained, since they introduce an element of self-interest into the relationship between researched and researcher. Respectable journalists should not pay their sources, she explained, lest the objectivity of their reporting become distorted by conflicts of interest. Now and then they may appropriately pick up the check for a modest shared lunch, but they should never lavish large sums on their interviewees' children's tuition and other needs.

Of course, we anthropologists do these things because of how we understand the importance of our personal relationships in the field research process. Many of our relationships are built over long periods, and it is through—not despite—participating in them materially that we gain many of our most robust insights. Instead of holding ourselves apart from those we study so as to maintain an illusory neutrality, we often seek close involvement in their lives as a means to deep understanding. It is only a part of ethnography to report on the manifest content of interviews. It is at least as important to place statements in context and to learn from our own experience of participating in the worlds of the people we study, dealing with similar circumstances, power structures, assumptions, expectations, and so on. Necessarily, this opens us to their ethics—to evaluating our conduct and relationships in their terms. It is from this perspective, where local culture, history, and ethics are of the utmost importance, that researchers in the field are apt to consider the conduct of their fieldwork predecessors and the responsibilities they have left them.

In Alitoa, strange as it felt to be mistaken for Margaret Mead's children, Lise Dobrin and I grasped that our visit was being understood in terms of a longstanding Arapesh model of an exchange partnership (*buanyin*) that is inherited along a family line.[27] Such a relationship linking partners in different localities is itself considered a valuable resource. So, in the villagers' eyes, Mead and Fortune had long ago forged a partnership with Alitoa—indeed, with the ancestors of the owner of the meeting place where we sat. For us to step into their place in that long-dormant relationship, arriving with the characteristic anthropological paraphernalia of notebooks, camera, and so on, itself practically amounted to a claim to a kind of descent from them. The question, were they our parents or grandparents, was thus a prompt for us to elaborate upon our genealogical connection to our predecessors, who in the villagers' view must also be our ancestors.

In the local ethics of discourse, it would have been most appropriate for us to reply simply and emphatically that, yes, we *were* Mead's descendants, though afterward we might have let slip that we were not her children genetically but only through teachers, the connection of shared work, and receiving her influence by reading her work. At the time, however, we didn't manage to think of that. Instead, we gracelessly protested again that we were not in fact Mead's descendants. The villagers seemed disappointed. Eventually they asked, at least did we *know* her descendants? They brightened to hear that we were in touch with them and asked us to please relay word to them that they were welcome—indeed invited—to come visit Alitoa and maintain the relationship their ancestors had instituted. It was a place where fieldwork predecessors called out for fieldwork successors.

NOTES

I wish to thank the panelists at the "Voicing the Ancestors" conference session at the AAA meeting in Minneapolis on November 17, 2016: Sebastian Braun, Margaret Bruchac, Robert Hancock, Ira Jacknis, Mindy Morgan, Saul Schwartz, and Joshua Smith, with an added measure of thanks to Mindy for initially proposing the session and for organizing the lunch where we began planning to revise the conference papers for publication in this HOAA theme section. I thank HOAA's editors, Fred Gleach and Regna Darnell, for generously supporting the project from its inception, and the two anonymous reviewers for HOAA for their comments. I am especially grateful to the colleagues and friends who read drafts and offered suggestions which helped me improve the paper (and widened my knowledge in different ways): Grant Arndt, Marge Bruchac, Lise Dobrin, Richard Handler, Jeffrey

Hantman, Saul Schwartz, and Josh Wayt. It was Lise Dobrin's idea to repatriate those photos to Alitoa, and my thinking about fieldwork ethics takes inspiration from our conversations and her steady work over many years to present textual and other research materials in ways that will be meaningful to the source community.

1. About Alitoa, see Roscoe 2002, xxviii–xxx.
2. From a community's perspective, the relevant predecessors may be non-anthropologist researchers in other fields or even journalists and state social service workers who write articles, ask probing questions, and so on. To us, these are separate occupations, their institutional homes unrelated to our academic departments, but anthropologists have had the experience of having to prove to community members that they are different from such outsiders, for example, in the aftermath of disliked press coverage, health research, or censusing.
3. For example, I found my way to the Orokaiva region of Papua New Guinea where I began doing fieldwork in 1991 after reading Erik Schwimmer's writings about his research there in the 1960s, visiting him in Montreal, and receiving his encouragement. There is also the opposite case, namely, territoriality, where a past researcher seeks to block new field research in the same community (Schneider 1995, 135–36; Dobrin and Bashkow 2010, 98).
4. On the multifarious role of local assistants, see Sanjek 1993; Schumaker 2001; Middleton and Cons 2014; Bruchac 2018b; and Jacknis, this volume.
5. Papers from the previous sessions have been published in two collections edited by Richard Handler (Handler, et al. 2016, 2017). An additional collection edited by Bashkow is in press (Bashkow in press).
6. See, for example, the attempt to represent these relationships in a "family tree" format at https://academictree.org/anthropology, accessed March 8, 2019, or the discussion of the cultural politics of intellectual kinship by Bandeh-Ahmadi 2016.
7. For more on this history, see the essay by Schwartz in this volume.
8. Some of this history is traced in the classic paper by Jacob Gruber (1970) that appears to have introduced the term "ethnographic salvage." See also Haddon 1903; Jacobsen 1977, ix.
9. For example, Gruber 1970; Trigger 1980.
10. See Berliner 2014; Sahlins 2001.
11. For keys to the large literature on collaborative approaches to research in anthropology, archaeology, and linguistics, see Atalay 2012; Colwell-

Chanthaphonh and Ferguson 2008; Cook 2015; Dobrin and Schwartz 2016; Lassiter 2005; Parezo 2015; and Schwartz and Lederman 2011.

12. Boas 1911, 60–61, quoted by Schwartz in this volume.

13. Frank Speck letter to Edward Sapir, July 10, 1913, quoted in Bruchac this volume.

14. Speck had a long career of outspokenness and activism on varied fronts. In the 1920s, for example, he fought on behalf of Indians in Virginia against the infamous eugenicist Walter Plecker, and in the 1930s he actively supported the formally incorporated Eastern Chickahominy Tribe in seeking federal recognition (Adkins and Adkins 2007, 88–92, 116, 186, 196, 225–26; Rountree 1990, 215–36, 274). Remarkably, this long-sought recognition was granted to the Eastern Chickahominy and five other Virginia Indian tribes in 2018 (Portnoy 2018). For more on Speck, see Bruchac 2018b.

15. This question is discussed by Schwartz and Lederman 2011.

16. Rietz is the subject of a paper by Joshua Smith that was presented in the 2016 "Voicing the Ancestors" conference session and is expected to be published in a future volume of HOAA.

17. On Tax's "Action Anthropology," see Smith 2015; Stocking 2000, 191–96.

18. Smith 2016.

19. Florence Speck letter to Edmund Carpenter, October 27, 1972, quoted by Bruchac in this volume.

20. For the full story, see Bruchac 2018a.

21. Deloria 1969, 78.

22. Deloria 1969, 82.

23. Deloria 1973, quoted in Hancock, this volume.

24. Deloria 1969, 81, 95. The larger political significance of this is discussed by Biolsi and Zimmerman 1997, 15–17.

25. In Custer, where Deloria criticized anthropologists for failing to help Indian communities practically and politically, he was of course ignoring those anthropologists who were already actively doing so, for example, Sol Tax and Nancy Oestreich Lurie, both of whom were fervent, long-time activists and knew Deloria well. Lurie would later complain that younger anthropologists, themselves ignorant of the "exceptions and counter-traditions" that Deloria had omitted "for rhetorical effect," effectively turned "Deloria's critique into a self-justifying cliché that erased memories of anthropologists like Sol Tax, D'Arcy McNickle, Alexander Lesser, and Phileo Nash who worked with

American Indian leaders in struggles for rights and sovereignty in an era when such work was out of sync with the standards of disciplinary recognition" (Arndt forthcoming; Castile 2004, 275). About Deloria and Tax, see Smith 2015, 445 (quoting Deloria's eulogy for Tax), and the essays by Braun and Hancock in this volume.

26. Deloria 1973 quoted in Hancock, this volume.
27. See Dobrin and Bashkow 2006, Dobrin 2014, 135.

REFERENCES

Adkins, Elaine, and Ray Adkins. 2007. *Chickahominy Indians—Eastern Division: A Brief Ethnohistory*. Bloomington: Xlibris.

Arndt, Grant. Forthcoming. "Rediscovering Nancy Oestreich Lurie's Activist Anthropology." In Bashkow, et al.

Atalay, Sonya. 2012. *Community-Based Archaeology: Research with, by, and for Indigenous and Local Communities*. Berkeley: University of California Press.

Bandeh-Ahmadi, Hoda. 2016. "Insiders, Outsiders, and Intellectual Kinship #UniversityCrisis." *Allegra Lab*, http://allegralaboratory.net/insiders-outsiders-and-intellectual-kinship-universitycrisis/.

Bashkow, Ira, Carolyn Rouse, Grant Arndt, Arzoo Osanloo, and Rena Lederman. Forthcoming. "Vital Topics Forum: Voicing the Ancestors: Readings for the Present from Anthropology's Past." *American Anthropologist*.

Berliner, David. 2014. On Exonostalgia. *Anthropological Theory* 14, no. 4: 373–86.

Berman, Judith. 2001. Unpublished Materials of Franz Boas and George Hunt: A Record of 45 Years of Collaboration. In *Gateways: Exploring the Legacy of the Jesup North Pacific Expedition, 1897-1902*, eds., Igor Krupnik and William Fitzhugh, pp. 181-213, Washington DC: Smithsonian Institution, National Museum of Natural History, Arctic Studies Center. https://archive.org/details/gatewaysexplorin12001krup

Biolsi, Thomas, and Larry Zimmerman, eds. 1997. *Indians and Anthropologists: Vine Deloria, Jr., and the Critique of Anthropology*. Tucson: University of Arizona Press.

Bruchac, Margaret M. 2018a. "Broken Chains of Custody: Possessing, Dispossessing, and Repossessing Lost Wampum Belts." *Proceedings of the American Philosophical Society* 162, no. 1: 56–105.

———. 2018b. *Savage Kin: Indigenous Informants and American Anthropologists*. Tucson: University of Arizona Press.

Castile, George Pierre. 2004. "Federal Indian Policy and Anthropology." In *A Companion to the Anthropology of American Indians*, edited by Thomas Biolsi, 268–83, Oxford: Blackwell.

Colwell-Chanthaphonh, Chip, and T. J. Ferguson, eds. 2008. *Collaboration in Archaeological Practice: Engaging Descendant Communities*. Lanham MD: Altamira Press.

Cook, Samuel. 2015. "The Activist Trajectory and Collaborative Context: Indigenous Peoples in Virginia and the Formation of an Anthropological Tradition." *Collaborative Anthropologies* 7, no. 2, 115–41.

Deloria, Vine, Jr. (1969) 1988. *Custer Died for Your Sins*. Norman: University of Oklahoma Press.

Devereux, George. 1967. *From Anxiety to Method in the Behavioral Sciences*. The Hague: Mouton.

Dobrin, Lise. 2014. "Language Shift in an 'Importing Culture': The Cultural Logic of the Arapesh Roads." In *Endangered Languages: Beliefs and Ideologies in Language Documentation and Revitalization*, edited by Peter Austin and Julia Sallabank, 125–48, Oxford: Oxford University Press.

Dobrin, Lise, and Ira Bashkow. 2010. "'The Truth in Anthropology Does Not Travel First Class': Reo Fortune's Fateful Encounter with Margaret Mead." *Histories of Anthropology Annual*, vol. 6, 66–128.

———. 2006. "'Pigs for Dance Songs': Reo Fortune's Empathetic Ethnography of the Arapesh Roads." *Histories of Anthropology Annual*, vol. 2, 123–54.

Dobrin, Lise, and Saul Schwartz. 2016. "Collaboration or Participant Observation? Rethinking Models of 'Linguistic Social Work.'" *Language Documentation and Conservation* vol. 10, 253–77.

Gruber, Jacob. 1970. "Ethnographic Salvage and the Shaping of Anthropology." *American Anthropologist* 72, no. 6: 1289–98.

Haddon, Alfred Cort. 1903. "The Saving of Vanishing Data." *Popular Science Monthly* 62: 222–29.

Handler, Richard, Ira Bashkow, Jacqueline Solway, Lee Baker, and Gregory Schrempp. 2016. "Voicing the Ancestors: Readings in Memory of George Stocking." *HAU: Journal of Ethnographic Theory* 6, no. 3: 367–86.

Handler, Richard, Robert Brightman, Pauline Turner Strong, and Alexander King. 2017. "Voicing the Ancestors II: Readings in Memory of George Stocking." *HAU: Journal of Ethnographic Theory* 7, no. 1: 461–88.

Hantman, Jeffrey. 2018. *Monacan Millennium: A Collaborative Archaeology and History of a Virginia Indian People*. Charlottesville: University of Virginia Press.

Jacobsen, Johan Adrian. (1884) 1977. *Alaskan Voyage, 1881–1883; from the German text of Adrian Woldt*, translated by Erna Gunther. Chicago: University of Chicago Press.

Lassiter, Luke Eric. 2005. *The Chicago Guide to Collaborative Ethnography*. Chicago: University of Chicago Press.

Middleton, Townsend, and Jason Cons. 2014. "Coming to Terms: Reinserting Research Assistants into Ethnography's Past and Present." *Ethnography* 15, no. 3: 279–90.

Parezo, Nancy. 2015. "Introduction: Scholarly Collaboration: Past, Present, and Future." *Collaborative Anthropologies* 7, no. 2: 25–31.

Portnoy, Jenna. 2018. "Trump signs bill recognizing Virginia Indian tribes." *Washington Post*, January 30, 2018. Accessed June 12, 2018. http://www.washingtonpost.com/local/virginia-politics/trump-signs-bill-recognizing-virginia-indian-tribes/2018/01/30/8a46b038–05d4–11e8–94e8-e8b8600ade23_story.html.

Roscoe, Paul. 2002. "Introduction to the Transaction Edition." In *The Mountain Arapesh by Margaret Mead*, xv–xxxi, New Brunswick NJ: Transaction.

Rountree, Helen C. 1990. *Pocahontas's People: The Powhatan Indians of Virginia Through Four Centuries*. Norman: University of Oklahoma Press.

Sahlins, Marshall. 2001. "Reports of the Death of Culture Have Been Exaggerated." In *What Happens to History: The Renewal of Ethics in Contemporary Thought*, edited by Howard Marchitello, 189–213. New York: Routledge.

Sanjek, Roger. 1993. "Anthropology's Hidden Colonialism: Assistants and their Ethnographers." *Anthropology Today* 9, no. 2: 13–18.

Schneider, David. 1995. *Schneider on Schneider: The Conversion of the Jews and Other Anthropological Stories*, edited, transcribed, and with an introduction by Richard Handler. Durham NC: Duke University Press.

Schumaker, Lyn. 2001. *Africanizing Anthropology: Fieldwork, Networks, and the Making of Cultural Knowledge in Central Africa*. Durham NC: Duke University Press.

Schwartz, Saul, and Rena Lederman. 2011. "Collaborative Methods: A Comparison of Subfield Styles." *Reviews in Anthropology* 40, no. 1: 53–77.

Smith, Joshua. 2016. "Robert Rietz's Action Anthropology: Radical Caring and the Non-Use of Power." Presentation at Annual Meeting of the American Anthropological Association, Minneapolis, November 17, 2016.

———. 2015. "Standing with Sol: The Spirit and Intent of Action Anthropology." *Anthropologica* 57, no. 2: 445–56.

Stocking, George W., Jr. 2000. "'Do Good, Young Man': Sol Tax and the World Mission of Liberal Democratic Anthropology." In *Excluded Ancestors, Inventible Traditions: Essays Toward a More Inclusive History of Anthropology*, edited by Richard Handler, 171–264. Madison: University of Wisconsin Press.

Trigger, Bruce. 1980. "Archaeology and the Image of the American Indian." *American Antiquity* 45, no. 4: 662–76.

8

No Object without Its Story

Franz Boas, George Hunt, and the Creation
of a Native Material Anthropology

The role of Franz Boas (1858–1942) in shifting the institutional center of American anthropology from the museum to the academy is well known (Jacknis 1985). In his own career this was embodied in his transition from the American Museum of Natural History (1895–1905) to Columbia University (1896 until his formal retirement in 1936). Despite this, Boas's own reorientation of museum anthropology itself is less fully understood.[1] Boas's museum anthropology was naturally predicated upon a conception of what he took to be the aims of ethnology. These were two-fold. The first was to document the Native worldview. An ethnography should be, as he wrote in 1909, "a presentation of the culture as it appears to the Indian himself" (Jacknis 1996, 197). His second goal was to reconstruct cultural history, which was largely responsible for creating such worldviews (Stocking 1974, 8–9).

In implementing his vision, which may be partially glossed as the salvage paradigm, Boas called for the creation of a permanent record of non-literate cultures: the need of the anthropologist to acquire existing objects (especially the oldest available) or to create new ones (by the use of recording technology, such as pen and paper, cameras, or phonographs) (Stocking 1977). While Boas certainly valued highly the visual and material realms of Native cultures, ultimately he circumscribed their role, arguing that much of culture was ideational and what was visible might, in fact, be deceiving (Jacknis 1996).

In addition to his theoretical aims, Boas's museum anthropology was shaped by circumstance. Unable after 1900 to do much field collecting himself, he worked with others. In particular, he turned to George

Hunt (1854–1933), establishing a decades-long relationship which itself influenced and extended Boas's museum anthropology in significant ways. Of mixed English and Tlingit parentage, Hunt grew up among the Kwakwa̲ka̲'wakw (Kwakiutl) community in the intercultural trading post of Fort Rupert, British Columbia. Ironically, given his lifelong study of their culture, Hunt was not a Native Kwakwa̲ka̲'wakw, although he was bilingual in English and Kwakwala and was successively married to two Kwakwa̲ka̲'wakw women. In fact, as Berman argues, Tlingit may have been his first language, and he derived much of his social position from his maternal inheritance of ceremonial privileges, privileges that were honored by the Kwakwa̲ka̲'wakw. Hunt's "Native" identity, like that of many Native Americans, was thus not a simple reflection of Indigeneity. Although Hunt had many occupations over his long life, most important was his work as a key cultural mediator for a succession of ethnographers. Since Boas spent relatively little time among the Kwakwa̲ka̲'wakw, his resulting ethnography was a mutually constituted series of texts, created by exchange and dialog largely in an epistolary mode (Berman 1996).

FRANZ BOAS AND THE OBJECT

The core of a Boasian theory of material culture was present from his very first Northwest Coast fieldwork. On a trip to northern Vancouver Island in 1886, Boas encountered difficulties in carrying out his mission of documenting the earlier artifact collection at the Berlin ethnographic museum, gathered by Johan Adrian Jacobsen. He soon discovered that unless he could identify and speak with the original owners of these objects, and obtain their stories, he would not be able to learn their significance in Native cultures. Thus, he concluded that there was an inherent disjunction between cultural form and meaning (Boas 1890, 7).

The following year, Boas generalized what he had learned in a defining debate with Smithsonian anthropologists Otis T. Mason and John W. Powell in the pages of *Science* (Stocking 1968, 1974, 1977, 1994). Boas argued that cultural classifications based on external appearances were deceiving because "the character of an ethnological phenomenon is not expressed by its appearance, by the state in which it *is*, but by its whole history. . . . The outward appearance of two phenomena may be identical, yet their immanent qualities may be altogether different" (1887b, 589). If one could not depend on surfaces, then what should one study? Boas argued instead that "from a collection of string instruments, flutes, or drums of 'savage' tribes and the modern orchestra, we cannot derive any conclusion but that similar means have been applied by all peoples to make music. The character of their music, which is *the only object worth studying, and which determines the form* of their instruments, cannot be understood from the single instruments, but requires a complete collection of the single tribe" (1887a, 486, emphasis added).

Thus, the anthropologist needed to systematically reconstruct holistic cultural contexts. As his museum career evolved, Boas extended this perceived disjunction between form and meaning in his study of primitive art (Jacknis 1992b), a position that also lay at the heart of the doctoral dissertation of his first Columbia PhD, Alfred Kroeber (1901). By 1907, two years after leaving the American Museum of Natural History, Boas summarized his position on materiality in anthropology. Speaking of the vast assemblages of artifacts in museum collections, Boas argued that "almost all of them receive their significance only through the thoughts that cluster around them" (1907, 928), He continued, "Thus it happens that any array of objects is always only an exceedingly fragmentary presentation of the true life of a people. For this reason any attempt to present ethnological data by a systematic classification of specimens will not only be artificial, but will be entirely misleading. The psychological as well as the historical relations of cultures, which are the only objects of anthropological inquiry, cannot be expressed by any arrangement based on so small a portion of the manifestation of ethnic life as is presented by specimens" (1907, 928). This firm belief in the fundamental ideational and symbolic character of culture and the corresponding circumscription of the material world effectively marked a radical transformation, if not the end, of the "museum age" in American anthropology.

GEORGE HUNT'S IMPLEMENTATION OF A BOASIAN THEORY

Despite his formulation of a comprehensive theory of material anthropology, Franz Boas was able to spend only limited time in the field col-

Fig. 22. Franz Boas and the George Hunt family, Fort Rupert. Photograph by Oregon C. Hastings, 1894. American Philosophical Society.

lecting for museums. Instead, to execute his vision he relied on a large roster of collecting agents, most notably George Hunt.

Artifact Collecting

Over his career, George Hunt assembled many large and important artifact collections, a task for which he was well prepared (Jacknis 1991,

2002). As the son of a Hudson's Bay Company clerk in Fort Rupert, he learned to read and write, keep accounts, and became skilled in logistical matters of packing and shipping. As a young man, he worked as a translator for governmental surveys (in 1877, 1878, 1879), on the last assisting Israel Wood Powell on a collecting trip for the Canadian Geological Survey, which was Hunt's first involvement with artifact collecting. His first substantial collecting experience came in 1881 when he assisted J. A. Jacobsen with his collecting for Berlin's Royal Ethnographic Museum.

Franz Boas and George Hunt first met in Victoria, BC, in 1888. After taking down several texts, Boas continued to seek him out on subsequent trips to the Province. In 1891, he commissioned Hunt to assemble a Kwakwaka'wakw collection (the first that Hunt made entirely on his own) for the World's Columbian Exposition, to be held in 1893. After a summer in Chicago of intensive ethnographic collaboration, the pair was reunited in the fall of 1894, when Boas visited Hunt's village to collect for both the U.S. National Museum and the American Museum of Natural History, collections that Hunt supplemented the following year.

The most important collection that Hunt made was the one he gathered for the Jesup North Pacific Expedition (1897–1905) of the American Museum of Natural History. This, his largest collection (1,022 Kwakwaka'wakw, 283 Nuxalk, and 219 Nuu-chah-nulth items), was his most comprehensive. It was also the best documented—the artifacts themselves as well as the collecting process.

After the close of the Jesup Expedition, Hunt was hired by George G. Heye to collect for what later became the Museum of the American Indian (1906–1910). Later still, Hunt assisted in the collecting and photography of Edward S. Curtis (1911–14), Samuel A. Barrett of the Milwaukee Public Museum (1915), and Pliny E. Goddard, also at the American Museum of Natural History (1922–24). Given his training in ethnography by Boas, all of Hunt's work can be seen as an implementation of Boasian theory. Boas's position can best be seen in a series of letters that he sent to his field collectors, including Hunt. First, Boas felt that museum specimens needed to be well documented. For example, at the start of their work for the Jesup Expedition, in 1897, Boas

Fig. 23. Kwakwa̱ka̱'wakw (Kwakiutl) dish for fish oil, collected by George Hunt, 1897. American Museum of Natural History, cat. no. 16/2263.

wrote, "You will, of course, have to keep a note-book on all things you will collect in Bella Coola, and I suppose it will be simplest if you put a tag with the name of the specimen on each, and then write in your notebook again the name of the specimen, and the number, and what you have learned about it."[2]

Second, museum collections needed to be comprehensive. After a few years of collecting, Boas felt, however, that they were not getting everything that they needed: "It strikes me that we have not yet a full collection of the simple every day implements."[3] In calling for these domestic objects, Boas appealed to Hunt's Native understandings: "The best thing you could do would be to sit down and think what the Kwakiutl used for cooking, including every thing from beginning to end, then what they used for wood-working, for painting, for making basket-work, for fishing, for hunting, etc."[4]

Objects, however, were not enough, no matter how well-documented they might otherwise be. The domestic collections made in response were fully described in texts in Kwakwala and English translation, which Boas and Hunt subsequently published (1921). In arguing for texts, Boas explained, "Only we must remember that we want to have the tales and songs belonging to all of them," and "it is better for us to get a few pieces less and the story belonging to each. We do not want to grab everything and then not know what the things mean."[5]

In the face of Boas's constant goading for results, Hunt responded to his mentor in Boasian fashion: It "takes time to Do it Right."[6] Later he added, "Only one thing I see it will be harder for me this year, then it was at the World's fair [Chicago in 1893], for I got to get the stories and songs."[7] He added, "It is slow work for me to write the stories and buying at the same time."[8]

One of the most indicative examples of Hunt's internalization of a Boasian methodology came in response to Boas's complaint about the high price ($65) that his assistant had paid for a large feast dish in the form of a *tsonoqua* (wild woman of the woods): "The price that you had to pay for the Dzo'noq!ua dish is very high; and, although I presume you were very much interested in this specimen, I do not think the purchase was a very good one."[9] In response to this admonishment, Hunt explained that a similar one had just been sold for $100, and claimed that "The owner would not sell it for that Price so I thought I got it very cheap for if we write about the ways the Indians Handle it in the large feast I think you would like it."[10]

Finally, in order to address his aim of documenting culture history, Boas advocated for collecting the oldest artifacts that were available. Of old house posts, Boas wrote, "We cannot get enough of these; and the older they are, the better."[11] Along with the old, Boas often requested the good and the beautiful, which for him seem to be have been conflated: "The few old masks from Koskimo, and the old skull rattles, are also very good. I wish you could get more of these old carvings. They are much finer than the new ones. . . . What we need most are good old carvings."[12]

In his quest for old things, Hunt was guided by his personal experience. Of the old sandstones used to smooth down wood, he told Boas, "I use to see them when I was a little boy," and he searched around especially for the old time things he remembered.[13] He also discovered things that even he did not know about: "Yet I have lots of truly

Fig. 24. Kwakwa̱ka̱'wakw
(Kwakiutl) *tsonoqua*
feast dish, collected
by George Hunt, 1902.
American Museum of
Natural History, cat. no.
16/9013–14.

Fig. 25. Kwakwa̱ka̱'wakw
(Kwakiutl) skull rattle,
collected by George Hunt,
1899. American Museum
of Natural History, cat. no.
16/6897.

old fations [*sic*] things to send to you this year that you and I not no
any thing about of [until] you Read the stories carefully. for in the old
times I found out that there was no masks made of wood. for they Had
no knives to carve with. so all the masks was made out of Red cedar
Bark or LagEkw."[14]

Fig. 26. Kwakwạkạ'wakw (Kwakiutl) cedar bark mask, collected by George Hunt, 1899. American Museum of Natural History, cat. no. 16/6758.

Evidently, Hunt could not find any extant cedar bark masks, so he had them made. Boas was quite happy to accept newly made commissions, as long as they reflected traditional norms: "In regard to other things, I understand perfectly well that they are reproductions of older implements that have gone out of use, and that your friends are making them in order to show what the Indians used to do in olden time. In cases of this sort, I should even be satisfied if you had made them yourself, as long as they are made correctly."[15] Not everything the team collected, however, was old and an expression of pre-contact cultures. Among their accumulated collections were several objects of acculturation, such as a dance apron made of recycled commercial cloth (Jacknis 2002, 42). Undoubtedly, the justification was that these were vital artifacts for contemporary Kwakwa̱ka̱'wakw culture.

As a "Native" collector, George Hunt was more than just a facilitator for Boas. As Boas hoped he would, on numerous occasions Hunt initiated projects. As soon as he returned to Fort Rupert from the Chicago exposition in January 1894, he was out looking for masks, even though Boas was not collecting at the moment. It was Hunt who suggested collecting in late winter, searching in caves for old things, and seeking permission from the Indian agent. Once Hunt went ahead on his own, buying up all the carved stone heads he could find, then asking Boas if he wanted any. In December 1899 Hunt managed to combine personal experience and professional rationale in a typically perfect combination. Hunt's wife had been sick, and "one of this Indian medicine I am using on my wife this last five weeks and it is the only thing that is doing lot of good—so I think it is good to have all this in you museum."[16] Upon Boas's reply that it was a splendid idea and that his museum did not have such material, Hunt proceeded to make a rather extensive and unique collection of Kwakwa̱ka̱'wakw medicines (Jacknis 1991, 220).

Hunt was also Native in his collecting pragmatics. He was able to draw upon his circle of family and friends, and because he was a ceremonial practitioner he knew what objects were available. Once he was able to purchase a Nuu-chah-nulth (Nootka) whaler's shrine by trading some Kwakwa̱ka̱'wakw songs (Jacknis 1991, 211). None of this would have been possible for Boas.

Photography

In addition to collections of artifacts, which were made by Natives, Boas was eager to take photographs of the Kwakwa̱ka̱'wakw material world (Jacknis 1984). Hunt had participated intimately during Boas's 1894 field season in Fort Rupert, when the anthropologist hired O. C. Hastings, a commercial photographer from Victoria, to make 189 photographs of houses, crafts, people, and ceremonies. With Boas's example before him, Hunt soon demanded a camera so that he, too, could contribute to these aims of Boasian material anthropology. Like his mentor, Hunt's goal in his photography was to document a Native vision with its cultural meanings, which he usually glossed as "stories" (Jacknis 1992a).

Repeatedly in their early years of collaboration, Hunt cried out for a camera. As early as 1896, after witnessing a series of dramatic dances, he wrote: "Oh, if I Had your camera with me."[17] Hunt exclaimed, "I think we ought to done [it] long ago," for it would "make our work correct." Several years later Hunt again appealed to Boas, "I think it would show this things plain if we can get it taken in that way,"[18] and "for lots of this things is [sic] Done and I cant Explain it."[19]

Sometime between 1901 and 1903, Hunt finally obtained a camera, either from Boas or from his brother-in-law, who was a photographer. Almost all of Hunt's approximately ninety extant photos are now preserved at the American Museum of Natural History. Mostly taken on the Jesup Expedition, between 1901 and 1905, they illustrate a wide range of subjects: scenery (villages and places of mythological occurrences); subsistence (women drying seaweed and halibut, stringing clams, and roasting salmon); artifacts and technology (canoes and canoe-making, totem poles, potlatch figures, and grave monuments); portraits (his family, ritual leaders); potlatches (repaying marriage debts, giving away blankets, and buying coppers); and ceremonialism (costumed dancers, chiefs in regalia carrying coppers, shamans, and men gambling).

In good Boasian fashion, many of these images document artifact contexts. One notable example depicts a dancer wearing a bee mask with its full costume, both of which Hunt managed to collect.

In his photography, Hunt's pictures clearly illustrated a Native vision. Unlike most non-Native photographers, particularly collector Charles F. Newcombe, Hunt's primary subject was, in fact, not objects, but social activity, especially ceremonialism. For instance, as an initiated shaman himself he was able to produce the only known photographs of Kwakwaka'wakw shamans, even if they were staged.

This approach is also apparent from his photographs of potlatches, which Anglo cameramen also captured. Invariably, he is much closer to the Native action, and he clearly reveals the ordering of ceremonial space, with its vertical piling up of blankets and its horizontal array of participants sitting in a square.

Fig. 27. Kwakwa̱ka̱'wakw (Kwakiutl) bee mask and costume, collected and photographed by George Hunt, ca. 1904. American Museum of Natural History, cat. nos. 16/9587, 9624; neg. no. 13797.

Fig. 28. Kwakwa̲ka̲'wakw (Kwakiutl) shaman and patient. Photograph by George Hunt, ca. 1902. Hunt's caption: "Doctor Healing sick man with a Basket and sharp Pointed stick to Drive the Evel spirit away and spruce tree for the same." American Museum of Natural History, neg. no. 22868.

In many ways, Hunt's photographs are better documented than Boas's own. For ceremonies, he usually notes its kind, its stages and action, its participants and place, accompanied with a Kwakwala gloss. Like Boas and a few other anthropologists, he exposed photos in ritual series (such as the hamatsa dancer; fig. 31, 32); and repeatedly captured subjects in alternate times and spaces (such as marriage debt repayment potlatches in both Fort Rupert and Alert Bay, figs. 29 and 30).

As he matured, Hunt came to freely espouse a Boasian critique of other photographers, even those he assisted, such as Edward S. Curtis. Of a picture of his wife dressed for her marriage, Hunt complained, "He Dont [sic] know what all the meaning and the story of it. for on that Picture you cant see the four carved Post under it."[20] Curtis was interested in visual surfaces, not cultural meanings: "about the photo of my wife there is story belong to it. But Mr Curtice did not take the story or did not care as long as he get the picture taken."[21]

Figs. 29 & 30. Kwakwa̱ka̱'wakw (Kwakiutl) potlatches. Photographed by George Hunt, in Alert Bay and Fort Rupert BC, 1902–05. American Museum of Natural History, neg. no. 104463, and American Museum of Natural History, neg. no. 104473, respectively.

Figs. 31 & 32. Kwakwaka'wakw (Kwakiutl) hamatsa dancers. Photograph by George Hunt, ca. 1902: Initiate's return from the woods, and initiate being restrained. American Museum of Natural History, neg. no. 22866, and no. 22858.

Fig. 33. Francine Hunt, wife of George Hunt; "Nakoaktok chief's daughter."
Photograph by Edward S. Curtis, ca. 1910–14. Curtis 1915: plate 334.

In his photography, perhaps even more so than in his artifact collecting, Hunt was extending a Boasian methodology in profound ways.
Although going beyond Boas's own practice, his mentor would surely
have appreciated its value.

This intense focus on the material and visible world served as the
foundation for the pair's Kwakwa̱ka̱'wakw ethnography. Following

Boas's move to Columbia in 1905, they turned increasingly to the creation of texts of various sorts (Jacknis 1996; Berman 1996). Desiring no object without its story, in time they would focus on the stories themselves as the privileged entrée into Native worlds.

A BOASIAN LEGACY

At its root, the Kwakwa̱ka̱'wakw ethnography generated by Franz Boas and George Hunt was mutually constituted. Each helped form the other, over a span of decades. The nature of their relationship was emblematically demonstrated in a letter that Boas wrote to the Kwakiutl, which he asked Hunt to read at a feast in 1897:

> My friend, George Hunt, will read this to you. . . . It is good that you should have a box in which your laws and your stories are kept. My friend, George Hunt, will show you a box in which some of your stories will be kept. It is a book that I have written on what I saw and heard when I was with you two years ago. It is a good book, for in it are your laws and stories. Now they will not be forgotten. Friends, it would be good if my friend, George Hunt, would become the storage box of your laws and of your stories.[22]

The book, *The Social Organization and the Secret Societies of the Kwakiutl Indians* (for which Boas was sending the page-proofs), would be published later that year. Bearing the authorial credit, unprecedented for its time, "By Franz Boas, Based on Personal Observations and on Notes Made by Mr. George Hunt," it attested to their already close professional partnership. Boas and Hunt had many different sorts of relationships: Boas acted as teacher and mentor, as well as supervisor (for payment from institutions like the American Museum of Natural History or the Bureau of American Ethnology). For all of its constrictions and asymmetries (Berman forthcoming; Bruchac 2018), this was a professional relationship based on friendship, as Boas told the community at Fort Rupert. And as in any true collaboration, each contributed to a final product that neither could fully determine himself.

By the end of their lives, George Hunt and Franz Boas had jointly created a storage box of Kwakwa̱ka̱'wakw traditions. As Boas knew, boxes were key symbols in Northwest Coast cultures, both for the storage of

Fig. 34. Franz Boas and George Hunt, with Kwakwaka̱'wakw crafts demonstrator, Fort Rupert BC. Photograph by Oregon C. Hastings, 1894. American Museum of Natural History, neg. no. 11604.

food and other forms of material wealth, as well as metaphorically for the inheritance of ancestral rank and ceremonial privilege. The boxes of the museum and the book that Boas and Hunt were filling would thus contain both the forms of indigenous culture and, perhaps more importantly, their meanings.

The Native material anthropology that Boas and Hunt created around 1900 was thus a double challenge to the contemporary practice of curators such as Otis T. Mason. Instead of a universalistic evolutionism based on substance and surface appearance, they advocated for relativistic descriptions rooted in the concepts and beliefs, historically derived, held by the Native makers and users of those objects accumulating in museums.[23] At a time of severe cultural upheaval and dislocation, Franz Boas and George Hunt together sought to create a Native material anthropology.

NOTES

1. During my years of graduate study in anthropology at the University of Chicago (1974–79), I worked closely with George Stocking, the

dedicatee of the Stocking symposia at the meetings of the American Anthropological Association. In preparation for my intended career as a museum curator, I was inspired to apply Stocking's formulations of Boasian anthropology to the material and visual world, a topic that my mentor had relatively neglected (Jacknis 2016). This essay, which draws upon details presented in several of my publications (see the References section of this chapter), essentially elaborates insights on Boas's theories first discussed by Stocking. This essay also draws upon two earlier conference presentations: "Franz Boas, George Hunt, and the Development of a Native Anthropology in British Columbia," delivered in 2012 at Victoria University, Wellington, New Zealand, and "Native Anthropologists of the Northwest Coast, ca. 1900–50," given in 2014 at the Australian Museum, Sydney, Australia. I am currently extending this work in a collaborative research project devoted to Boas's pathbreaking Kwakwa̱ka̱'wakw monograph of 1897 (Glass et al. 2017). For his helpful comments, I am grateful to Ira Bashkow.

2. Franz Boas to George Hunt, April 14, 1997, AMNH acc. 1897–43; see Jacknis 1991, 190.

3. Franz Boas to George Hunt, January 13, 1899, AMNH acc. 1899–50; see Jacknis 1991, 190.

4. Franz Boas to George Hunt, January 13, 1899, AMNH acc. 1899–50, see Jacknis 1991, 190.

5. Franz Boas to George Hunt, April 14, 1897, AMNH acc. 1897–43; see Jacknis 1991, 190.

6. George Hunt to Franz Boas, April 23, 1895, AMNH acc. 1895–4; see Jacknis 1991, 190. In keeping with the conventions of the literature on George Hunt, his original orthography has been retained. As Berman argues (forthcoming), this is actually a key clue to his linguistic positioning in regard to the many languages he spoke (Tlingit, Chinook Jargon, Kwakwala, and English).

7. George Hunt to Franz Boas, May 24, 1897, Franz Boas Papers, American Philosophical Society, Philadelphia (hereafter APS); see Jacknis 1991, 190.

8. George Hunt to Franz Boas, February 28, 1899, APS; see Jacknis 1991, 190.

9. Franz Boas to George Hunt, June 17, 1902, AMNH acc. 1902–46; see Jacknis 1991, 197.

10. George Hunt to Franz Boas, July 4, 1902, AMNH acc. 1902–46; see Jacknis 1991, 197–99.

11. Franz Boas to George Hunt, April 30, 1897, APS; see Jacknis 1991, 190, 192.
12. Franz Boas to George Hunt, September 13, 1899; AMNH acc. 1899–50, APS; see Jacknis 1991, 192.
13. George Hunt to Franz Boas, July 4, 1899, APS; see Jacknis 1991, 211.
14. George Hunt to Boas, April 24, 1899, APS; see Jacknis 1991, 192–93, 194–95.
15. Franz Boas to George Hunt, January 3, 1900, APS; see Jacknis 1991, 192.
16. George Hunt to Franz Boas, December 6, 1899, APS; see Jacknis 1991, 220.
17. George Hunt to Franz Boas, February 15, 1896, APS; see Jacknis 1992a, 144.
18. George Hunt to Franz Boas, March 27, 1900, APS; see Jacknis 1992a, 144.
19. George Hunt to Franz Boas, February 5, 1900, ms. no. 1927, APS; see Jacknis 1992a, 92, 144.
20. George Hunt to Franz Boas, May 4, 1920, APS; see Jacknis 1992a, 145.
21. George Hunt to Franz Boas, June 7, 1920, APS; see Jacknis 1992a, 145.
22. Franz Boas to the Kwakiutl, April 14, 1897, AMNH acc. 1897–43; see Jacknis 2002, v, 393.
23. The possibilities of a Native anthropology had been a persistent, if limited, tradition in the Americanist tradition. Even before Boas, Lewis Henry Morgan had depended on the insights of Iroquois Ely Parker, as had Alice C. Fletcher with Francis LaFlesche, an Omaha. That Boas's own interests in developing a Native anthropology were more broadly based than his work with Hunt may be seen by his similar—although less substantial—research with two other Northwest Coast natives: Tsimshian William Beynon and Tlingit Louis Shotridge, as well as his encouragement of Ella Deloria (Dakota), Archie Phinney (Nez Perce), and Zora Neale Hurston (African American), all of whom he mentored during the 1920s and 1930s.

REFERENCES

Berman, Judith. Forthcoming. "Raven and Sunbeam, Pencil and Paper: George Hunt of Fort Rupert, British Columbia." In *"To Put It Down Right": Essays in the Franz Boas-George Hunt Collaboration*. Proposal accepted by University of British Columbia Press, Vancouver BC.
———. 1996. "The Culture as It Appears to the Indian Himself: Boas, George Hunt and the Methods of Ethnography." In *Volksgeist as Method and Ethic: Essays on Boasian Ethnography and the German Anthropological Tradition*, edited by George W. Stocking Jr., 215–56. Madison: University of Wisconsin Press.
Boas, Franz. 1921. "Ethnology of the Kwakiutl, Based on Data Collected by George Hunt." *Bureau of American Ethnology Annual Report for 1913–14*, no. 35.

———. 1909. "The Kwakiutl of Vancouver Island." *The Jesup North Pacific Expedition, Memoir of the American Museum of Natural History* 8, no. 2. New York: G. E. Stechert.

———. 1907. "Some Principles of Museum Administration." *Science* 25, no. 650: 921–33.

———. 1897. "The Social Organization and the Secret Societies of the Kwakiutl Indians." *Annual Report of the U. S. National Museum for 1895*: 311–738.

———. 1890. "The Use of Masks and Head-ornaments of the Northwest Coast of America." *Internationales Archiv für Ethnographie* 3: 7–15.

———. 1887a. "The Occurrence of Similar Inventions in Areas Widely Apart." *Science* 9, no. 224: 485–86.

———. 1887b. "Museums of Ethnology and Their Classification." *Science* 9, no. 228: 587–89.

Bruchac, Margaret M. 2018. "Finding Our Dances: George Hunt and Franz Boas." In *Savage Kin: Indigenous Informants and American Anthropologists*, 20–47. Tucson: University of Arizona Press.

Curtis, Edward S. 1915. *The Kwakiutl. The North American Indian*, vol. 10. Norwood MA: Plimpton Press.

Glass, Aaron, Judith Berman, and Rainer Hatoum. 2017. "Reassembling *The Social Organization*: Collaboration and Digital Media in (Re)making Boas's 1897 Book." *Museum Worlds: Advances in Research* 5: 108–32.

Jacknis, Ira. 2016. "Doing the History of Anthropology as the History of Visual Representation." *History of Anthropology Newsletter* 40, no. 1.

———. 2002. *The Storage Box of Tradition: Kwakiutl Art, Anthropologists, and Museums, 1881–1981*. Washington DC: Smithsonian Institution Press.

———. 1996. "The Ethnographic Object and the Object of Ethnology in the Early Career of Franz Boas." In *Volksgeist as Method and Ethic: Essays on Boasian Ethnography and the German Anthropological Tradition*, edited by George W. Stocking Jr., 185–214. Madison: University of Wisconsin Press.

———. 1992a. "George Hunt, Kwakiutl Photographer." In *Anthropology and Photography, 1860–1920*, edited by Elizabeth Edwards, 143–51. New Haven: Yale University Press.

———. 1992b. "'The Artist Himself': The Salish Basketry Monograph and the Beginnings of a Boasian Paradigm." In *The Early Years of Native American Art History: The Politics of Scholarship and Collecting*, edited by Janet Catherine Berlo, 134–61. Seattle: University of Washington Press.

———. 1991. "George Hunt, Collector of Indian Specimens." In *Chiefly Feasts: The Enduring Kwakiutl Potlatch*, edited by Aldona Jonaitis, 177–224. New York: American Museum of Natural History.

————. 1985. "Franz Boas and Exhibits: On the Limitations of the Museum Method of Anthropology." In *Objects and Others: Essays on Museums and Material Culture*, edited by George W. Stocking, 75–111. Madison: University of Wisconsin Press.

————. 1984. "Franz Boas and Photography." *Studies in Visual Communication* 10, no. 1:2–60.

Kroeber, Alfred L. 1901. "Decorative Symbolism of the Arapaho." *American Anthropologist* 3: 308–36.

Stocking, George W., Jr. 1994. "Dogmatism, Pragmatism, Essentialism, Relativism: The Boas/Mason Museum Debate Revisited." *History of Anthropology Newsletter* 21, no. 1:3–12.

————. 1977. "The Aims of Boasian Ethnography: Creating the Materials for Traditional Humanistic Scholarship." *History of Anthropology Newsletter* 4, no. 2:4–5.

————, ed. 1974. *The Shaping of American Anthropology: A Franz Boas Reader, 1883–1911*. New York: Basic Books.

————. 1968. *Race, Culture, and Evolution*. New York: Free Press.

MARGARET M. BRUCHAC

9

Encounters in Ontario

Acts of Ethnographic Search and Rescue

"Wampum $50.00." This simple notation appears in the midst of a list of accounts, in a dusty reddish-brown account book vaguely catalogued as "Montagnais-Naskapi" and housed in Frank Gouldsmith Speck's Papers at the American Philosophical Society. Fifty pages record an eclectic array of travel expenses and purchases in Algonquin, Montagnais, Naskapi, Cree, Nipissing, and other First Nations Aboriginal communities in Quebec and Ontario during the summers of 1912–14.[1] Sample entries include: rail fare for two from Philadelphia to Ottawa, $27; travel by canoe and hotel in North Temiskaming, $56.50; an array of miscellaneous expenses at Bear Island (including boat, "Indian Dance," pipes, strawberry soda, candy, and specimens), $172.00; and rail travel to Montreal via private Pullman car (plus incidentals), $26.00.[2] During this journey, Speck collected more than three thousand ethnographic objects; the single most expensive purchase was wampum. That transaction reflects a particu larly fraught entanglement of tradition, survival, salvage, and expediency.

For Speck, the logistics of the 1912–14 field seasons were a bit of a challenge. He had successfully financed earlier expeditions to Beo-thuk, Penobscot, and Nanticoke territory by selling Indigenous artifacts to George Gustav Heye at the Museum of the American Indian and George Byron Gordon at the University Museum (now the University of Pennsylvania Museum of Archaeology and Anthropology, or Penn Museum). But in 1912, as a relatively new faculty member at the University of Pennsylvania (Penn), he had no graduate students, no research assistants (other than his wife Florence), and no guaranteed funding. He did, however, have a new patron: Edward Sapir, recently appointed head of the Canadian Anthropology Division at the Victoria Memorial Museum (now the Canadian Museum of History).[3]

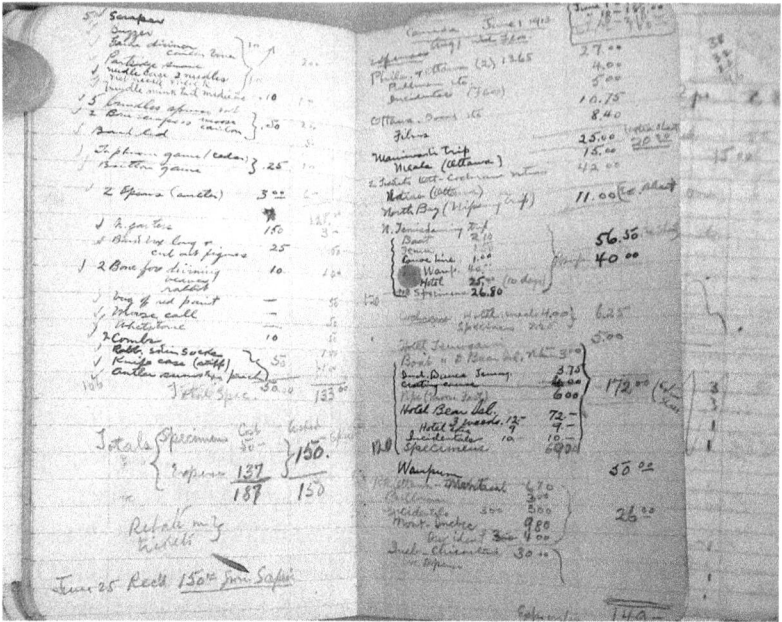

Fig. 35. Pages from Frank Speck's Account Book, showing some of his expenses for travel and ethnographic purchases in 1913. Courtesy of the American Philosophical Society.

Speck and Sapir were old friends; they had attended Columbia University together as students of Franz Boas, held successive appointments as Harrison Fellows at the University Museum, and taught in the emerging department of Anthropology at Penn.[4] Their families had even shared a house in Philadelphia, but their lives diverged when Sapir found a new position in Canada (Witthoft 1991, 6). The two men bridged the distance with dense correspondence, writing as often as twice a week to share anecdotes and insights, devise theories and research plans, and negotiate the values of material in their respective collections.

Their otherwise chatty correspondence took on a suddenly urgent tone in July 1912, when Speck discovered that his Indigenous research informants were, quite literally, starving due to their loss of access to fish and wild game, and dying from accidentally introduced diseases, with no apparent rescue in sight. In response, the two anthropologists devised a research plan that went far beyond mere salvage anthropology. As their correspondence reveals, they decided to meld ethnographic research with political activism. To articulate how this strategic intervention took shape, I have interwoven snippets of their correspondence, with explanatory text, into a series of dramatic acts and scenes.

ACT ONE: ENTERING THE TERRITORY

During the 1910s, Indigenous communities on both sides of the Canadian and U.S. border were struggling to retain territorial control, political sovereignty, and economic stability in the face of continuing encroachment by colonial settler descendants (Miller 2004; Morantz 2002; Scott 1988). When salvage anthropologists arrived in this middle ground, they faced Indigenous subjects who were not necessarily keen to be collected. Some were intrigued by the financial benefit that might come from selling crafts and working as guides, but others were wary of unwelcome outsiders (Bruchac 2018a; Ettawageshik 1999). A few savvy individuals recognized the potential of enlisting researchers like Speck as allies in cultural survival.

Scene One: The Natives Are Dying Like Sheep

When Frank and Florence Speck first visited Montagnais territory at Lake St. John in April 1912, nothing seemed amiss; they made some productive research connections and collected one hundred and forty ethnological specimens.[5] By the time they returned in July, however, circumstances had changed dramatically. In a hasty note to Edward Sapir, Frank wrote:

> As you must know, these rivers have been leased to American millionaires & the natives are forbidden to fish them, so they are starving and dying off like sheep from measles, smallpox & consumption with no medical assistance. The present overseer is a doctor but takes no concern for them. Mr. Gallienne is able to explain what has impressed me as the most atrocious outrage Canada has permitted against her natives. Yours in haste. (Speck July 7, 1912)[6]

Speck was shocked to discover that the traditional lifeways he sought to study were in danger of disappearing, as were the wild game populations that people depended upon. Indigenous communities had attempted to assert their long-standing free-range resource-gathering rights in specific territories under the agreements encoded in treaties, but their political status was shifting vis-à-vis the colonial settlers who surrounded them. Under Canada's "Indian Act" of 1876, they had been designated as "Aboriginal" wards of the state, who were not allowed to directly manage their own affairs or to negotiate with non-Aboriginals.[7] The state intended to segregate Aboriginal people from the rest of the Canadian population to ensure their "civilization, protection, and assimilation" (Dougherty and Madill 1980). The First Nations bands that relocated to reserve communities received some government assistance (commodities, health care, education, etc.), but they were also exposed to social disorder, cultural loss, and physical abuse (Coates 2008; Morantz 2002). The most vulnerable groups were Algonquin, Innu (Naskapi and Montagnais), Anishinaabe (Ojibway), and Cree people who had long depended upon hunting and fishing for their survival, and who were increasingly being forced to compete with colonial settlers and tourists for those same resources (Pulla 2016).

Until this moment, Speck and Sapir had largely followed their own interests and inclinations in field research. They had gone wherever they wished, interviewed whoever seemed most knowledgeable, observed whatever seemed most authentic, collected whatever they found interesting, and published whatever they pleased. Although they had experienced the loss of key elderly informants, it had not, apparently, occurred to them that they might be witnessing the impending loss of an entire research population and the destruction of a way of life. Suddenly conscious of both the urgency of the situation and their privileged positions as intellectual authorities, they decided to intervene. Speck took the first step by making a personal visit to the Canadian Parliament. He wrote to Sapir:

> Did I tell you in any of my letters that I went to the Parliament at Quebec to make a complaint at the Dept. of Fisheries against selling the salmon-fishing monopoly & letting the Indians at Moisie starve? (!) Yes I registered a big kick with M. Dufault, the Minister of Fisheries & he was glad I saw him (I was backed by some "wise ones" in Quebec) and he sent a telegram to the fish warden at Moisie to investigate and if the conditions were bad to allow them to take fish etc.

So you see I got one stone turned, & am not done yet. If they don't do something for these poor devils, I'll threaten to let the whole thing out in the Amer. papers & that, as I happen to know from friends of the Inds. in Quebec, is what some of the political grafters are afraid of. You didn't know I had developed into a sort of (political) missionary, but if you were to see those poor devils you would not wonder. (Speck July 7, 1912)

Speck did not specify who the "wise ones" were in Quebec, but his threat to alert the American newspapers was not an empty boast. Canada's tourist economy was, at that time, heavily reliant on American sport hunters and tourists (Pulla 2016).

Sapir, in his turn, immediately penned a letter to the Canadian Department of Indian Affairs, telling Speck "I have not forgotten your appeal in behalf of the Montagnais Indians." He went on:

I have written to Pedley, the Superintendent General of Indian Affairs, quoting the pertinent passage from your letter from Seven Islands and from your letter of introduction of Mr. Gallienne.... As I do not know Mr. Pedley personally I am having a carbon copy of my letter sent to Mr. D. C. [Duncan Campbell] Scott, who is Chief Accountant and at the same time Superintendent of Indian Education, and also to Mr. C. A. [Charles A.] Cooke, a Lake of the Two Mountains Iroquois in the Indian service. Both of these I know personally. I hope something may come of it to give added strength to your complaint lodged with the Department of Fisheries. (Sapir July 12, 1912)

Scott was the most highly placed Indian agent in Canada. Cooke, a Mohawk from Kanesatake who worked as a translator and clerk for the Department of Indian Affairs, was also the former editor of the newsletter *Onkweonwe* (Edwards 2010). As an Indigenous activist with both Iroquoian and Algonkian kinship ties, Cooke could be expected to spread the news to First Nations communities across Quebec and Ontario.

After interviewing "the educated people at Seven Isls. & Moisie and the Inds. themselves," Speck largely blamed the situation on a corrupt Indian agent:

Dr. Mc Dougall is not at all what he should be, neglecting his duties, and what shows more than anything his caliber, entirely out of sympathy with the Indians & their welfare. Although I did not see him during my stay, I heard from a number of quarters very unfavorable accounts of his indifference, inebriacy and medical neglect. This as you must realize is personal and I do not wish to bring charges against him nor involve you or me in controversy. To be plain with you Mc Dougall is evidently a crook Ind. agent (typical one) in the job for whatever he can get, and the devil with his wards. He prevents other worthy persons from aiding the Inds. as they have been accustomed to in past years medically on the grounds of a regulation restricting competitive practice which is in vogue in the province. . . . Had the Inds. received any care while at the coast they would not have succumbed to measles & smallpox after they had taken fright & fled to the woods. Here, of course, the Fisheries Dept. comes in. As long as they can not support themselves fishing while at the coast they have no recourse but to go inland to hunt & starve if the game fails. . . . These are the true circumstances as I see them; others down there too. Of course one of the greatest faults lies in the fisheries monopolies which prevents natives from fishing in leased territory. (Speck July 21, 1912)

Speck urged Sapir to convey these sentiments to Scott, while emphasizing that he did not wish to "involve you or me in controversy" (Speck July 21, 1912). Yet, controversy was inevitable, given the conflicting desires of the parties involved.

Scene Two: Making the Map

Speck insisted, based upon his observations thus far, that far-flung travels for seasonal hunting were not incompatible with part-time settlement at the Hudson Bay Trading Company posts and missions. He told Sapir that "even under a nomadic hunting life the natives can prosper if they have care, sympathetic medical attendance and some economic privileges." Technically, this hunting life was not truly "nomadic;" First Nations people traditionally timed their travels between sea and shore, and adapted to the seasonal availability of wild marine, floral, and faunal resources (Armitage 1990). Most non-Natives (especially American and Canadian sportsmen), however, imagined that these resources were naturally abundant in fixed locations nearly year-round. Failing to recognize the specialized ecological knowledges at work, they viewed Aboriginals as merely opportunistic hunters and scavengers.

In his 1912 report, Indian agent Armand Tessier attempted to counter this stereotype:

> The Indian is reputed to be careless and improvident. I contend on the contrary that so far as concerns fur-hunting he is endowed with a fineness of perception and a prudence that a white man has not. . . . Accompanied by his family, the Indian carries on his operations over a tract of land along a river or in the neighborhood of a lake, and that is what he calls his "hunting ground." That is his patrimony. It has been bequeathed to him by his father, who himself got it from his ancestors. From father to son these hunters have at the same place followed the fur animals, killed the beaver each year, and each year they have found it again and there always are some. There is nothing astonishing in that to anyone who knows how the Indian acts.[8]

Around the same time this report was released, Frank Speck seems to have suddenly "discovered" family hunting territories. Did he meet with a family hunting party? Was there a story recounted around a campfire in the north woods? Or did he read Tessier's report? Excited by the possibility of recording ancestral practices, Speck decided to interview hunters and chart the bounds. Sapir assisted by procuring an up-to-date geographical survey map.

The interviews began with Chief Aleck Paul of the Teme-Augama Anishinaabe at Bear Island on Lake Temagami, Ontario. Paul and other chiefs, Speck told Sapir, were "putting in a fine job marking territories," while also providing new information on totems and clans (Speck July 6, 1913):

> These people are Ojibways proper having totemism, paternal animal clans, the *Midewin* in the past, *Nenebuc* as their culture-hero, the *wisana*, or animal namesake (something I stumbled on to by accident never having heard of it before). . . . They, indeed, rec-

ognize the dividing line between Ojib. & Algon. I have had pretty good luck with myths, and social data and am making a sort of census of individuals showing name, totem, *Wisana*, nickname, family hunting territory or family name, & reason or story explaining the name. . . . I am getting what I wanted about totems clans & hunting family groups.

By the way please get another of those maps & send as a present to Chief Aleck Paul, Bear island, *Temagami P. Q.* as I have promised it to him. These fellows help me an awful lot to get among the people. (Speck July 6, 1913)[9]

Virtually all of the hunters that Speck met with appear to have enthusiastically joined in the process. He was eager to map familial and tribal attachments to specific ecosystems, but he also learned of relationships that transcended human kinship. In general, these Indigenous hunters adhered to the ontological construction of totemic animal ancestors, supernatural culture heroes, and wild animals as "other-than-human" kin and neighbors. Some of these other-than-human beings (in corporeal form or manifesting as dream spirits) communicated demands that, when respected, would ensure a successful hunt (Hallowell 1960; Speck 1917). Ritually proscribed weapons, charms, and containers were more than mere tools; they were imbued with intentions that solicited and reflected reciprocal human-animal relationships.

For example, many Algonkian hunters kept discrete and distinctive "meat pans" in the form of round, stitched, decorated birchbark dishes marked with etchings of the desired animals who had communicated, in dreams, their willingness to be hunted (Speck 1917, 18). The artistry of these meat pans was instrumental to the success of the hunt, as an Algonquin hunter named Kakwa explained:

It is known that when a beaver once comes to tell something it is never in vain that he speaks. . . . He also wants his meat pan made to look pretty. After it is done and decorated just as he wants it, he never fails (to supply his beneficiary with instructions where to find his game). Yet he does not wish different kinds of meat to be cooked in his meat pan, only his own kind of meat he wants to have eaten in it. (Speck 1917, 17)

Speck collected examples of these meat pans and other seemingly utilitarian objects—knives, fish spears, snares, tobacco bags, etc.—to illustrate the material components of Indigenous hunting traditions. These objects, however, did not communicate on-the-ground relations across space and time as effectively as the map.

The speed with which Speck constructed the map (over the course of only two field seasons in 1913 and 1914) was remarkable, given the fact that he personally traveled to so many of the tribal communities represented. Within only a few days of starting the project, he told Sapir:

> The map is now blocked out from Wanapitei Lake & to Temiskaming & Kipaua, & north to Matachewan Post with hunting territories. It is quite interesting but complex and important, especially to the Indian. It has been quite a job to see the various proprietors themselves of the domains and get the bounds accordingly. These are very strict among the bands and families. (Speck July 10, 1913)

As an illustration of scale, in one large area alone—roughly two hundred by three hundred miles between the St. Lawrence River and an area northwest of Lake Mistassini—Speck delineated fifty-five distinct family hunting territories for the Lake St. John (Innu) (Montagnais), including four for Chicoutimi, and nine for Tadousac and Escoumains (Speck 1927). The cartography was not without contention. In some places, several families claimed portions of the same territory, and Speck went to considerable effort to translate their concerns. Some chiefs saw the map as a political tool, and demanded that Speck speak to Parliament on their behalf. "The Ojibway," he told Sapir, were "more of a spunky aggressive bunch. They want me to put up a rec'd [record] for them at Ottawa" (Speck July 10, 1913).

With this in mind, it seems fair to ask: Was this map a marker of memory, or a snapshot in time? Did all of these hunters and tribal nations recognize these particular territories as ancestral? It seems possible that, during Speck's interviews and negotiations, the map may have shape-shifted into a strategic cartographic performance, with the intended goal of making Indigenous land use visible and comprehensible to white settler colonials.

Scene Three: Selling the Map

Apart from the practical goal of charting physical boundaries, the map provided evidence for three key claims: Indigenous people had utilized these territories before colonial contact; the territories had clear boundaries; and Indigenous families maintained proprietary rights to territories passed down from father to son. Interestingly, this representation neatly aligned with the restrictions encoded in the 1876 Indian Act. Technically, the Crown had limited Indigenous hunting and harvesting to only those reserved lands to which a band held state-sanctioned title. No one, not even a member of another "Indian band," was allowed to "settle, reside or hunt upon, occupy or use any land or marsh," outside of the lands assigned to them by the state.[10] The assertion of inherited hunting grounds thus conceptually extended title to Indigenous lands in multiple directions: temporally into the past, lineally through families, seasonally with the game, and geographically across a broad swath of territory. By arguing that they had always utilized these resources, Indigenous hunters testified to having tribally and individually occupied lands located outside of the reserves where the government intended to keep them. In effect, they asserted that the physical boundaries of the reserve traveled with them wherever they hunted.

When publicizing his conclusions, Speck indulged in an academic performance by exerting what could be called his "authorial authority." As articulated by Robert Paine, anthropological researchers must always consider these questions when representing their subjects: "Is it, then, our duty to 'arrange' what Otherness says, so that context appears by our authorial wisdom, i.e. privilege? Or is it our duty to let Otherness speak for itself (himself, herself)—to give it the stage?" (Paine 1989, 35)

I would suggest that Speck chose to do both by positioning himself as an esteemed authority on the Indigenous Others of Canada and by encouraging those Others to share space on the stage he had created. He finessed the performance of his data to simultaneously highlight Indigenous strategies of survival, resistances to modernity, and the durability of ancient traditions.

The title of Speck's first newspaper article on the topic says it all: "Penn Professor's Discovery Confounds Indian 'History': Doctor

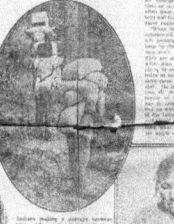

Fig. 36. Front page of the *Philadelphia Public Ledger* for November 23, 1913, highlighting Frank Speck's research on hunting territories. Courtesy of the American Philosophical Society.

Speck Establishes That the American Redskin Hunts on His Own Family Ground, is a Protector of Game, and is No Mere Rover Through the Forests" (Lovell 1913). Canada's Aboriginal hunters were, he argued, forest "farmers." The reporter for the Philadelphia *Public Ledger* noted: "[Speck is] known to the red men as their friend and protector. Many times he has interceded for them in Quebec and Ottawa, and the Indians know this and appreciate it, and it was therefore to him that they have given proof of their ownership of the forests not as tribes merely but as individuals thus upsetting all established data" (Lovell 1913).

The article, heavily illustrated with drawings and photographs, was so compelling that a reader might imagine themselves inside the tent, in the smoke of the fire, peering over Speck's shoulder as the map came into focus:

> To get this accurate map, [Speck] carried with him through his trips a large Government section map on which the Indians he visited drew with their own hands the boundaries of their lands. The map would be spread on the floor of the tent, and a family council would be held to ensure the accuracy of the drawing. Sometimes the head of the family whose lands abutted would be summoned, and a minute question of line would be settled. When the limits of their land were completely outlined, Doctor Speck would continue his journey with his guides to the home of the next family, where a similar process would be gone through with. (Lovell 1913)

Speck suggested that Indigenous regulations were, of necessity, conservationist in practice, since wild game was crucial for survival. The Hudson Bay posts were not modern capitalist intrusions; they were new resource-gathering and exchange places that had been almost seamlessly integrated into existing subsistence patterns (Morantz 2002). As Speck observed,

> The Montagnais subsist entirely upon the products of the hunt, trading the furs that they obtain during the winter for the necessities of life at the Hudson's Bay Company's posts. Accompanied by his family, the Montagnais hunter operates through a certain territory,

known as his "hunting ground" (*oti'tawin*), the boundaries determined by a certain river, the drainage of some lake, or the alignment of some ridge. This is his family inheritance, handed down from his ancestors. (Speck 1915, 294–95)

Speck quoted Chief Aleck Paul explaining how the restrictions operated, using comparisons that (Speck must have hoped) would resonate with white Canadian farmers:

We Indian families used to hunt in a certain section for beaver. We would only kill the small beaver and leave the old ones to keep breeding. Then when they got too old, they too would be killed, just as a farmer kills his pigs, preserving the stock for his supply of young. The beaver was the Indians' pork; the moose, his beef; the partridge, his chicken; and there was the caribou or red deer, that was his sheep. All these formed the stock on his family hunting ground, which would be parceled out among the sons when the owner died. . . . We were to own this land so no other Indians could hunt on it. Other Indians could go there and travel through it, but could not go there to kill the beaver. Each family had its own district where it belonged, and owned the game. (Speck 1915, 295)

Paul insisted that Indigenous people had managed and policed their territory since time immemorial to preserve the abundance and diversity of game. In subsequent publications, Speck dug deeper, unearthing (and promoting) further evidence of precolonial territorial arrangements (Speck 1927).

ACT TWO: THEY TRUSTED HIM

Speck was an extraordinarily successful salvage anthropologist. As Irving Hallowell recalled, "If there is an art to collecting, Speck had mastered it" (Hallowell 1951, 70). Edmund Carpenter recalled that Speck's informants "trusted him, often more than they trusted their own children," and that he frequently spent his own money purchasing significant cultural objects that might otherwise be lost (Carpenter 1991, 80). Native people liked and trusted Speck, but some of that trust might have been misplaced, given the fact that he was always on the lookout for valuable items that could be profitably sold to cover his field research expenses.

Scene One: Expansive Relations and Expensive Gifts

Speck was eager to find objects that appeared to be the last of their kind, including some that eloquently reflected the diminishing natural resources. For example, he was excited to procure a large canoe, telling Sapir: "Don't say it is too large as it is a *beauty* & of the larger size formerly called '*war*' canoe' by these people. They have entirely gone out of use now & I suppose can not be made for want of large enough bark" (Speck June 25, 1913). Field collecting was costly, especially in locales where Indigenous artisans had learned the value of their work. In the Adirondacks, he noted, "all of these Indians, through contact with tourists, sports etc. have an exaggerated idea of the value of their heirlooms and hold to them for fancy prices which I had to pay." Similarly, at Bear Island, "Prices are quite high as they sell a good deal to Amer. Sportsmen, as high as $3.00 to $3.50 for beaded moccasins" (Speck June 30, 1913).

Interviews were becoming more costly: "I also had to pay for information, at rate of $1.50 to $2.00 per day at Temagami" (Speck July 21, 1913). Even the informants who contributed to charting hunting territories expected to be paid:

> I have to pay fairly well for information giving something to everybody who contributes his knowledge. Some of them have worked pretty steady, for Inds., marking bounds and discussing divisions.... So I have had to pay out quite a little for info, something that I have gotten off easily with further east. (Speck July 10, 1913)

This raises important questions about motives. Were Speck's informants contributing to the mapping project solely out of their desire to both communicate and negotiate boundaries? Or was it also an opportunity to collect some extra income from a generous researcher?

In addition to the costs of paying informants and purchasing objects, Speck was especially attentive to protocols of gift-giving. At Bear Island, he honored his host Chief Paul and thanked the community by holding a "potlatch" feast:

Fig. 37. *Chief and group of Ojibways at Bear Island.* Photograph by Frank G. Speck, DOM # 2391, February 5, 1914. Courtesy of the American Philosophical Society.

Last night I gave this band a little feast and they gave us a dance in the bush. Almost 150 Ind[ian]s. came & we were the only white people permitted on hand, although there are a half dozen or so on the island. The ceremony opened with a round dance, a kind of "reverser." Then I had soft drinks passed around, & a Duck Dance followed, very pretty figure to it. Then they gave a Bear Dance "*Magwace.*" Then my "potlatch man" passed around bags of candy, cakes, peanuts, pipes & tobacco. Then another old man gave a solo dance while they were eating & I followed with a little speech which the chief translated in stentorian basso-relievo, & another round dance wound up my "potlatch." Needless to say my speech was a little complimentary & they gave me a good "Migwetc!" shout. (Speck July 6, 1913)

Notes like this are corroborated by expense accounts archived at the Penn Museum. Speck was the only Penn professor (and perhaps the only anthropologist) to make bulk purchases of candy and tobacco before heading out to the field (Bruchac 2018a, 162).[11]

Scene Two: Valuable Discoveries

Only a few days after the potlatch at Bear Island, Speck happened upon a remarkably valuable find. In Temagami, he met Jean Baptiste Delay, a French Canadian artifacts dealer who had, in his possession, two wampum belts that had been recently removed from the First Nations community at Lac des Deux Montagnes (Lake of Two Mountains, the Oka Reserve now known as Oka and Kanesatake) (Bruchac 2018b). Speck immediately recognized these as authentic and valuable. He told Sapir:

> I am very glad that I have a little piece of good luck to report. What I wrote you several days ago regarding wampum has turned out well and I have the belts here now and will send them by tomorrow by registered mail. There are two of them, beauties I must say. They come from the Iroquois at Oka Reserve and of course are very old. I got them from a Frenchman who had married an Ind. woman. He had brought them with him from Oka where an old chief had sold him the pieces, telling him that the white figures on a blue background denoted "chiefs," the more elaborate the figure, the higher in rank was the chief. This information is of course worthless scientifically. (Speck July 10, 1913)

Delay's interpretation was "worthless" simply because it was patently false; on wampum belts, the relative sizes of figures do not reference ranking chiefs; instead, they represent tribal nations, bands, or gathering places (Beauchamp 1901).

Speck described the belts to Sapir, proposing to sell them to the Victoria Museum (now the Canadian Museum of History) to cover his field expenses. Sapir confirmed that these were "certainly fine" and worth whatever one had to pay to get them: "It is too bad that their last possessor was not able to give explicit data in regard to the interpretation of the belts, but even so, they are great things to have" (Sapir July 18, 1913). They then indulged in some good-natured haggling over how much they could charge the museum:

> Now about the wampum (which incidentally I am worried about until I hear you get it), I could put the price of $125.00 for the two

belts, but do you think this is high enough. You might drop me a line personally & let me know what you think of it & if you think it is worth more, give me an idea. It nearly knocked me over to see those belts. I won't dicker with the price on these until I hear from you and you can figure it out & let me know. Of course if I do get a little ahead on this wampum deal it will pay up some of Flo's [his wife, Florence's] expenses in the field and help me out in some of my future work which is now all the more urgent & complete parallel studies at Lake St. John, St. Lawrence r[iver] & elsewhere, not to speak of Oldtown [Penobscot territory in Maine]. (Speck July 21, 1913)

When Delay offered up two additional Kanesatake wampum belts from the same source a short time later, Speck purchased those as well, hoping to sell them just as quickly.

Here it is important to note that the Oka Reserve, at that time, reflected an almost unique arrangement of Algonkian (Algonquin, Huron, and Nipissing) and Iroquoian (Mohawk) families, situated in two small, politically distinct villages—Oka and Kanesatake—located on either side of the Sulpician Church (Swain 2010; York and Pindera 1991).[12] Despite long-standing traditions of seasonal travel for hunting, the Algonkian families living at Oka had settled down (some more easily than others) to year-round farming (Speck 1923). Despite having converted to Catholicism, the Mohawk families at Kanesatake maintained longhouse traditions and political relations with Haudenosaunee nations elsewhere (Beaulieu and Sawaya 2000; Blanchard 1983). To the Mohawk chiefs, the wampum belts that Speck purchased had, in fact, served as significant material markers of their ongoing political relations with the Six Nations Haudenosaunee Confederacy (Bruchac 2018b; Nelson 2009).

Speck, however, treated these wampum belts as a fortuitous and lucrative discovery. He purchased all four wampum belts for a total of about $100, and immediately sold two to Sapir for $200 (Bruchac 2018b, 77).[13] The profits paid for his travel expenses and provided seed funding for further studies of hunting territories in Quebec, but his plans were interrupted by another unexpected call for help.

Scene Three: Strategic Alienations

In the spring of 1914, only ten months after the wampum deal, Speck and Sapir were contacted by Haudenosaunee (Six Nations Iroquois) chiefs at Grand River, Ontario with an urgent request. A collection of wampum belts improperly removed from tribal custody had been smuggled into the United States and sold to a collector. Chief Josiah Hill sent Speck a photograph of ten belts that had left the custody of Wampum Keeper John Buck under mysterious circumstances (Speck May 4, 1914). Speck asserted (incorrectly, as it turns out) that he had seen the belts in the Heye collection (which was then housed at Penn), but he was concerned that "divulgence of all the facts relative to the belts may make it unpleasant for the University Museum" (Speck May 13, 1914) and himself, since Penn was his place of employment.

At Speck's urging, Sapir wrote to Scott at the Canadian Department of Indian Affairs, suggesting that Heye be "given a chance to restore the belts without unnecessary unpleasantness," while asking "that as little use as possible be made of either Dr. Speck's or my own name in this matter" (Sapir May 16, 1914).[14] When it came to wampum, Sapir told Scott, communal property rights rather than individual property rights must be asserted: "it will be absolutely necessary to have the Indians prove that the belts were tribal, and not individual property, and that they were stolen from the tribe as a whole, and not rightfully sold by an individual. Once this is done, there should be no essential obstacle to the restitution of the stolen property" (Sapir May 16, 1914).

Scott then wrote to Heye, informing him that wampum was tribal patrimony that "could not be sold or disposed of in any way without the consent of the Tribes, which was never given" (Scott October 28, 1914).[15] Six chiefs—Richard Hill, Johnson Williams, Abram Charles, David Sky, John Buck Jr., and Robert Davy—signed an affidavit to back up their claims (Six Nations Council January 28, 1915), but Heye flatly refused to cooperate.[16] During this same time, a number of other wampum belts went missing under equally mysterious circumstances, generating confusion that has yet to be clearly resolved (Bruchac 2018b; Hill 2001).

Curiously, Speck and Sapir made no effort whatsoever to inform either Native chiefs or Canadian authorities about the four wampum belts they had personally purchased from Delay.[17] Speck quietly held onto two of these wampum belts (one with a five-diamond motif and one with a six-diamond motif) for sixteen years before finally transferring (likely selling) them to George Gustav Heye.[18] These acts of purchase and concealment seem out of character for men who had so passionately argued for the return of wampum belts under other circumstances. Did they regard the wampum they purchased as their own private property? Did they regard Oka and Kanesatake as less deserving of assistance in reclaiming cultural heritage?

At times, Speck was a man full of contradictions. In a 1916 article, he had insisted that Kanesatake's wampum belts were merely decorative relics and no longer used in a ceremonial manner (Speck 1916, 122). Then, in a 1923 article, he argued the opposite, claiming that "wampum ceremonialism" had persisted at Kanesatake, since the Mohawk were "strong enough to resist influence through contact with the restless Algonkian" (Speck 1923, 2019). However, at the same time, he insisted there was a strict divide between the settled Iroquoian "maternal-agricultural complex" and the nomadic Algonkian "paternal-hunting complex" (Speck 1923). By that logic, any tribal community that appeared to have blended these practices would have no valid claim to either a fixed reserve or a hunting territory. These published assertions were not merely theoretical; the words of academic authorities carried power amidst the already fraught relations with the state, and they generated misleading representations that have persisted into the present (Miller 2004; York and Pindera 1991).

This wampum transaction is best understood by looking at two key pieces of evidence: the account book that plainly records Speck's ethnographic expenses, purchases, and sales, and the information contained in a letter from another witness to the events: Frank's wife, Florence Speck. In 1972, six decades after their trip to Temagami and two decades after Frank's death, Florence wrote to Frank's former student, Edmund (Ted) Carpenter. She was dismayed to hear that some Haudenosaunee ritual masks collected by Frank were recently sold at a Sotheby's auction, and the news stirred an old memory of another sensitive collection. She told Ted that tribal leaders had been pleading with her for years for the return of their wampum:

The Indians have been trying to buy back the wampum belts which Frank had bought from a man in Canada. I was with him when we went there. . . . I carried the belts in a dark green bag, like all the students carried with their books. Later on we took the beaded belts to the State Museum [NYSM] at Albany and gave them for safe keeping. The Indians have been trying to get them back but Frank always said, they would sell them again and they are safe there. (Florence Speck October 27, 1972)[19]

She recalled that in some cases, Frank had purchased and donated ritual objects to unscrupulous tribal individuals who only re-sold them to dealers. She also recalled that, since Canadian authorities had been actively engaged in a search for stolen wampum, her "dark green bag" had offered a convenient means of concealment when she and Frank crossed the border. Sadly, Carpenter never responded to Florence's concerns about wampum belts. His colleague William Fenton concluded that "Mrs. Speck's memory was faulty," since he had no knowledge of Speck having deposited wampum at either the NYSM or MAI. Florence's "potentially embarrassing" letter was then tucked away in uncatalogued private museum archives.[20]

Over the course of a century, the wampum belts that Speck purchased from Delay wound their way into and out of public and private collections; each step in their travels inspired new labels that identified them as inherently unidentifiable relics and art objects, rather than Indigenous patrimony (Bruchac 2018b). When one of those belts resurfaced at a Sotheby's auction in 2009, Condoled Chief Curtis Nelson testified that an elder chief, ninety-four-year-old Tekharihoken (Samson Gabriel), recalled the circumstances of its loss: "It is known that Frank Speck wrongfully purchased this Wampum Belt and other Wampum items from a French man named J. B. Delay who was married to a Kanesatake woman. People at Kanesatake and other Mohawk communities at Grand River Territory tried to get all the stolen Kanesatake Belts returned but were not successful at that time" (Nelson 2009).

Two of the wampum belts that Speck purchased were eventually repatriated—the six-diamond belt one in 2014, and the five-diamond belt in 2018—but two remain in the collections of the Canadian

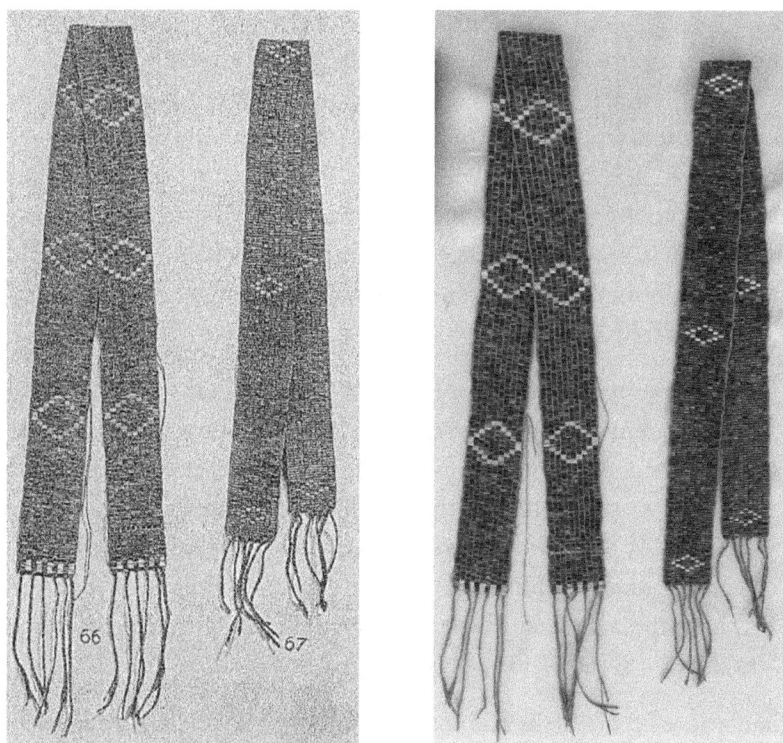

Fig. 38. (Left) The six-diamond wampum belt and five-diamond wampum belt from Kanesatake are shown in a black and white photograph taken by Frank G. Speck in 1915. (Right) The same two wampum belts are shown at Kanesatake after their reunification, in a photograph taken by Margaret M. Bruchac in 2018.

Museum of History (Bruchac 2018b). Many other patrimonial items are still missing, and the search to recover them continues today.

EPILOGUE

Why revisit these letters from the early days of anthropology? Correspondence can preserve important records of personal opinions, social negotiations, and intellectual theories as they evolve into political representations and actions that may have lasting effects. Salvage anthropologists were forced to take an abrupt turn when faced with the imminent extinction of their subjects. These letters capture the moments when researchers were rushing to capture materials before their subjects vanished, while also wielding the power to decide how those materials would be represented in museums and in texts.

In retrospect, it is worth considering just what was in the minds of those hunters who labored to place their marks on the map they constructed, in collaboration with Speck. In a world where power can be conceptually invested in spoken words (e.g., ritual speech) and in apparently inanimate objects (e.g., wampum), words on paper could become a potent weapon for cartographically reclaiming territory. Chief Paul told Speck:

> You can write this down for me. . . . What we Indians want is for the Government to stop the white people killing our game, as they do it only for sport and not for support. We Indians do not need to be watched about protecting the game, we must protect the game or starve. . . . When the treaty was made, about sixty years ago, the Government said, "You Indians own the game. . . . These Indians need to have their rights in the land recognized and protected as much as the new settlers." (Speck 1913, 24)

Paul was referring to the Robinson-Huron treaty, which had explicitly promised hunting and fishing rights to the Teme-Augama Anishnaabe, but Ontario had refused to set aside a reserve. Ironically, some Native people then became dependent on income gained from working as guides and fire rangers for the non-Native hunters, tourists, settlers, and surveyors who sought to displace them (Thorpe 2012, 52). With this in mind, Speck's informants were not "primitives" stuck in the past; they were savvy people in a modern world, using ancient logics to tap into any available resources to survive.

The desires of museums and the market economy had, to a considerable degree, fueled the economic engines of ethnographic salvage. Native people were not merely passive victims in this trade, however. Some artisans crafted utilitarian and decorative objects—canoes, hunting equipment, baskets, tourist art, etc.—explicitly for sale (Ettawageshik 1999). Objects like these reflected, not an "impersonal trade" dependent upon a market exchange of goods and service, but something closer to a face-to-face "mutuality" in a shared landscape (Gudeman 2009, 63–64). Speck, through his generous gift-giving and craft purchases, was a key participant in this mutuality, but he also trans-formed some of the sensitive objects he collected into marketable com-modities. Those sales were expedient at the time, but they sometimes caused the very kinds of cultural loss he sought to prevent.

In the end, Speck's "family hunting territory" argument was a quali-fied success. As an interventional strategy, it restored some hunting and fishing rights, but as a foundational understanding, it provoked unend-ing debate around the relative time-depth of Indigenous hunting tradi-tions. During the 1930s, Diamond Jenness argued that "primitive" and "migratory" tribes owned no "real property," and that the boundaries were merely a carry-over from colonial fur trading with the Hudson Bay Company (Jenness 1932). Then, Eleanor Leacock argued that patrilineal territories were a patriarchal, capitalist intrusion into earlier matrilineal and communal systems (Leacock 1955). Calvin Martin suggested that hunting traditions had died out generations earlier when Indigenous "masters of the game" were enticed by the bounty of the fur trade to destroy their animal brethren (Martin 1978). Harvey Feit later praised Speck's moral advocacy but characterized his research as an "ethno-graphic error" (Feit 1991). Shephard Krech insisted that Native people had never been natural preservationists to begin with (Krech 1999). Yet, these arguments miss the point: the various forms of Indigenous engagement with resources—cooperation, preservation, market trade, reciprocity, ritual—need not be mutually exclusive. The emphasis on ethnic essentialism appears to have prevented some observers from understanding that Aboriginal hunters could be perfectly capable of selectively employing differing responses to differing circumstances.

I would suggest that what Speck and Sapir devised, in collabora-tion with their Indigenous interlocutors, was a clever approach to a fraught situation. By placing the primary *public* responsibility for game management with male heads of families, while under-emphasizing other equally important relationships, they promoted an interpreta-tion that would fit the restrictions of the Indian Act, wherein land ownership, hunting rights, and chiefly title were vested conspicuously (and, apparently, solely) in men. From the outside, it would appear as though ritual hunting practices had been secularized, transmuted into the practical "farming" of wild fauna. Yet, the spirits of the game still spoke to those who listened. Thus, one style of negotiation took place in *private* spaces where both men and women interacted with other-than-humans, away from the prying eyes of both state agents and anthropologists. Another style of negotiation took place in public spaces, where one was expected to navigate settler state protocols. Canadian authorities cooperated, to a degree, by preserving some tribal and patrilineal hunting and fishing rights on both treaty lands and "unoccupied" Crown lands, but many significant areas are still unprotected and contested today.[21]

In the twenty-first century, as Colin Scott has demonstrated among the Cree, the family hunting territory model has gained new respect as what is, and likely always was, a highly effective means of managing wildlife resources in remote locales "where cooperation between households is most important," and is, in fact, critical for survival (Scott 1988, 170). Sovereignty and self-determination, as Anna Willow observes among the Anishinaabe, can be also exerted through the practice of counter-narratives and "counter-mapping" to restore traditional understandings that have been warped by settler colonialism and historical injustices (Willow 2013). By re-marking, re-claiming, and re-utilizing traditional territories and ecosystems, Indigenous people (in Canada and elsewhere) are demonstrating that Indigenous maps need not be rooted in the past and fixed in time, but can be a savvy (and, if necessary, fluid) response that employs whatever tools are necessary to effectively communicate sovereign rights while grappling with the colonial situation at hand.

NOTES

1. The term "Aboriginal" designates the First Nations people in the traditional territories that are often mapped as part of the colonial settler nation of Canada. Many historical sources also use the terms "Indians" or "natives." In this text, the term "Indigenous" will be used to refer broadly to Native Americans, also known as American Indians, in the United States and First Nations, also known as Aboriginals, in Canada.

2. "Account book for field trips," in Subcollection I, Series I Research Material, II Circumboreal, B Montagnais-Naskapi, 1 General Information, Box 2, Frank G. Speck Papers, Mss. Ms. Coll. 126, American Philosophical Society (APS).

3. Notations of sales to patrons can be found in Speck's account book and ledger 1908–49, in Series III, Personal: B. Accounts, box 8, folder 6, Frank G. Speck Papers, E44, Phillips Library, Peabody Essex Museum (PEM).
4. "Anthropology, Department of," University Relations Files, UPF 8.51 box 14, University Archives and Records Center, University of Pennsylvania.
5. Speck account book, APS.
6. Unless otherwise noted, these letters are archived in the Sapir Correspondence 1-A-236M, Box 634 f.1 (1911–1912), and Box 634 f.2 (1913–1914), Canadian Museum of History (CMH).
7. Formerly the "Gradual Enfranchisement Act" in Laws of Canada, Chapter 18: "An Act to amend and consolidate the laws respecting Indians (April 12, 1876)," "Indigenous and Northern Affairs Canada," Government of Canada, accessed May 30, 2017, www.aadnc-aandc.gc.ca/eng/1100100010252/1100100010254.
8. Armand Tessier. 1912 Report in Department of Indian Affairs Records, Public Archives of Canada, Ottawa, vol. 6750, file 420–10, January 13, 1913.
9. Underlining is in the original text.
10. 1876 Indian Act in Laws of Canada, Chapter 18 (April 12, 1876).
11. See, for example, "Expense Accounts for 1910–1911" in Speck Papers box 10 folders 4–5, Penn Museum Archives, University of Pennsylvania Museum of Archaeology and Anthropology.
12. The entanglement of these communities happened in the early 1700s, during the relocation of the Sault au Recollet Indian Mission founded by the Saint Sulpice Seminary in Montreal (Beaulieu and Sawaya 2000; Swain 2010). By the 1910s, despite existing treaties and promised lands, Native titles to the land were under attack by the Sulpicians, who were actively engaged in efforts to sell off thousands of acres (Swain 2010, 21–22).
13. The wampum belts only cost about $90, but Speck was obligated to purchase other objects from Delay in order to get the wampum. A few of Delay's letters are archived in "Wampum—Misc. Notes" in Subcollection I, Series I Research Material, III Northeast, A. General, Box 3, in the Frank Speck Papers at the American Philosophical Society.
14. "Six Nations Agency—Reports, Correspondence and Memoranda Regarding the Theft of Eleven Wampum Belts from the Six Nations Reserve." Library Archives of Canada 1900–1915, Record Group 10, Volume 3018, File 220, 155.
15. "Six Nations Agency," 155.
16. "Six Nations Agency," 155.

17. The two wampum belts that Speck sold to Sapir still reside in the collections of the Canadian Museum of History today, where they are catalogued as CMH #III-I-929 and #III-1-930.
18. The two wampum belts that Speck sold to Heye were catalogued as MAI #16/3826 and MAI #16/3827; both have since been returned to Kanesatake (Bruchac 2018b).
19. Florence Speck to Edmund Carpenter, October 27, 1972, letter archived in uncatalogued curatorial files at the New York State Museum Archives, Albany NY.
20. George Hamell to William Fenton, June 15, 1994, letter archived in uncatalogued curatorial files at the New York State Museum Archives, Albany NY.
21. See, for example, the "Numbered Treaties" in northern Ontario, Manitoba, and elsewhere, described in "Treaties with Aboriginal people in Canada," *Indigenous and Northern Affairs Canada*, Government of Canada, accessed June 10, 2017, www.aadnc-aandc.gc.ca/eng /1100100032291/1100100032292.

REFERENCES

Armitage, Peter. 1990. *Land Use and Occupancy Among the Innu of Utshimassit and Sheshatshit*. Sheshatshiu: Innu Nation.

Beauchamp, William M. 1901. "Wampum and Shell Articles Used by the New York Indians." *New York State Museum Bulletin* 41: 321–480.

Beaulieu, Alain, and Jean-Pierre Sawaya. 2000. "L'importance strategique des Sept-Nations du Canada." *Bulletin d'Historie Politique* 8 no. 2–3: 87–107.

Blanchard, David. 1983. "The Seven Nations of Canada: An Alliance and a Treaty." *American Indian Culture and Research Journal* 7, no. 2: 3–23.

Bruchac, Margaret M. 2018a. *Savage Kin: Indigenous Informants and American Anthropologists*. Tucson: University of Arizona Press.

———. 2018b. "Broken Chains of Custody: Possessing, Dispossessing, and Repossessing Lost Wampum Belts." *Proceedings of the American Philosophical Society* 62, no. 1: 56–105.

Carpenter, Edmund. 1991. "Frank Speck: Quiet Listener." In *The Life and Times of Frank G. Speck, 1881–1950*, edited by Roy Blankenship, 78–84. Philadelphia: University of Pennsylvania Department of Anthropology.

Coates, Ken. 2008. "The Indian Act and the Future of Aboriginal Governance in Canada." Research Paper for the National Centre for First Nations Governance. Accessed April 22, 2019. http://fngovernance.org /ncfng_research/coates.pdf.

Dougherty, Wayne, and Dennis Madill. 1980. *Indian Government under Indian Act Legislation, 1868–1951.* Ottawa: Department of Indian Affairs and Northern Development, Treaties and Historical Research Centre.

Edwards, Brendan F. R. 2010. "'A most industrious and farseeing Mohawk scholar': Charles A. Cooke (Thawennensere), Civil Servant, Amateur Anthropologist, Performer, and Writer." *Ontario History* CII, no. 1: 83–110.

Ettawageshik, Frank. 1999. "My Father's Business." In *Unpacking Culture: Art and Commodity in Colonial and Postcolonial Worlds,* edited by Ruth B. Phillips and Christopher B. Steiner, 20–29. Berkeley: University of California Press.

Feit, Harvey A. 1991. "The Construction of Algonquian Hunting Territories: Private Property as Moral Lesson, Policy Advocacy, and Ethnographic Error." In *Colonial Situations: Essay on the Contextualization of Ethnographic Knowledge,* edited by George W. Stocking Jr., 109–34. Madison: University of Wisconsin Press.

Gudeman, Steve. 2009. *Economic Persuasions.* New York: Berghan Books.

Hallowell, A. Irving. 1960. "Ojibwa Ontology, Behavior and World View." *Culture in History: Essays in Honor of Paul Radin,* edited by Stanley Diamond, 19–52. New York: Columbia University Press.

———. 1951. "Frank Gouldsmith Speck, 1881–1950." *American Anthropologist* 53, no. 1: 67–75.

Hill, Richard. 2001. "Regenerating Identity: Repatriation and the Indian Frame of Mind." In *The Future of the Past: Archaeologists, Native Americans and Repatriation,* edited by Tamara Bray, 127–37. New York: Garland Publishing.

Jenness, Diamond. 1932. *The Indians of Canada,* Bulletin 45. Ottawa: National Museum of Canada.

Krech, Shephard, III, ed. 1999. *The Ecological Indian: Myth and History.* New York: W. W. Norton.

Leacock, Eleanor. 1955. "Matrilocality in a Simple Hunting Economy (Montagnais-Naskapi)." *Southwestern Journal of Anthropology* 11, no. 1: 31–47.

Lovell, Malcom Read. 1913. "Penn Professor's Discovery Confounds Indian 'History': Doctor Speck Establishes That the American Redskin Hunts on His Own Family Ground, is a Protector of Game, and is No Mere Rover Through the Forests." *Public Ledger,* November 23, 1913.

Martin, Calvin. 1978. *Keepers of the Game: Indian-Animal Relationships and the Fur Trade.* Berkeley: University of California Press.

Miller, James R. 2004. *Reflections on Native-Newcomer Relations*. Toronto: University of Toronto Press.

Morantz, Toby. 2002. *The White Man's Gonna Getcha: The Colonial Challenge to the Crees in Quebec*. Montreal: McGill-Queen's University Press.

Nelson, Chief Curtis. 2009. "Declaration to the Haudenosaunee Standing Committee on Burial Rules and Regulations." Unpublished manuscript, testimony provided to the Haunosaunee Standing Committee; copy in author's possession.

Paine, Robert. 1989. "Our Authorial Authority," *Culture* 9, no. 2: 35–48.

Pulla, Siomonn P. 2016. "Critical Reflections on (Post) Colonial Geographies: Applied Anthropology and the Interdisciplinary Mapping of Indigenous Traditional Claims in Canada during the Early 20th Century." *Human Organization* 75, no. 4: 289–304.

Scott, Colin. 1988. "Property, Practice and Aboriginal Rights Among Quebec Cree Hunters." In *Hunters and Gatherers 2: Property, Power and Ideology*, edited by Tim Ingold, David Riches, and James Woodburn, 35–51. Oxford: Berg.

Speck, Frank G. 1927. "Family Hunting Territories of the Lake St. John Montagnais and Neighboring Bands," *Anthropos* 22, no. 3/4: 387–403.

———. 1923. "Algonkian Influence upon Iroquois Social Organization." *American Anthropologist*, New Series 25, no. 2: 219–27.

———. 1917. "Game Totems among the Northeastern Algonkians." *American Anthropologist* 19, no. 1: 9–18.

———. 1915. "The Family Hunting Band as the Basis of Algonkian Social Organization." *American Anthropologist* 17, no. 2: 289–305.

———. 1916. "Wampum in Indian Tradition and Currency." *Proceedings of the Numismatic and Antiquarian Society of Philadelphia* 27: 121–31.

———. 1913. "The Indians and game preservation," *Red Man* 6, 21–25.

Swain, Harry. 2010. *Oka: A Political Crisis and Its Legacy*. Vancouver: Douglas and McIntyre.

Thorpe, Jocelyn. 2012. *Temagami's Tangled Wild Rice: Race, Gender, and the Making of Canadian Nature*. Vancouver: University of British Columbia Press.

Willow, Anna J. 2013. "Doing Sovereignty in Native North America: Anishinaabe Counter-Mapping and the Struggle for Land-Based Self-Determination." *Human Ecology* 41, no. 6: 871–84.

Witthoft, John G. 1991. "Frank Speck: The Formative Years." In *The Life and Times of Frank G. Speck, 1881–1950*, edited by Roy Blankenship. Philadelphia: University of Pennsylvania Department of Anthropology.

York, Gregory, and Loreen Pindera. 1991. *People of the Pines: The Warriors and the Legacy of Oka*. Boston: Little, Brown.

10

The Boas Plan

A View from the Margins

It is well known that Franz Boas considered published texts in American Indian languages to be "the foundation of all future researches" ([1905] 1974, 123). Like Bronislaw Malinowski, whose *Corpus Inscriptionum Kiriwiniensium* (1922, 24) and *Corpus Inscriptionum Agriculturae Quiriviniensis* (1935, 75–210) were inspired by the nineteenth-century corpora of classical philology, the "Boas plan" for American Indian languages (Stocking 1992, 60–91; Voegelin 1952) drew on philology to chart what turned out to be a more enduring but nonetheless contentious textual tradition in Americanist anthropology (Bauman and Briggs 2003, 255–98; Darnell 1990b; Epps, Webster, and Woodbury 2017; Silverstein 2015). Addressing a joint meeting of the American Anthropological and Philological Associations in 1905, Boas noted:

> There are very few students who have taken the time and who have considered it necessary to familiarize themselves sufficiently with native languages to understand directly what the people whom they study speak about, what they think and what they do. There are fewer still who have deemed it worth while to record the customs and beliefs and the traditions of the people in their own words, thus giving us the objective material which will stand the scrutiny of painstaking investigation. I think it is obvious that in this respect anthropologists have everything to learn from you; that until we acquire the habit of demanding such authenticity of our reports as can be guaranteed only by philological accuracy of the record, can we hope to accumulate material that will be a safe guide to future studies. ([1906] 1974:184–85)

By and large, however, future generations of anthropologists have not shared Boas's enthusiasm for philology. Beginning with some of his own students, anthropologists have found fault with Boas's textual legacy, with criticism focusing in particular on Boas's own corpora—how they were collected and presented and what purpose, if any, they serve. As Dell Hymes, who embraced a Boasian-Nietzschean philological anthropology (1981, 382–83), noted: "It was not surprising that the attention of the recorders was focused on recording itself, on publication of the texts, on preparation of grammars to help elucidate the texts. What is strange is that no scholarly tradition arose of continuous work with those texts" (1981, 382–83). Few anthropologists today elicit, transcribe, gloss, translate, and publish native-language texts—activities that now fall within the province of linguistics proper—even as source communities revitalizing their languages and cultures are rediscovering and repurposing archival documentation from anthropology's salvage era. Given these ambivalent evaluations and extra-disciplinary beneficiaries of Boas's textual bequest, further attention to its original provenance and ongoing significance seems warranted. Here, I offer a case study of the Boas plan in action during Boas's lifetime and outline its methodological framework and approaches to social relations in the field. I then discuss three texts produced during the course of the Boas plan, describe the communicative contexts in which they were elicited, and discuss how community linguists have recontextualized them for tribal members today. I conclude with a brief reflection on the history and future of salvage anthropology.

BOAS, MARSH, AND THE SMALLS

In the summer of 1936, Boas sent Gordon Harper Marsh, a nineteen-year-old novice fieldworker who had just graduated from Columbia College, to Perkins, Oklahoma, to study Chiwere, a Siouan language spoken by the Ioway and Otoe-Missouria Indians (Image 38). Marsh was gifted in languages and linguistics, even perhaps something of a prodigy, and Boas was doubtless drawn to Marsh's philological background and ambitions. As an undergraduate, Marsh had taken Boas's linguistics seminar, which, Marsh wrote Boas, "over the two years' time has meant more than almost any other single class at Columbia, and

Fig. 39. Gordon Marsh in 1957 after he left his position at the University of Alaska to become a Russian Orthodox priest. University of British Columbia Archives [UBC 5.1/2023].

I am obliged to you in every way for what I have got out of it."[1] By the time he graduated from Columbia, he was proficient in Latin, Greek, French, German, and Russian. He then pursued a diploma in comparative philology at Oriel College, Oxford,[2] where he found himself "hounded by Gothic, Old Norse, Old English, Old High German, Old Saxon, Old Irish, Welsh and Sanskrit."[3]

In preparation for his summer of fieldwork between graduating from Columbia and leaving for Oxford, Marsh studied Boas and Swanton's chapter on Dakota in the *Handbook of American Indian Languages* (1911, 875–966) as well as Paul Radin's appended Winnebago text.[4] Boas also arranged a meeting in New York between Marsh and William Whitman, one of his graduate students. While Whitman was not a linguist, he did ethnographic fieldwork with Otoe-Missourias in Oklahoma in 1935. Among his informants was an Otoe woman named Julia Small, and Whitman gave Marsh a letter of introduction to Julia's husband, Robert.[5] Whitman and Marsh were not the first anthropologists with whom the Smalls had worked. In 1922, Alanson Skinner had gathered a collection of Ioway myths and tales from Robert while working for the Public Museum of the City of Milwaukee. The Smalls's complementary backgrounds and skills made them an attractive pair of consultants for a succession of anthropologists. Julia, who spoke little or no English, was Otoe and the last living member of the Iowa Medicine Lodge (Whitman 1937, xvi), while Robert had "an excellent command of the English language" in addition to the Ioway dialect of Chiwere; he was also a "first-class interpreter" (Skinner 1922, 17; 1925, 27). With monolingual Julia, Marsh was able to obtain "traditional tales" in Otoe, while with bilingual Robert he conducted translational elicitation and collected "colloquial texts" in Ioway (Whitman 1947a, 233).[6]

Marsh's first letter to Boas after he arrived in Perkins records his initial impressions of the Smalls:

> After collecting my mail at the post office, I immediately looked up my informant, Bob Small, to whom I had a letter from Whitman. In the evening I found him home. I believe he is the best sort of informant. He is a Sac and Fox chief who was orphaned as a small child and was brought up by his Ioway grandparents. He speaks Ioway exclusively, having forgotten his Sac and Fox tongue, since he never used it after the age of ten. His wife is an Ioway and Oto and speaks very little English. The two converse in Ioway all the time. Bob Small is much interested in his language and has been observing it I guess ever since he worked with Skinner some years ago. (En passant—Skinner nearly spoiled the business by paying $5.00 for 5 hours and

Fig. 40. The Small homestead as photographed by Marsh in July 1936. Marsh pitched his tent in the yard and boarded with the Smalls during his summer of fieldwork. Gordon H. Marsh, Materials for a Study of the Iowa Indian Language, American Council of Learned Societies Committee on Native American Languages, American Philosophical Society.

having his informant live at the hotel over in Cushing (15 miles) where he himself was staying.) I figure that I can afford to pay $2.50 for five hours. I board with the family and have my tent in their yard so that it is very convenient and Mr. Small likes the arrangement. He has a foreman's job on a PWA project, which he is hoping will continue. He also rents his farm and one room of his house to a white farmer. He is not so poorly off. He has several farms which he rents out and an oil lease for pumping oil thru his land.

He is heavy-set, stocky and paunchy like so many of the Indians, and his wife is a heavy person too. His good nature and interest are a tremendous help. Whenever we find an Ioway word that's like a Dakota one, he gets as much kick out of it as I do, and laughs heartily and tells his "old lady" (as he calls his wife), who is usually at

Fig. 41. Robert Small in September 1936 shortly before Marsh returned to New York and from there to Oriel College, Oxford. Gordon H. Marsh, Materials for a Study of the Iowa Indian Language, American Council of Learned Societies Committee on Native American Languages, American Philosophical Society.

Fig. 42. Julia Small in September 1936. Gordon H. Marsh, Materials for a Study of the Iowa Indian Language, American Council of Learned Societies Committee on Native American Languages, American Philosophical Society.

hand to consult since he uses so much English, he doesn't always have the less common Ioway words on the tip of his tongue, but he can always get them from Mrs. Small. Besides Ioway he knows Oto and tells me the differences.[7]

A letter from two months later reflects Marsh's growing sense of rapport, even friendship, with his consultants. Marsh attended events with Robert Small, including Elsie Springer's funeral feast and the dedication of a PWA-funded community hall—events that Small described in the "colloquial texts" he gave Marsh. Marsh also entertained community members by reading his texts aloud and reciting Chiwere tongue twisters. Insinuating that by these means he had built better relationships in the field than Whitman, Marsh offered to elicit data on doctoring from Julia Small that Whitman had hoped but was unable to obtain and asked Boas for advice on how to collect such information:

I have been living with the Indians and associating with them all this time. My informant and I are friends now and I know many of the other Indians. They all seem to be fine people. Whitman warned me about lending any of them money. As yet none of them has asked to borrow any. By associating with them we do a lot of interesting things. I went with my informant, Mr. Small, to the funeral feast of the wife of that Missouri fellow I mentioned. The Indians built themselves a new community hall with PWA funds and we went to the dedication and to a dance they held there two weeks ago. Tomorrow they are to have another dance to raise money to equip the hall. I hope to learn to do square dances as well as Indian dances. I want to learn some of their songs too. Maybe I can also get my informant to teach me how to shoot a bow and arrow. He has two bows he made and has been making some arrows the last few days. If I learn all these beside the language I'll be quite an Indian when I return, to say nothing of having become tan too. I can say a few words and simple sentences and can ask for food at the table. The Indians get a great kick out of hearing me talk. Sometimes I read them parts of my text, a lot of which they have never heard, and they say it sounds very natural to them and they all understand it. They are pleased when I say 8888 for them. It is supposed to be the hardest thing to say and some of them say they can't say it themselves. It is simply: kóge glelábļĭ glébļą húyą glelábļįną glébļą glelábļĭ agļĭ glelábļĭ. . . .

By the way, last year Whitman was going to get some medical and medicinal information from Mrs. Small, who is a doctor. He returned before obtaining it. Would it be something worth my looking for? Would it be valuable knowledge or useful to anyone? I think she would be willing to tell me quite a bit, but I don't want to bother with it unless it is something somebody wants. If I do get it, what is the best way of collecting the information about herbs, etc.?[8]

Marsh confronted a number of linguistic challenges during his field-work, and the bulk of his letters to Boas are dedicated to those difficulties. In this context, the selections above, in which Marsh describes the interpersonal dimensions of his research, are peripheral to the central concerns of his correspondence, and they received no uptake from Boas: Boas's replies, where extant, are brief and focused exclusively on linguistic topics. Excluding salutations and valedictions, Boas's reply to Marsh's preceding letter consists of five staccato sentences addressing linguistic difficulties Marsh spent pages detailing and ignores the Smalls completely:

> In Dakota the demonstrative corresponding to your *ga* means something distant but visible. For this reason it is hardly ever used for derivatives expressing time. Probably one of the greatest difficulties in Dakota are always presented by particles which give a very definite tone to the subject matter but which it is almost impossible to translate. I can appreciate your difficulty in regard to the sonants and medials. On the whole in Indian languages the medials begin unvoiced and end slightly voiced.[9]

If Marsh wanted to collect information about "herbs, etc.," he would have to figure out how to go about it on his own.

COLLECTING TEXTS AND BUILDING RAPPORT

Boas's dedication to collecting and publishing corpora in their original languages is demonstrated by his own work. Drawn to the "object-like character" of texts, Boas switched his ethnographic focus "from the tangible to the textual" over the course of his career (Jacknis 1996, 197–98) and amassed in the process his (in)famous "five-foot shelf" containing thousands of pages of Kwakiutl texts.[10] In addition, Boas worked tirelessly to promote text collection and publication through the Committee on Research in Native American Languages (Leeds-Hurwitz 1985) and by founding journals like the *International Journal of American Linguistics* (Boas 1917).

As with many aspects of Boas's legacy, his research program for American Indian languages has received mixed evaluations. On the one hand, we are encouraged to "honor his pioneering efforts" to make otherwise marginalized and silenced native voices central to his work (Lewis 2001b, 402) thereby providing a precedent for "cooperative" and "collaborative" processes of ethnographic co-authorship (Berman 1996, 217; Clifford 1982, 138; Lassiter 2005, 26–29; Marcus and Fischer 1986, 71). On the other hand, there are "the problematic aspects of his legacy" (Epps, Webster, and Woodbury 2017, 45). Like other salvage anthropologists, Boas has been criticized for prioritizing the data over his consultants and source communities. Boas covered up compromising "methodological shenanigans" (Harkin 2001, 396), concealed the processes by which his texts were collected, backgrounded the identities of consultants like George Hunt and Henry Tate (Berman 1996, 230; Maud 1989, 2000; Radin 1933, 114), and "denied American Indian informants like Hunt power and agency" (Lassiter 2006, 28).

Charles Briggs and Richard Bauman argue that Boas's methods must be situated within "the larger contours of colonial domination that increasingly deprived Native American communities of land, material wealth, and cultural and linguistic autonomy" (1999, 516), and that he was "complicit in naturalizing white control of Native American communities" (1999, 519; Bauman and Briggs 2003, 255–98; Lewis 2001a, 448; Lewis 2008, 187–88). According to Briggs and Bauman, the role of consultants like Hunt in his research process "was largely limited to exchanging words for low wages" (1999, 517), and Boas did not hesitate to use financial coercion to produce results (1999, 488). This is not the Boas who "garbed himself in Kwakiutl blankets and had himself given potlatch feasts," but the Boas who could be "'a little rough' with informants in order to make 'their attitude improve'" (Stocking 1968, 204).

Whether "boon or bane" (Lewis 2008), the moralistic tone that characterizes discussions of Boas's methods perhaps suggests that presentist concerns and expectations regarding fieldwork are being projected back on Boas and the textual tradition he promoted.

While Boas's own work is an essential starting point for making sense of the Americanist textual tradition, his work does not exhaust the practices and possibilities of the broader Boas plan. Boas was only the central figure in an elaborate institutional and interpersonal network, and his technique of text collection via long-term correspondence was only one (relatively unrepresentative) example of the methodological scenarios he envisioned. Though Boas consistently emphasized the advantages of texts recorded by native speakers themselves, he also outlined a hierarchy of text collection methods for visiting fieldworkers. At the bottom of this hierarchy he placed "unsatisfactory" methods like using interpreters and pidgin languages, which produce data that "can be used only with a considerable degree of caution" (1911, 59). The "ideal aim" was to have investigators with a "practical knowledge" of the field language (1911, 60). However, Boas characterized this ideal as "under present circumstances, entirely beyond our reach" due to the lack of fieldworkers, the number of mutually unintelligible American Indian languages, and the fact that researchers could not spend "long continuous periods with any particular tribe, so that the practical difficulties in the way of acquiring languages are almost insuperable" (Boas 1911, 60). In such cases, Boas suggested that a "theoretical knowledge" of the language—enough to transcribe, read back, and perhaps even understand texts as they were dictated—was the next best option. While there were certainly theoretical considerations behind Boas's textual turn, it was also to some degree pragmatically motivated. Boas presented text collection as a methodological compromise between using interpreters or pidgins and becoming fluent in the field language. Since the former option was inadequate and the latter impractical, Boas concluded that "under present conditions we are more or less compelled to rely upon an extended series of texts as the safest means of obtaining information from the Indians" (Boas 1911, 61, [1906] 1974, 1917; Berman 1996, 222–23).

If a view from the margins could enhance our Boas-centric understanding of his eponymous plan, Marsh seems like a good candidate.

In one sense, Marsh may be even more representative than Boas, since he was conducting precisely the kind of short-term fieldwork described above. Marsh was recruited, however, as Boas's own career was winding down—Boas retired from Columbia while Marsh was in Oklahoma. In the early 1930s, the ethnographic monograph was gaining ground on the corpus in the discipline's generic hierarchy (Darnell 1990, 247–52), and by 1936, the Committee on Research in Native American Languages was out of money and would be dissolved the following year (Leeds-Hurwitz 1985, 153). Ultimately, the Americanist textual tradition would be transported, transmitted, and transformed beyond anthropology as Sapir's students made linguistics the discipline with primary responsibility for language documentation (Duranti 2003, 324–26; Silverstein 2015, 83–84). This incipient division of anthropological labor is visible between the lines of Marsh's letters as he responds to Whitman, his ethnographic predecessor.[11] In the preface to his dissertation, Whitman delegated responsibility for Chiwere phonology to a future linguist (1937, vii). Whitman understood his own task as one of cultural reconstruction (see below), which required neither theoretical nor practical knowledge of Chiwere, and he used interpreters when, for example, a bilingual informant insisted on telling his clan origin story in Chiwere.

Meanwhile, Marsh followed established procedures in using the field language to build rapport. Drawing on extracts from Boas's letters and diaries from the field,[12] some have suggested that Boas's textual obsession compromised his fieldwork, making him an "austere visitor" (Jacobs 1959, 127) who never tried to "became personally acquainted with the people (White 1963, 49) and who "chose to transcribe and edit texts instead" of engaging with contemporary cultural and colonial realities in indigenous communities (Sanjek 1990, 203). For Boas, however, the alternative to collecting texts in speakers' native languages was not "participant observation," which was not yet cultural anthropology's signature method, but using an interpreter or pidgin to collect texts in translation. In this context, Boas credits his scenario of a fieldworker capable of transcribing, understanding, and reading back texts in the native language with an improvement in rapport: "how much better is the information obtained by observers who have command of the language, and who are on terms of intimate friendship with the natives, than that obtained through the medium of interpreters" (Boas 1911, 61). When Marsh declares that "my informant and I are friends now" and sows doubts about how well Whitman really knew "the Indians," Marsh takes a page straight from Boas's *Handbook*, which associates linguistic mediation via interpreter or jargon with social distance and use of the field language with social intimacy.

The specific techniques Marsh used, such as reading texts aloud to community audiences, were also established protocol. Boas recommended reading texts because it deceived consultants into thinking that the fieldworker understood more than he or she did. This deception was effective, however, because of the equally instrumental motivation Boas attributed to consultants: they "are eager to be put on record in regard to questions that are of supreme interest to them" (Boas 1911, 60–61). This mutually instrumentalizing orientation, in which anthropologists want to record texts and consultants want to go on record, contrasts with the picture of Boas threatening to withhold paltry wages to get results. It is arguably a better fit for Boas's work with Hunt and is certainly a better fit for Marsh's fieldwork. By his own admission, Marsh was offering low wages (half as much as Skinner had paid fourteen years earlier), but the Smalls were "not so poorly off," and based on Marsh's description, financial incentives were not their main motivation for participating. Rather, the work seems to have appealed to Robert's meta- and inter-linguistic awareness, and as will be described below, the texts Marsh collected suggest that the Smalls were interested in something like going on record.

While quibbling over terminology, Mead (1939) and Lowie (1940) shared Boas's methodological judgments regarding field languages and emphasized the instrumental role of language use in building rapport (Mead 1939, 196–99). Even Marsh's tongue twister trick had been tried before. As Lowie wrote of his Crow fieldwork: "I constantly assumed droll relationships with my interlocutors, both for their entertainment and to familiarize myself with the kinship nomenclature. I learnt a tongue-twister to confound unsuspecting strangers. I recorded an occasional funny tale not only for textual analysis, but to read and re-read it to a never-to-be-surfeited Crow audience. I composed a mock-account of a vision resulting in my capturing twenty picketed horses and striking countless coups" (1940, 83).

Marsh, too, developed a droll field persona, entertaining community members by reciting tongue-twisters, reading texts, and joking about going native—Lowie's "mock-account of... striking countless coups," corresponds to Marsh's comments to Boas that he would be "quite an Indian" when he returned tanned to New York after learning their language, songs, dances, and how to shoot bows and arrows. Ioways and Otoe-Missourias seem to have been in on the joke. As Marsh reported, they "got a great kick out of hearing me talk" and claimed that even some of their own were unable to say 8,888.[13]

In sum, Marsh implemented contemporary Boasian methodological recommendations for short-term fieldwork by using the native language and other strategies to build rapport with (and, by his own account, befriend) the Smalls. The portions of his letters describing his interpersonal successes contrast with those describing his linguistic difficulties, sending Boas the message that the data collection part of his fieldwork was going well even if his linguistic analysis was not. Boas may not have taken the time to respond to Marsh's descriptions of his relations with the Smalls since they conformed so closely to the template he had outlined in the *Handbook* and other writings. Marsh's relationships were, however, subsidiary to his linguistic objectives. There is no indication that Marsh's research was collaborative in the modern sense, nor was he, like some of his contemporaries, planting the roots of that tradition (Lassiter 2005, 25–47).

THE SOCIAL LIVES OF THE TEXTS

When Boas wrote, after pointing out the inadequacy of early missionary grammars, "as we require a new point of view now, so future times will require new points of view and for these the texts, and ample texts, must be made available" ([1905] 1974, 123), it seems improbable that he had the future needs of source and descendent communities in mind. Nor did Marsh, whose immediate goal was to get enough data for a Chiwere grammar, anticipate that his work might someday be useful to Ioways and Otoe-Missourias themselves. In a 1976 letter to community linguist Jimm Goodtracks, Marsh wrote, "When I collected that material in Perkins . . . I had no idea that some time it would be of some value to the Indian people themselves. But I am very glad if it can help them."[14] Indeed, the products of the Americanist textual and philological tradition have accumulated value as they have been not only reread and recontextualized by researchers but also reclaimed and revitalized by communities (Buckley 1996: 293–94; Golla 1995; Jacknis 1996, 209; Powell 2015; Thom 2003, 7). From this perspective, Boas's salvage orientation might be retrospectively justified: "Boas was right," Hymes wrote, "in putting first the need to preserve texts for the future, texts that the future would not be able to obtain. We are now able to recover and repatriate them, as it were, in more adequate form" (Hymes 2003, 35; Gruber 1970).

I turn now to three examples of how Ioways and Otoe-Missourias have recovered Marsh's archival language documentation "in more adequate form" by reworking his texts for community audiences. In 1971, Marsh, turned Reverend Priestmonk Innocent of the Russian Ortho-dox Church, donated the results of his three months of fieldwork from thirty-five years earlier—circa one thousand manuscript leaves, four thousand cards (a slip file dictionary database), seventy-five bluebooks of four leaves each, and several photographs—to the American Phil-osophical Society, where they have since been accessed by academic and community-based researchers.[15] In this section, I focus on the social lives of three texts: Robert Small's "The Girls Go Fishing" and "This Land Here," and Julia Small's "My Grandmother." On one level, these texts (read in conjunction with other contemporary sources) contain information about their own dialogic genesis in an interaction between Marsh and the Smalls in 1936, during which Robert and Julia Small used the opportunity Marsh gave them "to be put on record" (Boas 1911, 60–61) to challenge salvage anthropology's methods and assumptions. At the same time, the texts have ongoing social lives in the present: community linguists have retranscribed, retranslated, and reframed Marsh's documentation in order to create new versions ori-ented toward community purposes today. While these new versions have been transformed in various ways from Marsh's archived originals, they are still recognized and circulate as the same texts. In my conclu-sion, I address the distinctive value of the Americanist textual tradition within salvage anthropology by contrasting these processes of textual circulation with salvage anthropology's material cultural collections, which do not circulate in the same ways.

The multiple social lives of Marsh's materials are visible from two versions of "The Girls Go Fishing," a brief account of fishing and turtle hunting by Robert Small. It was among the first texts that Marsh collected, and its lexical, morphological, and syntactic simplicity reflect Small's accommodation to Marsh's language skills toward the beginning of his fieldwork. While the text is grammatically uncomplicated, its message is more complex. The final sentence, "People say the turtle has different kinds of meat," ends with áñe, "they say" or "it is said," a Chiwere genre marker for "speaking the past"—that is, emphasizing the "secondhand nature and traditional character of what is said" (Kroskrity 1998, 105–6; Schwartz 2018, 83). The text thus presents the persistence of traditional subsistence practices and knowledge, a topic of interest to Marsh (recall his interest in Small's bows and arrows) and one with implicit significance in light of salvage anthropology's assumption that traditional culture existed only as a memory or survival rather than as an ongoing practice with contemporary relevance (see below).

While "The Girls Go Fishing" has relatively little value for linguistic analysis, its grammatical accessibility makes it ideal for literacy-based language maintenance and revitalization today. In 1977, "The Girls Go Fishing" was recontextualized as Lesson sixteen in a book produced by community linguist Jimm Goodtracks and missionary linguist Lila Wistrand-Robinson to help Ioways and Otoe-Missourias learn Chiwere as a second language (Otoe and Iowa Language Speakers 1977, 84). Its transformation from archival documentation to pedagogical resource was accomplished by Goodtracks and Wistrand-Robinson retranscribing, reglossing, and retranslating the text in order to make it more accessible to language learners. For example, the pedagogical text isolates into separate, simpler words, morphemes that Marsh agglutinates into long, complex words: hó-giϴìge-ahíñe 'fish-catch-they arrive going' becomes ho githíge ahínye 'fish catch arrive', and p'í-wa'ų̃ñeną 'good-they make them-and' becomes pi wa'únye na 'good make-they and.' The retranscription also accommodates to the Anglophone background of language learners by spelling words in ways

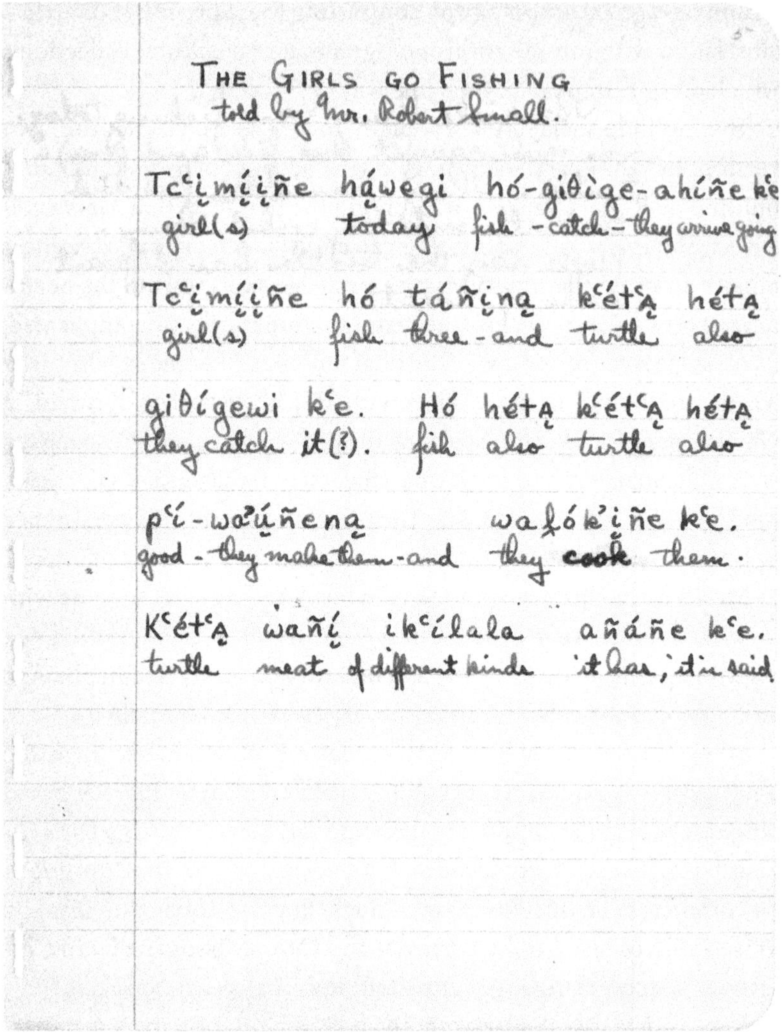

THE GIRLS GO FISHING
told by Mr. Robert Small.

Tc⁽ɨ́m̨ɨ́ɨñe   háwegi   hó-giθige-ahíñe k̓e
girl(s)   today   fish - catch - they arrive going

Tc⁽ɨ́m̨ɨ́ɨñe   hó táñina k̓étᴀ hétᴀ
girl(s)   fish three - and turtle also

giθígewi k̓e.   Hó hétᴀ k̓étᴀ hétᴀ
they catch it (?). fish also turtle also

p⁽í-waⁱúñena   waɫók̓iñe k̓e.
good - they make them - and   they cook them.

K̓étᴀ waññí ik⁽ílala   añáñe k̓e.
turtle meat of different kinds it has; it is said

Fig. 43. Marsh's manuscript of Robert Small's text "The Girls Go Fishing."
Gordon H. Marsh, Materials for a Study of the Iowa Indian Language, American
Council of Learned Societies Committee on Native American Languages,
American Philosophical Society.

that help English speakers produce proper pronunciations. Unlike in
English, aspiration in Chiwere is phonemic: voiced stops, such as [d],
are allophones or variants of the corresponding unaspirated voiceless stops, such as [t], but contrast with the aspirated voiceless stops,
such as [tʰ]. Thus, taɲi or daɲi is three, but tʰaɲi is soup. Since English

LESSON 16

THE GIRLS GO FISHING

As told by Robert Small

Chihmínye hanwegi ho githíge ahínye ke.
girls   today fish catch arrive

Chihmínye ho danyi na ketan hedan githígewi ke.
girls   fish three and turtle also   catch

Ho hedan ketan hedan pi wa'únye na walók'inye ke.
fish also turtle also good make-they and cook-they

Ketan wanyí ikílala anyánye ke.
turtle meat   different say-they

The girls went fishing today. They caught three

fish and a turtle. They cooked the fish and the turtle

to make them good. It is said that turtle is a different

kind of meat.

Vocabulary:
githi-ge   'to catch'
ahi-nye   'they arrive'
wa'un-nye 'they make'
walok'i-nye 'they cook, fry'
anya-nye   'they say'

Fig. 44. "The Girls Go Fishing" recontextualized for language revitalization. Otoe and Iowa Language Speakers 1977, 84. Courtesy of Jimm Goodtracks.

speakers naturally aspirate word initial voiceless stops, they would likely read Marsh's *táñį* [three] as tʰaɲi [soup]. Thus, the pedagogical text's *danyi* substitutes the voiced variant [d] for the unaspirated voiceless stop [t] Marsh recorded. It also replaces graphs and diacritics from Americanist phonetic notation with less technical English digraphs: <th> is used for the dental fricative rather than theta <θ> and <ny> is used for the palatal nasal rather than tilde < ˜ >. Finally, the pedagogical text appends a list of vocabulary words that frame "The Girls Go Fishing" as a vocabulary building opportunity for language learners. Recontextualized as a resource for language revital-ization, "The Girls Go Fishing" has reached a far wider, community-based audience than Marsh's original documentation at the American Philosophical Society.

Another example of recontextualization giving ongoing relevance to materials Marsh collected comes from the Ioway Cultural Insti-tute, an online resource on Ioway history, language, and culture devel-oped by Lance Foster, who is now the Tribal Historic Preservation Officer for the Iowa Tribe of Kansas and Nebraska. Foster presents a re-transcription as well as an interlinear and free translation of "This Land Here," another text Marsh elicited from Robert Small. The text describes how allotment affected the community following the Dawes Act of 1887:

> Way back, 46 years ago, the chief took the pen and signed a treaty and we divided up the land. Our village was broken up and from that time we have tried to educate our children. The whiteman then opened up the rest of the land for themselves, and then they made the animals, the birds, everything disappear, all rubbed out. Because of all of this, it can never be today the way it used to be, when we moved around. We will never again be that way.
>
> The government's officials arrived, and made promises if we would accept allotment, tempting us with everything good. Because of these promises, we accepted allotment. However, we soon found that everything they said was untrue. Indeed they even gave less money to us than they had promised.
>
> In the old days, we never divided up the land. Before allotment, we all walked together in a good way, we lived well. We did not want for anything. We never lacked meat. Anywhere on the land we wanted to camp, that is where we camped. We used to have many horses. When the whiteman came, the land was divided up, and indeed, because of this allotment, we now have nothing. (Foster 1999)

Following the text, Foster adds, "This page then is dedicated to the spirits of these two men, Robert Small and Gordon Marsh, that their efforts may be known and remembered" (1999), lending their work a retrospective collaborative aura.

Marsh's correspondence shows that he did not conceive of his work with Small as collaborative research in the current sense of the term. Even so, Marsh's act of transcribing and preserving Small's discourse has a co-constructed dimension that would be overlooked if the text collecting project were viewed as the mirror of an overly simplified, one-sided relation of colonial domination, with the anthropologist alone determining the agenda and orchestrating the interaction (and its products) to support his own monologic authority. "This Land Here" (and "The Girls Go Fishing") reflects a decision by Small to give Marsh "colloquial texts" about current issues and events, as opposed to "traditional tales." Small's deep knowledge of the latter is attested by the extensive collection of $wéka^n$ 'myths' he had given Alanson Skinner in 1922 (Skinner 1925, 27–28). But Small chose to speak with Marsh primarily about contemporary topics like turtle hunting, allotment, a PWA-funded community hall project, and Elsie Springer's funeral. In order to understand why he did so, it is helpful to consider what Small would have known about anthropologists from his previous encounters with them.

Based on his fieldwork with Otoes in 1935, Whitman reported:

Due to the complete breakdown of the old culture there was nothing for an anthropologist to observe, and I had therefore to rely for my information on the memories of the old, a few of whom remembered as children the days of the buffalo hunt, who could recall the words of their fathers and grandfathers. "My friend," said one informant when I explained to him the purpose of my visit, "you have come to us fifty years too late." (Whitman 1937, xv)

And after visiting Ioway communities in 1914 and 1922, Skinner concluded:

Practically speaking, Ioway native culture, in all its branches, is dead. Of the seventy-nine survivors of the tribe in Oklahoma or the one hundred sixty-two less primitive members in Kansas and Nebraska on the Nemaha Reservation, not one today keeps up the ancient rites, or even believes in them. The last pagan was the late Chief David Tohee, who died during the great influenza epidemic a few years ago. The rest of the tribe are either Peyote devotees or Christians. At the present writing, hardly an object of native manufacture remains in their hands, and the data presented in this paper have been gleaned from the memories of the older men and women of this once important tribe, or from specimens collected by the writer or in several museums. (Skinner 1926, 190)

These statements suggest that Skinner and Whitman did not consider their consultants' current cultural realities worthy of anthropological attention. They were interested instead in reconstructing the culture of three or four generations before by recording (in English) what current elders remembered about their "pagan," buffalo-hunting ancestors and by acquiring "specimens" that their consultants had inherited from that era.

In this connection, it is interesting to revisit Marsh's joke to Boas that associates being Indian with, among other qualities, shooting bows and arrows. While Whitman wrote that "we cannot discuss the material culture of the Oto because there is nothing left of it" (1937, xiv), and Skinner considered that "hardly an object of native manufacture remains in their hands" (1926, 190), Skinner was able to find one contemporary example of a bow and arrows made by Robert Small, who "bears the reputation of being an expert bow and arrow maker," even though "bows and arrows are virtually things of the past" (1926: 287–88). Skinner goes on to warn that Small's "modern examples . . . may not have been made according to the old style" and reproduces a photograph of Small's arrows in Plate XLII of his *Ethnology of the Ioway Indians* (1926, 326–27) alongside a "warrior's headdress" (described as a "slightly degenerate modern survival of the handsome garments of this type worn in earlier times" [1926, 258–59]), and a Ghost Dance rattle (the Ghost Dance being a "modern religious cult" compared to earlier bundle- and pipe-based ceremonies [1926, 248]). Skinner's Plate XLII, then, compared to the preceding plates of war bundles, gens pipes, and Buffalo Society and Grizzly Bear Society doctors' bundles, groups together temporal anomalies or, more pejoratively, dubious modern facsimiles of older authentic artifacts. As a manufacturer of such "survivals," Robert Small was the material cultural counterpart of

Julia Small, "the last survivor of the Iowa Medicine Lodge" (Whitman 1937, xvi). And just as Robert made arrows for Skinner, he made another set for Marsh, who donated them to the anthropology museum at the University of British Columbia in 1959, where he was then a lecturer in the Slavonic Studies department teaching a course on "The Peoples of the Soviet Union."

If Whitman's consultant, who might have been Small himself, was being relatively precise when he told him that he had arrived fifty years too late, he was dating the end of the "old culture" to around 1885—that is, the years immediately preceding the passage of the Dawes Act. In "This Land Here," Small dates the transition to 1890 ("way back, 46 years ago"), the year allotment was implemented on the Ioway reservations. Given his interactions with Skinner, Whitman, and Marsh, Small was undoubtedly familiar with much of what motivated salvage anthropologists, including their interest in cultural practices associated with the pre-Dawes Act past of mobile communal life over current cultural conditions, and to some degree, Small seems to agree that Ioway history is a narrative of decline culminating in an impoverished material and cultural present. Skinner, Whitman, Marsh, and Small are all nostalgic in their own ways for older iterations of Ioway and Otoe-Missouria life, but unlike Skinner, Whitman, and Marsh, Small's narrative identifies colonization as responsible for the transformations his community has undergone. Whitman found "nothing for an anthropologist to observe" in 1935 "due to the complete breakdown of the old culture" but provides no account of how exactly a culture breaks down to nothing—his syntax itself resists responsibility. Small, however, could not be clearer: "because of this allotment, we now have nothing."

Moreover, while in "This Land Here" Small seems to agree with salvage anthropology's depiction of the Indian present as culturally degenerate, his other "colloquial texts" resist the imputation that he, his family, and community are culturally lacking, and that the traditions they still practice are mere "survivals" from a past that has outlived its currency. Instead, these texts show contemporary Ioways and Otoe-Missourias maintaining their traditions authentically, carrying on subsistence practices and customs like funeral feasting, while renew-

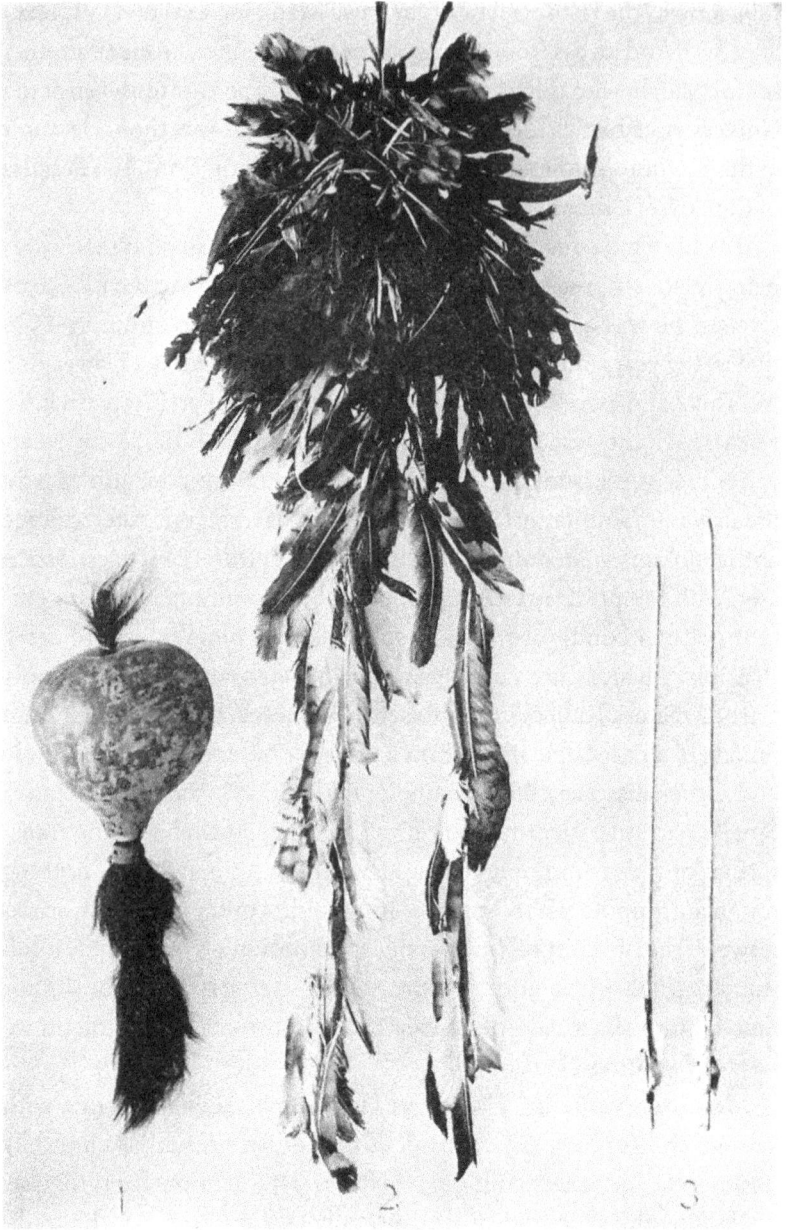

Fig. 45. Plate XLII from Alanson Skinner's *Ethnology of the Iowa Indians* (1926, 326–27). A "pair of pointed, headless arrows" made by Robert Small are on the right, next to a headdress and gourd rattle.

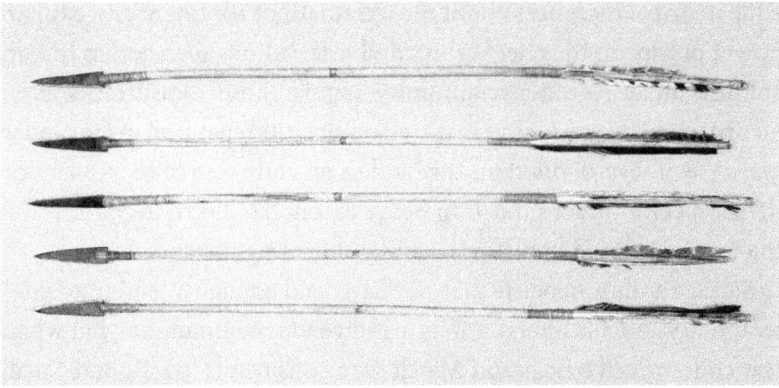

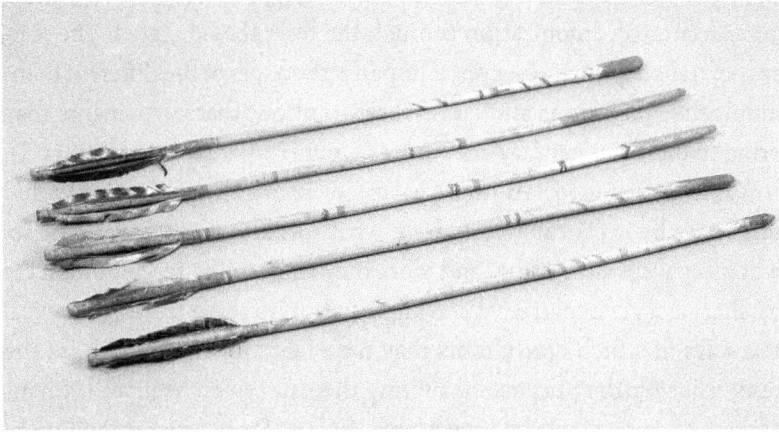

Figs. 46 & 47. Arrows made by Robert Small collected by Marsh and donated to the University of British Columbia Museum of Anthropology in 1959. The arrows on the left have metal points for hunting deer, while the arrows on the right have wooden points for hunting birds and squirrels. Image 45 photo by Jessica Bushey [D2.82 a-e], Image 46 photo by Derek Tan [D2.81 a–e]; courtesy of UBC Museum of Anthropology, Vancouver, Canada.

ing other traditions by adapting them to new conditions—for example, constructing a community hall for dances using PWA funds. In other words, in "This Land Here" and other texts, Small anticipates, acknowledges, and resists negative cultural evaluations of Ioways and Otoe-Missourias by anthropologists and the wider society they represent. Indeed, this is surely part of why the texts Small gave Marsh resonate so strongly with the aims of community linguists today. Over time, community linguists like Foster have used "This Land Here" to educate tribal members about the aftermath of allotment and explain how it produced the checkerboarded reservations seen across Indian country today. Another community linguist, Jimm Goodtracks, even incorporated this text into a math lesson since its repetition of the phrase *máyan wathrége* 'divided up the land' is an early source for a term for division (Goodtracks n.d.). In being recontextualized in these ways, the text has gained in historical and political significance.

Salvage anthropologists may not have paid enough attention to contemporary colonial interventions in indigenous communities, but when text collectors like Boas and Marsh gave consultants like Robert Small an opportunity to go on record, they were able to foreground their own perspectives on colonization through the texts they dictated. The process of transcription preserves, if imperfectly, traces of the different communicative intentions and cultural assumptions that participants may bring to the documentary encounter (Dobrin 2012; Nevins 2013, 113–51, 2015; Silverstein 1996). At times, we can recover information that would otherwise be irrevocably lost about what speakers were responding to, who they were addressing, and what they were trying to communicate by sharing a given narrative. Paying attention to these traces can reveal the ways in which consultants may have been trying to "address the researcher for the purpose of altering the latter's perspective" (Nevins 2013, 144). In the texts he gave Marsh, Robert Small was responding to and challenging underlying assumptions of salvage anthropology itself.

Another text from Marsh's corpus that contains interesting clues that the speaker was trying to address and educate the researcher is Julia Small's "My Grandmother." The story describes how Small's grandmother survived an epidemic after falling sick while on a hunting expedition and getting separated from her group by a fog. She came across a tobacco-smoking grizzly bear who came to her rescue and promised to guide her home. Due to the grizzly bear's power, Small's grandmother made it home safely and did not suffer from fatigue, hunger, or thirst on the journey. The narrative concludes after Small's grandmother arrives home, but she then adds a coda to the story:

1. My grandmother had the spiritual power of the bear.
2. And it seems *(that)* my grandmother's spirit/soul is with the bear.

3. There is a way, it seems.

4. My grandmother liked to smoke tobacco every day.

5. Even during the night, she sat puffing tobacco.

6. It was the big grizzly who had taught her, it seems.

7. And my grandmother was a doctor.

8. And today it is, the *(same)* medicines indeed *(she used)*, I use them *(for)* my own ones.

9. And today, the medicines my grandmother told me about they are *(the ones)* I use them *(for)* my own.

10. Today, I got talking about my grandmother.

11. It does not make me feel good *(to)*day.

12. It has been almost fifty years since she left me.

13. Today it is, I reminisce about her.

14. The country where the great grizzly is, I think my grandmother is there with him.

15. And I hope in the future, *(the one)* they call him God's son, that when he comes down to this land, I hope he takes my grandmother for me.

16. Há, my grandmother it is, I am telling about her, my own one. She knows me, her own one, it seems.

17. And pitifully I am speaking, *(for)* she thinks of me, *(her)* spirit, it seems.

18. That is the last *(as)* I am talking for myself.

19. Today, that it is, it is the end, it seems. (Goodtracks 1998, 7)

One way that this text has been read by community linguists is as a stylistic exemplar. In the introduction to his retranscription and retranslation of "My Grandmother," Jimm Goodtracks notes: "Julia did not speak English; she only spoke Chiwere. As such, she spoke the language in a classical style of former days. In terms of literary standards, she exemplifies the fine narrative skills of the older monolingual speakers, who accentuated proper grammatical form with syntax variation to provide an eventful and explicit view of life from the traditional Ioway and Otoe-Missouria perspective.... Subsequent generations have tended to speak in a more simplified version of the language" (Goodtracks 1998, 2). Goodtracks presents the text in a two-column format with

Chiwere on the left and a facing English translation. As can be seen in Goodtracks's translation of the coda above, he employs a number of denaturalizing devices that draw attention to the translation's status as a text derived from originally Chiwere discourse. For example, Goodtracks's italicized parentheticals mark interpolations that clarify the meaning of phrases that are difficult to follow in their literal translation. He also indicates where Small used the evidential ášgu^{n} by including "it seems" in his translation, as in lines two and three above: "And it seems *(that)* my grandmother's spirit/soul is with the bear. There is a way, it seems" (Goodtracks 1998, 7). Marsh's translation, in contrast, achieves a more natural English prose style in part by omitting these evidentials: "My grandmother's spirit is with the bear's. There is a way." By preserving features like evidentials in his translation, Goodtracks hopes to give readers of the English text a sense of traditional Chiwere narrative conventions. As language shift advances in American Indian communities, translations become increasingly important ways of presenting texts to tribal members who may only be able to (or are only interested in) accessing heritage language texts in translation.

While community linguists like Goodtracks present "My Grandmother" as an exemplar of a "classical" Chiwere style, the text—and the coda in particular—can also be read for what it reveals about Small's perspective in its context of production. Small begins her coda with a short preface that mentions a spiritual connection between the bear and her grandmother (line one) and positions them presently occupying a shared space *ída*—that is, distant from the space shared by the speaker (Small) and addressee (Marsh) (lines two and three). She then alludes to a past event in the story she has just recounted—when her grandmother first met the bear, "he was smoking tobacco and the smoke went up now and again *(as)* he sat puffing, it seems" (Goodtracks 1998, 5)—by describing an example of something that the bear taught her grandmother, that is, how to smoke tobacco (lines four through six). She goes on to say that her grandmother taught her doctoring, emphasizing that the medicines she uses today are the same ones her grandmother told her about (lines seven through nine). In this way, she narratively embeds her own medical knowledge within the relationships between herself and her grandmother, and her grandmother and the bear. Unlike the example of the bear teaching her grandmother how to smoke tobacco, however, themes of doctoring and medicine lack an antecedent in the story itself. Lines seven through nine are puzzling not only because their content lacks precedent in the story about her grandmother and the bear but also due to their placement just before the coda takes a reflexive turn. Beginning in line ten, Small characterizes her own discourse as "talking about my grandmother," and describes its effect on her (line eleven) and her grandmother, who knows what Small says and thinks of Small when Small speaks of her (lines sixteen and seventeen).[16] The last two lines of the coda are also speech about speech but signal the end of her discourse, saying, in effect, "I am done talking about my grandmother for today."[17] The position of lines seven through nine right before Small's discourse turns on itself suggest that they are the last element of the narrative sequence. They are what the story has been building up to, what it is in some sense about.

While the presence and placement of lines seven through nine appear undermotivated in the text as presented, they make perfect sense if they respond to a question from Marsh that has been edited out of the text itself. We can get a sense of the question Small might have been answering if we return to Marsh's letter to Boas. While Marsh's comparative evaluations of rapport sound a note of rivalry with Whitman, he also volunteered to collect medicinal information that Whitman had hoped but been unable to obtain from Small. If "My Grandmother" is understood as a reply or rejoinder to a question from Marsh about doctoring and medicine, then lines seven through nine and their position make sense: they gain a pragmatic warrant in Marsh's prior discourse, which is elided along with the rest of the text's dialogic scaffolding in the ultimate presentation of the monologic "My Grandmother" but is preserved in Marsh's letter to Boas.

Read as a response to medical questions from Marsh, "My Grandmother" tells the story of how Small learned to doctor from her grandmother, who was given spiritual power by a bear, and tells how, in telling the story, she is maintaining her relationship with her grandmother, whose spirit is with the bear. Unlike the past, when her grandmother told her about her medicines, and the future, when she expects God's son to reunite them (line fifteen), Small is spatially separated from her grandmother in the present but maintains a relationship with her in part by talking about her—her grandmother's spirit hears what she says and thinks of her. The word Small uses for "talking about my grandmother" in lines ten, sixteen, and eighteen is *ix^a^nhégragi* 'I am causing her, my own one, to live.' By making her grandmother alive, so to speak, through her speech, she maintains their relationship through time and across space. She furthermore contextualizes all of her preceding discourse, including the story of her grandmother being rescued by the bear and her account of her grandmother teaching her how to be a doctor, within this relationship-maintaining function of her speech. By placing both her medical knowledge and her speech about her medical knowledge within her relationship with her grandmother and her grandmother's relationship with the bear, she proposes a radically different, relationship-oriented framing of doctoring and indeed of discourse itself than Marsh's notion to "get some medical and medicinal information from Mrs. Small" on "herbs, etc."

CONCLUSION

In 2010, I accompanied a group of Ioways and Otoe-Missourias on a trip to the Milwaukee Public Museum to see some of the items there that Skinner had gathered on his 1922 collecting trip. Our small caravan made the over one-thousand-mile round-trip drive from the northern Ioway reservation near White Cloud, Kansas, to Wisconsin and back. As far as I can remember, we did not see Robert Small's arrows. Like Skinner, tribal members were primarily interested in bundles, pipes, and other objects with more spiritual resonance. We were permitted to handle the objects and take photographs (it fell to me to handle objects tribal members wanted to see but were wary of disturbing, proving the value of having an anthropologist along),[18] but at the end of the day, we left the museum and the objects stayed. After seeing the collections, some of the younger tribal members discussed repatriating them, but as the elders on the trip reminded them, one strand of community oral history has it that the last owners of the bundles and pipes entrusted them to the museum for safekeeping because there was no one left in the community who knew how to care for them. Without proper care, the bundles and pipes were dangerous to the community and therefore should remain in the museum in keeping with their last owner's wishes. Of course, it may happen someday that the consensus within the Ioway and Otoe-Missouria communities will shift toward repatriation and set in motion a complex institutional and legal apparatus that could, eventually, return some of what Skinner collected to their source community (Foster 1994).

The discursive objects that Marsh recorded, however, circulate differently than Skinner's specimens. While the notebooks within which Marsh inscribed the Smalls's narratives are currently located at the American Philosophical Society in Philadelphia and will, for the foreseeable future, remain there, the words themselves can be easily copied; they can be recontextualized or repatriated in any number of forms that are recognized as no less "the texts" than are the archived initial inscriptions. Nondiscursive objects can of course be entextualized, too, in photographs or museum catalogue descriptions, but such representations are not those artifacts in the same way that discourse recontextualized is itself that discourse (recontextualized). Skinner's Plate XLII is not Small's arrows, but "The Girls Go Fishing" in the pedagogical books for language learners, "This Land Here" on Foster's Ioway Cultural Institute, and Goodtracks's presentation of "My Grandmother" are as much those texts as are the versions in Marsh's notebooks.

Salvage anthropology has long functioned as a historicizing epithet, associating the researcher so labeled with a theoretically naïve and ethically suspect disciplinary past. One drawback of such a label is that it groups researchers together based on ideology rather than methodology and overlooks the ways in which research programs operating within a broadly similar theoretical framework could play out with subtle, but significant and far-reaching differences in practice. Boas's notion to "record the customs and beliefs and the traditions of the people in their own words" ([1906] 1974, 184–85) was no less ideologically overdetermined than any other salvage project. But once consultants were given the opportunity to go on record, there was no guarantee that they would stick to the anthropologists' expected ways of framing customs, beliefs, traditions, or whatever else the anthropologist was hoping to elicit. As long as the researcher faithfully recorded and archived what was said, the speaker's message can often still be recovered, no matter how much the pragmatic force of their discourse may be obscured by the fieldworker's own framing and editing.[19] Thus, the products of the Americanist textual tradition are distinctive among the objects preserved by salvage anthropology in that they reflexively preserve traces of their own interactional genesis in a cross-cultural encounter between fieldworker and consultant and can be relatively easily reproduced, which allows them to accumulate value as they are reframed for successive audiences. Read as "memories of the old," "The Girls Go Fishing," "This Land Here," and "My Grandmother" would fit neatly within Skinner's and Whitman's work to elicit information about the past. But in these texts, the Smalls not only provide information about nineteenth-century events, they are also speaking to Marsh in their present and, through the efforts of community linguists like Foster and Goodtracks, are taking on new significance as they are presented in forms that speak to the concerns and interests of community audiences today.

While Marsh eventually left linguistics, the languages he studied never left him: when Goodtracks contacted him in the 1970s (at a retirement home for Russian Orthodox clergy), he could still recite from memory the Chiwere texts he had collected forty years before. While Marsh did not envision that the texts he archived would be of value to their source communities, the Chiwere corpus that he and the Smalls co-constructed not only bears traces of the social-interactional context of its production but also invites an open-ended series of future recontextualizations that could not have been foreseen by its creators. In one sense, the Americanist textual tradition may not be as prominent in anthropology today as it once was, but in another sense, the Boas plan for American Indian languages is just beginning.

NOTES

1. Marsh to Boas, May 13, 1936, Franz Boas Papers, American Philosophical Society.
2. "Marsh, Berryman Given Fellowships to English Colleges," *Columbia Spectator*, March 10, 1936, 1.
3. Marsh to Boas, December 22, 1937.
4. Marsh to Boas, June 13, 1936.
5. Marsh to Boas, May 25, 1936.

6. As I have described elsewhere, Whitman 1947a is an incomplete version of a Chiwere grammar sketch Marsh drafted sometime before 1942 and which Voegelin and Harris (1945, 19) found among Boas's papers after his death (Schwartz 2014). For reasons that remain obscure, the manuscript bears Whitman's name and was published in *IJAL* with Whitman listed as the author. The grammar sketch was the only publication that emerged from Marsh's Chiwere fieldwork. Like Marsh, Whitman is a relatively obscure Boasian, though he makes a brief appearance as Jeannette Mirsky's lover in Mead's correspondence (Banner 2003, 340, 428). In addition to his dissertation, Whitman published a collection of Otoe folklore in English (1938) and a posthumous culture and personality style ethnography of San Ildefonso Pueblo (1947b). His career was cut short by his untimely death in 1939 "as a result of injuries received in an explosion at his residence" (American Anthropological Association 1940, 180).
7. Marsh to Boas, June 13, 1936.
8. Marsh to Boas, August 6, 1936.
9. Boas to Marsh, August 20, 1936.
10. Alluding to the marketing of the Harvard Classics (a multivolume anthology edited by Harvard President Charles Eliot) as "Dr. Eliot's Five-Foot Shelf of Books," Murdock complained that "despite Boas' 'five-foot shelf' of monographs on the Kwakiutl, this tribe falls into the quartile of those whose social structure and related practices are least adequately described" (1949, xiv, n. 5). Boas's "five-foot shelf" has since functioned as a metonym for the Boasian textual tradition in disciplinary polemic.
11. See also Epps, Webster, and Woodbury 2017, 52–53 on the nearly contemporary case of Harry Hoijer and Morris Opler with the Chiricahua Apache
12. As Boas wrote in a letter on October 12, 1886: "I had a miserable day today. The natives held a big potlatch again. I was unable to get hold of anyone and had to snatch at whatever I could get. Late at night I did get something [a tale] for which I have been searching—'The Birth of the Raven.' It is unfortunate that the work here has to stop for a while, since I have such fine leads" (Rohner 1969, 38).
13. Marsh's earnest (and one-sided) account of these interactions in his letters to Boas leverages seemingly positive local evaluations of his social and linguistic integration as proof of his progress and a claim of authority over his field site. In so doing, he (like many contemporary text collectors) overlooks some of the moral and communicative complexities of his research as a kind of colonially inflected cross-cultural encounter. While Marsh

certainly had at least some facility with Chiwere as a code, that Ioways and Otoe-Missourias would, after only two months of fieldwork, jokingly elevate Marsh's Chiwere abilities above their own suggests an ironic orientation toward Marsh and his linguistic performances that seems to have been lost on Marsh himself—his communicative competence, in other words, lagged behind his grammatical competence. In my own fieldwork since 2009, I have heard stories of how the last generations of native Chiwere speakers would make similar remarks to language learners in the 1960s-90s, even (or especially) when the students' pronunciations were nonstandard. Some of my consultants present these comments as sincere compliments that exemplify the traditional elders' positive outlook: they wanted to encourage language learners rather than draw attention to, and make them feel ashamed for, their mistakes. Others, however, have suggested that the audience for these compliments included other speakers and more advanced language learners, who recognized their ironic quality. This bears some similarity to teasing routines in other Native American communities, in which errors are complimented rather than directly corrected—the targets of the teasing learn to correct themselves as they become aware that the compliments have an ironic dimension (Nevins 2013, 61–62). While I would not want to propose an unproblematic continuity in Ioway and Otoe-Missouria teasing routines between the 1930s (as refracted through Marsh's letters to Boas) and accounts of native speakers in the 1960s-90s (that I've heard from consultants since 2009), the irony directed toward Marsh may reflect local forms of language socialization through teasing compliments, which could have taken on additional significance as they were applied to a nineteen-year old, non-Native researcher with an evident interest in "playing Indian" (Deloria 1998).

14. Rev. Prior Innocent to Jimm Good Tracks, June 7, 1976; letter in possession of Jimm Goodtracks.
15. Gordon H. Marsh, Materials for a Study of the Iowa Indian Language, American Council of Learned Societies Committee on Native American Languages, American Philosophical Society.
16. Marsh's translation is easier to follow here: "I speak about my grandmother she knows me (what I am saying). I poor thing when I am speaking her spirit thinks about me."
17. Marsh has "This is the last I (have to) talk about. Today this is the last."
18. A number of community members believe that handling sacred objects in an improper manner or context invites spiritual and physical harm (Foster 1994, 1).

19. This was one of the central insights of Hymes (1981, 2003), whose ver-
sified versions of texts Boas, Sapir, and Jacobs had rendered in prose
paragraphs drew attention to their poetic dimensions. Hymes saw it
as "a kind of repatriation . . . to help recover in older texts their linea-
ments of shaping artistry" (2003, 322). Silverstein (1996) and Nevins
(2013, 113–51, 2015) have re-examined texts collected by Sapir and Hoijer, respectively, to reveal speakers' communicative intentions mis-
recognized by the researchers. In a less historical but more reflexive
vein, Moore (1993, 2009, 2013) and Dobrin (2012) have applied similar
approaches to their own recordings and found that their consultants'
narratives were responding to and communicating with them in ways
that they did not fully appreciate during their fieldwork.

REFERENCES

American Anthropological Association. 1940. "News and Notes." *American
Anthropologist* 42, no. 1: 180–81.
Banner, Lois W. 2003. *Intertwined Lives: Margaret Mead, Ruth Benedict, and
Their Circle.* New York: Knopf.
Bauman, Richard, and Charles L. Briggs. 2003. *Voices of Modernity: Lan-
guage Ideologies and the Politics of Inequality.* Cambridge: Cambridge
University Press.
Berman, Judith. 1996 "The Culture as It Appears to the Indian Himself":
Boas, George Hunt, and the Methods of Ethnography." *In Volksgeist
as Method and Ethic: Essays on Boasian Ethnography and the German
Anthropological Tradition,* edited by George W. Stocking, 215–56. Madi-
son: University of Wisconsin Press.
Boas, Franz. 1917. "Introductory." *International Journal of American Linguistics* 1, no. 1 :1–8.
———. 1911. "Introduction." In *Handbook of American Indian Languages,* Part
1, edited by Franz Boas, 5–83. Washington: Government Printing Office.
———. (1906) 1974. "Some Philological Aspects of Anthropological
Research." In *The Shaping of American Anthropology 1883–1911: A Franz Boas
Reader,* edited by George W. Stocking, 183–88. New York: Basic Books.
———. (1905) 1974. "The Documentary Function of the Text." In *The
Shaping of American Anthropology 1883–1911: A Franz Boas Reader,* edited
by George W. Stocking, 122–23. New York: Basic Books.
Boas, Franz, and John R. Swanton. 1911. "Siouan: Dakota (Teton and Santee
Dialects) with Remarks on the Ponca and Winnebago." In *Handbook of*

American Indian Languages, Part 1, edited by Franz Boas, 875–965. Washington: Government Printing Office.

Briggs, Charles, and Richard Bauman. 1999. "'The Foundation of All Future Researches': Franz Boas, George Hunt, Native American Texts, and the Construction of Modernity." *American Quarterly* 51, no. 3 :479–528.

Buckley, Thomas. 1996. "'The Little History of Pitiful Events': The Epistemological and Moral Contexts of Kroeber's Californian Ethnology." In *Volksgeist as Method and Ethic: Essays on Boasian Ethnography and the German Anthropological Tradition*, edited by George W. Stocking, 257–97. Madison: University of Wisconsin Press.

Clifford, James. 1982. *Person and Myth: Maurice Leenhardt in the Melanesian World*. Berkeley: University of California Press.

Darnell, Regna. 1990a. *Edward Sapir: Linguist, Anthropologist, Humanist*. Berkeley: University of California Press.

———. 1990b. "Franz Boas, Edward Sapir, and the Americanist Text Tradition." *Historiographia Linguistica* 17, no. 1–2: 129–44.

Deloria, Philip J. 1998. *Playing Indian*. New Haven: Yale University Press.

Dobrin, Lise M. 2012. "Ethnopoetic Analysis as a Resource for Endangered-Language Linguistics: The Social Production of an Arapesh Text." *Anthropological Linguistics* 54, no. 1:1–32.

Duranti, Alessandro. 2003. "Language as Culture in U.S. Anthropology." *Current Anthropology* 44, no. 3: 323–47.

Epps, Patience L., Anthony K. Webster, and Anthony C. Woodbury. 2017. "A Holistic Humanities of Speaking: Franz Boas and the Continuing Centrality of Texts." *International Journal of American Linguistics* 83, no. 1: 41–78.

Foster, Lance M. 1999. "This Land Here." Accessed March 5, 2017. http://ioway.nativeweb.org/language/thislandhere.htm.

———. 1994. "Sacred Bundles of the Ioway Indians." MA thesis, Department of Anthropology, Iowa State University.

Golla, Victor. 1995. "The Records of American Indian Linguistics." In *Preserving the Anthropological Record*, edited by Sydel Silverman and Nancy J. Parezo, 143–57. New York: Wenner-Gren Foundation for Anthropological Research.

Goodtracks, Jimm G. n.d. "Báxoje Jiwére Wírawe: Ioway, Otoe-Missouria Mathematics." Accessed March 5, 2017. http://iowayotoelang.nativeweb.org/pdf/mathandtime.pdf.

———. 1998. "*Hinкúñi* My Grandmother." Baxoje-Jiwere Language Project. Accessed March 5, 2017. http://iowayotoelang.nativeweb.org/pdf/worage_hinkuni_feb_06.pdf.

Gruber, Jacob W. 1970. "Ethnographic Salvage and the Shaping of Anthropology." *American Anthropologist* 72, no. 6: 1289–99.

Harkin, Michael. 2001. "Comment." *Current Anthropology* 42, no. 3: 395–96.

Hymes, Dell. 2003. *Now I Know Only So Far: Essays in Ethnopoetics*. Lincoln: University of Nebraska Press.

———. 1981. *"In Vain I Tried to Tell You": Essays in Native American Ethnopoetics*. Philadelphia: University of Pennsylvania Press.

Jacknis, Ira. 1996. "The Ethnographic Object and the Object of Ethnology in the Early Career of Franz Boas." In *Volksgeist as Method and Ethic: Essays on Boasian Ethnography and the German Anthropological Tradition*, edited by George W. Stocking, 185–214. Madison: University of Wisconsin Press.

Jacobs, Melville. 1959. "Folklore." In *The Anthropology of Franz Boas: Essays on the Centennial of His Birth*, edited by Walter Goldschmidt, 119–38. San Francisco: Howard Chandler.

Kroskrity, Paul V. 1998. "Arizona Tewa Kiva Speech as a Manifestation of a Dominant Language Ideology." In *Language Ideologies: Practice and Theory*, edited by Bambi B. Schieffelin, Kathryn A. Woolard, and Paul V. Kroskrity, 103–22. New York: Oxford University Press.

Lassiter, Luke Eric. 2005. *The Chicago Guide to Collaborative Ethnography*. Chicago: University of Chicago Press.

Leeds-Hurwitz, Wendy. 1985. "The Committee on Research in Native American Languages." *Proceedings of the American Philosophical Society* 129, no. 2: 129–60.

Lewis, Herbert S. 2008. "Franz Boas: Boon or Bane?" *Reviews in Anthropology* 37: 169–200.

———. 2001a. "The Passion of Franz Boas." *American Anthropologist* 103, no. 2: 447–67.

———. 2001b. "Reply." *Current Anthropology* 42, no. 3: 400–403.

Lowie, Robert H. 1940. "Native Languages as Ethnographic Tools." *American Anthropologist* 42, no. 1: 81–89.

Malinowski, Bronislaw. 1935. *Coral Gardens and Their Magic*. Vol. 2, *The Language of Magic and Gardening*. Bloomington: Indiana University Press.

———. 1922. *Argonauts of the Western Pacific: An Account of Native Enterprise and Adventure in the Archipelagoes of Melanesian New Guinea*. London: Routledge.

Marcus, George E., and Michael M. J. Fischer. 1986. *Anthropology as Cultural Critique: An Experimental Moment in the Human Sciences*. Chicago: University of Chicago Press.

Maud, Ralph. 2000. *Transmission Difficulties: Franz Boas and Tsimshian Mythology*. Burnaby BC: Talonbooks.

———. 1989. "The Henry Tate—Franz Boas Collaboration on Tsimshian Mythology." *American Ethnologist* 16, no. 1: 158–62.

Mead, Margaret. 1939. "Native Languages as Field-Work Tools." *American Anthropologist* 41, no. 2: 189–205.

Moore, Robert E. 2013. "Reinventing Ethnopoetics." In *The Legacy of Dell Hymes: Ethnopoetics, Narrative Inequality, and Voice*, edited by Paul V. Kroskrity and Anthony K. Webster, 11–36. Bloomington: Indiana University Press.

———. 2009. "From Performance to Print, and Back: Ethnopoetics as Social Practice in Alice Florendo's Corrections to 'Raccoon and His Grandmother.'" *Text & Talk* 29, no. 3:295–324.

———. 1993. "Performance Form and the Voices of Characters in Five Versions of the Wasco Coyote Cycle." In *Reflexive Language: Reported Speech and Metapragmatics*, edited by John A. Lucy, 213–40. Cambridge: Cambridge University Press.

Nevins, M. Eleanor. 2015. "'Grow with That, Walk with That': Hymes, Dialogicality, and Text Collections." In *The Legacy of Dell Hymes: Ethnopoetics, Narrative Inequality, and Voice*, edited by Paul V. Kroskrity and Anthony K. Webster, 71–107. Bloomington: Indiana University Press.

———. 2013. *Lessons from Fort Apache: Beyond Language Endangerment and Maintenance*. Chichester UK: Wiley-Blackwell.

Otoe and Iowa Language Speakers with Lila Wistrand-Robinson. 1977. *Otoe and Iowa Indian Language*. Book I. Park Hill OK: Jiwele—Baxoje Language Project.

Powell, Timothy B. 2015. "Anthropology of Revitalization: Digitizing the American Philosophical Society's Native American Collections." In *The Franz Boas Papers*, Vol. 1, *Franz Boas as Public Intellectual—Theory, Ethnography, Activism*, edited by Regna Darnell, Michelle Hamilton, Robert L. A. Hancock, and Joshua Smith, 331–44. Lincoln: University of Nebraska Press.

Radin, Paul. 1933. *The Method and Theory of Ethnology*. New York: Basic Books.

Rohner, Ronald P., ed. 1969. *The Ethnography of Franz Boas: Letters and Diaries of Franz Boas Written on the Northwest Coast from 1886 to 1931*. Chicago: University of Chicago Press.

Sanjek, Roger. 1990. "The Secret Life of Fieldnotes." In *Fieldnotes: The Makings of Anthropology*, edited by Roger Sanjek, 187–270. Ithaca: Cornell University Press.

Schwartz, Saul. 2018. "Writing Chiwere: Orthography, Literacy, and Language Revitalization." *Language & Communication* 61: 75–87.

———. 2014 "Who Wrote Whitman's Grammar?" Siouan and Caddoan Languages Conference, Madison WI, May 23, 2014.

Skinner, Alanson. 1926. "Ethnology of the Ioway Indians." *Bulletin of the Public Museum of the City of Milwaukee* 5, no. 4:181–354.

———. 1925. "Traditions of the Iowa Indians." *Journal of American Folklore* 38, no. 150: 425–506.

———. 1922. "A Summer Among the Sauk and Ioway Indians." *Yearbook of the Public Museum of the City of Milwaukee* 2: 6–22.

Silverstein, Michael. 2015. "From Baffin Island to Boasian Induction: How Anthropology and Linguistics Got into Their Interlinear Groove." In *The Franz Boas Papers*, Vol. 1, *Franz Boas as Public Intellectual—Theory, Ethnography, Activism*, edited by Regna Darnell, Michelle Hamilton, Robert L. A. Hancock, and Joshua Smith, 83–127. Lincoln: University of Nebraska Press.

———. 1996. "The Secret Life of Texts." In *Natural Histories of Discourse*, edited by Michael Silverstein and Greg Urban, 81–105. Chicago: University of Chicago Press.

Stocking, George W. 1992. *The Ethnographer's Magic and Other Essays in the History of Anthropology*. Madison: University of Wisconsin Press.

———. 1968. *Race, Culture, and Evolution: Essays in the History of Anthropology*. New York: Free Press.

Thom, Brian. 2003. "The Anthropology of Northwest Coast Oral Traditions." *Artic Anthropology* 40, no. 1: 1–28.

Voegelin, C. F. 1952. "The Boas Plan for the Presentation of American Indian Languages." *Proceedings of the American Philosophical Society* 96, no. 4: 439–51.

Voegelin, C. F., and Z. S. Harris. 1945. "Index to the Franz Boas Collection of Materials for American Linguistics." *Language* 21, no. 3: 1–3. Language Monograph No. 22: Index to the Franz Boas Collection of Materials for American Linguistics.

White, Leslie A. 1963. "The Ethnography and Ethnology of Franz Boas." *Bulletin of the Texas Memorial Museum* 6. Austin: Texas Memorial Museum.

Whitman, William. 1947a. "Descriptive Grammar of Ioway-Oto." *International Journal of American Linguistics* 13, no. 4: 233–48.

———. 1947b. *The Pueblo Indians of San Ildefonso: A Changing Culture*, edited by Marjorie W. Whitman. New York: Columbia University Press.

———. 1938. "Origin Legends of the Oto." *Journal of American Folklore* 51, no. 200: 173–205.

———. 1937. *The Oto*. New York: Columbia University Press.

11

Look Once More at the Old Things

Ruth Underhill's O'odham Text Collections

Most biographical essays concerning Ruth Underhill mention that in 1979, when Underhill was ninety-seven years old, the Tohono O'odham hosted a traditional banquet in her honor and invited her to serve as Grand Marshall at their annual community parade (Colwell-Chanthaphonh and Nash 2014; Lavendar 2006; Zepeda 1993). A description of the events surrounding the commemoration, published in *Anthropology News*, signaled the importance not just to Underhill personally, but to the field of Americanist Anthropology (Herold 1980). During the festivities, Enos Francisco, tribal vice-chairman, presented her with a plaque that thanked Underhill, saying that she "captured the spirit of our O'odham through her writing and made it possible for those of us today and tomorrow to appreciate the richness of our O'odham heritage" (Herold 1980, 3). Underhill viewed this honor by the O'odham community as "the crowning part of [her] life" (Herold 1980, 3). The events were a testament to the generosity of the O'odham tribe and a reminder of the benefits of anthropological research when mutual respect and trust is engendered between the researcher and community.

What is particularly striking about the celebration is that it occurred nearly forty years after Underhill's original research among the O'odham. The community, first known by Underhill as the Papago, changed significantly during that period.[1] But as the testimonies demonstrate, Underhill's publications remained accessible and relevant to the community throughout the intervening decades. The community viewed Underhill's work not as remnants of previous generations but as a productive component of ongoing O'odham cultural life. The long-standing relationship between Underhill and the O'odham tribe provides an especially rich example of how Indigenous communities participated in early twentieth century anthropology, not just as research subjects and collaborators, but also as readers and consumers of the scholarly texts produced about their communities.[2] Underhill's work with the O'odham and the afterlife of the texts that were produced encourages readers to look beyond the moment of ethnographic research to consider how exchanges between local groups and fieldworkers continue over time, including across generations as cultural texts are engaged, interpreted, and repurposed by Indigenous communities. As Saul Schwartz observes in this volume, stories are examples of discursive acts that are entextualized in ways much different than objects of material culture. While ethnographic collecting often implies the removal of an object from a community and from wider circulation, stories are able to be retold by various orators and reinscribed by different observers. Importantly, these types of texts carry with them the imprint of exchange which, as Schwartz discusses (herein) enhances rather than diminishes cultural meaning through their continued circulation. Stories, songs, and other oral performances that were written down in the late nineteenth and early twentieth centuries have created a corpus of textual materials that tribal members have revived and used in novel ways such as in contemporary Indigenous language programs (Morgan 2009, 247–49). Underhill's publications of O'odham songs and stories in the 1930s and 1940s are a primary example of this circulatory process.

In the early 1930s, Underhill elicited a sequence of O'odham ceremonial songs and speeches that became the basis for many of her scholarly works including the books *Singing for Power* (1938) and *Papago Indian Religion* (1946). While the books are examples of early twentieth century salvage ethnography intended to preserve cultural practices, the text collections that form the core of both works have not remained static, and their continued circulation within the O'odham community has imbued them with significant value. Not only have they been published and republished in various forms, they have also served as the basis for retranslation and reinterpretation by others. In 1979, O'odham speakers Baptisto Lopez, Jose Pancho, and David Lopez, along with the anthropologist Donald Bahr, published portions of Underhill's collection as *Rainhouse and Ocean: Speeches for the Papago Year*. The book was the culmination of a multiyear project to retranslate Underhill's texts back into O'odham and to provide deeper analysis of the songs and ceremonial cycle (Underhill et al. 1997). Almost two decades later, Ofelia Zepeda, the O'odham linguist and poet, offered her own interpretation of Underhill's work in an introduction to a new edition of *Singing for Power*. In her essay, Zepeda acknowledges the significance of Underhill's collection and credits her for engaging in an early form of collaborative and community-based research (Zepeda 1993, xi). These various collections are not repetitive, but rather build on the previous work's analysis and understanding of the distinctive O'odham song and speech cycle. While Underhill could not have anticipated the ways in which her texts would be used and reused, she was prescient in creating works that not only served the interests of the current generation in preserving O'odham culture but also provided a foundation for revitalization efforts among generations yet to come.

UNDERHILL'S COMMITMENT TO A PRACTICAL ANTHROPOLOGY

Underhill began her studies in anthropology under Ruth Benedict and Franz Boas when she was forty-six years old and looking for a new start after her divorce.[3] When she entered Columbia University in 1929, Americanist Anthropology was still centered on Indigenous communities in the U.S., and she joined other scholars such as Edward Kennard, Elsie Clew Parsons, and Gladys Reichard in focusing on Southwestern tribes. Though frustrated at times by the challenges of being an older student, Underhill felt that her maturity helped her both focus in her studies and establish rapport with tribal members, particularly women, during her fieldwork (Underhill 2014, 139–40, 160). She made her first trip to the Tohono O'odham reservation in 1931 and returned frequently over the course of the next four years. During her first summer, Underhill met Maria Chona and began a friendship and collaboration that would result in the book, *Papago Woman*, an early example of feminist anthropology and Indigenous life history (Berry Brill de Ramirez 2015). These fieldwork sessions also included her elicitation of the song texts and speeches from male ritual leaders that became the basis for her writing and analysis of O'odham religion and social structure.

Much of Underhill's professional career was spent as an applied anthropologist in the federal government. Although initially she hoped for a university position after completing her degree, the limited opportunities of the 1930s forced her to seek employment outside of the academic setting. In 1934, she found temporary government work by assisting Gladys Reichard in teaching Navajo to local students at the bicultural and bilingual Hogan school. Shortly after, John Collier, the Commissioner of Indian Affairs, hired Underhill to review the proposed constitution for the Tohono O'odham that had been drafted under the newly passed Indian Reorganization Act. Collier expected her to be supportive of the effort; however, Underhill was critical of the resulting document because she believed it failed to recognize the particularities of O'odham social and political structures. As a result, Collier barred her from working with the community on further issues of reorganization (Lavendar 2006, 110). Seeking reliable employment and unable to continue government work with the O'odham, Underhill successfully sat for the civil service exam in 1935. She subsequently accepted a position consulting on issues of tribal land management with the Soil Conservation Survey. Underhill was unhappy in this position, and in 1937 she transferred to the Indian Education Department, remaining there for the next ten years. As part of her appointment, she trained teachers assigned to reservation communities about Native communities and authored booklets for the *Indian Life and Custom Series* based on her continuing ethnographic research among various tribes (Underhill 2014, 194–95).

After leaving government service entirely in 1948, she spent four years teaching anthropology at the University of Denver. She then began a productive post-retirement career, writing, lecturing, and serving as a popular commentator on television and radio programs. During this period, she wrote the general textbooks *Red Man's America* (1953) and *Red Man's Religion* (1965), and continued to look for opportunities to publish for non-academic audiences. She believed firmly that anthropology needed to be accessible to the wider public; however, she also wanted to be taken seriously as a scholar (Underhill 2014; Lavendar 2006). This tension between scholarly legitimacy and popular reach created difficulties for Underhill at various points in her career. In a 1975 letter to a publisher, she suggested that some of her previous books should be reissued to a more general audience, noting that most of her books were published "through universities, although they were in sufficiently popular style so that my colleagues criticized me for seeming unscientific" (Papers of Ruth M. Underhill, n.d.). During her career, Underhill witnessed the discipline move increasingly to more abstract and theoretical discussions; however, she remained skeptical of these efforts and was determined to keep anthropological findings relevant to wider society. Fortunately, she lived long enough to see the discipline shift again and to respond to Indigenous community concerns about the ethics of anthropological research and encourage new collaborations between anthropologists and tribes. Underhill passed away in 1984, a few years after the receiving honors from the O'odham community and just before her 101st birthday.

SINGING FOR POWER: TODAY AND TOMORROW

The O'odham songs and speeches that comprise *Singing for Power* were collected by Underhill over fourteen months in Santa Rosa, Arizona. She was content to spend most of her time in the field talking with women, but she realized that she would have to work with old men if she was to learn about the seasonal ritual cycle and the special, archaic language of song. Her principal intermediary was Juan Xavier, a young O'odham man who had lived in Phoenix while attending a theological school and learning English. Xavier spoke the everyday language of O'odham life fluently; however, he was untrained in ritual speech and thus viewed his work with Underhill as an opportunity to expand his own ceremonial knowledge (Underhill et al. 1997, 3). Underhill would transcribe the ceremonialist's speeches phonetically in O'odham; Xavier would then work with the speaker to review the O'odham text, offering corrections and providing a word-by-word translation in English. Finally, Underhill crafted an English gloss for the interlinear translation that she believed captured the inherent poetry within the songs. Later, she reflected the purpose of her collecting: "The reason was so that these could be written down and used by Papagos for many years to come. The old priests were dying, and some had not taught their ceremonials to younger men. If this continued, the beautiful language and all the actions connected with it might be lost" (Underhill et al. 1997, 3). While Underhill's focus was on documentation and preservation, she saw how textual collections could generate new possibilities for the community and elicited the texts with the intention that the songs could be used by the community itself, in ways that they deemed appropriate later on.

Singing for Power begins with Underhill's extended discussion of the songs and speeches, their origin, their rhythmic form, and the special role of ceremonialists in O'odham society. In the following sections, Underhill offers short contextual descriptions of the rituals, including the participants' roles and structure of the ceremonies, in addition to her English versions of the speeches. As Underhill observes, "Since the songs are magic tools, it has not seemed possible to present them without some description of the magic they are supposed to work. Such description is almost a part of the translation, for without it, the emotional weight of the songs could not be understood" (Underhill 1993, 8). She includes songs for "pulling down the clouds," the crucial ritual of making and drinking the fermented saguaro cactus wine, as well as shorter songs that are associated with particular forms of power such as animal magic. She uses ethnographic vignettes to frame the speeches and songs, and either offers descriptions of the accompanying ceremonies or connects the content of the songs to O'odham cosmology. Underhill's descriptions pay attention to the performative aspects of the ceremonies including the setting and accompanying material objects. This is best exemplified in her lengthy description of the drinking ritual where she observes the various steps from the procurement of the cactus fruit to the preparation of the wine. These descriptions are active and draw the reader into the events as they unfold as well as providing more general cultural information. For example, she describes how "the women return to the shelter and dump their bushels of juicy pulp in the cooking pot. . . . When the juice is boiled, and strained through a basket, there is still a pulp, one of the few sweets known to the Papagos, and there are the oily seeds which supply both grease and flour" (Underhill 1993, 23). Her analysis of the actual songs is limited, and most are presented without any elaboration of the content. In her introduction to the songs associated with animals and healing, she states, "The songs, like all Papago magic, are not prayers. They are only descriptions and it does not matter whether they praise or ridicule. . . . The point is to visualize the animal with all the peculiarities which are to evoke him and make him real. . . . They are little vignettes of desert life, humorous, exquisite, and friendly" (Underhill 1993, 50). She presents the reader with an experience of the songs rather than an extended analysis of form or content. As part of her descriptive contextualization, she includes illustrations from three young artists, Avellino Herera, Sia Pueblo, and Ben Pavisook, which depict scenes of daily O'odham life, local flora and fauna, and ceremonial objects that are mentioned in the texts (Underhill 1993, xv). What does not appear, however, is the O'odham language itself nor any extended discussion of its grammatical rules or structure.

In the first few chapters, Underhill indicates some of the difficulties with translating and representing songs and speeches. After a lengthy commentary regarding her decision regarding how to render O'odham into a readable English text, Underhill admits that her free translations are inconsistent, with some closely adhering to O'odham grammatical form and others taking considerable liberty with structure to satisfy an assumed contemporary English-speaking reader. In regard to the verb-final word order in O'odham, Underhill writes, "There is a beauty and a rhythm in the arrangement which we can appreciate; but we could hardly read sentence after sentence in that order without weariness . . . and therefore I have only suggested the idea where it could be done easily. If it sounds like an imitation of the classics, I have but to apologize to the Papagos, for they worked out the system for themselves, and I only wish I could render it better" (Underhill 1993, 17). In her discussion, she also gestures to the complexities inherent in any ethnographic project; while research is always accomplished at a specific time and place, the resulting text can and will be read outside of this context. Underhill considers this when deciding on how to represent tense in the English translations, and she makes the decision to keep the songs and descriptions active despite her admission in the introduction that many aspects of O'odham rituals are no longer performed.[4] Underhill justifies the decision based largely on who she sees as her primary audience: "In describing the ceremonies, I do so in the present tense. . . . I have preferred to use the method of the old men who gave me the poetry and to draw the picture as though all of it were still to be found in the present" (Underhill 1993, 8–9). Here Underhill refers to the decline of traditional ceremonialism but also, importantly, positions her account in a way that rejects a trend in American anthropology that was growing during this period.

In the 1930s, the Boasian project of "salvaging" culture by eliciting retrospective accounts of myths and "old ways" remembered by elderly informants had come to seem old-fashioned to many anthropologists. Older questions regarding cultural history gave way to newer approaches such as acculturation studies, which drew heavily on sociology and detailed how communities were adapting to new social and political structures as a result of contact with others (Murray 2013, 52–55). Underhill was well acquainted with these works as a result of her time in government service. Anthropologists, particularly those she worked with at the Office of Indian Affairs, viewed acculturation studies as being better suited to inform public policy and rejected previous approaches that focused on pre-reservation or pre-contact Indigenous culture. (Morgan 2017, 17–19). It is telling that Underhill never employed this theoretical positioning in her own scholarly writings but rather continued to hew closely to Boas's advice to concentrate on the stories and remembrances of tribal elders. This was not done out of naivety, nor a paternalistic idea about collecting for science, but rather to acknowledge O'odham values and concerns. In her introduction to *Singing for Power*, she observes that the O'odham "have put on the white man's clothing and built adobe houses. There are government wells in what was once the waterless desert, and government schools. But until the old men who knew the other ways are gone, the core of the ancient life will remain" (Underhill 1993, 9). In this light, salvage anthropology is less about creating a record of a vanishing culture and more about documenting ongoing cultural practices that communities themselves identified as distinctive and significant (Jacknis herein). In her writings, Underhill always assumes that the O'odham, while certainly changing, will continue to persist as a distinctive community within the larger U.S. polity. Her act of collecting ceremonial songs and speeches, as well as the decision to present them in the present tense in *Singing for Power*, can be seen as her support of an accessible form of anthropological knowledge that she believed would ultimately benefit the O'odham themselves.

That Underhill constructed *Singing for Power* in a way that could be useful to the future O'odham community is consistent with her own practice of using and reusing her own ethnographic data for multiple purposes and in a variety of publications—government, popular, and scholarly. In each, she framed the basic content in ways that anticipated the needs of her perceived readership. The songs that appear in *Singing for Power*, which was always intended for a more popular audience, were reprinted in her larger, more scholarly work, *Papago Indian Religion* (1946). In this book, the song translations are virtually identical, but she substitutes her popular descriptive style for a more analytical tone in contextualizing and discussing the texts. For example, she begins the section on Mockingbird speeches in *Singing for Power* with the simple description of the two messengers "whose duty it is to call neighbors to the feast" and where "the invitation to the Sit-and-Drink was 'given' in the unknown past, in magic words, that help to bring the rain" (Underhill 1993, 29). In *Papago Indian Religion*, she begins with a lengthy description of the drinking ceremony with comparative examples from four different villages, paying particular attention to performative style. She continues, "The speeches, both of invitation and of response, were hereditary and were somewhat different, at least in later days, for each village. . . . They were delivered not in abrupt, staccato style of the war and salt speeches, but were smooth and flowing, with heavy emphasis on the last word in each sentence. They mention a supernatural about whom none of the speakers could tell anything, but who resembles the rain gods of Mexican tradition" (Underhill 1946, 52). Unlike in *Singing for Power*, Underhill identifies the community (Archie) from which her version of the song originates. Details such as this occur throughout *Papago Indian Religion* but are strikingly absent from the earlier work. While the English renditions of the song texts are the same in the two published works, the discussion and contextualization are divergent enough to create books with vastly different scopes and aims.

Portions of her text collections also appear earlier in the Office of Indian Affairs periodical, *Indians at Work* (IAW), a magazine intended for employees of the CCC-Indian Division (Underhill 1936; Morgan 2017). Here, she reflects the spirit of the periodical by connecting O'odham game-playing to economic exchange, thereby demonstrating the commensurability of O'odham culture with modernity. In the introductory paragraph, Underhill writes that games "were the one real method of trade. Anyone writing a book on Indian economics might do worse than start with the subject of games" (Underhill 1936, 40). Descriptions of "intervillage games" also appear in *Papago Indian Religion*, where the argument regarding economic exchange in the IAW article is sublimated to a lengthy discussion regarding how the games fit into the larger ritual cycle. Though she mentions economic exchange, and that games could be "said to take the place of a market," this is only passing reference in an extended description of songs, races, and ceremonies (Underhill 1946, 116–34). In each of these occurrences, her descriptions are slightly modified, illustrating Underhill's own awareness of the flexibility of ethnographic writing and the need to alter text to fit the expectations and needs of the audience.

That Underhill intended her work to be read in this flexible and expansive way may also be inferred from the way she closes *Singing for Power*. She shows in detail that, notwithstanding the loss of many old songs and rituals, new ones were still being composed by ritual leaders, inspired by dreams. In the book's final pages, she tells of an old man who dreams that he has been taken to a city where he meets an O'odham clown who has also become lost. Together, the two return home. When they arrive back in O'odham country, it is surprisingly filled with traditional ritual objects, of exactly the kinds that he knew had become very scarce. The clown instructs the dreamer to "Look at these things. . . . Our people are ceasing to use them. It may be that this is right and that they should take over the white man's ways. But, before you decide, come here. Look once more at the old things. Be sure" (Underhill 1993, 158). The dream responds directly to the progressive abandonment and loss of O'odham culture, but what is particularly striking is its insistence that the change is neither inevitable nor irrevocable. By ending with the dream in which the ritual leader is challenged to "look once more at the old things," Underhill seems to be inviting the reader, who could very well be O'odham, to look back over the texts in the book itself as a way to begin. Those texts, which from one perspective are ethnographic "material," produced through research, are from another perspective repositories of knowledge that preserve it until the O'odham people will once again find it useful. Read in this way, the O'odham are not only responsible for cultural maintenance and renewal, but also for the consequences if they choose to let the practices lapse. In effect, Underhill meant for her ethnography to become part of the existing O'odham discursive repertoire and, as such, stimulate dialogue across generations.

FUTURE READERS RESPOND

Beginning in 1975, three highly regarded O'odham speakers—Baptisto Lopez, Jose Pancho, and David Lopez—collaborated with the anthropologist, Donald Bahr, on a project to create a new edition of O'odham ceremonial speeches and songs based on Underhill's fieldnotes and text collection. The resulting book, *Rainhouse and Ocean,* provides O'odham text with parallel English translations, analyses of O'odham oratorical practices, and expanded discussions about the significance of the various ceremonies. Rather than relying on Underhill's published free translations as a source, the speakers based their English translations on their knowledge of the language and analysis of the O'odham found in Underhill's field notebooks. They worked with Bahr to retranscribe the O'odham texts into a new orthography and supplemented them with the speakers' own knowledge of the ceremonies and rituals. In some cases, the speakers taped new versions of the ritual speeches to be transcribed and included in the published version.

Throughout the work, the authors drew comparisons and distinctions from Underhill's works and discussed the ways in which the song and speech texts were transformed through the act of retranslation (Underhill et al. 1997, 47). They noted that the differences in orthography were significant and impacted the translation and interpretation of the songs. Underhill used an orthography that was largely idiosyncratic, while Lopez, Pancho, Lopez, and Bahr used a contemporary orthography developed in the 1970s and adopted for use by the tribe.

Critically, the new orthography preserved consonantal variations that Underhill's transcriptions failed to note. The authors of *Rainhouse and Ocean* also used Underhill's literal translations of the O'odham found in her fieldnotes, rather than her previously published texts to guide their own work because they believed these translations preserved more of the O'odham oratorical style (Underhill et al. 1997, 14).

While variances in translation are subtle, they do provide a different sense of the songs as a whole. The following are excerpts from the first stanza of the preparatory songs for the Salt ritual and are illustrative of the differences that appear throughout the two works. The first text is an example of Underhill's gloss that appears in *Singing for Power*; the second is the O'odham text and English translation by Lopez, Pancho, Lopez, and Bahr.

SINGING FOR POWER

I rose and across the bare spaces did go walking,
Did peep through the openings in the scrub,
Looking about me, seeking something.
Thus I went on and on. Where there was a tree that suited me,
Beneath it prone and solitary I lay,
My forehead upon my folded arms I lay
There was an ancient woman.
Some lore she had somehow learned
And quietly she went about telling it
To me she spoke, telling it.
Then did I raise myself upon my hands;
I put them to my face and wiped away the dust,
I put them to my hair and shook out the rubbish (Underhill 1993, 115).

RAINHOUSE AND OCEAN

Nt ha'ap am wu : ṣ,
Ta am ṣaṣdkam oidk i himhi, ia ta'ataj

G je: jeg oidk ne : nhoga hab cem ñ-wuihim
Nta ha'ap ñ-juccuhim.
Nt a hebai g u:s ap'ecudk weco am kupal

hejel ñ-wua
Nt a no : nhoi si ka:kiobink tua, kuawak
wo'iwa
Ka wuḍ hemak wi'ikam oks
Ta hebai ja'icu s-ma cok
An cem s-ba; bagi e-a:g
O wa g am s-ñ-a; gidam kaij
Nt a am ñ-da; gṣk i wam
Nt a ñ-wuhio mawua
Nt a g jeweḍ am i dagkwa
Nt a g ñ-mo'o eḍa mawua
   Nt a g tanhadag gi: gim.

I set out
Went among scattered plants, trying to hide
behind them
Went among open places trying to look
Thus I continued
Somewhere found a good tree and below it
face down threw myself
Crossed my arms and put them down, put
my forehead down.
There was one ancient woman
Somewhere she had learned something
Slowly she told it
Wanting to tell me she spoke.
I pressed down and arose
Touched my face
Rubbed off the dirt
Touched my hair
Shook out the trash

(Underhill et al. 1997, 50)

In addition to the most obvious addition of O'odham in *Rainhouse and Ocean*, there are clear distinctions regarding pronoun use, voice, and word choice, which collectively forms a style distinctive from Underhill's free translation.

Similarly, the contextual descriptions of O'odham social and religious life differ significantly between Underhill's prior publications and *Rainhouse and Ocean*. For example, while Underhill gives only one version of the salt pilgrimage, Lopez, Pancho, Lopez, and Bahr provide four. They also include a lengthy description of the pilgrimage itself written in 1897 in English by Jose Lewis Brennan, an O'odham community member (Underhill et al. 1997, 38–47). Whereas *Singing for Power* portrays a singular, anonymous speaker, *Rainhouse and Ocean* provides multiple versions and voices. This allows the authors an opportunity to comment on these differences as well as ultimately providing a more complex and nuanced depiction of the song cycle. Despite differences, the authors remained generous to Underhill's initial work and collection. They commented, "We feel that the new version is correct, but that correctness is a matter of degree... Our interpretation could have missed something, too. Yet, we have not hesitated to differ from the earlier translations. It is felt that two available translations, consistently made, are better than one" (Underhill et al. 1997, 15).

Similar to Underhill's original rationale for collecting the song texts, the coauthors of *Rainhouse and Ocean* claimed that the impetus for publishing the translated works was to create a lasting text for the benefit of the O'odham community. After stating that their primary audience is the O'odham community, they write, "The writers hope that young Papagos in the year 2000 will find this book informative and that old Papagos of today will find it truthful" (Underhill et al. 1997, 5). Rather than viewing it as a static relic, the authors saw the text collection as iterative and productive among the community. Throughout the collection, the coauthors express their appreciation and admiration for Underhill's work despite the differences in interpretation. David Lopez was quoted in relation to the 1979 celebration of Underhill: "I think hers are the most accurate of the books written. They give you a picture of how it was. You can pick them up and read again and again" (Herold 1980, 3).

However, *Rainhouse and Ocean* is ultimately a product of the collaboration between Bahr, Lopez, Pancho, and Lopez. While based on her texts, the collection represents an analytical development in O'odham scholarship by providing examples of variations within the song cycle. A note in the introduction to the collection states that while Underhill was supportive of the work as a whole, "she does not necessarily subscribe to the interpretations covered in the body of this book" (Underhill et al. 1997, 5). There is a clear distancing from the previously published versions of the same speeches and songs. At the same time, they suggest that Underhill's collaborative work with Xavier, which produced the notebooks of songs and speeches, and the first English translations, amounted to an important "first stage." Their work—returning the texts to the original language, elaborating on their meanings, and providing some oratorical analysis—constituted a "second stage." Importantly, they admit that while they present the texts in O'odham, there is still little linguistic analysis, and that there would likely be a "future 'stage three'" that would take the conditions of performance even more seriously (Underhill et al. 1997, 15).

While not necessarily extending the oratorical analysis envisioned by the authors in *Rainhouse and Ocean*, a "third stage" in the analysis of Underhill's text collection did appear in a new introduction by Ofelia Zepeda in the 1993 republication of *Singing for Power*. Zepeda began her career as a teacher of the O'odham language, but she later decided to pursue a PhD in Linguistics at the University of Arizona. Her linguistic work focused on O'odham morphology, and in 1983 she produced the first comprehensive grammar of Tohono O'odham. Zepeda has also published collections of poetry in both O'odham and English, including the books *Ocean Power: Poems from the Desert* (1995) and *Where Clouds Are Formed* (2008), that illustrate the continuing vitality of the language. In 1999, Zepeda was recognized with a MacArthur Foundation grant for her work on Indigenous language maintenance and revitalization.

Zepeda's reconsideration of Underhill's work came at a time when issues of Indigenous language loss were receiving greater public attention. She had helped create the American Indian Language Development Institute (AILDI) in the late 1970s and early 1980s, which promoted grassroots collaborations between linguists, speakers, and language teachers. In the 1990s, the institute found a permanent home at the

University of Arizona where Zepeda was an Assistant Professor of Linguistics (Zepeda and Hill 1991; McCarty et al. 1997). AILDI was a major center of language revitalization work during this time and supported many local language initiatives as well as working on a national level to help pass the 1990 and 1992 Native Languages Acts.[5] As part of this language activism, scholars began to seek ways to connect communities with the linguistic resources amassed in the early twentieth century as a result of anthropological research. Suddenly, old collections were given new attention.

This energy is reflected in Zepeda's introduction to *Singing for Power*. She uses the introduction to emphasize the importance of Underhill's work and as evidence for the maintenance of many O'odham ritual celebrations despite earlier concerns about their obsolescence (Zepeda 1993, ix–x). She also references *Rainhouse and Ocean* in the introduction and describes the process through which it was created. Zepeda includes an excerpt from the text "The Running Speech" in both O'odham and English and writes, "I have used this excerpt to illustrate that the work performed by Dr. Underhill in 1938 is essentially timeless. The beauty of the language and rhythm she felt important enough to capture though the English language was still very much alive in 1978. Even as we approach the year 2000, there are still small handfuls of orators and would-be orators who struggle to memorize parts of these speeches and songs" (Zepeda 1993, x). Importantly, by including portions of *Rainhouse and Ocean* in an introduction to *Singing for Power*, Zepeda reinforces their unity as part of a singular collection; they are merely two textual variations of the enduring O'odham song cycle. While Zepeda believes that the O'odham are ultimately responsible for the maintenance of the ritual cycle, she writes, "Underhill contributes indirectly to the continuation of ritual for the O'odham. Her descriptions, interpretations, and translations of what was said will for years be acknowledged as a work that has helped the people and their collective memory of what was said and why" (Zepeda 1993, viii). Zepeda reinforces Underhill's view of the fundamental utility of ethnography as a cultural resource that can be repurposed for the community's benefit.

In a remarkable passage, Zepeda retells the story from Underhill's book in which the clown implores the O'odham man in a dream to "look at these things." She agrees that the passage is an exhortation for cultural preservation and renewal; however, she claims that, unlike the collections in 1938 and 1979, the future has arrived and younger generations are actively reclaiming the practices of the past. Zepeda writes, "Today many young O'odham and in particular the teachers of these young people are reaching around and in back of them into the recent past to attempt systematically to revive old customs and rituals" (Zepeda 1993, xiii). This cultural production, which is fully within the control of the community, signals an important revaluation of the early twentieth century anthropological project. Works by anthropologists such as Underhill do not serve merely as codas to abandoned cultural practices, but themselves connect past and present forms, and facilitate conversations between previous and future generations.

Looking back over *Rainhouse and Ocean*, as well as the various editions of *Singing for Power*, important linkages emerge between the different iterations and editions of the text collection. They all argue for cultural repatriation—making texts and materials from earlier times available to speakers and teachers of today. While not excusing the ideological and ethical problems of the salvage project, Underhill's collections allow for a different perspective where the primary inheritors of the information are not the scientific community, but rather the source communities that Underhill always assumed would be there to resuscitate the practices. This work of reclaiming earlier anthropological works for contemporary projects is ongoing, and continues to generate new insights and understandings (Epps et al. 2017; Schwartz herein). In *Singing for Power*, Underhill seems to understand that texts she collected had the capacity to travel beyond her and beyond her collaborators for the generations yet to come. Instead of offering larger theories of social change, Underhill chose to present the speeches and songs largely as they were given to her, documenting the exchanges and always positioning herself within the transactions. In this way, she makes an important theoretical as well as methodological choice by giving primary voice to tribal members who contributed to the project. While these voices are mediated, Underhill's attention to audience, as well as her consideration of the afterlife of texts, have made them productive. Decades later, the descendants of the interlocutors became the authors, insuring that "old things" such as Indigenous language texts can continue to inspire new intergenerational collaborations.

NOTES

1. The Tohono O'odham (Desert People) is the self-designated term for the community and the official name of the tribe. It was formally recognized by the U.S. government in 1986 when the most recent tribal constitution was adopted. The term O'odham refers both to the community and language. Previously, the community was known as the Papago. This was a colonial derivation of the neighboring Pima's name for the tribe and was used historically by both the Spanish as well as the United States. The tribe was known officially as the Papago when Ruth Underhill started her fieldwork in the 1930s and the term was used in the first tribal constitution in 1937.

2. Phillip H. Round (2015) has argued for more attention to be given to the ways in which American Indian people participated in what he terms the "reading revolution" within the United States. While he focuses mostly on the late nineteenth century and schoolchildren, the same call for viewing tribal communities as consumers of texts applies to ethnographic works of the twentieth century.

3. Underhill is well known in Americanist circles, and her career has been documented in a number of volumes dedicated to women anthropologists, particularly those working in the American Southwest (Lavendar 2006; Parezo 1993; Berry Brill de Ramirez 2015). Her autobiography focusing on her early life and career has been published and provides insight into her views regarding the usefulness of anthropological research (Underhill 2014).

4. This approach to writing in the "ethnographic present" was, of course, the focus of much criticism of anthropology in the 1980s. Authors such as Johannes Fabian (1983), and James Clifford and George Marcus (1986), took issue with the ways in which ethnography constructed a "timeless" present and ignored historical contexts. I argue that Underhill chose to write in this way, not to disregard history, but as a means of supporting continuing cultural practices.

5. The 1990 Native American Language Act was passed to rectify past injustices regarding the maintenance of Indigenous languages. In addition to recognizing the active suppression of the languages in the past, the law states that the United States is responsible for working with

communities to help maintain Indigenous languages. The Native American Language Act of 1992 went further and allowed the government to award grants for the study of and development of Indigenous languages.

REFERENCES

Berry Brill de Ramirez, Susan. 2015. *Women Ethnographers and Native Women Storytellers: Relational Science, Ethnographic Collaboration, and Tribal Community*. New York: Lexington.

Clifford, James, and George Marcus, eds. 1986. *Writing Culture: The Poetics and Politics of Ethnography*. Berkeley: University of California Press.

Colwell-Chanthaphonh, Chip, and Stephen E. Nash. 2014. "Introduction." In *An Anthropologists Arrival: A Memoir* by Ruth Underhill, edited by Chip Colwell-Chanthaphonh and Stephen E. Nash, 1–24. Tucson: University of Arizona Press.

Epps, Patience, Anthony K. Webster, and Anthony C. Woodbury. 2017. "A Holistic Humanities of Speaking: Franz Boas and the Continuing Centrality of Texts." *International Journal of American Linguistics* 83, no. 1: 41–78.

Fabian, Johannes. 1983. *Time and the Other: How Anthropology Makes Its Object*. New York: Columbia University Press.

Herold, Joyce. 1980. "Papago Tribe Honors Ruth Murray Underhill." *Anthropology News* 21, no. 3: 3.

Lavendar, Catherine. 2006. *Scientists and Storytellers: Feminist Anthropologists and the Construction of the American Southwest*. Albuquerque: University of New Mexico Press.

McCarty, Teresa, Lucille J. Watahomigie, Akira Yamamoto, and Ofelia Zepeda. 1997. "School-Community-University Collaborations: The American Indian Language Development Institute." In *Teaching Indigenous Languages*, edited by Jon Reyhner, 85–104. Flagstaff AZ: Northern Arizona University.

Morgan, Mindy J. 2017. "Anthropologists in Unexpected Places: Tracing Anthropological Theory, Practice, and Policy in *Indians at Work*." *American Anthropologist* 119, no. 3: 435–47.

———. 2009. *The Bearer of This Letter: Language Ideologies, Literacy Practices, and the Fort Belknap Indian Community*. Lincoln: University of Nebraska Press.

Murray, Stephen O. 2013. *American Anthropology and Company*. Lincoln: University of Nebraska Press.

Papers of Ruth M. Underhill. n.d. Ruth Underhill Publications, 1932–1934. Box 11, Folder 17, "Multiple Publications—Correspondence, 1955–1979." Denver Museum of Science and Nature, Denver CO.

Parezo, Nancy. 1993. *Hidden Scholars: Women Anthropologists and the Native American Southwest.* Albuquerque: University of New Mexico Press.

Round, Phillip. 2015. "America's Indigenous Reading Revolution." In *Why You Can't Teach United States History without American Indians,* edited by Susan Sleeper-Smith, Juliana Barr, Jean M. O'Brien, Nancy Shoemaker, and Scott Manning Stevens, 165–80. Chapel Hill: University of North Carolina Press.

Underhill, Ruth. 2014. *An Anthropologist's Arrival: A Memoir,* edited by Chip Colwell-Chanthaphonh and Stephen E. Nash. Tucson: University of Arizona Press.

———. 1946. "Papago Indian Religion." *Columbia University Contributions to Anthropology.* Vol. 33. New York: Columbia University Press.

———. (1938) 1993. *Singing for Power: The Song Magic of the Papago Indians of Southern Arizona.* Tucson: University of Arizona Press.

———. 1936. "The Old Intervillage Games of the Papago." *Indians at Work* 4, no. 7: 40–2.

Underhill, Ruth M., Donald Bahr, Baptisto Lopez, Jose Pancho, and David Lopez, eds. (1979) 1997. *Rainhouse and Ocean: Speeches for the Papago Year.* Tucson: University of Arizona Press.

Zepeda, Ofelia. 2008. *Where Clouds Are Formed.* Tucson: University of Arizona Press.

———. 1995. *Ocean Power: Poems from the Desert Sun.* Tucson: University of Arizona Press.

———. 1993. "Foreword." In *Singing for Power: The Song Magic of the Papago Indians of Southern Arizona* by Ruth Underhill, vii–xiv. Tucson: University of Arizona Press.

———. (1983) 2016. *A Tohono O'odham Grammar.* Tucson: University of Arizona Press.

Zepeda, Ofelia, and Jane Hill. 1991. "The Condition of Native American Languages in the United States." In *Endangered Languages,* edited by Robert Robins and Eugenius Uhlenbeck, 135–55. Oxford: Berg.

12

Rereading Deloria

Against Workshops, for Communities

Custer Died for Your Sins by Vine Deloria Jr. has for half a century been regarded as a damning attack on anthropology and anthropologists. It is a famous attack that has been said to divide North American anthropology into two epochs: "BD and AD—Before and After Deloria" (Stull 1999, 63). But the book is more often quoted than read. As Bea Medicine wrote, "readers seemingly do not go beyond page 100" (2001, 3). Today, many seem to not read it at all. When read, the book's most incendiary passages, which are of course its most quoted, are easily misunderstood. In this essay I show that, far from a broadside against anthropology generally, *Custer* criticizes a particular strain of anthropology that Deloria saw as misguided.[1] Like Rob Hancock (herein), I am disappointed at how Deloria has been read. When reread carefully, it becomes apparent that, far from an "indictment" of anthropology (Thornton 2000, 762), he was distinguishing between bad and good anthropology and, likewise, between bad and good American Indian Studies; and that he aimed to convince anthropologists to do things better (and Indians to let them).

Like all texts, *Custer* has to be read in the context of its time and of its author's biography. Vine Deloria Jr. was the son of Vine Deloria Sr.; the grandson of Philip Joseph Deloria or *Tipi Sapa*, two very influential ministers; and the nephew of Ella Deloria. The Delorias came from a line of leaders in their Yankton community; conversion to Christianity was a necessary adjustment to new realities (Deloria 1999, 35). It is not a coincidence that Vine Jr., like his cousin, Bea Medicine, understood that Native "peoples and communities must adapt and adjust in order to survive" (Brayboy et al. 2007, 234–35). He graduated from

Iowa State University with a BS in General Science in 1958, went on to earn a Master's degree in Sacred Theology from the Lutheran School of Theology in Chicago in 1963, and then became executive director of the National Congress of American Indians (NCAI) from 1964 to 1967, after which he earned a JD in 1970 (DeMallie 2006, 932). His position as director of the NCAI, an organization that served and still serves as the umbrella organization for tribal governments, is crucial to understand *Custer* and the work to follow.

In *Custer*, Deloria did not attack, lampoon, or disavow anthropology or anthropologists in general. He criticized "workshop anthropologists," a reference to the Workshop on American Indian Affairs that had first been organized by anthropologists Sol Tax and Fred Gearing in 1955.[2] This was a six week immersive summer course, usually held in Colorado, and taught until 1972. Hanson writes that it "focused on Indian history and participants were indoctrinated to current social science concepts of personality, society, and culture" (1997, 201). In fact, the workshop was a place where future Native leaders could learn about federal Indian policies and their consequences; included in that were larger discussions about colonialism, oppression, and alternative economic and political theories. Sol Tax himself (1977, 229) saw the workshop as a tool to teach Native college students more about American Indian affairs; too often, they could not answer to expectations from non-Native students and faculty, who assumed that as Indians they were experts on everything Native. While "it did not occur to [Tax] that simply bringing them together to compare notes would be the beginning of an American Indian youth movement" the workshop would indeed have a large influence on the leadership of the National Indian Youth Council (NIYC) (Shreve 2011), the radical organization that, perhaps ironically, was partially founded in response to the outcome of the Chicago Indian Conference, organized by Sol Tax, in 1961. Day thought that the NIYC was founded based on "general impatience and frustration with shifts in national Indian policy, with the continued paternalism of the BIA and with the limited goals and cautious tactics of the NCAI leaders" (1972, 507). However, he also described an evolving "debate between NYIC and NCAI moderates" beginning at the same time (1972, 517).

The positions the NCAI represented were informed by the lived reality of reservation communities. Compromises and adjustments in all areas from sovereignty to jurisdiction, from social welfare to traditional ceremonies, often informed daily decisions by tribal governments, who were pragmatic in their relations with local, state, and federal governments and policies. Vine Deloria Jr. wrote, "Every conceivable problem that could occur in an Indian society was suddenly thrust at me from 315 directions" (1972, 503). Pragmatism in solving these problems was one of the very things that the radical movement was fed up with, and so the NCAI often found itself at odds with the more radical notions of various Red Power organizations, of which NIYC was one of the first. Darcy McNickle wrote that older men had been unwilling "to challenge the forces around them," and so "the anger of the young was in part directed at them" (1973, xii). In fact, NIYC gave voice to those fed up with and opposed to the notion that the situation of American Indians could be improved from within the system, through court cases, collaboration, and reform.

Deloria was a good choice for the NCAI because he was not an old Indian: he was young, educated, and articulate. Shirley Hill Witt, herself an influential member of the NIYC, wrote, "The 1964 NCAI convention in September produced new evidences of intertribal and intergeneration unanimity with the election of the NIYC's Vine Deloria, Jr, as its executive director. There appeared a fusing of philosophy within the Indian word [sic] heretofore lacking" (1965, 67). Hazel Hertzberg, on the other hand, saw it quite differently when she wrote, "Many of these Indian young people are quite as sophisticated as their white counterparts, and also as angry and alienated. They are familiar with 'the identity crisis,' 'alienation,' and 'the marginal man,' terms which they apply freely to their own situation. They are deeply respectful of what they believe to be the values of Indian life, as well as that of tribal institutions and tribal elders, an attitude that they do not always apply to their elders in the NCAI" (1971, 292). Understanding the debate in terms of a contradiction, however, might be culturally inappropriate and thus unproductive. Meyer wrote that while the NCAI had "played a most significant role in helping to create the consciousness behind the current political actions of the more activist groups," it was ignoring "certain important issues" because "their radical and controversial nature is a threat to the overall tribal body" (1971, 86). Over the tenure of Deloria at NCAI, however, Day argued, there might have been a rapprochement; "the accelerated Indian militancy of 1970," it seemed to him, "had the tacit, if not the explicit, support of most leaders of the NCAI and NIYC organizers" (1972, 528). Steiner's account seems to corroborate that (1968), even though underlying differences continued to exist and would break into the open in the 1970s.

Deloria saw these differences, and pinned them on one crucial political issue: the emerging coalition between traditional "old-timers" and the NIYC was opposed to the NCAI over the question of what a "tribe" is. As Deloria asked, "Is it a traditionally organized band of Indians following customs with medicine men and chiefs dominating the policies of the tribe, or is it a modern corporate structure attempting to compromise at least in part with modern white culture?" (1972, 504). Tribalization, or perhaps re-tribalization, Deloria felt, was inevitable. But it could not mean the artificial exclusion of modernity. "The anthropological message to young Indians has not varied a jot or tittle in ten years," he wrote in *Custer* (1969, 87). "It is the same message these anthros learned as fuzzy-cheeked graduate students in the postwar years—Indians are a folk people, whites are an urban people, and never the twain shall meet." This idea, to the Deloria family, as well as to others in reservation communities, was unacceptable. In *x-marks*, Scott Lyons writes, "If modernity does not make space for the Indian, the Indian may respond by denying the validity of modernity and becoming a culture cop. At least in that role he or she will be valued" (96). There was never any question about modernity not making space for the Delorias (Deloria 1999). In the 1960s, however, when a conscientious revitalization of historical Lakota culture began to slowly gain traction, such an embrace of a modern Lakota identity started to become complicated, at least as perceived by some. Those for whom modernity made no space were prone to become culture cops, and workshop anthropologists were supporting them.

Deloria's beef with workshop anthros was that they defined and continue to define Native people as premodern: "Folk theories pronounced by authoritative anthropologists become opportunities to escape responsibilities. If, by definition, the Indian is hopelessly caught between two cultures, why struggle? ... Workshops have become [...] summer retreats for non-thought rather than strategy sessions for leadership enhancement" (1969, 89).

At the same time that Deloria blasted workshop anthros, he laid blame at workshop Indians: "Herein lies the Indian sin against the anthropologist," he points out. "Only those anthropologists who appear to boost Indian ego and expound theories dear to the hearts of workshop Indians are invited to teach at workshops. They become human recordings of social confusion which are played and replayed every summer to the delight of people who refuse to move on into the real world" (1969, 89). What he meant here—and this stayed a recurrent critique of his—was that anthropology, to be more than a workshop discipline, has to engage with modern indigenous peoples as modern peoples. The past was gone, and while it should not be forgotten, to constantly orient oneself to the past meant not to live in reality, and not being able to adjust to "the real world" in ways that would be beneficial. One could choose to be a traditional tribe, of course, but a modern corporate structure was so much more efficient in the political dealings with the federal government.

According to Miller (2013, 32), in 1970, Vine Deloria Jr. told Raymond DeMallie that he reminded him of Ella Deloria, "whom he characterized as 'always being interested in old things that were irrelevant today,'" and "asked him, 'Why don't you do something useful?'" The initial encounter did not prevent them from becoming friends and close collaborators, and Deloria seemed to reconsider his position. "No matter how Indians approached their problems, the answer appeared to be the same. If one was primarily a political activist, one could not remain in the field for long before the question of religious morality and history asserted itself," he wrote a few years later (1974, 251). However, this made it all the more important that history not be misconstrued, and that it be continued and applied to contemporary situations: "the tribe must stand before history and reclaim its political and cultural identity and independence" (250). Could historical accounts that only look at traditional life "have correctly informed the reader on the struggle of the Navajo and Hopi against Peabody Coal Company at Black Mesa,"

Deloria asked (2003, 26). To drive the point home, he wrote in 1997 that most anthros believe "that tribal people represent an earlier stage of human accomplishment and that we can learn about our past by studying the way existing tribal peoples live" (214). I am convinced (in part by his enduring friendships with anthropologists) that Deloria knew better, but he made a necessary point that was and remains an important critique. As Rob Hancock (herein) points out, one of the anthropologist friends of Vine Deloria Jr. was none other than Sol Tax. The Workshop on American Indian Affairs was what Deloria wanted, as it focused on contemporary issues. Where it led, though, was not where Deloria wanted to go. The dichotomy within Deloria can be explained by this conflict, which rests on his reluctance to accept that one strategic weapon to fight contemporary battles over sovereignty and legal rights had become the re-appropriation by Native activists of American stereotypes of Native people. To reclaim one's political and cultural identity, for Deloria, who was an unabashedly modern traditionalist, could not mean to accept historical stereotypes as contemporary reality, yet for those who saw, sought, and built essentialized differences to American society, one of the readily available strategies was to appropriate those notions.

In *We Talk, You Listen*, Deloria (1970) would expound on the consequences of this expectation that Native peoples are and forever will be folk people. Workshop anthropologists and workshop Indians, who play to and legitimize the notion of non-modern Native peoples, create other, related expectations on identity and authenticity. Once those expectations become the accepted, dominant discourse, the only accepted representatives of Native peoples are those that play to those expectations. "Much contemporary leadership in racial communities," he wrote, "is recognized only in liberal circles. These leaders earn their living by attending liberal conferences as performing animals suited only for 'telling it like it is.' Never have so many done so little for so few and so expensively" (74). This situation, he argued, was amplified because "the white liberal establishment" was caught in a logical circle of paranoia in which everything is interpreted according to the mythology of oppression," and so, "under the guise of racial integrity for racial minorities, [has] successfully lifted the ancient 'white man's burden' from the souls of white folk" (74). Because of that, important legal, political, economic, and social realities were overlooked because they either did not register as reality, or because all minorities were simply classified as "minorities," without differentiation.

> Liberals have tended to equate the Southern red-necked sheriff and the Bureau of Indian Affairs. Thus we have had people ask us how we got off the reservation, how often we are beaten by government agents, and how they can help us to become free. They continue to talk about "organizing" the poor Indians as if we were some conglomerate slum population that was dependent upon their goodwill for survival, in spite of the fact that Indian tribes have been organized as federally chartered corporations under the Indian Reorganization Act of 1934 for over a generation. (79)

This was the point of Deloria's critique: that the people he called liberals, and in which we can include workshop academics as well as workshop Indians, did not take the time to look at reality. As Temin (2018) points out, this "discourse of civic inclusion" ironically staged cultural oppression and erasure.

I have argued elsewhere that I read Vine Deloria Jr. as defender of the primacy of specific cultural realities as lived in communities over "essentialized or selected anthropological knowledge" (Braun 2013a, 150), an argument against "procedural landscapes" (Braun 2013b). When Deloria talked about reality, he meant the lived reality of modern Native communities, as compared to the "social confusion" of people who are trying to relive a traditional past. Here the conflicts—between tribal councils and urban movements; between the NCAI and the NIYC or the American Indian Movement (AIM); between the Native ranchers, farmers, and workers, who live Native reality; and those people who want to recreate a different, assumed traditional Native reality—came to the forefront.

These conflicts would break out into the open in the most extreme way at Wounded Knee, in 1973, and on Pine Ridge over the next several years. During those events, Deloria wrote, he was waiting to see "whether a central party emerged in the crisis so that we could begin to sort out issues and personalities." When that did not happen, he "told most of the people who had contacted [him] to stay out of the situation" (1980, 561). Deloria, in other words, was looking for pragmatic politics that respected the past, but at the same time recognized and demanded respect for present needs. He did not see that in much of the Red Power organizations or their workshop allies, who, in their "social confusion" instead became records that played and were played in their own world. Deloria articulated this very succinctly in a 1998 article:

> This generation of Indians now coming to power shows a strange alienation from the community setting. For all the talk about the grass roots and reverence of elders, we see very little concern for the people on the homelands. Everyone is proud to claim a tribal heritage, but many times it appears not as a commitment but as a status symbol of "Indianness." Individual self-determination and intellectual sovereignty are scary concepts because they mean that a whole generation of Indians are not going to be responsible to the Indian people, they are simply going to be isolated individuals playing with the symbols of Indians. (28)

This was in alignment with his earlier assessment of the Red Power movement: "Indians were well represented in the media from the Alcatraz occupation through the Wounded Knee trials, but, unfortunately, each event dealt primarily with the symbols of oppression and did not project possible courses of action that might be taken to solve problems" (Deloria 1994, 31). Again, Deloria was concerned with the usefulness of academic engagement with Native communities. As he wrote, "*Self-determination, sovereignty, hegemony, empowerment,* and *colonialism* are nice big words that philosophers and intellectuals use, but what do they really mean? I often feel they assist us creating a set of artificial problems, wholly abstract in nature, that we can discuss endlessly without having to actually do something" (1998, 25).

Vine Deloria Jr. was not an ordinary member of a reservation community—nor was he a community member at all, in the sense of being a resident—but he believed in the possibility, potential, and necessity to engage communities directly; to learn from community members about their daily lives, their issues, and their (modern, contemporary, lived) culture; and to then craft pragmatic, useful solutions.

Deloria engaged with and critiqued anthropology and anthropologists not because he did not like the discipline, but because he saw it as important and as potentially making a positive contribution to Indian life. As Rob Hancock points out, too (herein), it was an important tool—too important to let it go astray. It is important to read Deloria not simply as an academic, but as a Yankton man.[3] As Hancock notes, the humor is purposeful; those who read Deloria literally are missing many points. Perhaps more importantly, however, not only is teasing something reserved for one's cousins, but if Deloria would not have cared for and about anthropology, he would have simply ignored it.

While he did not give up on critiquing anthropologists, Deloria saw they did have, in general, at the very least, a good understanding of culture and community. In his concluding chapter for an edited volume in honor of the twenty-fifth anniversary of *Custer Died for Your Sins*, he wrote about religion and religious appropriation: "a self-righteous piety has swept Indian country, and it threatens to pollute the remaining pockets of traditionalism and produce a mawkish unreal sentimentalism that commissions everyone to be 'spiritual' whether they understand it or not.... It is totally disheartening to see Indians interviewed in the seemingly endless documentaries about the environment and find them telling us that the earth is our mother. The interviewer nods wisely, the Indian looks solemn, and the destruction continues." Here, he also wrote: "With a few exceptions anthropologists have not contributed to this bastardization of tribal religion and have maintained a respectful distance, hoping that Indians will come to their senses" (1997, 212–13).

How, then, should anthropology (and history, American Indian Studies, legal studies, social work, etc.) engage Native communities, according to Vine Deloria Jr.? I think we can find a set of ideas he presented on what would constitute good practice in academia dealing with American Indian issues by decolonizing Deloria—that is, by stripping away that layer of outside expectations that has been heaped upon his image that turn him into somebody he was not. Deloria writes about the 1960s and 1970s: "What we dealt with for the major portion of a decade was not American Indians, but the American conception of what Indians should be" (2003, 33). I think that this time frame can be extended and applied to Deloria, himself—we are dealing too often with the American and the Native American conceptions of what Deloria stands for rather than with who he was and what he said. He has been appropriated by those whom he relentlessly criticized, namely workshop Indians and workshop anthropologists.

When I cut to what Deloria asks from anthropology (and other academic endeavors), and simultaneously asks from American Indian people, I come up with a short list:

Look reality in the face and describe it as it is, not as it should be.

Do not trivialize the power of traditional knowledge. That includes essentializing, romanticizing, and appropriating it.

Recognize that anybody you speak with is your contemporary, a modern person like yourself, not a survival of the past.

Acknowledge that people know what they are doing, even if they seem to be doing things that you or others do not approve of.

Understand that culture is not essentialized unless it is politicized, and then it is bastardized into ethnicity.

Respect the fact that cultures change, that people have different ideas, and that it is not those most exotic who speak for the community or have traditional knowledge.

Understand that traditional knowledge is known and lived, not worn, performed, sold, profusely claimed, or demanded.

Do something useful with your research based on the reality as lined out in the first point; this does not need to be directly political, but it should address communities as they are.[4]

This condensation should not be mistaken for the complexity of actual work in the field. However, I also think that we gain from being clear on positions and approaches; everything else follows from them (in complex, paradoxical, and sometimes contradictory ways). Anthropology done right could lead to a better understanding of Indian realities, better policies, and better communities. Done wrong, it would worsen all those things. Much was (and is) at stake.

Looking at Deloria as a figure of the past has turned him and his writings into aesthetics, ready to be used to adorn our resumes, to be dropped in a conversation to assure our own status, and to prop up our credentials. What he was actually demanding was not unlike what bell hooks calls "theory as a liberatory practice":

> Just as some elite academics who construct theories of "blackness" in ways that make it a critical terrain which only the chosen few can enter—using theoretical work on race to assert their authority over black experience, denying democratic access to the process of theory making—threaten collective black liberation struggle, so do those among us who react to this by promoting anti-intellectualism by declaring all theory as worthless. By reinforcing that there is a split, both groups deny the power of liberatory education for critical consciousness, thereby perpetuating conditions that reinforce our collective exploitation and repression. (1994: 68–69)

"Deloria," wrote Brayboy et al., "was ahead of many in examining the detrimental effects of the (self-)colonization of Indigenous peoples and our cultures" (2007, 235). This is very true. But we should remember that Vine Deloria Jr. might still object that (self-)colonization, or settler colonialism, or any other terms that are de rigueur and in vogue, are abstractions and distractions from the problems at hand. These seem to be reiteration of old concepts in new clothes. Colonization had meaning as expropriation, and because it extinguished treaty rights. These concrete and specific issues demand specific, focused action. Academic discussions can help find and define the appropriate action, but only if they are specific, focused, honest, and based on reality. In other words, we should "do something useful."

NOTES

1. This text has profited enormously from several very kind readings by Ira Bashkow that have contributed much to cohesion and argumentation. It has also benefitted from conversations with Richie Meyers, David Posthumus, and others. All errors and mistakes are obviously mine.
2. Vine Deloria Jr. and Sol Tax were good friends, and Deloria appreciated the initial workshops. His critique, as I argue below, was more

directed to what he perceived the workshops turned into once they became more controlled by the students themselves (hence his critique of a vicious cycle of teachers and students no longer challenging viewpoints, but simply reifying preconceived assumptions).

3. Vine Deloria Sr. transferred the family's tribal enrollment from Yankton to Standing Rock, and Vine Deloria Jr. was born on Pine Ridge. However, based on comments from friends and colleagues from Pine Ridge, I hesitate to characterize Vine Deloria Jr. as Lakota. It needs to be remembered that Standing Rock is not only home to Lakota, but to a large Yanktonai community, too.

4. After a conversation with Philip J. Deloria, I want to clarify that I do not think this necessitates long-term, ongoing contacts in, kinship with, or living in communities. What it does necessitate is an understanding of specific community concerns, histories, and cultures— that is, an active listening to community concerns and an inductive, not deductive, epistemology (DeMallie 1993). I thank Phil Deloria for helping me to clarify this point.

REFERENCES

Braun, Sebastian Felix. 2013a. "Imagining Unimagined Communities: The Politics of Indigenous Nationalism." In *Tribal Worlds: Critical Studies in American Indian Nation Building*, edited by Brian Hosmer and Larry Nesper, 141–60. Albany: SUNY Press.

———. 2013b. "Against Procedural Landscapes: Community, Kinship, and History." In *Transforming Ethnohistories: Narrative, Meaning, and Community*, edited by Sebastian Felix Braun. 201–21. Norman: University of Oklahoma Press.

Brayboy, Bryan McKinley Jones, K. Tsianina Lomawaima, and Malia Villegas. 2007. "The Lives and Work of Beatrice Medicine and Vine Deloria Jr." *Anthropology and Education Quarterly* 38, no. 3: 231–38.

Day, Robert C. 1972. "The Emergence of Activism as a Social Movement." In *Native Americans Today: Sociological Perspectives*, edited by Howard M. Bahr, Bruce A. Chadwick, and Robert C. Day, 506–32. New York: Harper & Row.

Deloria, Vine, Jr. 2003. *God is Red: A Native View of Religion*. Golden CO: Fulcrum Publishing.

———. 1999. *Singing for a Spirit: A Portrait of the Dakota Sioux*. Santa Fe: Clear Light.

———. 1998. "Intellectual Self-Determination and Sovereignty: Looking at the Windmills in Our Minds." *Wicazo Sa Review* 13, no. 1: 25–31.

———. 1997. "Anthros, Indians, and Planetary Reality." In *Indians and Anthropologists: Vine Deloria, Jr., and the Critique of Anthropology*, edited by Thomas Biolsi and Larry J. Zimmerman, 209–21. Tucson: University of Arizona Press.

———. 1994. "Alcatraz, Activism, and Accommodation." *American Indian Culture and Research Journal* 18, no. 4: 25–32.

———. 1980. "Schlesier, Other Anthropologists, and Wounded Knee." *American Anthropologist* 82, no. 3: 560–61.

———. 1972. "This Country was a lot Better off when Indians were Running It." In *Native Americans Today: Sociological Perspectives*, edited by Howard M. Bahr, Bruce A. Chadwick, and Robert C. Day, 498–506. New York: Harper & Row.

———. 1970. *We Talk, You Listen: New Tribes, New Turf.* New York: Delta Publishing.

———. 1969. *Custer Died for Your Sins.* New York: Avon Books.

DeMallie, Raymond J. 2006. "Vine Deloria Jr. (1933–2005)." *American Anthropologist* 108, no. 4: 932–40.

———. 1993. "'These Have No Ears': Narrative and the Ethnohistorical Method." *Ethnohistory* 40, no. 4: 515–38.

Hanson, Jeffery R. 1997. "Ethnicity and the Looking Glass: The Dialectics of National Indian Identity." *American Indian Quarterly* 21, no. 2: 195–208.

Hertzberg, Hazel. 1971. *The Search for an American Indian Identity: Modern Pan-Indian Movements.* Syracuse: Syracuse University Press.

Hill Witt, Shirley. 1965. "Nationalistic Trends among American Indians." *Midcontinent American Studies Journal* 6, no. 2: 51–74.

hooks, bell. 1994. *Teaching to Transgress: Education as the Practice of Freedom.* New York: Routledge.

Lyons, Scott Richard. 2010. *x-marks. Native Signatures of Assent.* Minneapolis: University of Minnesota Press.

McNickle, Darcy. 1973. *Native American Tribalism: Indian Survivals and Renewals.* London: Oxford University Press.

Medicine, Beatrice. 2001. *Learning to Be an Anthropologist and Remaining "Native": Selected Writings*, edited with Sue-Ellen Jacobs. Urbana: University of Illinois Press.

Meyer, William. 1971. *Native Americans: The New Indian Resistance.* New York: International.

Miller, David Reed. 2013. "Borders and Layers, Symbols and Meanings: Raymond J. DeMallie's Commitment to Ethnohistory, with Nods to Thick Description and Symbolic Anthropology." In *Transforming Ethnohistories: Narrative, Meaning, and Community*, edited by Sebastian Felix Braun, 23–42. Norman: University of Oklahoma Press.

Shreve, Bradley G. 2011. *Red Power Rising: The National Indian Youth Council and the Origins of Native Activism*. Norman: University of Oklahoma Press.

Steiner, Stan. 1968. *The New Indians*. New York: Harper & Row.

Stull, Donald D. 1999. "Review of *Indians and Anthropologists: Vine Deloria, Jr., and the Critique of Anthropology* Edited by Thomas Biolsi and Larry J. Zimmerman." *Great Plains Quarterly* 19, no. 1: 63–64.

Tax, Sol. 1977. "Anthropology for the World of the Future: Thirteen Professions and Three Proposals." *Human Organization* 36, no. 3: 225–34.

Temin, David Myer. 2018. "Custer's Sins: Vine Deloria Jr. and the Settler-Colonial Politics of Civic Inclusion." *Political Theory* 46, no. 3: 357–79.

Thornton, Russell. 2000. "Indians and Anthropologists: Vine Deloria, Jr., and the Critique of Anthropology. Thomas Biolsi and Larry J. Zimmerman. Eds." *American Ethnologist* 27, no. 3: 762–63.

ROBERT L. A. HANCOCK

13

"Let's Do Better This Time"

*Vine Deloria Jr.'s Ongoing Engagement
with Anthropology*

For an Indigenous scholar and a non-anthropologist, Vine Deloria Jr. occupied, and continues to occupy, an outsized space in the discipline's image of itself. A recent demonstration of this fact can be found in a new Canadian four-field introductory textbook, which includes an excerpt from Deloria at the beginning of its first chapter, "Introduction: Viewing the World through the Lens of Anthropology" (Muckle and González 2016). Here is how the authors introduce him: "Although there were certainly some good relationships between anthropologists and Indigenous peoples, it is justifiable to state that until the latter part of the twentieth century, the relationship was largely exploitative. Anthropologists would often take much from the Indigenous peoples in regard to their cultural knowledge and beliefs, as well as hundreds of thousands of human skeletons and millions of artifacts, while providing nothing or very little in exchange. Anthropologists were advancing their own careers, filling museums, and making contributions to the discipline of anthropology at the expense of Indigenous peoples" (Muckle and González 2016, 16–17).

Following this is a heavily abridged excerpt from Deloria's 1969 essay, "Anthropologists and Other Friends," highlighting his critique of negative roles that anthropologists have played in Indigenous communities. Muckle and González implicitly present Deloria's perspective as marking the low point in the relationship between Indigenous peoples and anthropologists. They sum it up by writing, "The relationship between Indigenous peoples and anthropologists has significantly improved in recent decades. . . . In many ways, the relationships that anthropologists have with Indigenous peoples can now be characterized as supportive, rather than exploitative" (Muckle and González 2016, 17).

I find this representation of Deloria's perspective unsettling. I recognize the challenges and constraints of introducing anthropology to students in a first-year course; even so, I am not satisfied with the kind of narrative of progress that Muckle and González exemplify. While I do not contest that as a whole anthropology's relationships with Indigenous peoples have changed in positive ways in the nearly half-century since Deloria published "Anthropologists and Other Friends," his position in that essay is more complex and more compelling than a simple rejection of the work done by anthropologists (see Braun, herein).[1] Indeed, this was made clear by Deloria himself after the essay appeared.

SETTING THE STAGE

We can gain a more nuanced perspective on Deloria's position on the relationship between anthropologists and Indigenous communities from his presentation at a symposium that was convened in response to his "Anthropologists and Other Friends" article, which was published in the August 1969 issue of *Playboy* magazine (Deloria 1969a; Deloria 1969b; chapter four). The symposium, entitled, "Anthropology and the American Indian," ran alongside the 1970 American Anthropological Association conference in San Diego, supported by the Bureau of Indian Affairs and the National Indian Training and Research Center and published by the Indian Historian Press. Deloria appears to have been a significant presence at these AAA meetings; for example, Nancy Lurie mentioned at the beginning of her symposium presentation that "the reason that I am going to have to leave shortly after this paper is that Vine Deloria is giving a paper in another session in which I am attacked by name, and I am a little curious to hear what he has to say" (Lurie 1973, 4).

At the same time, and in contrast to Deloria's approach, the participants in the session did not engage with Deloria's work in a sustained way, although at least one of the organizers and one of the presenters also wrote reviews of *Custer Died for Your Sins* at around the same time (Officer 1970; Ortiz 1971). Some presenters and commentators refer to his work, or his ideas, only in passing, while others outline disagreements with his approach, sometimes even while admitting that they had not read the book (e.g., page 19).[2] The most direct responses to Deloria came in papers from Margaret Mead and Alfonzo Ortiz. Mead adopted an informal but defensive posture in her piece, comparing Deloria's work to his aunt Ella Deloria's earlier pieces: "You know, Vine, that you wouldn't have written your book 25 years ago. I read your Aunt Ella's novel, which she never let me publish, but it wasn't like yours. It was called *Water Lily* and it was a lovely book, but she never let me have it. So who was exploited? But you, Vine, you wouldn't have written *your* book *then*. What you are writing belongs to *now*. And, it is part of the whole generation gap, and the change in the world" (Mead 1973, 74; emphases in original).

In contrast, Ortiz struck a much more conciliatory tone and offered a more generous reading of Deloria's work:

We are here because anthropologists are under attack by Vine Deloria and by many other Indians who have taken up his call, and because there are many just grievances involved. I would like to think that Vine was just testing his bowstring to see if it was taut enough, to use his own imagery, and that his intended purpose is achieved when both sides can get together, along with those of few of us [*sic*] who are unwittingly cast in the role of mediator, and talk—really talk—about healing the strains of the relationship. As such, I am here to offer an Indian anthropologist's perspective on anthropology. (Ortiz 1973, 85–86)

In the end, however, the conversation never really got started as the papers each went in their own direction.

The morning session included papers from Lurie ("Action Anthropology and the American Indian"), Philleo Nash ("Applied Anthropology and the Concept of 'Guided Acculturation'"), and Omer Stewart ("Anthropologists as Expert Witnesses for Indians: Claims and Peyote Cases"), with commentary from Mary Natani, Ken Martin, Abbott Sekaquaptewa, and D'Arcy McNickle. The afternoon session included papers from Mead ("The American Indian as Significant Determinant of Anthropological Style"), Bea Medicine ("Anthropologists and American Indian Studies Programs"), Ortiz ("An Indian Anthropologist's Perspective on Anthropology"), and Deloria, with commentary from Roger Buffalohead, Gerald One Feather, Marilyn Halpern, Agnes Savilla, and Gloria Emerson. The book was reviewed in the *American Anthropologist*, where the reviewer noted, "although there is little in the book that the American Indian specialist will find new, it is rare to find such a diversified collection of opinions and personalities under one cover" (Stucki 1976, 404).

The symposium was organized by James Officer and chaired by him and Edward Dozier, both professors of anthropology at the University of Arizona. Officer and Francis McKinley, the director of the National Indian Training and Research Center, wrote that the intention of the symposium was to "bring Indians and anthropologists together to discuss the virtues and deficiencies of past and present relationships, and help chart a course for the future" (Officer and McKinley 1973, xiii). In his opening remarks for the morning session, Officer explained that his goal was "to elucidate most of the traditional relationships which have embraced Indians and anthropologists, to attempt some appraisal of these relationships in terms of mutual benefits or liabilities and to commence a dialogue which may yield insights into new directions such relationships must take. I do not believe we can settle all these issues in a one-day session, but I anticipate taking a long initial step in that direction" (Officer 1973, 2). Deloria spoke last, and was introduced by Dozier, who chaired the afternoon session: "Our next speaker is famous Vine Deloria, author, attorney, Standing Rock Sioux" (92). The title of his presentation was, "Some Criticisms and a Number of Suggestions."

(TALKING ABOUT) TALKING BACK TO ANTHROPOLOGISTS

The tone of Deloria's opening comments is lost in the transcripts, though one later commentator notes, "his writing style is uniquely filled with cynicism and sarcasm in depicting the injustices wreaked upon American Indians by colonization" (Meyers 2008, 8–9), which might guide our reading. His presentation offers a stark contrast with the bureaucratic language of Officer's introduction, beginning with his remarks on his choice of clothing, where he made explicit his perception of the relationship of his work to that of the other speakers: "I deliberately dressed in a dark shirt and Levi's so that those of you who are of Indo-European tribal descent—the group that ravaged from the Himalayas to Catalina Island—would be able to identify the symbolism in your own terms: the bad guys always wear dark clothes" (Deloria 1973, 93). He began his presentation by commenting on the presentations by Ortiz and Mead, perhaps in response to their direct engagement with his work. There is definitely an edge to his remarks, and he started off by setting an aggressive tone.

Deloria then shifted to a discussion of his intention in writing "Anthropologists and Other Friends" and laid out the position that he saw contemporary anthropologists take in relation to the situation of Indigenous communities:

> The point that I had hoped to bring out in the *Playboy* article, the chapter in my book, and in subsequent speeches falls half-way between what I am credited with saying and what Miss Mead has said. I do not believe that *you* maliciously harm Indians—what I am saying is that you can have the best of intentions of helping the Indians and the results of *those* actions may be bad for Indian people. This is the point that I tried to raise and if I were really mad at you I would *not* have done it in a satirical way or put a chapter on humor into what others think is an Indian manifesto.
>
> What I would like to bring out is that I feel that the anthropological discipline, as *that* discipline which is devoted to the preservation of knowledge of Indian communities, cultures, and tribal societies, has unconsciously fallen into the position of blocking very significant movements in the American Indian community by perpetuating an idea of Indians of yesteryear so that we are judged on the body of knowledge that you have preserved and not on what we are today. Consequently that is why you find a great deal of reluctance by Indian people to be associated with anthropologists. That is why you have attitudes such as "we never tell them much." . . . We are thrust back into the past when we deal with you or the knowledge you preserve. (Deloria 1973, 93–94; emphases in original)

These points succinctly delineate the key concerns of his presentation: that anthropologists are not helping Indigenous communities in their current political struggles, mirroring issues raised by Sol Tax in "The

Freedom to Make Mistakes" (1956); and that anthropologists are in fact holding these communities back by continuously comparing current situations and contexts to earlier representations from the discipline.

At this point, he turned his attention to Stewart's paper, arguing that the fact that some Indigenous communities are able to pay for professional research on their own behalf does not mean that all anthropologists are engaged in research relationships based on ideals of equity and service to the community. He is especially blunt in his criticism of anthropologists for not speaking up on behalf of communities facing termination:

> You have some responsibility to the Indian community if we are on a one-to-one basis to help us when we need help and not simply when *you* want to study us. We must see that responsibility in areas where we need your professional skill. And we must see it on the basis of friendship and not solely on the basis of contingency fees in claims cases. When we need your body of knowledge to defend ourselves it must be given, since it is partly our work product also, if we are on a one-to-one basis with you. (Deloria 1973, 95; emphasis in original)

Deloria is calling on anthropologists to see Indigenous communities as partners in research, and to work with and for Indigenous communities, rather than to treat them as sources of funding or academic prestige. This connects directly to the issue of anthropological control of knowledge, as seen in challenges communities faced in accessing unpublished materials, or in the ways that current communities were judged by external standards based on older ethnographies, which is at the core of Deloria's commentary.

He then switched his attention from anthropologists to contemporary Indigenous communities and what he saw as anthropology's obligation to engage with them:

> At the present time there is a tremendous Indian movement afoot and this movement is very confused. We have people landing on every unoccupied island and national monument across the country with little or no understanding of the issue involved. Yet, there are significant things in America's past that make these little islands and

national monuments important if we had the information for our people and we could raise significant social issues with our activism. An outstanding example that I can give you is the deprivation from the Sioux Indians of the Pipestone Quarry—the religious significance of that national monument to the Sioux. We must have material to balance, against the government's right of eminent domain, the religious meaning for the tribes of that area, in order to resolve the question. If we are going to have any meaningful social progress we must work as colleagues on situations like this one.

I do not find this situation. Instead I find a significant number of anthropologists consistently going against Indian people and Indian movements because they stand there as authority figures and say "since the National Congress of American Indians doesn't represent all the Indians, therefore by implication it really doesn't represent *any* of the Indians. Therefore I, the scholar, the authority figure, am the person who really knows. Therefore what I say is right and what they say is wrong, or at least not to be trusted." I think that this is the thing that Indian people are trying to tell you.

There's not a responsible Indian in the country who would stand up and say, "I represent Indians and this is what Indians think." We raise issues among ourselves consistently but there's not one of us that would stand up and say, "This is what really is." How can anthropologists make such pretensions when we can't? And, what I have been trying to do is explore the attitudes that we find in the academic disciplines, particularly the anthropologists, that makes them feel they have this right or knowledge.

Al Ortiz maintains that the Bureau of Indian Affairs has a much more significant role in the Indian community than the anthropologists, and I would certainly agree with him. But there are procedures of checks and balances that we can use with the Bureau of Indian Affairs so that we can stop or hamper the bad things that it is doing. And those of you who have been observing Indian affairs know that if the tribal council does not like what the Bureau of Indian Affairs is doing on their reservation they can get on the 747 air flight and go to Washington and they are in the Secretary of Interior's office the next day and they raise all kinds of hell and changes are effected in the Bureau of Indian Affairs—sometimes. At least we have a chance. But with the missionaries and anthropologists there are no procedural checks and balances that we can use, other than satire, exclusion—the things you have been objecting to in this last year. We have no way to relate to people who are on reservations as volunteers. Protest is the only mechanism we have to communicate with you that perhaps we don't like what some of you are doing. (Deloria 1973, 96–97)

Deloria did not end on this note, however; he went on to outline his vision of how the relationship between Indigenous people and anthropologists could improve the years to come and wrapping up with an encouragement:

Consequently, I want to close this presentation with a number of suggestions. I don't believe, in view of the awakening of the non-Western European peoples in this country, that an observational science can be a valid science if the person observing is not intimately tied in with the community that he's observing and shares some of the burdens and responsibilities for what's happening in that community. By his very presence in that community he has changed things. And this is what I would say: that it is time for the Indian organizations and the American Anthropological Association to sit down and discuss what issues are relevant in the Indian community; what studies you have that are relevant to the things that we are doing; what needs we have that would be relevant to future research that you might want to undertake on a professional basis.

Gerald Brown (a member of the Flathead Indian tribe of Montana) and I came to an American Anthropological Association meeting in Denver in 1966 and suggested this idea. Almost no response. Let's do better this time. (Deloria 1973, 97–98)

Rather than calling for a rejection of the discipline, or its eradication, Deloria sought to reimagine the relationship—including the balance of power—between anthropologists and Indigenous communities. He was advocating for a closer, more equitable relationship, one in which anthropologists' support for Indigenous causes would not only strengthen their position in Indigenous communities but also lead to better research.

CONCLUDING THOUGHTS

It should be clear from the foregoing that Deloria is misunderstood by those who represent his position as a categorical indictment and repudiation of anthropology and anthropologists. In fact, Deloria had close and long-standing connections with anthropologists, particularly Sol Tax (Cobb 2008, 139, 143–44), going so far as to serve as a eulogist at Tax's memorial service (Smith 2015b, 445, 454). Deloria also wrote a touching introduction to the work of his aunt, Ella Deloria, who had been a student of Franz Boas and who published significant works of ethnography, linguistics, and fiction (Deloria 1998). I think that the misunderstanding of Deloria's commentary on anthropology, reducing it to a unidimensional polemic, reflects anthropologists' own simplified understandings of the politics of past anthropological research. As I have argued elsewhere (Hancock 2015), historians of anthropology should counter this tendency by bringing more attention to the real complexities of the political contexts in which past anthropologists worked. We need to understand politics broadly—that is, not only in terms of collusion or intervention with state authorities, but also in the political dimensions of social relationships, theories, and methodology.

Deloria's commentary on the discipline is a good example of this, since it must be understood in the context of a continuing history of relationships between researchers and Indigenous people. The contemporary reader of Deloria's 1969 article and chapter is often ignorant of Tax's work that actually embodies many of the ideals for which Deloria was advocating (Lurie 1998; Tax 1958, 1975; Gearing, Netting, and Peattie 1960; Cobb 2007; Smith 2010, 2015a, 2015b). Deloria's longstanding engagement with anthropology (he participated in another AAA session on the twentieth anniversary of *Custer Died for Your Sins*, in 1989 (Deloria 1997; Biolsi and Zimmerman 1997) can be read as a reflection of his faith in anthropology as much as of his frustration with it.

My intention with this short piece has been to correct some of the misunderstanding of Deloria's engagement with anthropology, deep and long-standing as it was. Anthropologists reveal their own estrangement from the history of their discipline when they caricature his views as simply condemnatory. We can continue to read Deloria's piece as a mere cataloging of the discipline's shortcomings, or, building on the context he offered, we can read it as an argument about anthropology's potential to contribute to Indigenous communities and the need for anthropologists to improve in this regard. I think the key clue in this regard is Deloria's comment that he would not have resorted to humor or satire were he truly mad at anthropologists, and I think that anthropologists' angry response to his chapter—overlooking this very fact, among others—speaks to a challenge that historians of anthropology have to face in considering the relationships between Indigenous communities and our disciplinary predecessors.

Deloria's chapter and his commentaries represent a protest—a call for equity, relevance and respect, and a call to action. In particular, his closing exhortation, to "do better this time," remains a powerful message and continues to resonate. He is not rejecting anthropology, but trying to remind anthropologists both of our responsibility to Indigenous communities and of the potential ways that we can live up to that responsibility. At the same time, as historians of anthropology, we also have to answer his call to do better, to ensure that we do a good job of understanding and representing the relationships the discipline has had with Indigenous communities. When we think about doing better, we need to think not just in terms of working with Indigenous communities but also in terms of understanding and representing those relationships.

If anthropologists take later commentators such at Muckle and Gonzáles at face value, it is important also to ask from whose perspective the relationship has improved, and to ensure that those changes and that assessment reflect the perspectives and needs of the Indigenous communities with whom anthropologists work. The misunderstanding of earlier commentators, such as Deloria, can lead to two equally problematic, if opposed positions: it can mean either jettisoning the discipline as irredeemably flawed, or embracing the current positions and perspectives adopted by anthropologists as unproblematic advancements over an unenlightened past. Neither perspective serves students well, and it is our responsibility as historians of the discipline to answer his call.

NOTES

I am grateful to Mindy Morgan and Ira Bashkow for organizing the AAA session in Minneapolis for which an early version of this paper was originally prepared and for offering me an opportunity to participate. I would also like to thank the other presenters for the conversations that started there. Ira Bashkow offered crucial editorial interventions for which I am thankful, as have Fred Gleach and the readers for HOAA. I also want to acknowledge Joshua Smith for our ongoing conversations about Sol Tax's work and its continuing resonances.

1. A detailed examination of the processes by which this reading of Deloria's critique became hegemonic in mainstream American anthropology remains a crucial project, one that unfortunately exceeds the scope of this brief reflection.

2. Citations that include only the page number refer to sections that are not part of individual papers (e.g., introductory remarks or comments from the audience).

REFERENCES

Biolsi, Thomas, and Larry J. Zimmerman, eds. 1997. *Indians and Anthropologists: Vine Deloria, Jr., and the Critique of Anthropology*. Tucson: University of Arizona Press.

Cobb, Daniel M. 2008. *Native Activism in Cold War America: The Struggle for Sovereignty*. Lawrence: University Press of Kansas.

———. 2007. "Devils in Disguise: The Carnegie Project, The Cherokee Nation, and the 1960s." *American Indian Quarterly* 31, no. 3: 465–90.

Deloria, Vine, Jr. 1998. "Introduction." In *Speaking of Indians*, by Ella Deloria, ix–xix. Lincoln: University of Nebraska Press.

———. 1997. "Conclusion: Anthros, Indians and Planetary Reality." In *Indians and Anthropologists: Vine Deloria, Jr., and the Critique of Anthropology*, edited by Thomas Biolsi and Larry J. Zimmerman, 209–21. Tucson: University of Arizona Press.

———. 1973. "Some Criticisms and a Number of Suggestions." In *Anthropology and the American Indian: Report of a Symposium*, 93–99. San Francisco: Indian Historian Press.

———. 1969a. "Custer Died for your Sins." *Playboy* 16, no. 8: 131–32, 172–75.

———. 1969b. *Custer Died for Your Sins: An Indian Manifesto*. New York: Macmillan.

Gearing, Fred, Robert M. C. C. Netting, and Lisa Peattie, eds. 1960. *Documentary History of the Fox Project: A Program in Action Anthropology*. Chicago: University of Chicago Press.

Hancock, Robert L. A. 2015. "Franz Boas, Wilson Duff, and the Image of Anthropology in British Columbia." In *Franz Boas as Public Intellectual: Ethnography, Theory, Activism*, edited by Regna Darnell, Michelle A. Hamilton, Robert L. A. Hancock, and Joshua Smith, 237–61. Lincoln: University of Nebraska Press.

Lurie, Nancy O. 1998. "Selective Recollections on Anthropology and Indians." *Current Anthropology* 39, no. 4: 572–74.

———. 1973. "Action Anthropology and the American Indian." In *Anthropology and the American Indian: Report of a Symposium*, 4–15. San Francisco: Indian Historian Press.

Mead, Margaret. 1973. "The American Indian as a Significant Determinant of Anthropological Style." In *Anthropology and the American Indian: Report of a Symposium*, 68–74. San Francisco: Indian Historian Press.

Meyers, Richard Thomas. 2008. "Anthropology, American Indians, Research, and the Ensuing Identity 'Plague.'" PhD diss., Arizona State University.

Muckle, Robert, and Laura Tubelle de González. 2016. *Through the Lens of Anthropology: An Introduction to Human Evolution and Culture*. Toronto: University of Toronto Press.

Officer, James E. 1970. "Review of *Custer Died for Your Sins: An Indian Manifesto* by Vine Deloria." *Arizona and the West* 12, no. 3: 292–94.

Officer, James E., and Francis McKinley. 1973. "Preface." In *Anthropology and the American Indian: Report of a Symposium*, xi–xvi. San Francisco: Indian Historian Press.

Ortiz, Alfonzo. 1973. "An Indian Anthropologist's Perspective on Anthropology." In *Anthropology and the American Indian: Report of a Symposium*, 85–92. San Francisco: Indian Historian Press.

———. 1971. "Review of *Custer Died for Your Sins: An Indian Manifesto* by Vine Deloria." *American Anthropologist* 73, no. 4: 953–55.

Smith, Joshua. 2015a. "'Last on the Warpath': The Spirit and Intent of Action Anthropology." PhD diss., University of Western Ontario.

———. 2015b. "Standing with Sol: The Spirit and Intent of Action Anthropology." *Anthropologica* 57, no. 2: 445–56.

———. 2010. "The Political Thought of Sol Tax: The Principles of Non-Assimilation and Self-Government in Action Anthropology." *Histories of Anthropology Annual* 6: 129–70.

Stucki, Larry R. 1976. "Review of *Anthropology and the American Indian: Report of a Symposium.*" *American Anthropologist* 78, no. 2: 404.

Tax, Sol. 1975. "Action Anthropology." *Current Anthropology* 16, no. 4: 514–17.

———. 1958. "The Fox Project." *Human Organization* 17, no. 1: 17–19.

———. 1956. "The Freedom to Make Mistakes." *America Indigena* 16: 171–77.

CONTRIBUTORS

IRA BASHKOW, Department of Anthropology, University of Virginia. email: bashkow@virginia.edu

MARGARET M. BRUCHAC, Department of Anthropology, University of Pennsylvania. email: mbruchac@sas.upenn.edu

SEBASTIAN F. BRAUN, American Indian Studies Program, Iowa State University. email: sfbraun@iastate.edu

REGNA DARNELL, Department of Anthropology, University of Western Ontario. email: rdarnell@uwo.ca

FREDERICO DELGADO ROSA, Department of Anthropology, CRIA-FCSH/ NOVA University, Lisbon, Portugal. e-mail: fdelgadorosa@fcsh.unl.pt

FREDERIC W. GLEACH, Department of Anthropology, Cornell University. email: fw1@cornell.edu

ROBERT L. A. HANCOCK, LE, NONET, University of Victoria. email: rola @uvic.ca

IRA JACKNIS, Phoebe A. Hearst Museum of Anthropology, University of California, Berkeley. email: jacknis@berkeley.edu

SHARON LINDENBURGER, Department of English, University of Western Ontario. email: slinden@uwo.ca

KATHY M'CLOSKEY, Department of Sociology, Anthropology and Criminology, University of Windsor. email: mcloskey@uwindsor.ca

MINDY MORGAN, Department of Anthropology, Michigan State University. email: morgan37@msu.edu

NANCY J. PAREZO, American Indian Studies (emerita), University of Arizona. email: parezo@email.arizona.edu

CLAUDIA SALOMON TARQUINI, CONICET-National Scientific and Technical Research Council, National University of La Pampa, Argentina. email: claudia.salomon.tarquini@humanas.unlpam.edu.ar

SAUL SCHWARTZ, Department of Comparative Literature, University of California, Berkeley. email: saulgschwartz@berkeley.edu

DEANA L. WEIBEL, Department of Anthropology, Grand Valley State University. email: weibeld@gvsu.edu

www.ingramcontent.com/pod-product-compliance
Lightning Source LLC
Chambersburg PA
CBHW030906270326
41929CB00008B/596